RENATA WHURR
2 ALWYNE ROAD
LONDON N1 2HH
ENGLAND
01-226-1729

D1795832

Speech Perception by Ear and Eye: A Paradigm for Psychological Inquiry

Dominic William Massaro

Program in Experimental Psychology
University of California, Santa Cruz

LEA LAWRENCE ERLBAUM ASSOCIATES, PUBLISHERS
1987   Hillsdale, New Jersey   London

The cover was adapted from an illustration by
Bishop John Wilkins, An Essay Towards a Real Character
and a Philosophical Language, 1668

Copyright © 1987 by Lawrence Erlbaum Associates, Inc.
All rights reserved. No part of this book may be reproduced in
any form, by photostat, microform, retrieval system, or any other
means, without the prior written permission of the publisher.

Lawrence Erlbaum Associates, Inc., Publishers
365 Broadway
Hillsdale, New Jersey 07642

Library of Congress Cataloging-in-Publication Data

Massaro, Dominic W.
    Speech perception by ear and eye.

    Bibliography: p.
    Includes index.
    1. Human information processing. 2. Speech perception.
3. Auditory perception. 4. Visual perception. I. Title.
[DNLM: 1. Psychology, Experimental. 2. Speech Perception.
WV 272 M414s]
BF444.M37   1987   153.6   87-5375
ISBN 0-8058-0061-1
ISBN 0-8058-0062-X (pbk.)

Printed in the United States of America
10 9 8 7 6 5 4 3 2 1

To Pia, Andrew, and Karen

Theories are nets to catch what we call "the world": to rationalize, to explain, and to master it. We endeavor to make the mesh ever finer and finer

Karl R. Popper, 1959, p. 59

Strong inference, and the logical tree it generates,....offers a regular method for reaching firm inductive conclusions one after the other as rapidly as possible

John R. Platt, 1964, p. 347

A theory is only overthrown by a better theory, never merely by contradictory facts

J. B. Conant, 1947, p. 36

The measure of success in moving toward scientific explanation is the degree to which a theory brings out relationships between otherwise distinct and independent clusters of phenomena

William K. Estes, 1979, p.47

To improve its (the organism's) bet, it must accumulate and combine cues

Egon Brunswik, 1955, p. 207

First, we view the human as a processor of information

Donald A. Norman, 1969. p. 3

The work in this research program has shown that stimulus integration often obeys simple algebraic rules

Norman H. Anderson, 1981, p. 3

In general, such concepts are fuzzy in the sense that they correspond to classes of objects or constructs which do not have sharply defined boundaries

Lotfi Zadeh, 1965, p. 251

Preface

This book is about the processing of information. The central domain of interest is face-to-face communication in which the speaker makes available both audible and visible characteristics to the perceiver. Articulation by the speaker creates changes in atmospheric pressure for hearing and provides tongue, lip, jaw, and facial movements for seeing. These characteristics must be processed by the perceiver to recover the message conveyed by the speaker. The speaker and perceiver must share a language to make communication possible; some internal representation is necessarily functional for the perceiver to recover the message of the speaker. That is, the perceiver must evaluate the external characteristics against some representation specifying the relationship between the audible and visible characteristics and the meaningful units of the message. On the basis of this process, some decision can be made about the intended message. The perceiver, in this regard, is processing information and this research is the study of information processing.

One claim is that the nature of the information processing can be studied without necessarily first knowing exactly what information is used. Logically, discovering what information is used cannot be determined without knowing something about information processing. Psychophysical methods, so useful for discovering what information is used, depend on some understanding of information processing. The current study integrates information-processing and psychophysical approaches in the analysis of speech perception by ear and eye.

The research framework is grounded in the testing of multiple hypotheses of the phenomena of interest. Binary oppositions are constructed and tested in a variety of experimental tasks and with several independent and dependent variables. The goal is to have multiple tests of contrasting hypotheses so that the rejection of a hypothesis does not rest on a single outcome.

The experimental tasks are designed following the principles of information processing and information integration. Factorial designs, along with an elaboration of these designs, are used to manipulate multiple independent variables independently of one another. The tasks are also designed to tap particular stages of information processing in order to gain insight into how the processes work, rather than simply the output of the processes. In many instances, the questions of interest demand a fine-grained analyses of the results. The experimental tests in these cases involve the quantitative testing of mathematical-process models of performance. Fine-grained analyses appear to be essential for this enterprise. Kepler was bothered by a deviation of 6′ of arc between the actual orbit of Mars and that predicted by Ptolemaic theory. Concern over this small deviation contributed to the eventual theory of elliptical rather than circular orbits. Fine-grained analyses and the testing of process models offer the potential for discovering how some action, such as pattern recognition, is actually achieved rather than simply postulating one of many possible models that could produce the action.

The guiding theoretical principle is that multiple sources of information are evaluated and integrated to achieve speech perception. The outcomes of the binary contrasts constrain how evaluation and integration must work. Contrary to decades of discreteness, evaluation of a source information (e.g., a feature) provides information about the degree to which alternatives are presented. Sources of information are evaluated independently of one another and the integration occurs in such a fashion that the least ambiguous sources have the most impact on the judgment. The nature of the processes in the speech-perception domain do not differ significantly from those involved in other forms of similar behavior. The discoveries in the speech domain are shown to inform a variety of behaviors ranging from person impression and categorization to sentence interpretation and decision making.

The ambitious goal of the book has been implemented by embedding messages at multiple levels. A research framework for psychological inquiry, experimental design, and model testing is presented hand in hand with the discoveries of speech perception by ear and eye and how these discoveries illuminate behavior in a variety of other domains.

Acknowledgements

My teachers, colleagues, and students have had a substantial influence on my work. In graduate school, John Moore and Jerry Myers instilled the appreciation of the benefits of experimentation and quantitative models in psychological inquiry. Don Norman and Dave Rumelhart were helpful experts during my postdoctoral years when I was developing my information-processing approach to the study of the mind. Norman Anderson offered not only a critical mind and the framework of information integration but an ideal model of scientist and person. Bill Epstein, Shelly Ebenholtz, and Dave Grant were my supportive colleagues on the fourth floor during my Wisconsin years. Gregg Oden and Lola Lopes brought new energy to the midwest and have been constant sources of stimulation. The unwavering support of John Theios has been extremely important. Dick Venezky has helped keep things in perspective. My students John Barresi, Wendy Idson, Howard Kallman, Michael Cohen, Joe Hary, and Laura Thompson have been and continue to be a source of pride. At Santa Cruz, the consistent encouragement of the members of the PEP group has been very valuable.

Michael M. Cohen provided significant contributions at all stages of the project, from ideas and commentary to implementing the experimental work and the model testing to mastering the system to produce camera-ready copy. Laura Thompson, Brigid Barron, Tracy Elser, Elizabeth Laren, Michael Glasgow, and Philip Pillin tested subjects. Astrid Roggen, Pat Sanders, Carole Degen, and Melessa Hemler, Nicoletta Bolas, Diana Jordan, and Rosalva Vieyra typed parts of the manuscript. Jan Robinson did a valuable copy editing of the book. Neil Appel helped with the references and index. Debbie Johnson programmed a few of the figures. Special thanks also to the children, students, and senior citizens that participated in the experiments. Margaret Ann Krzyzostan and the teachers at the University Child Care deserve a special gratitude for the extended run of the van game. The teachers at Westlake and Natural Bridges Schools were generous in providing the opportunity to test children during class time.

The first draft was written while I was a resident scholar for the project, Perception and Action, at the Zentrum für Interdisziplinäre Forshung der Universität Bielefeld. The excitement, bread, beer, and rain each contributed its share to the enterprise. Both home and abroad, Karen, Andrew, and Pia helped distract me from the project. Norman Anderson, Michael Birnbaum, Alvin Liberman, Brian MacWhinney, Melanie Mayer, Doug Medin, Bruno Repp, and Brian Walden were kind enough to make available results of their studies and to grant permission for use in the present framework. Ray Gibbs made valuable comments on an earlier draft of the book. His suggestions helped to enhance the message and to leave fewer stones unturned. Thanks also go to Jennifer Gille, Brian MacWhinney, Bruno Repp, Lex van der Heijden, and Annie Vinter for comments on specific aspects of the research enterprise.

The writing of this book and the research reported herein were supported, in part, by NINCDS Grant 20314 from the Public Health Service and Grant BNS-83-15192 from the National Science Foundation. This support is gratefully acknowledged.

Dominic William Massaro

Santa Cruz, California
1987

Contents

Table of Phonetic Symbols

Phonetic symbol	Key word	Phonetic symbol	Key word
i	eve	d	day
I	it	k	key
ɛ	met	g	go
æ	at	h	he
a	father	f	for
ɔ	all	v	vote
ʊ	foot	θ	thin
u	boot	ð	then
ɜ	word	s	see
ʌ	up	z	zoo
ə	about	ʃ	she
eI	say	ž	azure
aI	I	tʃ	church
ɔI	boy	dž	judge
aʊ	out	m	me
oʊ	go	n	no
Iu	new	ŋ	sing
p	pay	j	you
b	be	r	read
t	to	l	let
x	loch	w	we

Chapter 1: Scientific Framework for Psychological Inquiry

In face-to-face communication, the perceiver both sees and hears the speaker. The goal of the research reported in this book is to develop a psychological description of how the perceiver recognizes what the speaker says. Given the preceding century of psychological inquiry, it would not be inappropriate to bypass metatheoretical and methodological preliminaries and to get on with it. The hypotheses, experimental tests, and analyses stand on their own merit and reduce uncertainty about the processes involved in bimodal speech recognition. Preliminaries are necessary, however, because the relevance of the research stretches well beyond understanding speech perception into diverse domains of perceptual and cognitive performance. The goal of the book, therefore, is more ambitious than the goal of the research because the book confronts fundamental issues in experimental psychology and cognitive science, as well as the information and processes supporting speech perception. To set the stage for the research and to illustrate its relationship to extant issues, an important theoretical (or perhaps metatheoretical) principle is presented and evaluated.

1. Modularity of Mind

The present research addresses an engaging issue in extant psychological theory, defined as modularity by Fodor (1983). The thesis of modularity is apparent in a variety of domains ranging from Chomsky's language organ (1975) and Pylyshyn's (1984) impenetrable processes to Forster's (1985) modular lexicon. I will follow Fodor's presentation of the issue because it is the most complete and influential one to date. Fodor's thesis is that there are independent psychological systems making up much of our mental life. These input systems are to be distinguished from more cognitive or central systems. We can and have learned a lot about input systems, but have not and cannot learn very much about general or central cognitive systems. What properties, then, do input systems have that make them good candidates for a successful psychological inquiry? Fodor gives nine properties that define input systems and distinguish them from central systems.

First, input systems are domain-specific, and Fodor manages to define about six of them—five corresponding to the traditional senses and one more for language. There are qualitative differences in processing among these input systems. For example, the psychological mechanisms in vision that mediate object perception would differ significantly from the processes contributing to sentence interpretation. Second, the operation of input systems is mandatory; we can't help but read roadside signs. Third, there is only limited central access to the mental representations that input systems compute. Fourth, input systems are fast. The fifth and maybe most important property of input systems is that they are informationally encapsulated; the information available for processing by any input system is limited to specialized bottom-up properties. Sixth, the input analyzers have shallow outputs, or simply solve the task they were designed to solve. The seventh property of input systems is that they are associated with the fixed neural architecture. The eighth property is that input systems exhibit characteristic and specific breakdown patterns; specific brain injury creates specific deficits. Finally, in his ninth characteristic, Fodor argues for the innateness of input systems in which the ontogeny of input systems exhibits a characteristic pace and sequencing.

The nine properties of input systems are best understood when contrasted with the description of central systems. The main distinction here involves what the input systems compute as opposed to what the organism believes. When we use language to communicate our views, we draw on all of what we have seen, heard, remembered, or think. The cognitive mechanisms must have an interface among the outputs of all of the input systems. Perhaps it is this attribute of having available multiple sources of information that makes Fodor pessimistic about understanding central systems. The thesis of the present endeavor, however, is that input systems also have multiple sources of information available, and they should not be distinguished from central systems in terms of the number of sources of information. In speech, for example, there are multiple, audible, visible, and contextual sources of information supporting perception.

The contribution of the current approach has to do with the question of the uniqueness of the processes that have been uncovered in bimodal speech perception. The hypothesis is that the processes involved in bimodal speech perception are similar to those involved in a number of other domains of perceptual and cognitive functioning. After developing an understanding of speech perception by ear and by eye, I explore several domains and ask whether similar or analogous processes occur across these domains. The domains include person impression, learning of arbitrary categories, sentence interpretation, probability judgments of possible events, and judgments of category membership. Following Fodor's classification, these domains include both input modules and central systems. It should not be possible to provide the same process description across these domains, especially a description developed from another unique input domain of bimodal speech perception. To the extent that the present framework can provide a unified account of this broad range of phenomena, modularity is not a reasonable guideline for psychological inquiry.

1.1 Speech Perception

Liberman and Mattingly (1985) have adopted Fodor's modularity principle in their revision of the motor theory of speech perception. According to their view, a biologically distinct system (a module) is responsible for the perception of phonetic information without translation from preliminary auditory impressions. Speech perception results from the input module's specialization for phonetic gestures. Given the assumed biological link between perception and production, listeners are prevented from hearing speech as ordinary sound. Articulatory gestures are perceived because of the lawful dependencies among gestures, articulatory movements, vocal-tract shapes, and signal. In a similar fashion, Eimas (1985) has proposed that infants arrive with innate perceptual mechanisms to detect discrete phonemic categories. These claims for specialization of speech would offer little hope for our research framework on two counts. First, approaching the study of bimodal speech perception from the perspective of prototypical pattern recognition must fail. By definition, a specialized process should not follow general principles. Second, the laws uncovered for bimodal speech perception should have little applicability to other domains of human performance.

To anticipate the outcome of the current enterprise, my claim is that both expectations from the modularity principle have failed to materialize. The research has succeeded in uncovering principles of bimodal speech perception; principles that are highly representative of bimodal speech perception prove to be relevant to a variety of behaviors ranging from person impression to the utilization of arbitrary categories. In each domain, the perceiver evaluates multiple sources of both bottom-up and top-down information, integrates these sources with respect to representations in memory, and classifies the pattern on the basis of the relative goodness of match among the relevant categories. The findings also offer a much more optimistic view of language use by the hearing-impaired. To the extent that speech perception is not specialized, we should be able to substitute the sounds of speech with other functionally-valid cues. Lipread information combined with transformation of acoustic signal into tactile, visible, or electrical forms should be sufficient to support language perception and understanding.

The remaining charge of the first chapter is to articulate the research paradigm and place it in the context of contemporary theory. Although familiar to most readers, the research strategies of falsification and strong inference are reviewed. The present use of the research strategy of testing between alternative hypotheses has succeeded in providing major constraints on any contending theory of speech perception. Two different approaches to experimental psychology are described and contrasted. The historical link to the current research is presented in terms of Egon Brunswik's probabilistic functionalism and the contemporary reference belongs to Norman Anderson's theory of information integration. There are also important relationships to the highly informative work on natural categories (Mervis & Rosch, 1981) and the descriptive framework of Fuzzy Set Theory (Zadeh 1965, 1984).

2. Research Framework

One framework for scientific endeavor has been expressed most succinctly by Karl Popper (1959). The central assumption is that hypothesis testing must follow deductive rather than inductive methods. Following Hume, Popper claims that we are not justified in inferring universal statements from singular ones. Any conclusion drawn inductively might always turn out to be false. Although we can generate many instances of positive results, the theory might still be exposed as false. As scientists, we should guard against trying to verify a particular hypothesis by demonstrating that it works in specific instances. Given that new instances can always falsify a given statement, no experimental observation can verify a hypothesis.

2.1 Falsification

Popper proposes that a hypothesis, once constructed, must be subjected to the following analysis. The investigator begins by comparing the conclusions derived from the hypothesis in order to determine whether they are internally consistent. An analysis of the conclusions will also indicate whether or not the hypothesis is testable. By contrasting this hypothesis with other hypotheses, the investigator determines whether the theory is unique and whether it would constitute a scientific advance should the hypothesis survive experimental tests. If the conclusions drawn from the hypothesis meet these requirements, it is worthwhile to subject its conclusions to experimental tests.

Experimental tests will decide how well a hypothesis or theory survives. If a theory survives the experimental tests, we should not discard it. On the other hand, if the experimental tests falsify conclusions drawn from the theory, then the theory should be rejected or modified accordingly. In a more recent contribution, Popper (1976) acknowledged that models could be modified indefinitely to incorporate inconsistent results. This prolongation of falsification is called immunization. Successive modification of a model keeps it alive and holds off its eventual death. In this case, an alternative conceptualization would be a better contribution than another inconsistent experimental result. As observed by Conant (1947, p. 36): "A theory is only overthrown by a better theory, never merely by contradictory facts."

Surviving a particular experimental test only temporarily supports a theory because another investigator may very soon provide a test that overthrows it. A critical feature of Popper's scientific framework is that verifiability and falsifiability do not have a symmetrical relationship. Although theories can be falsified, they cannot be truly verified. Popper proposes that it is best to conclude that positive results only corroborate a particular theory; they do not verify it.

2.2 Strong Inference

Building on Popper's approach to scientific endeavor, John Platt (1964) encourages scientists to employ a strong-inference strategy of testing hypotheses. In contrast to generating a single hypothesis, Platt would have the scientist generate multiple hypotheses relevant to a particular phenomenon of interest. The experimental test would be designed to eliminate (or in Popper's words, falsify) as many of these hypotheses as possible. The results of the experimentation would allow the generation of new hypotheses which could be subjected to further tests. Both Platt and Popper adhere to David Hume's axiom prohibiting inductive arguments. The message is that the scientist should not attempt to confirm a single pet hypothesis. However, Platt's solution is more productive in that at least one of the multiple hypotheses under test should fail and, therefore, can be rejected.

Table 1 illustrates the falsification and strong inference strategies of hypothesis testing. Strong inference has the potential of providing more information than falsification. If an experiment can be designed to falsify one hypothesis with one outcome and another hypothesis with another outcome, then there is a greater likelihood of rejecting a hypothesis. By making two hypotheses mutually exclusive, the experiment should be able to falsify one of the hypotheses. However, other outcomes might be possible; for example, neither or both of the outcomes may obtain. The bottom panel of Table 1 acknowledges the fact that any experimental test of a hypothesis usually requires auxiliary assumptions relevant to the specific experimental situation. It could be the case that certain observations do not disprove a hypothesis if the assumptions involved in testing the hypothesis are not appropriate. Thus, following Garner, Hake, and Eriksen (1956), we should exploit the idea of converging operations, or in the strong-inference framework, converging tests that lead to the same outcome. When very different tests lead to the same result, we are less likely to be wrong.

Table 1. Illustration of the strategies of falsification and strong inference in hypothesis testing

	falsification		*strong inference*	
prediction	$H \Rightarrow O$		$H_1 \Rightarrow O_1, H_2 \Rightarrow O_2$	
observation	$\neg O$	O	O_1 and $\neg O_2$	$\neg O_1$ and O_2
conclusion	$\neg H$	none	$\neg H_2$	$\neg H_1$
prediction	$H + A \Rightarrow O$		$H_1 + A \Rightarrow O_1, H_2 + A \Rightarrow O_2$	
observation	$\neg O$	O	O_1 and $\neg O_2$	$\neg O_1$ and O_2
conclusion	$\neg(H + A)$	none	$\neg(H_2 + A)$	$\neg(H_1 + A)$

H = hypothesis, O = observation, A = assumptions, $\neg X$ = the negation of X, $\Rightarrow$ = implies

3. Two Approaches to Psychological Inquiry

Most studies in experimental psychology represent one of two metatheoretical frameworks. The psychophysical approach aims to discover laws relating the physical world to observable behavior. The value of psychophysics requires little emphasis and is illustrated by progress in domains of color perception, tone perception, and the near hit of Weber's law. Psychophysical methods have also been successful in determining the influence of higher-order visual properties on visual perception and action. The second framework aims to discover how the stimulus world is processed in order to result in some observable behavior. The value of this information-processing approach is apparent in the progress that has been made in understanding pattern recognition, memory, and decision making. The current research utilizes both psychophysical and information-processing methods and a brief overview of these approaches is warranted.

3.1 Psychophysics

The psychophysical approach was inaugurated by Fechner (1860) and has remained central to experimental psychology. Some stimulus is manipulated under highly controlled conditions in a task requiring some judgment or action from the participant. Given the experimental control and direct manipulation of the stimulus, it is possible to determine causal relationships between stimulus and behavior. I have distinguished between Titchenerian and Gibsonian psychophysics (Massaro, in press c). The first approach assumes that the whole is composed of component parts and that these parts can be isolated and studied individually. Research within this framework has used relatively simple stimuli and relatively simple tasks, such as judging the loudness of a pure tone varying in amplitude. Theorists within the Gibsonian framework ask that investigators focus on the higher-order structure of the environment and relate it to behavior (Gibson, 1979; Haber, 1983; Turvey, 1977; Turvey & Shaw, 1979). The implicit assumption in this proposal is that there are complex environmental invariants responsible for much of behavior and the goal is to discover these properties to explicate behavioral observations. Studying behavior in a natural situation is dictated by this assumption. If higher-order invariants of the environment are eliminated, as supposedly occurs in simple laboratory tasks, then they cannot be discovered. Gibson (1950, 1966) and his followers have reminded us about one traditional problem in scientific inquiry called external validity or the degree to which one can generalize from the experimental to the natural situation.

The Gibsonian framework is similar in many important respects to the Titchenerian paradigm, however. Both paradigms dictate the discovery of relationships between objective and subjective worlds without fundamental concern for the intervening mental processes and representations. In contrast to the Titchenerian assumption of the whole being composed of component parts, however, the neo-Gibsonians, like the Gestaltists, believe that higher-order invariants are directly perceived and will stand on the left side of the S-R chain. Although fundamentally different with regard to the nature of the information, research on component-cues as well as research on higher-order invariants is grounded in the domain of psychophysics.

3.1.1 Limitations of Psychophysics

These two approaches to the study of the world of information have produced somewhat disappointing results (Massaro, 1985b). Gibsonians and neo-Gibsonians have not yet delivered with respect to discovering higher-order invariants (see Shebilske, in press; von Hofsten, in press). Looking out my window at grass, weeds and trees, there is no apparent single higher-order invariant that can capture my experience of depth and object constancy. The knowledge acquired in the psychophysical study of component cues has also been relatively limited. Although many cues have been proposed, there is very little insight into how the perceiver evaluates and utilizes the cues in perception. We have not learned the relative importance of the cues nor how the multiple cues work together. (A recent study by Cutting and Millard (1984) has, at least, begun to address the relative importance issue.) One strategy in the traditional psychophysical approach has been to ask how one cue works when other cues are neutralized or held constant. This single-factor design strategy is particularly apparent in most studies of visual localization of points of light because these studies are carried out in the absence of visual context. The single-cue paradigm not only fails to define how the particular cue would operate in a more natural situation; it also does not address the issue of how the perceiver evaluates and integrates multiple cues in perceptual processing.

3.2 Information-Processing Theory

In information-processing theory, the individual is viewed as a processor of information (Broadbent, 1958, 1971; Massaro, 1975a; Neisser, 1967). It should be noted that the information-processing theory is a metatheoretical framework (Massaro, 1986b; Palmer & Kimchi, 1986) and is much more general than any particular methodology such as the additive-factor method (Sternberg, 1969). The researcher attempts to understand what happens to the information as it is perceived, interpreted, and acted upon by the individual. The processing of environmental information depends on the nature of the relevant sensory systems, some representation of past experiences, the relevant motor systems, and the goals of the participant.

One central assumption of research within the information-processing paradigm is that observed performance in some domain involves a sequence of processing stages. The onsets of these processing stages are successive and each stage operates on the information available to it. The operations of a particular stage take time and transform the information available to it. The transformed information is made available to the next stage of processing. Two theoretical constructs are important in this approach. First, the memory construct describes or defines the nature of the information at a particular stage of processing. Second, the processing construct describes the operations performed by a stage of information processing. The information-processing paradigm provides a framework that can be implemented using a variety of experimental methods, manipulations, and dependent variables. Examples of informative research areas include the additive-factor method and backward recognition masking.

A major implication of the information processing approach is that it is necessary to account for each of the processing stages involved in performance. This principle requires that the investigator make explicit the implicit assumptions inherent in the experimental task. Failure to do so severely limits what can be learned from the results. The precise analysis given by the information-processing methodology can be thought of as a microscope. It allows the experimenter to see what is not directly observable. As an example, the additive-factor methodology has been reasonably successful in providing glimpses at recognition, memory search, and response selection processes (Massaro, 1984a; Sanders, 1980; Sternberg, 1975; Theios, 1975).

3.2.1 Limitations of Current Information-Processing Models

A prototypical information-processing model aims to specify 1) the time course of mental operations, 2) the nature of mental operations, and 3) the nature of memory structures that hold information. In contrast to what might be expected from their name, information-processing models have not really been all that concerned with information. Information is taken to mean the actual aspects of the environment that are informative. Noting the failure of an earlier enterprise, information theory in explaining psychological phenomena, Neisser helped shape the view of information in the information-processing model: "information is what is transformed and the structured pattern of its transformations is what we want to understand" (p. 8, 1967). This statement seemed to give license to relegating information to a minor role in information processing.

Within the information-processing framework, many researchers sought to define the time course and nature of mental operations without specifying the nature of the information used in particular domains. These researchers used rather arbitrary stimuli (tones, lights, letters, words) without really being concerned with their function in the real world. The implicit assumption was that the time course and nature of mental operations could be defined independently of the nature of the stimuli being processed. Although this research was a profitable enterprise, one obvious legacy is a model in search of a natural domain to describe.

The limitations of pure information processing became apparent to this writer when I and a group of students applied the model to language processing (Massaro, 1975b). Consistent with the information-processing approach, many facets of understanding language were illuminated by accounting for the stages of processing involved. For example, isolating the perceptual unit functional in speech perception required analyzing the memory structures and psychological processes involved in the task of perception. What became obvious, however, is that the language information is as important or more important than the processing of that information. A complete theory of language perception has to describe not only what is done with information but also what is used as information.

Consider the role of time. The time available for processing information is important in speech perception as it is in domains with simple artificial signals (Massaro, 1975b). However, time also is information in speech in that some speech distinctions, such as vowel identity and consonant voicing, are cued by the duration of the speech segments (Massaro, 1984c). Thus, the potential information in the language signal and its utilization by the language user has to be described as well as the time course of perception, decision, and memory. The information-processing paradigm is still the best game in town because it provides a coherent framework for the finding of analogous processes in speech perception and reading (Massaro, 1975b, 1978, 1979). Even so, it is now clear that a model of information processing must include the nature of information and its utilization in addition to its processing.

3.3 Integrating Information and Information Processing

My goal in this essay is to integrate the information processing approach with the study of the world of information. The paradigm that makes this resolution possible can be attributed, in part, to Brunswik (1952, 1955, 1956), who anticipated some of the trends currently in vogue in psychology. In contrast to Helmholtz's (1856) idea of perception guided by unconscious logic, he viewed perception as a primitive and autonomous process. This view subsumes Fodor's (1983) thesis of separate and autonomous modules for different psychological functions such as visual perception and language. Brunswik also called for the study of natural situations rather than artificial experimental tasks. Thus, calls to natural ecology in the study of perception such as those by Neisser (1976) and Haber (1983) were in the psychological literature decades ago. For the present framework, Brunswik's significant contribution was the acknowledgement of multiple but ambiguous sources of influence on behavior. He proposed the concept of probabilistic functionalism based on the idea that many cues determine behavior. However, the cues were seen as equivocal and only probabilistically related to behavior. Before articulating the extension of these ideas to the study of speech perception, an overview of pattern identification is appropriate.

4. Pattern Recognition

Recognition, identification, and categorization of patterns appear to be central to perceptual and cognitive functioning. Pattern recognition has been found to be fundamental in such different domains as playing chess, examining x-rays, and reading (Chase & Simon, 1973; Lesgold, 1984a, 1984b; Massaro, 1984a). It is important to consider to what extent these three acts involve the same fundamental processes. That is, does categorization of an instance involve processing of a different nature than that required for recognition of the instance? We consider these three acts to entail the same fundamental processes. In addition, all of these acts have in common the possible characterization and classification as choice experiments in which the subject, given a stimulus, chooses one of a set of alternative responses (Bush, Galanter, and Luce, 1963).

We must also consider to what extent the processing of a pattern depends on the empirical domain involved. Does recognition of a chessboard configuration involve the same processes as recognition of the syllable /ba/ or does the utilization of multiple cues to object and depth perception differ qualitatively from integrating prosodic, syntactic, and semantic information in sentence interpretation? This issue addresses the notion of modularity of cognitive functioning postulated by Fodor (1983). In contrast to modularity, pattern recognition seems to involve similar operations regardless of the specific nature of the patterns (see Chapter 9). Evidence supporting this thesis is one of the products of the current endeavor. Third, what is the developmental progression of the processes involved in pattern recognition? There do not appear to be qualitative changes in speech perception across different stages of development, as might be expected from Piagetian theory (see Chapter 8). Analogous to similar processes across empirical domains, the same fundamental processes seem to occur across development. Fourth, what is the appropriate methodological and theoretical framework for studying pattern classification behavior? The goal of such research would appear to be defining the nature of the information in the environmental situation; the sensory, perceptual, and conceptual representations of that information; the representation of the alternatives in memory; the operations involved in matching the present event with the appropriate memory representations; and the selection of some action such as choosing a response on the basis of the outcome of these operations.

4.1 Multiple Sources of Information

The most salient aspect of the current approach to pattern recognition involves the idea of integrating multiple sources of information. Consider recognition of the word *performance* in the written sentence

The actress was praised for her outstanding performance.

Recognition of the critical word is achieved via a variety of bottom-up and top-down sources of information. Top-down sources include semantic and syntactic constraints and bottom-up sources include visual features and letters making up the word (Massaro, 1984a; Massaro, in press c). Orthographic constraints also have been shown to contribute to perceptual recognition at the word level (Venezky & Massaro, in press). The current research enterprise revolves around the fundamental processes involved in the evaluation and integration of audible and visible sources in bimodal speech perception. Although the focus is on bimodal speech, a central assumption is that these processes are fundamental to any pattern recognition situation and that there should be considerable overlap in the processes across different domains.

5. Integrating Information from Multiple Sources

Integrating multiple sources of information appears to be a natural function of human endeavor. Integration appears to occur to some extent regardless of the goals and motivations of the perceiver. Brunswik, more than anyone else, deserves recognition for the early acknowledgement of the multiple but ambiguous sources of influence on behavior. He stressed "the limited ecological validity or trustworthiness of cues . . . To improve its (the organism's) bet, it must accumulate and combine cues" (1955, p. 207).

Brunswik is best known for his lens model, illustrated in Figure 1 within a more contemporary format. With respect to the world of information, Brunswik distinguished between two kinds of validity. Ecological validity defines what cues are informative about the structure of the world. As an example, height in the vertical plane can be shown to be correlated with distance of the object from the observer. Functional validity defines what cues people actually use in perceptual processing. Given this distinction, it can be seen that a concern for ecological validity is not sufficient, given that some ecologically valid property of the physical world may not be used and hence not be functionally valid. One might expect that functionally valid cues might always be ecologically valid, but many counterexamples exist. The gambler's fallacy of using the outcome of a preceding roll of the dice to guide prediction of the current roll is one of many ecologically invalid decision heuristics. A complete description of the environmental-behavior relationship requires an analysis of both ecological and functional validity.

Brunswik and Kamiya (1953) found some ecological validity for the proximity of two lines as a cue to those lines defining the boundaries of a single object. Similarly, Seidner (Brunswik, 1956) found that vertical position of points was positively correlated with distance from the observer. It should be noted, however, that these latter two observations were only demonstrations of ecological validity given that they did not evaluate functional validity in terms of the extent to which these cues are utilized in perception and recognition.

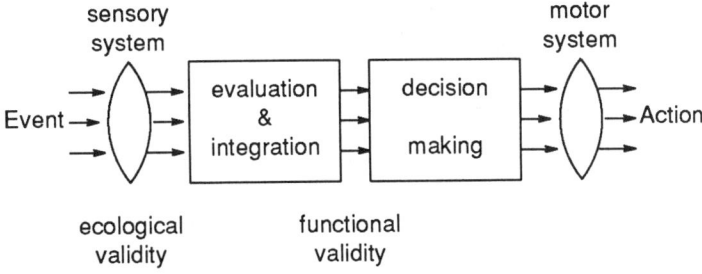

Figure 1. Schematic diagram of the Lens model of Brunswik, illustrated in a more contemporary format. Ecological validity refers to the aspects of the physical and sensory world that are informative about some object or event. Functional validity refers to those aspects that are actually utilized by the observer in perception and action.

The finding of only moderate ecological validity for various cues probably contributed to Brunswik's development of probabilistic functionalism, meaning that objects and goals in the environment are only probabilistically related to the available cues. A cue such as height in the vertical plane is an equivocal, and thus a probabilistic, cue to depth in that it only predicts depth with some probability. Having been informed by the development of fuzzy sets (Zadeh, 1965) and continuous information (Massaro & Cohen, 1983a), however, an equivocal cue might be better thought of as providing information to some degree rather than providing probabilistic information. That is, a depth cue provides continuous information about the degree to which a given depth is present. The fundamental difference between discrete (categorical) and continuous information is one central concern of the current study.

Consider an early experiment of Brunswik (1934). Subjects were asked to equate two groups of stamps that varied in number, size, and monetary value. When subjects were instructed to use just one of these three dimensions, their judgments were nonetheless significantly influenced by the irrelevant dimensions. Told to equate two groups of stamps with respect to number, subjects were influenced by the size and value of the stamps. Our present goal is to determine the appropriate experimental paradigm for the study of integration. Before doing so, the reader may have been bothered by my inexact use of the concept of information and I am now able to define it more explicitly.

5.1 Data and Information

The distinction between ecological and functional validity in the lens model of Brunswik can be used to clarify the use of information in the current endeavor. Like Brunswik, I believe it is necessary to distinguish between environmental properties that are potentially informative about some object or event and the properties actually used in perception and recognition of the object or event. The former might be called data and the latter information. As apparent from the examples of ecological and functional validity mentioned earlier, there is no reason to expect a one to one correspondence between data and information (or between ecological and functional validity).

Given the distinction between data and information, it is also possible to study one of these somewhat independently of the other. We have seen examples of evaluating ecological validity without a concern for functional validity. Our work might be characterized by a primary concern for how information is evaluated and integrated (without a detailed assessment of what is actually informative). Auditory and visual properties of the speech event are manipulated independently of one another, but without a specific assessment of the actual aspects of these properties that are functional (informative).

5.2 Brunswik's Representative Design

Complementing the theoretical notions of probabilistic functionalism, Brunswik (1955) proposed a unique methodological framework for psychological study. The framework called for representative designs or designs that are random samples of natural ecology. Thus, only correlational rather than experimental methods could be used because behavior must be studied within the context of the multiple cues as they co-occur in the natural world of the observer. Brunswik argued that single-factor and factorial designs are artificial because they decorrelate naturally occurring cues. For this reason, Brunswik contended that experimental results cannot be generalized to the real world. He made a distinction between internal and external validity. The results derived from a factorial design may be internally valid but not externally valid given that they have no generality outside the experiment itself.

Brunswik's concept of representative design is nicely illustrated in a study of size constancy (Brunswik, 1944) in which he followed up a laboratory study of size constancy with a representative design. A graduate student was interrupted in her daily routine at irregular intervals and asked to make judgments of the object she currently viewed. The subject was asked to estimate the size of various objects in a natural setting across a wide range of sizes and distances. The subject judged the size of trees, telephone poles, bookcases, inkwells, and so on. The primary measure of performance was a correlation between the subjective estimates and objective physical size. The study included five different kinds of perceptual judgments and produced subjective estimates of objective size, projective size, and distance. The data analyses were centered around correlations between the various aspects of the judgments and the environment. The largest and most impressive (to Brunswik) correlation was between perceived objective size and actual size. The correlation between estimated projective size and actual projective size was low. These results are identical in principle to classical laboratory studies of size constancy, and, therefore, the two kinds of study seem to converge on similar results. The question is whether the representative design of Brunswik offers a more informative study of the phenomenon and whether it can address the issue of the cues used in perception.

Hilgard (1955) provided important criticisms of representative designs and correlational analyses that are still relevant today. High correlations between perceived size and actual size can be obtained even with a relatively high error in the estimation of size. Some of the errors in Brunswik's observations were as great as 3 to 1. Hilgard conjectures that repeating the experiments with a blind subject also would produce high correlations. If the blind subject were given a name of the objects, the estimations would have correlated with the actual size of the object and not with the object's projective size. The subject would not have a basis for estimating the projective size given that the distance of the object would not be known. The main conclusion that would be reached is that size constancy of visual perception would be obtained even with a subject who could not see. In the representative design there is an artificial link between the known size of the object and the perceived size of the object. This kind of error in a representative design would not be obtained in a laboratory study of size constancy in which known object size would not be available because artificial stimuli would be used.

Hilgard's observations made two important points. First correlation or the more contemporary use of multiple regression can be a highly misleading index of environmental influences (see also Anderson & Shanteau, 1977; Birnbaum, 1973). Second, a representative design is not capable of discovering causal influences on behavior. As Hilgard observes, it is difficult to see how a naturalistic study of recovery from pneumonia ever would have found that Penicillin speeds up recovery. Analogously, it is hard to see how the relationship between diabetes and insulin could have resulted from just a correlational study. In both cases we expect and believe that some sort of experimental intrusion was necessary to discover these causal factors. In our work with speech perception it would not be possible to determine the relative influences of audible and visible speech without independent manipulation of these two potential sources of information.

5.3 Limitations of Representative Designs

Representative designs impose a major constraint on the type of psychological investigation that can be done. If two cues do not occur independently in the natural world, then they cannot be manipulated independently in the psychological investigations using representative designs. For this reason, representative designs are inadequate for psychological inquiry. The creation of artificial situations by utilizing factorial designs, on the other hand, can be very illuminating as I hope to demonstrate in our study of bimodal speech perception. With respect to external validity, one needs only a good theory that will allow generalization from a particular experiment to the real world, even if the experiment is not representative of the real world. A good theory is one that predicts exactly the experimental results and, without additional assumptions, rationalizes (or is at least is consistent with) naturalistic observations.

5.4 Information-Integration Framework and Factorial Designs

Loosely speaking, Anderson (1968, 1974, 1981, 1982) can be viewed as an intellectual descendant of Brunswik's probabilistic functionalism, but not of representative designs. Within the framework of information integration, it is accepted that there are multiple sources of information; the goal is to define the sources of information and to assess how they are integrated in perception and decision. In contrast to Brunswik's representative design, however, information integration is studied by utilizing factorial designs that manipulate independently multiple aspects of the environment. In our study of bimodal speech perception, we combine the information-integration paradigm with the research strategy of strong inference. It is also necessary to formulate quantitative models of performance in order to test among various alternative hypotheses.

5.5 Bimodal Speech

The availability of auditory and visual information in speech perception provides a relevant example of the multiplicity of cues in the natural situation. One might expect that the validity and reliability of the cues would be perfectly correlated. However, variation and noise in the environment and in the relevant sensory systems could differentially alter these two sources of information given that they are somewhat independent. For example, the perceiver might have a varying view of the speaker's face and extraneous background noise might vary randomly over time. Thus, for any particular speech event, the quality of the auditory aspect of the speech event is not necessarily correlated with the quality of the visual aspect of the event. Even if one adhered to the tenets of representative design, it seems reasonable to manipulate the auditory and visual sources independently of one another. Given that the two cues are not perfectly correlated in the natural situation, the factorial manipulation of the cues will not be completely new to the perceiver.

6. A Theoretical Framework for Pattern Recognition

According to the present framework, well-learned patterns are recognized in accordance with a general algorithm, regardless of the modality or particular nature of the patterns (Massaro, 1979; Oden & Massaro, 1978). The model has received support in a wide variety of domains and consists of three operations in perceptual (primary) recognition: feature evaluation, feature integration, and pattern classification. Continuously valued features are evaluated, integrated, and matched against prototype descriptions in memory, and an identification decision is made on the basis of the relative goodness of match of the stimulus information with the relevant prototype descriptions. The model is called a fuzzy logical model of perception (abbreviated FLMP). The concept of fuzzy logic and how it has influenced the development of the model is discussed more fully in Chapter 7.

6.1 Fuzzy Logical Model of Perception (FLMP)

Central to the FLMP are summary descriptions of the perceptual units of the language. These summary descriptions are called prototypes and they contain a conjunction of various properties called features. A prototype is a category and the features of the prototype correspond to the ideal values that an exemplar should have if it is a member of that category. The exact form of the representation of these properties is not known and may never be known. However, the memory representation must be compatible with the sensory representation resulting from the transduction of the audible and visible speech. Compatibility is necessary because the two representations must be related to one another. To recognize the syllable /ba/, the perceiver must be able to relate the information provided by the syllable itself to some memory of the category /ba/.

Prototypes are generated for the task at hand. In speech perception, for example, we might envision activation of all prototypes corresponding to the perceptual units of the language being spoken. For ease of exposition, consider a speech signal representing a single perceptual unit, such as the syllable /ba/. The sensory systems transduce the physical event and make available various sources of information called features. During the first operation in the model, the features are evaluated in terms of the prototypes in memory. For each feature and for each prototype, featural evaluation provides information about the degree to which the feature in the speech signal matches the featural value of the prototype.

Given the necessarily large variety of features, it is necessary to have a common metric representing the degree of match of each feature. The syllable /ba/, for example, might have visible featural information related to the closing of the lips and audible information corresponding to the second and third formant transitions. These two features must share a common metric if they eventually are going to be related to one another. To serve this purpose, fuzzy truth values (Zadeh, 1965) are used because they provide a natural representation of the degree of match. Fuzzy truth values lie between zero and one, corresponding to a proposition being completely false and completely true. The value .5 corresponds to a completely ambiguous situation whereas .7 would be more true than false and so on. Fuzzy truth values, therefore, can represent not only continuous rather than categorical information, they can represent different kinds of information. Another advantage of fuzzy truth values is that they couch information in mathematical terms (or at least in a quantitative form). This allows the natural development of a quantitative description of the phenomenon of interest.

Feature evaluation provides the degree to which each feature in the syllable matches the corresponding feature in each prototype in memory. The goal, of course, is to determine the overall goodness of match of each prototype with the syllable. All of the features are capable of contributing to this process and the second operation of the model is called feature integration. That is, the features (actually the degrees of matches) corresponding to each prototype are combined (or conjoined in logical terms). The outcome of feature integration consists of the degree to which each prototype matches the syllable. In the model, all features contribute to the final value, but with the property that the least ambiguous features have the most impact on the outcome.

The third operation during recognition processing is pattern classification. During this stage, the merit of each relevant prototype is evaluated relative to the sum of the merits of the other relevant prototypes. This relative goodness of match gives the proportion of times the syllable is identified as an instance of the prototype. The relative goodness of match could also be determined from a rating judgment indicating the degree to which the syllable matches the category. The pattern classification operation is modeled after Luce's (1959) choice rule. In pandemonium-like terms (Selfridge, 1959), we might say that it is not how loud some demon is shouting but rather the relative loudness of that demon in the crowd of relevant demons. An important prediction of the model is that one cue has its greatest effect when a second cue is at its most ambiguous level. Thus, the most informative cue has the greatest impact on the judgment.

The FLMP defines a representational system for the processing of speech. Following the illuminating analyses of Palmer (1978), five attributes must be specified for any representational system. These attributes and their implementations for bimodal speech perception are given in Table 2. The represented world is speech, and the representing world is the human listener. The aspects of the represented world, the aspects of the representing world, and their correspondences are listed in attributes 3, 4, and 5, respectively. The value of presenting the model in these terms is that it makes explicit attributes of speech that would have to be included in almost any reasonable representational system. The attributes listed in the representing world are those assumed by the FLMP and are subject to falsification in experimental and theoretical tests.

Table 2. Five attributes of the representational system assumed by the fuzzy logical model of speech perception

1. the represented world -- speech

2. the representing world -- perceiver

3. aspects of the represented world being modeled --
    audible and visible characteristics of the speech,
    speech segments (syllables, words), memory of speech,
    integration of characteristics, decision, and
    classification processes.

4. aspects of the representing world doing the modeling --
    features, truth values, integration operations,
    prototype descriptions, and classification algorithms.

5. correspondences between represented and representing
    worlds --

represented	representing
1. speech characteristics	1. features
2. speech segments	2. perceptual units
3. memory for speech	3. prototypes
4. integration of characteristics	4. prototype matching
5. decision/classification	5. pattern classification

6.2 Model Tests

An attractive feature of the FLMP is that it generates quantitative predictions of many experimental situations. The FLMP not only can be tested directly against a broad range of results, it is capable of being tested against other quantitative models of performance. It follows that the primary level of data analysis in the present monograph involves quantitative testing of models of performance. When possible, the predictions of the model are tested against the results of individual subjects. In cases in which tests of the model involve the results from other experiments, or when individual subjects are not tested for a sufficient number of trials, the model is applied to the average results. In all cases, the quantitative predictions of the models are determined by using the program STEPIT (Chandler, 1969). Each model is represented to the program in terms of a set of prediction equations and a set of unknown parameters. By iteratively adjusting the parameters of the model, the program minimizes the squared deviations between the observed and predicted points. The outcome of the program STEPIT is a set of parameter values which, when put into the model, come closest to predicting the observed results. Thus, STEPIT maximizes the accuracy of the description of each model.

Although it is convenient to describe hypothesis testing as a qualitative enterprise with a binary outcome, in reality, it is quantitative and the outcome is best interpreted in terms of the degree to which the model survives a test. Given that no single test is likely to be sufficiently informative, the goal is to implement an array of experimental tests of a given hypothesis. By having multiple tests, uncertainty is reduced beyond what would be available in a single test (Garner et al., 1956). In this manner, our scientific strategy resembles the theoretical framework assuming continuous sources of information in pattern recognition. Any measure of goodness-of-fit must, therefore, be interpreted in relatively continuous terms. There is no robust statistic that can give acceptable values of goodness-of-fit of a model relative to the number of independent observations and free parameters.

The goodness of fit that is used is the root mean square deviation (RMSD). The RMSD is simply the standard deviation or a measure of the variability of a set of scores that provides an indication of the average amount by which the scores deviate from the mean of the distribution. In the present usage, the concern is with the deviations between the predicted and observed results and the RMSD is the square root of the average squared deviation between the predicted and observed points. Given that the proportion of choosing a particular response alternative is between zero and one, and rating judgments are transformed to values between zero and one, the RMSD value is easily evaluated in terms of goodness of fit. The RMSD values can lie between zero and one and we usually have accepted RMSD values less than five percent as indicating a fairly good description of the results by a particular model. In addition to this absolute criterion, the relative difference in RMSD values for two different models provides another indication of goodness of fit.

It should be noted that the RMSD value is a much better index of the goodness of fit of a model than is the correlation between the predicted and observed values. We have found that some models may give very large RMSD values of around 20 percent, and yet the predicted and observed values will correlate about .95. Thus it is important to beware, as noted by Birnbaum (1973) and Anderson and Shanteau (1977), that high correlations do not necessarily reflect a good description by a particular model.

6.3 Application of the FLMP

To illustrate the FLMP, I analyze a classic study carried out by Denes (1955) because it was one of the few early studies directly concerned with multiple cues to a given speech distinction. The noun and verb pronunciations of *use* differ in the voicing of the final consonant. Analysis of natural productions of these words revealed that they differed in both vowel duration and consonant duration. The voiced alternatives /juz/ tends to have a longer vowel and a shorter consonant frication relative to the voiceless alternative /jus/. Denes manipulated the speech signal to create syllables that varied systematically on these two dimensions. The two variables were manipulated to give a range of values going from the ideal values for /juz/ to the ideal values for /jus/. Five levels of frication duration were factorially combined with four levels of vowel duration to give 20 unique syllables. Subjects were asked to identify the syllables as one of the two alternatives.

In the framework of the FLMP, the prototypes corresponding to the two syllables specify information about the durations of the vowel and frication segments

/juz/ : Long Vowel & Short Frication
/jus/ : Short Vowel & Long Frication

Given these contrasting alternatives, it can be assumed that Short is the negation of Long. Negation is implemented as the additive complement in the model giving the prototype descriptions

/juz/ : Long Vowel & Not(Long Frication)
/jus/ : Not(Long Vowel) & Long Frication

Given a test syllable, feature evaluation determines the degree to which the featural information in the test syllable matches the ideal values given for those features in the prototype descriptions. If v_i represents the degree to which the vowel has long duration and f_j represents the degree to which the frication has long duration, these values inserted into the prototypes would give

/juz/ : $v_i \,\&\, (1-f_j)$
/jus/ : $(1-v_i)\&f_j$

Integration of the features involves the product of the feature values to give a goodness of match

/juz/ : $v_i \times (1-f_j)$
/jus/ : $(1-v_i) \times f_j$

Given that these are the only two valid alternatives in the task, the probability of a /juz/ identification given a test syllable with vowel duration V_i and frication duration F_j is given by the pattern classification operation

$$P(/juz/ \,|\, V_i F_j) = \frac{v_i(1-f_j)}{v_i(1-f_j)+(1-v_i)f_j}$$

We do not know the ideal feature values, and therefore a free parameter for each unique level of vowel duration and frication duration must be estimated to predict the observed results. Nine free parameters are necessary to fit the 20 independent identification probabilities generated from the factorial combination of four levels of vowel duration and five levels of frication duration. The observed and predicted results are shown in Figure 2. Two important characteristics should be noted in both the observed and predicted results. There were main effects of both variables, and the effects were nonadditive. The effect of each variable was largest in the middle range of the variable. The middle range of each variable is the most ambiguous region, and the results illustrate that the effect of one variable is largest when the other variable is most ambiguous.

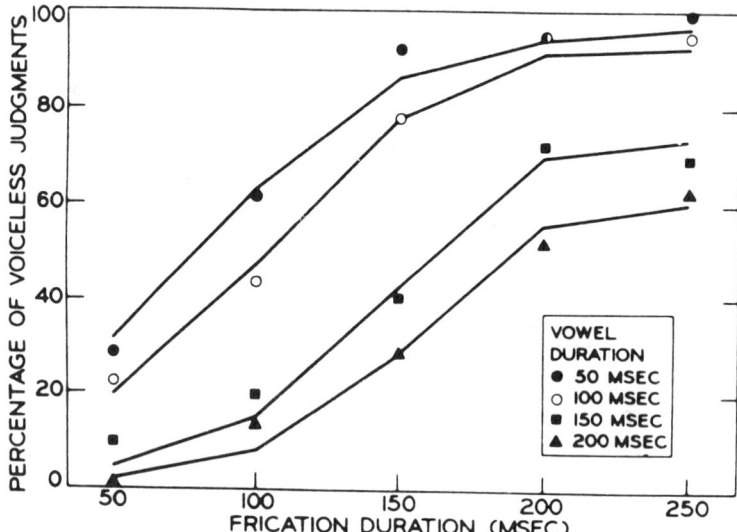

Figure 2. Observed (points) and FLMP predictions (lines) of the voicing judgments as a function of frication duration and vowel duration (observations of Denes, 1955; from Massaro & Cohen, 1977).

7. Speech Perception by Ear and Eye

The concern of the present monograph is the integration of auditory and visual information in speech perception. The relevance of visual information in speech perception was demonstrated most saliently in the phenomenon which has come to be known as the McGurk effect. McGurk and MacDonald (1976) reported that a perceptual illusion sometimes occurs if a speech sound is dubbed onto a videotape of a different articulation. As an example, subjects reported hearing /da/ when the sound /ba/ was paired with a /ga/ articulation. The outcome was called illusory given that hearing was influenced by the corresponding visual information. On the other hand, it might be more productive to view the phenomenon as the consequence of a natural tendency to integrate multiple sources of information in perceptual processing. (As an aside, it should be noted that this discovery was possible only because a situation that would not occur naturally was devised. Thus, we have a violation of Brunswik's (1952) and Neisser's (1976) dicta for psychological research.) What I aim to demonstrate is that the dissection of this phenomenon within the framework of binary oppositions, combined with the tools of information integration (Anderson, 1981, 1982) and model testing (Townsend, 1984), not only illuminates the phenomenon itself but also more general problems of perception and pattern recognition.

7.1 Binary Oppositions

The binary oppositions to be considered are arranged hierarchically in Figure 3. In some cases, the question at one level is dependent on the answers to the questions at higher levels. As an example, the issue of whether or not multiple sources of information are integrated (combined) in perception requires that multiple sources rather than just a single source be available to the perceiver. Similarly, questions about the nature of integration are meaningful only if integration occurs. On the other hand, whether sources of data provide continuous or categorical information can be assessed regardless of whether or not they are processed independently. Each question in Figure 3 demands one or two chapters.

The first question addresses the contribution of visual information to speech perception. Although we normally think of speech perception as a mapping between sound and hearing, there is good evidence for the utilization of visual information in face-to-face communication. Chapter 2 is devoted to a review of the literature supporting the conclusion of both auditory and visual sources of information in speech perception. The issue of audible and visible sources of information is easily motivated by the psychophysical approach because the causal influences of the stimulus world must be specified. The question also sets the stage for the information-processing approach, however, because influences of both audible and visible speech must engage significant processing. From this perspective, a more fundamental, challenging, and interesting question is addressed in Chapter 3. Are the two sources of information integrated (combined) in perception of speech or is only one source of information used at a given time? Pure psychophysics cannot address this question nor the remaining questions addressed in this book.

The next question is as psychophysical in spirit as it is process oriented because the answer specifies a psychophysical relationship as well as constrains the nature of the processing involved. Do perceivers have continuous or only

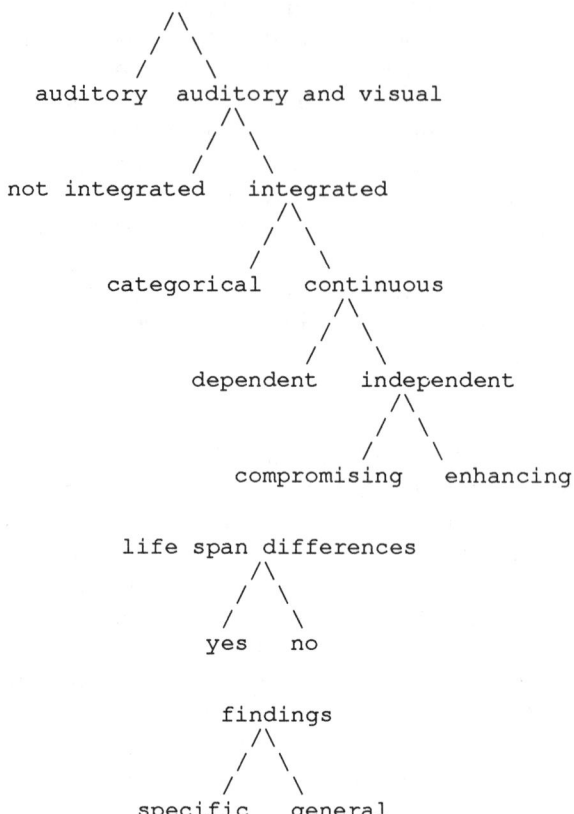

Figure 3. Trees of wisdom illustrating binary oppositions central to the domain of speech perception by eye and ear.

categorical information about speech? The traditional emphasis on categorical speech perception requires two chapters (4 and 5) rather than just one devoted to the issue of categorical versus continuous perception. Given the typical psychologist's belief in categorical perception, I expend a somewhat greater effort to reject this alternative in favor of continuous perception. Faced with continuous sources of information, are they treated independently of one another at some early stage of processing between stimulus and interpretation? This question, pursued in Chapter 6, has implications for psychophysics, in addition to implications for information processing. How the two sources of information are integrated, the most difficult question, is addressed in Chapter 7.

Given the value of both psychophysical and information processing approaches to psychological inquiry, it is encouraging that both approaches motivate the questions addressed in this monograph. As one moves from the top of the tree to the bottom, the emphasis changes from psychophysical to process concerns. This shift seems appropriate because some understanding of the information available is necessary to address the processing of the information. In turn, the nature of the processing is necessarily involved in understanding the information that is functional.

The binary oppositions can also be formalized within the information-processing model advocated here. Contrary to a common criticism of this class of models, the goal is to clarify the nature of processing within each stage rather than simply to distinguish among various stages. Figure 4 illustrates the three stages involved in pattern recognition. The auditory and visual sources of information are represented by uppercase letters. The evaluation process transforms these into psychological values (indicated by lowercase letters) that are then integrated to give an overall value. The classification operation maps this value into some response, such as a discrete decision or a rating. The issue of multiple sources of information in speech perception has to do with whether both auditory and visual properties are evaluated. The next two issues have to do with the evaluation of the sources in that we ask whether continuous information is available from each source and whether the output of evaluation of one source is contaminated by the other source. The issue of categorical versus continuous perception can also be asked with respect to the output of the integration process. The integration questions assess whether the components passed on by evaluation are integrated into some higher-order representation and how the two sources of information are integrated. The current research also addresses the process of classification, although no specific contrast is formulated.

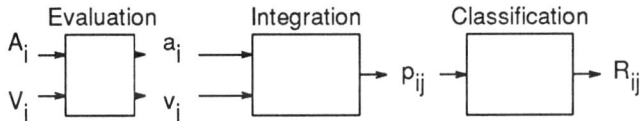

Figure 4. Schematic representation of the three operations involved in perceptual recognition.

The issues addressed in the strong-inference framework can be applied to developmental and life-span phenomena. One can ask simply to what extent the outcome of the binary contrast depends on development and aging. The confrontation of ontogenetic changes not only provides some information about potential boundary conditions on the outcomes, it delineates important facts about speech perception across the life span. In addition to the binary contrasts, the theoretical framework allows an important distinction between information differences and information-processing differences across development and aging. That is, differences might be due to differences in the information value of sources of information in speech perception, differences in the processing of the information, or both. Chapter 8 is devoted to reviewing striking similarities and differences in bimodal speech perception across development and aging.

The last chapter confronts the generality of the findings with respect to informing other domains of perception and cognition. Surprisingly, perhaps, a strong argument can be made for a cross-fertilization among disparate areas of inquiry. The processes uncovered in our study of bimodal speech perception offer a framework for the study of person impression, learning of arbitrary categories, sentence interpretation, probability judgments, and category goodness judgments. Although the case is not closed, it is now necessary to consider general processes along with the modular components in a specific domain of psychological inquiry. We begin in the next chapter with the issue of single versus multiple sources of information in speech perception.

Chapter 2: Single versus Multiple Sources of Speech Information: The Contribution of Visible Speech

In this chapter, support is gathered for multiple sources of information in speech perception. After reviewing prototypical studies of the utilization of multiple auditory and contextual sources, the contribution of visible speech is considered. Classic studies with speech in noise as well as more recent demonstrations with high quality natural auditory speech find evidence for a contribution from visible speech. More recently, experiments using synthetic auditory speech provide new insights into bimodal speech perception and offer the potential of illuminating the fundamental processes and structures in perceiving speech by ear and eye. In each experimental demonstration of multiple sources of information I will evaluate the results in terms of the general model introduced in the first chapter. The goal of the chapter is to give the reader a general flavor of the present framework while simultaneously making the case for the important contribution of visible information in face-to-face speech perception.

1. Audible Speech Perception

The argument for multiple auditory sources of information in speech perception comes from the discovery of many different cues or features that contribute to the discriminable contrasts found in speech (Massaro & Cohen, 1976; Massaro, Cohen, & Tseng, 1985; Massaro & Oden, 1980a). The phonetic difference between voiced and voiceless stop consonants in medial position appears to have up to 18 acoustic characteristics that could function as acoustic features (Lisker, 1978). The perceived distinction between /aga/ and /aka/ can be influenced by the preceding vowel duration, the silent closure interval, the voice-onset time, and the onset frequency of the fundamental (Cohen, 1979; Massaro & Cohen, 1983b; Port & Dalby, 1982). In addition to these bottom-up sources, phonological, lexical, and sentential constraints function as top-down sources of information in recognition (Ganong, 1980; Massaro, in press d; Massaro & Cohen, 1983d; Tyler & Wessels, 1983).

1.1 Multiple Acoustic Features

The formant structure and duration of vowels are ecologically valid because they both are correlated with vowel identity (Peterson & Barney, 1952; Peterson & Lehiste, 1960). An empirical question is whether these two properties are functionally valid. To answer affirmatively, it is necessary to illustrate how both vowel formants and vowel duration function as sources of information in vowel recognition. These sources of information are called acoustic features because they are a consequence of the acoustic properties of the speech signal and they have been shown to be functional in speech recognition. It is well-known that the vowel formants are the primary cues to vowel identity. The different vowels in English differ primarily in terms of tongue height and tongue advancement, which correspond to the position and the highest part of the tongue. Tongue height is the primarily determinant of the first formant, whereas tongue advancement is the primary determinant of the second formant. Massaro (1975b) reviews the studies supporting the psychological reality of the first and second vowel formants in vowel identification.

Vowel duration also appears to be functional in vowel identification. In English, about half of the vowels are relatively short in duration and the other vowels are relatively long (Peterson & Lehiste, 1960). It is only natural that listeners might utilize duration as a feature for identification of vowels. The importance of vowel duration as an acoustic feature has been demonstrated by Ainsworth (1972). Listeners identified synthetic vowels differing in the first and second formants (F1-F2) and in duration. Correct identification of the normally shorter vowels decreased as the vowel durations were increased. The converse held true for identification of the vowels which are somewhat longer in duration in normal speech.

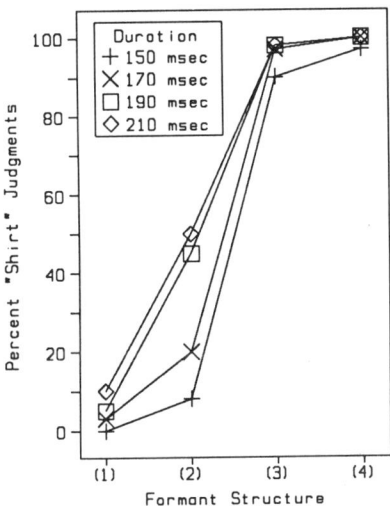

Figure 1. Predicted (lines) and observed (points) percentage of vowel identification as a function of the formant values; vowel duration is the curve parameter (observations taken from Bennett, 1968).

An important question is how duration information is combined with the information about the vowel formants. One of the few studies with the potential of addressing this question was carried out by Bennett (1968), who independently varied the duration and formant levels of British vowels in words using synthetic speech. In one set, the formant patterns were changed in four steps from the word *shut* to the word *shirt*. For each of the four formant patterns, the word was synthesized with four different vowel durations. British listeners identified each of the 16 stimuli as either *shut* or *shirt*. Figure 1 gives the proportion of *shirt* identifications as a function of the formant structure of the vowel; duration is the curve parameter. Changes in the formant structure changed the identification from one alternative to the other. Duration had a significant but smaller effect; the effect of duration was most noticeable at the second level of the formant structure.

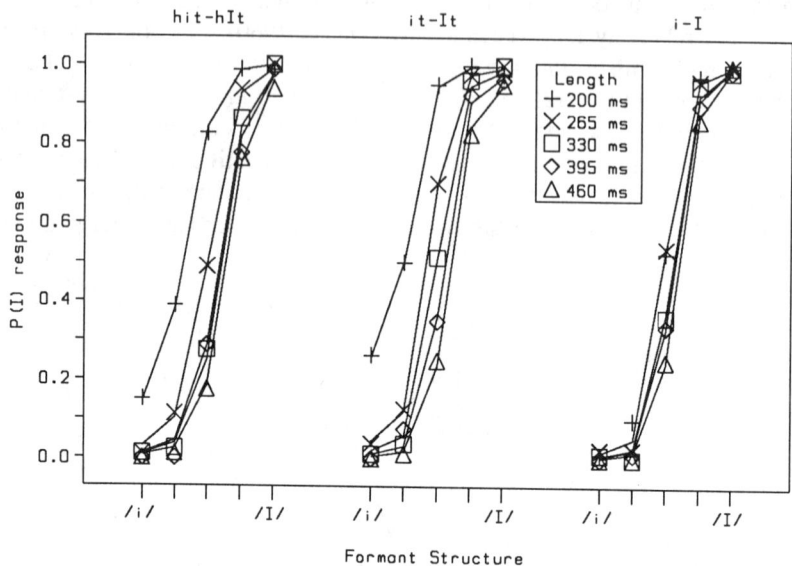

Figure 2. Predicted (lines) and observed (points) percentage of vowel identifications as a function of the formant values within three syllable contexts; vowel duration is the curve parameter (unpublished results).

In the present framework, formant structure and duration are treated as independent acoustic features defining the vowel alternatives (Massaro, 1984c). The predictions of the results are indicated by the lines in Figure 1. The model quantitatively describes the larger contribution of duration at the more ambiguous level of formant structure. In the model's description, the second level of formant structure is relatively ambiguous and, therefore, the influence of duration is made more apparent.

The Bennett (1968) study does not suggest a very convincing role for vowel duration nor does it provide a very strong test of the FLMP. Formant structure might be claimed to be the dominant cue because the effect of vowel duration is apparent only at one ambiguous level of formant structure. Given that most of the identification responses are near zero or one, they do not challenge quantitative models of performance. A more robust test of a model involves identification responses distributed across the complete interval between zero and one. To this end, we carried out an experimental study of the /i/-/I/ contrast, varying the formant structure and vowel duration (Massaro &

Cohen, unpublished results).

Five levels of formant structure were factorially combined with five levels of vowel duration. The vowels were placed in the syllable contexts /h-t/ and /-t/ and were also presented in isolation. College subjects classified the vowels as /i/ or /I/. Figure 2 gives the observed results for ten adult subjects, and reveals strong effects of both formant structure and vowel duration. The effect of one variable was largest at the ambiguous levels of the other variable. The predictions of the FLMP also shown in Figure 2 provide a good description of the average results with an RMSD value of .035.

1.2 Contextual Contributions

One important domain of evidence for multiple sources of information involves the contribution of higher-order context to speech perception. In the current view, the bottom-up information remains independent of the top-down information and the two sources are combined in the same manner as two bottom-up sources. When considered in this framework, one basic limitation in previous research is that it has been directed primarily at showing a positive contribution of context rather than at how context is integrated with information from the acoustic signal (Cole & Jakimik, 1978; Marslen-Wilson & Welsh, 1978; Pollack & Pickett, 1963). Recent research in our laboratory, along with other current studies, overcome these limitations in previous research and provide quantitative tests of the FLMP.

1.2.1 Phonological Context in Syllable Recognition

Massaro and Cohen (1983d) assessed how the information from the acoustic signal is combined or integrated with information about phonological constraints in English. Phonological constraints refer to the fact that languages are redundant in terms of the possible sequences of speech sounds. There are constraints on the ordering of speech sounds within English words such as /r/ but not /l/ following word- initial /t/. Seven listeners were asked to identify sounds along a continuum between /li/ and /ri/, which was made by varying the starting frequency of the third formant (F3) transition. These sounds were placed after each of four initial consonants. When the sounds are placed after the initial consonant /s/, /l/ is phonologically admissible in English, but /r/ is not. If phonological constraints influence perception, listeners should tend to hear /l/ following the sound /s/. Given an initial consonant /t/, however, listeners might be more likely to hear /r/ than /l/. In English, /l/ does not follow word-initial /t/. In addition to these two conditions, the contexts /p/ and /v/ are also included. Both /l/ and /r/ are phonologically admissible following /p/, but neither is admissible following initial /v/. The results not only provide a test of whether phonological constraints contribute to speech perception, the experimental design also allows quantitative tests of how context and an acoustic feature are integrated in speech perception.

Each speech sound was a syllable beginning with one of the four consonants, /p/, /t/, /s/, or /v/, followed by a glide consonant ranging in seven levels from /l/ to /r/ followed by the vowel /i/ (Massaro & Cohen, 1983d). On each trial, the syllable was randomly selected without replacement from the set of 28 syllables generated by the factorial combination of the four initial consonants and the seven F3 levels of the following glide. Subjects identified the sound by pressing one of eight buttons, labeled PLE, PRE, TLE, TRE, SLE, SRE, VLE, and VRE. Subjects were told that their task was to identify the syllable on the basis of what they heard. They were told that there was no correct response and simply to make the best judgment they could. Subjects were tested for two days with 28 practice trials and two sessions of 280 experimental trials each on each day.

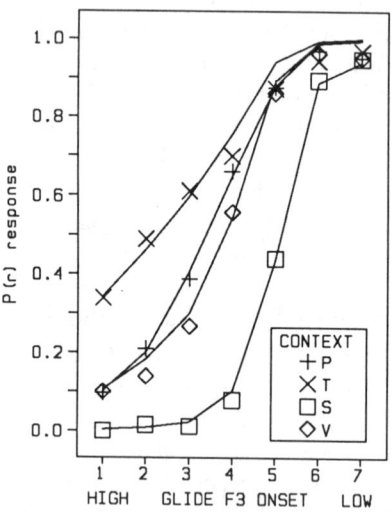

Figure 3. Observed (points) and predicted (lines) probability of an /r/ identification as a function of the F3 transition onset of the glide; the initial consonant is the curve parameter (from Massaro & Cohen, 1983d).

The recognition of the initial context consonant was very good, averaging about 95 percent correct. Figure 3 gives the overall probability of /r/ identifications pooled over the two days of the experiment. The points in the figure show that the identification of the glide is an orderly function of both F3 of the glide and the initial consonant. As expected, the proportion of /r/ identifications increased with decreases in the starting value of F3 of the glide. More importantly, an /r/ identification was more likely in the context of /t/ than in the context of /p/ or /v/ and least likely in the context of /s/. The effects of the initial context consonant were largest at the more ambiguous values of F3. In addition, the context effects did not appear to decrease with experience in the experiment. In summary, the results of the experiment show large effects of both the acoustic featural information of F3 and the phonological context of the initial consonant. The significant interaction of these two variables reveals that the magnitude of the context effect was largest at the more ambiguous levels of the acoustic featural information.

The lines in Figure 3 present the predictions of the fuzzy model of speech perception. One critical assumption of the model is that the featural information from the glide and the phonological context provide independent sources of information. The featural information representing the glide can be represented by the truth value T_i where the subscript i indicates that T_i changes only with the F3 transition. For the /l/-/r/ identification, T_i specifies how much R-ness is given by the critical F3 transition feature. This value is expected to increase as the onset frequency of the F3 transition is decreased. With just two alternatives along the continuum, it can further be assumed that the amount of L-ness given by the featural information is simply one minus the amount of R-ness given by that same source. Therefore, if T_i specifies the amount of R-ness given by the F3 transition, then $(1 - T_i)$ specifies the amount of L-ness given by that same transition.

The phonological context also provides independent evidence for R and L. The value C_j represents how much the context supports the consonant R. The subscript j indicates that C_j changes only with changes in phonological context. The value of C_j should be large when /r/ is admissible and small when /r/ is not admissible. Analogous to the treatment of the featural information, the degree to which the phonological context supports the consonant /l/ is indexed by $(1 - C_j)$.

The listener is assumed to have two independent sources of information. The total amount of R-ness and L-ness is determined by integrating these two sources. The amount of R-ness and L-ness for a given syllable can be represented by the conjunction of the two independent sources of information:

$$R-ness = (T_i \ \& \ C_j) \tag{1}$$

$$L-ness = [(1-T_i) \ \& \ (1-C_j)] \tag{2}$$

In this case, for pattern classification, the probability of an /r/- response is predicted to be

$$P(r) = \frac{T_i C_j}{T_i C_j + (1-T_i)(1-C_j)} \tag{3}$$

The model was fit to the proportion of /r/ identifications as a function of the F3 of the glide and the initial consonant context. Seven values of T_i are required for the seven levels of the F3 transition of the glide. Unique C_j values are required for each of the four different initial consonant contexts. Fitting the model to the observed data, therefore, requires the estimation of 11 parameters.

Figure 3 shows that the FLMP provides a good description of the average results, with an RMSD of .039. In addition, the parameter estimates of the model are meaningful. The T_i values, representing the degree of R-ness, increase systematically with decreases in the starting frequency of F3. The C_j values change systematically with phonological context; the degree of R-ness given by context is much larger for initial /t/ than for initial /s/. Relative to the context /v/, the context /p/ is somewhat more supportive of /r/ than of /l/. This could be due to the fact that, in natural English, initial /p/ is more likely to be followed by /r/ than by /l/ (Roberts, 1965).

1.2.2 Sentential Context in Word Recognition

Analogous to the question of the utilization of phonological context effects, we can ask whether there is a similar contribution of sentential context. A positive answer has been repeatedly found since Miller, Heise, and Lichten's (1951) seminal study, but little quantitative work has been aimed at assessing how sentential context is integrated with the sensory information. Following the framework of the FLMP, sentential context should provide an independent source of information made available to the word recognition process in perceiving continuous speech (Massaro & Oden, 1980b). To illustrate application of the model, a study of sentential context effects by Isenberg, Walker, and Ryder (1980) will be described and analyzed. They created a speech continuum between the function words *THE* and *TO* and placed each of these test words in two different sentence contexts. One context was appropriate for *THE* and the other for *TO*. This independent variation of the test word and sentential context allows a direct test of the FLMP.

The speech continuum was created by beginning with a natural utterance of the word *TO* and attenuating the onset energy between 14 and 36 dB in steps of 2 dB. With little attenuation, the word is heard consistently as *TO*; with a lot of attenuation, the word is heard as *THE*. Intermediate levels of attenuation give more ambiguous percepts. The test word was placed as the initial word in one of two sentence contexts

> *... GO IS ESSENTIAL.*
> *... GOLD IS ESSENTIAL.*

The only difference between the sentences is whether *GO* or *GOLD* follows the test word. Subjects were presented with the twelve versions of the test word in the two sentence contexts and were asked to identify the test words as *THE* or *TO*. The appropriate syntactic constructions are *TO GO* and *THE GOLD*, and the experimental question is how the sensory information and sentential context influence perceptual recognition of the test word.

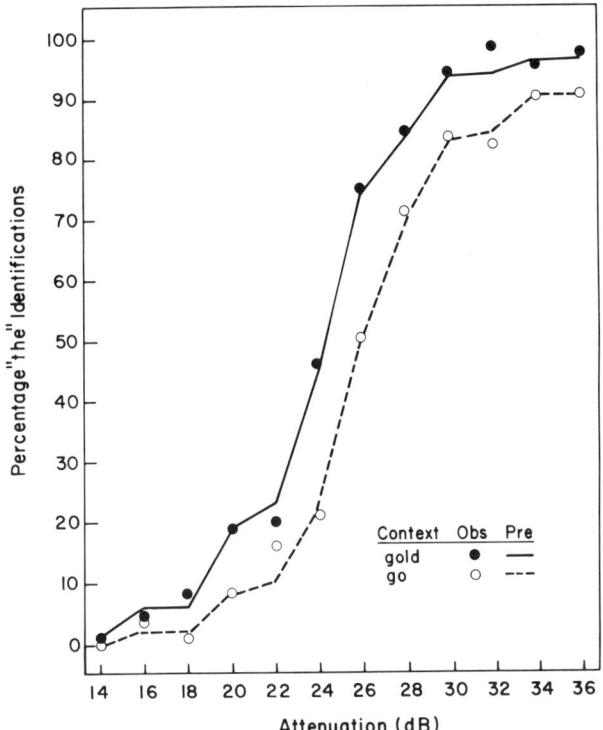

Figure 4. Observed (points) and predicted (lines) percentage of *THE* identifications as a function of the onset attenuation of the test stimulus and the sentential context (observations from Isenberg, Walker, & Ryder, 1980).

Figure 4 gives the observed results. As expected, the percentage of *THE* identifications increased systematically with increases in the attenuation of the onset of the test word. Sentential context also had an effect, especially at the intermediate levels of attenuation of the test word.

In terms of the FLMP, the acoustic features in the test word and the syntactic constraints given by the sentence provide independent sources of information for identification of the test word. The predictions of the model are identical in form to those given in the study of phonological constraints. If F_i is the featural information supporting the percept *THE*, and C_j is the syntactic information supporting this same percept, the probability of a *THE* identification given the contexts *GOLD* and *GO* are

$$P(THE \mid GOLD) = \frac{F_i C_j}{F_i C_j + (1-F_i)(1-C_j)} \tag{4}$$

$$P(THE \mid GO) = \frac{F_i(1-C_j)}{F_i(1-C_j) + (1-F_i)C_j} \tag{5}$$

It is assumed in Equations 4 and 5 that $(1-Fi)$ is the featural information supporting the percept **TO** and $(1-Cj)$ is the syntactic information supporting **TO**. Thus, Equation 4 gives the support for **THE** divided by the sum of support for **THE** and **TO** and analogously for Equation 5. Figure 4 also gives the predictions of the model. The model provides a good description of the average results with an RMSD of less than 2 percent.

2. Visible Speech Perception

We have seen how both multiple acoustic features and contextual constraints function as sources of information in speech perception. The question addressed here is whether speech also has visual information. Of course, visual information can be present only when the face of the speaker is visible to the perceiver. Although visual speech does not distinguish among all speech contrasts, it is ecologically valid (predictable) to some degree. Of psychological interest, of course, is whether visible speech is functionally valid. Anecdotal evidence comes from our dislike of dubbed movies, the seemingly extra effort to converse by telephone, and to listen to narrative over the radio. The habit of watching a person speaking and the greater reliance on the speaker's visible articulations within noisy and distracting environments and with hearing loss also support the impression of the substantial contribution from the visible domain of speech. O'Connor and Hermelin (1981) provide evidence that the deaf gain phonological information primarily from a code based on how words look when they are said. Similar phonological information is obtained by both deaf and hearing children suggesting that information can be derived from visual as well as auditory speech.

2.1 Consonant Contrasts

There have been informative studies describing the contrasts in speech that are visible in face-to-face communication. I begin with an analysis of the discriminable contrasts in consonant recognition. Recognizing visible speech without sound is called speechreading or lipreading. Walden, Prosek, Montgomery, Scherr, and Jones (1977) studied the visual recognition of consonants in 31 hearing-impaired adults. Subjects without any previous training appeared to discriminate among five categories of consonants. These categories that can be discriminated are usually called visemes, and are analogous to the concept phonemes describing the contrasts that can be recognized auditorily. Based on a criterion of 75 percent identification responses from within the viseme category, the five viseme categories that could be discriminated were /ðθ, fv, pbm, ʃž, and w/.

The subjects were then given systematic training in the recognition of the consonants. Training involved 14 one-hour sessions of intensive and individualized speechreading instruction, spread over a two-week period.

Subjects made same-different judgments to pairs of syllables and identified single syllables with immediate feedback. Replicating previous studies of training (e.g., Heider & Heider, 1940), the training succeeded in improving speechreading. The number of discriminable viseme categories increased from five to nine. Table 1 gives the performance for the nine visemes both before and after training.

Table 1. Percentage of within category identification responses for nine viseme categories. Results are given before and after training (after Walden et al, 1977)

Viseme	Pretraining	Posttraining
θ, ð̗	90.1	99.4
f, v	92.2	97.5
ʃ, ž	71.9	94.5
s, z	34.9	79.2
p, b, m	90.6	99.3
t, d, n, k, g, j	57.3	97.1
w	74.8	92.9
r	36.1	88.6
l	72.6	93.4

2.2 Vowel Contrasts

We might expect that vowels might be more difficult to discriminate than consonants because vowels can be more easily articulated with different vocal tract configurations (Ladefoged, Harshman, Goldstein, & Rice, 1978; Summerfield, 1983). However, there is evidence that untrained observers can discriminate among the vowels given just visible speech. Montgomery and Jackson (1983) asked observers to lipread 15 vowels and diphthongs in the context /h-g/. This context minimizes coarticulation effects on the visibility of the vowel. All of the test items were recognized at better than chance accuracy. Table 2 gives the performance for these items in terms of eight viseme categories, based on a criterion of 65% responses from within each category.

The stimulus-response confusion matrix was analyzed using multidimensional scaling. The representation derived from multidimensional scaling denotes the perceived relative similarity among the test items in terms of spatial distance. A two-dimensional representation of the vowels gave a reasonably good description of the confusions that were made. The two dimensions of this representation shown in Figure 5 can be interpreted in terms of physical measurements of the visible characteristics of the lips and tongue height. Figure 5 shows the recovery of the vowel quadrilateral similar to that

Table 2. Percentage of within category identification responses for eight viseme categories. Results are given for subjects without training (after Montgomery & Jackson, 1983)

Viseme	Performance
i, I	71.5
a, ɔ, ʌ	66.0
ʊ, 3	69.5
u	82.0
ɛ, æ, eI, aI	82.3
ɔI	82.2
aʊ	86.4
oʊ	76.9

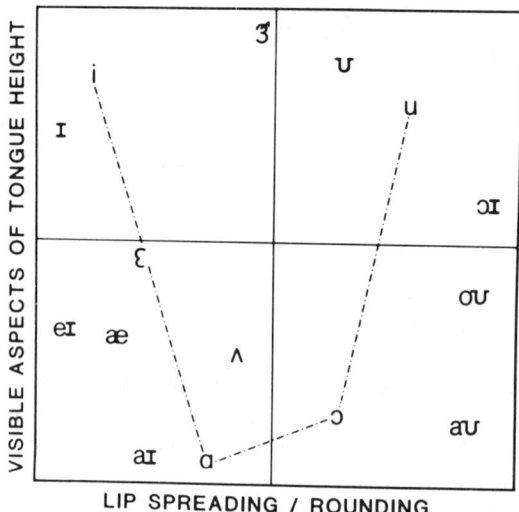

Figure 5. Two-dimensional representation of vowel confusions based on a multidimensional scaling analysis of the identification of 15 vowels (after Montgomery & Jackson, 1983).

determined in the analysis of the acoustic properties of speech. The vertical dimension distinguishes the high, mid, and low front vowels given that the opening of the mouth and the vertical separation of the lips varies concomitantly with tongue height. The horizontal dimension of lip spreading/rounding is a visible dimension correlated with front to back tongue placement. As can be seen in the figure, the vowels are fairly discriminable from one another on the basis of just these two properties.

2.3 Lipreading Ability

Lipreading, sometimes referred to as speechreading, involves speech perception given only visible speech. It might seem surprising, given the paucity of studies of speech listening ability, that there have been many studies of factors contributing to speechreading ability. On the other hand, speech listening is easy and individual differences are not readily observable. The factors that have been assessed have included many perceptual and cognitive correlates of lipreading performance (Jeffers & Barley, 1971, 1979). As noted by Summerfield (1983), the ability of postlingually-impaired listeners to lipread connected speech has been shown to correlate with a number of perceptual and cognitive skills. For example, positive correlations are found between lipreading of connected speech and visual memory span, non-verbal abstract reasoning, and the ability to lipread nonsense syllables. Given that the critical-processes approach has not proven to be completely successful in describing ability in other cognitive skills, it is not surprising that it has not defined the necessary correlates of lipreading. Although some of the correlations are fairly large, they may simply reflect the overall positive correlation among tests of different abilities.

Onset of deafness is negatively correlated with lipreading ability; that is, persons with earlier losses of hearing tend to be poorer lipreaders (Berger, 1972). If deafness occurs before language acquisition, there is no language basis to build on in the learning of lipreading (Conrad, 1979). This interpretation acknowledges the primacy of listening to language in the acquisition of spoken language.

Even though auditory speech might be considered to be primary, there is now evidence that visible speech influences the acquisition of phonology. Mills (1983, in press) observed that sighted and nonsighted children differ in their acquisition of phonology. Children between the age of one and two were videotaped, and transcriptions of a subset of their productions were made. Sighted children were found to acquire distinctions with visible articulation distinctiveness more quickly than those without articulation distinctiveness. For example, the production of /b, p, m/ and /f, v/ were more accurate than those of /d, t, g, k, n/. The idea is that acquisition would be easiest for segments having the fewest members in a viseme category. Thus, the labial and labial-dental consonants are acquired more quickly than the alveolar/velar consonants because the latter has a larger number of unique consonants in a viseme category. There is also some evidence that nonsighted children are slower in the acquisition of the distinctions with visible distinctiveness than are the sighted children. Given that only 3 children were observed in each group, these results and others must remain tentative. The results are intriguing and would provide strong evidence for the contribution of visible information in language acquisition. It would also be informative to test both perception and production to assess the importance of the visible information in both domains.

The most surprising correlation with lipreading skill is the visual-evoked response (VER) to light flashes (Samar & Sims, 1983; Shepherd, 1982; Shepherd, DeLavergne, Frueh, & Clobridge, 1977). In the Samar and Sims (1983) study, 18 subjects viewed 50 flashes of light generated at one second intervals during the collection of the VER. The latency of VN130 was identified in each subject's VER, which corresponds to a negative peak prior to the large positive peak. This latency correlated -.58 with accuracy of performance on the Utley (1946) speechreading test. This correlation was significantly lower than the earlier ones of .90 to .91 in the Shepherd (1982) in the Shepherd et al. (1977) studies.

To improve the correlation, Samar and Sims (1983) used a principal components analysis on the VERs. Three of the 10 components correlated significantly with lipreading accuracy, with a multiple correlation coefficient of .84. One component was a VF16 factor with a peak latency of 16 msec. As the authors point out, the very early latency of VF16 suggests that it is a correlate of individually fixed properties of neural organization or a correlate of attention to visual space. Attention does does not seem to be a viable candidate, however, because there is little evidence that attention can be directed so quickly (16 msec) after stimulus presentation. It is probably wise to be somewhat skeptical of these high correlations given the small sample size of 18 subjects and the many degrees of freedom involved in the principal components approach. However, it should not be surprising if lipreading skill, like other skills, is dependent on sensory/perceptual factors.

3. Bimodal Speech Perception

The results of speechreading without sound illustrate that visible speech is informative when presented alone. Of course, it is possible that visible speech might be rendered nonfunctional in the presence of audible speech. Thus, the important question is whether visual speech is also utilized by the perceiver given both audible and visible speech. The classic study of Sumby and Pollack (1954) was one of several demonstrations illustrating that what we see clearly influences what we perceive in speech perception by ear and eye (O'Neill, 1954).

3.1 Sumby and Pollack Study

Sumby and Pollack (1954) provided a quantitative measure of the visual contribution to speech intelligibility. Words were presented to the subjects under varying levels of background noise and with varying sizes of test vocabulary. Before each test the speaker recited the test vocabulary which also was available to the subject in written form. Subjects were instructed to select the word from the restricted vocabulary on the basis of any marginally available cues. Subjects either watched the speaker's facial movements directly as he spoke the word or faced away from the speaker. Words were presented over headphones and noise was mixed electronically with the speech signal.

As expected, speech intelligibility, as measured by correct word recognition, decreased with decreases in the speech-to-noise ratio. Speech intelligibility was much better with smaller vocabulary sizes, and the effect of vocabulary size was greatest at an intermediate speech-to-noise ratio. Most importantly, word recognition was significantly improved in the presence of visual information from the speaker's facial movements. The contribution of the visual information was much greater in an absolute sense with smaller speech-to-noise ratios. In addition, the contribution of visual information was greater for the smaller vocabulary sizes.

The authors also provided a relative measure of the contribution of visual information. This measure gives an assessment of the improvement in performance due to the visual information relative to the possible available improvement given performance in the absence of visual information. With smaller speech-to-noise ratios and, therefore, poorer performance, there would be more room for improvement given visual information. The authors discovered that the relative improvement was roughly constant across all levels of the speech-to-noise ratios.

This measure seems to provide a slightly different perspective on the greater contribution of visual information as the auditory information becomes ambiguous. In the framework developed in this monograph, there is a larger visual contribution as the auditory information becomes ambiguous because of a relatively sophisticated integration process. In the analysis given by Sumby and Pollack, the greater visual contribution with less auditory information is simply a consequence of poorer performance given just the auditory information. With poorer performance, there is greater room for improvement with the presence of visual information. We will find that the integration rule extends well beyond what could be explained simply on the basis of the overall level of performance.

The absolute contribution of visual information was greatest at the lowest levels of auditory information. This result is consistent with our finding of the greatest contribution of visual information at the most ambiguous level of the auditory information (see Chapter 3). In these previous studies of speech in noise, the most ambiguous level of the auditory information occurred with the smallest speech-to-noise ratios. Thus, the results in bimodal speech perception with large vocabularies and words presented in noise are consistent with the results of our experiments in manipulating auditory and visual information orthogonally in factorial designs.

The greatest contribution of visual information at the smallest speech-to-noise ratio contrasts somewhat with the observed contribution of sentence context to word recognition (Tyler & Wessels, 1983), and with the contribution of decreasing vocabulary size (Miller et al., 1951). The contributions of context and limited vocabulary size are greatest at an intermediate level of auditory information. This difference may simply reflect the fact that visual information presented alone is much more informative than contextual information from the sentence or a decreased number of possible alternatives. Thus the visual information in speech perception has a greater potential for making a large contribution without auditory information whereas the contextual information provided by a sentence or a limited vocabulary is not sufficient to disambiguate a test word when no stimulus information is provided about the test word. These results seem to simultaneously highlight the priority but not the dominance of bottom-up information and the characterization of visual information in speech perception as a bottom-up source of information.

3.2 Campbell Study

Campbell (1974) extended the traditional analysis of auditory recognition errors in noise (Miller & Nicely, 1955) to include visual and bimodal stimuli. In Experiment 1, subjects identified consonant/vowel syllables /bi/, /pi/, /di/, /ti/, /si/, and /zi/, presented on a television monitor, under auditory, visual, and auditory-visual (bimodal) conditions. Three different levels of auditory noise were added to the auditory and bimodal conditions. Subjects knew the six possible test alternatives and responded with one alternative on each trial. The confusion matrices were analyzed in terms of a hierarchical cluster scheme analysis. The results of this analysis were evaluated in terms of the discriminability of different phonetic features (Chomsky & Halle, 1968) under the three presentation conditions.

With the visual presentation, the features from most salient to least salient were coronal, continuant, and voicing. Thus, the alternatives /b/ and /p/ (minus coronal) were seldom confused with the other four alternatives which have a different place of articulation (plus coronal). The feature continuant was somewhat functional because the alveolar stops could be discriminated from the fricatives. The poorest discrimination involved the three pairs of alternatives sharing coronal and continuant and differing in voicing. In the auditory condition, the most salient feature was voicing and the least salient was coronal with continuant intermediate. These results illustrate an ideal complementarity of the auditory and visual dimensions. This complementary relationship proved functional in the auditory-visual condition given that there was much less confusion among the bimodal alternatives. The average percentage correct increased from 45 and 54 in the visual and auditory (-15 dB speech-to-noise ratio) conditions respectively to 88 in the bimodal condition. The percentages for each consonant are given in Table 3. In the auditory/visual condition, the salience of the features decreased from coronal to voice to continuant. This latter result is impressive in that coronal, the most salient visual feature, maintains this status in bimodal presentation.

Table 3. Proportion of correct identifications for each consonant for the visual, auditory and bimodal conditions in Campbell (1974, Experiment 1, -15 dB condition).

Consonant	Visual	Auditory	Bimodal
b	.238	.506	.910
p	.785	.581	.963
z	.338	.712	.926
p	.541	.580	.839
d	.200	.489	.893
t	.608	.358	.810

As was common at that time, Campbell (1974) assumed that linguistic phonetic features and their binary property were psychologically real. Campbell interpreted the results in terms of the processing of the phonetic features by a partitioning of the set of alternatives according to the binary nature of the features. The order of this serial processing is related to the discriminability of the features. Given auditory speech, the set would first be partitioned into the voiced and voiceless alternatives, then into sets also differing in continuant, and finally into the set of six alternatives also different in coronal. Given that processing was assumed to be serial, errors would be more likely to involve features processed later rather than earlier in time. An analogous process would occur for visual speech with only a change in the order of processing the features. In bimodal speech perception, the author proposed a combined phonetic matrix that contains the more discriminable value for each feature. For example, coronal would be cued by visual information whereas voicing would be cued by auditory speech. Research in other domains and in the present paradigm, however, indicates that the features might not be phonetic but are probably auditory and visual. In addition, the information from each feature is graded rather than binary, and both the auditory and visual correlates of a phonetic distinction such as coronal can contribute to bimodal speech perception. The features are combined following an algorithm in which the most informative feature has the most impact on the judgment.

The FLMP can be applied to the results in a straightforward manner. Subjects were limited to six alternatives and, therefore, these are the only relevant prototypes that have to be specified by the model. Each prototype has auditory and visual features. The important prediction of the FLMP is that the perceptual recognition of the bimodal syllable is jointly determined by both the auditory and visual sources. These sources provide continuous information and the information from one modality does not change with the presence or absence of the other modality. When integrated, the contribution of a given modality increases with increases in its information value and with decreases in the information value of the other modality.

With six alternatives stimuli and six responses under auditory, visual, and bimodal conditions, there are 6 x 6 x 3 = 108 independent observations. There are two ways that the model can be tested against the results. In the first test, the observations made in the auditory and visual conditions can be used to predict the results in the bimodal condition. These conditions provide estimates of the auditory and visual sources of information, respectively. In this case no free parameters are necessary to predict the 36 independent observations in the bimodal condition. In the second test, 72 free parameters are needed to estimate the auditory and visual sources of information and all 108 observations can be predicted. The FLMP provided a good description of the results with RMSD values of .020 and .015 for the first and second tests, respectively. Thus, the FLMP can describe unimodal and bimodal speech perception in noise-free tests.

3.3 Additional Studies

Erber (1972) studied bimodal speech perception with normal-hearing, severely hearing-impaired, and profoundly-deaf children. All groups were able to lipread the different places of articulation. The severely hearing-impaired could distinguish voicing and nasality through listening alone and, therefore, they achieved nearly perfect recognition given bimodal speech. The profoundly deaf children, on the other hand, gained nothing from the auditory domain, and gave similar performance in lipreading and bimodal speech perception. This result shows that sufficient hearing to resolve voicing and nasality but not place provides a situation in which bimodal speech can lead to essentially perfect performance. In this case, place of articulation information is available from the visible domain.

Dodd (1977) evaluated speech recognition in the presence or absence of visual articulation when the auditory signal was presented in white noise. Monosyllabic words were more accurately recognized with than without a simultaneous view of the speaker. Her results indicate that visual information is more important for front than for middle or back consonants. With just auditory information, Dodd found that front consonants are more poorly recognized than middle or back ones. Generally, there appears to be an auditory advantage for consonants articulated farther back in the mouth, perhaps because of greater resolution of the somewhat higher formant values. Thus, the greater contribution of visual information to the perception of front consonants most likely occurred because the noise interfered more with front than with middle or back consonants.

Replicating the paradigm of McGurk and MacDonald (1976) discussed in the next section, Dodd (1977) also opposed the visual and auditory dimensions by dubbing a visual articulation with a different speech sound. Subjects made more errors identifying the speech sound with the inappropriate articulation than identifying the speech sound presented alone. Although Dodd concluded that subjects attend more to the visual than the auditory sources, one might argue that the advantage enjoyed by the visual input may have been due to the noise added to the auditory input. We will find more direct support for Dodd's conclusion in the next chapter when attention to bimodal speech is assessed. Subjects find it somewhat easier to focus attention on the visual than on the auditory input.

3.4 McGurk Effect

In most research demonstrating a significant contribution of visible speech, the auditory signal was either absent or degraded by white noise, or presented to hearing-impaired listeners. Thus the ingenious manipulation of McGurk and MacDonald (1976) was significant in demonstrating that visual articulation has an important influence even when paired with perfectly intelligible speech sounds. We have all noticed the discrepancy of sight and sound in dubbed movies, but McGurk and MacDonald modified the situation to illustrate the power of visible speech. They dubbed a visible articulation such as /pa-pa/ with the speech sounds /na-na/. This gives a situation with perfectly intelligible auditory speech presented with a contradictory visual articulation. The surprising perceptual experience has come to be known as the McGurk effect.

Even though subjects were asked to indicate what they heard, a strong effect of the visual source of information was observed. Faced with the visible articulation /pa-pa/, paired with the sounds /na-na/, subjects often reported hearing /ma-ma/. Thus, the percept seems to result from a combination of visible place of articulation with auditory nasality and auditory voicing. The visual articulation is effective in modifying perception only when the visible place of articulation is different from that of the speech sound. For example, the visible articulation /p/ did not modify perception of the speech sound /b/ although the articulation /p/ did modify perception of the speech sound /d/. There were no differences within the class of articulations /d, t, g, k, n/ and none within the class /b, p, m/. For example, replacing an /n/ articulation of the sound /n/ with the articulation /g/ had no effect in that subjects always reported hearing /n/. The results are consistent with previous findings that visible articulation is not normally sufficient to distinguish middle from back stop consonants; neither is it able to distinguish voicing and nasality.

McGurk and MacDonald (1976) found that identification of place of articulation of a speech segment is influenced by the visible articulation. Subjects were instructed to identify what they heard, so it is natural to score accuracy with respect to the auditory event. The influence of front and back articulations on back and front sounds was not symmetrical, however. A nonlabial articulation had the largest influence on identification of place of articulation. When nonlabial articulations were paired with labial sounds, subjects made 73 percent errors in identifying the speech sound. Nonlabial sounds with labial lip movements produced 25 percent errors, many fewer than the reverse case. Summerfield (1979) also found a smaller influence of a labial relative to a nonlabial articulation in the perception of auditory voiced stop consonants. The asymmetry in the error rates could be due either to differences in the influence or perceptibility of visual labial and nonlabial articulations or to differences in the perceptibility of labial and nonlabial speech sounds.

More recently, Repp, Manuel, Liberman, and Studdert-Kennedy (1983) found less influence of contradictory visual information in the perception of auditory /d/ relative to auditory /b/, /v/, and /ð/. Thus, it appears that /d/ and possibly other alveolar or velar stop consonants are less influenced by contradictory visual articulation. The Repp et al. (1983) result seems to locate the asymmetry of influence in the speech sounds. The sound /d/ seems to be more robust and less influenced by contradictory visual information than the sounds /b/, /v/, and /ð/. Using the acoustic consequences of speech production as a guide, it might be argued that /d/ contains acoustic properties that are more robust than those of /b/. For example, Tillmann (1985) has argued that the first formant of the stop masks the second formant of /b/ more than it masks the second formant of /d/. This difference in masking occurs because of the proximity of the two formants in /b/ relative to /d/. In addition, a visible /da/ articulation does not appear to be a powerful cue to perceiving /da/. Subjects in the Repp et al. study seldom reported hearing /da/ when an articulation of /da/ was paired with another speech sound. Thus, the recognition of /d/ seems more directly linked with its auditory segment than do /b/, /v/, or /ð/. Repp et al. also found that subjects were more aware of the conflicting dubbing when an auditory /da/ was paired with /ba/, /va/, or /ða/ articulations. Subjects indicated their awareness by subjective ratings on a dubbed to not-dubbed continuum.

The errors in the MacDonald and McGurk (1978) study were also interesting in that listeners often reported hearing consonant clusters. When a labial articulation was paired with a nonlabial speech sound, doubled consonants such as /bd/ accounted for 84 percent of the errors. That is, all but 16 percent of the errors were reports of a consonant cluster. In contrast, given a labial sound with a nonlabial articulation, consonant clusters made up only about 1 percent of the error responses. This asymmetry is surprising and may reveal something about the differences in the temporal location of the auditory and visual information in a bimodal syllable (Massaro & Cohen, 1983c; Cohen, 1984). Spectrographic and video analysis indicate that a labial articulation is observable before an alveolar or velar articulation relative to the corresponding auditory speech event. The asymmetry also provides a challenging result for a theory of perception of bimodal speech as will be discussed in Chapter 3.

In an earlier study, McGurk and MacDonald (1976) found an interesting result when the labial speech sound /ba-ba/ was dubbed onto the articulation /ga-ga/. Subjects usually reported hearing /da-da/. This result, although somewhat attenuated, was also found for the sound /pa-pa/ dubbed onto the articulation of /ka-ka/. McGurk and MacDonald (1976) offer a reasonable interpretation of perceiving /da/ given auditory /ba/ and visual /ga/. Although perceiving /d/ when given information about only /b/ and /g/ may seem surprising, it should be remembered that middle and back articulations are not usually discriminated. Therefore, the condition is equivalent to having information about auditory /b/ and information about visual /d/ or /g/. Given this analysis, both the visual and auditory sources of information appear to influence perceptual recognition of place. The contribution of the visual input is apparent because a labial sound is sometimes heard as nonlabial when it is paired with a nonlabial visual articulation. The auditory information also contributes to the place judgment given that /d/ rather than /g/ is perceived and auditory /b/ is more similar to /d/ than to /g/.

McGurk and MacDonald's result—perceiving the middle stop given auditory front and visual back components—was not found when the speech sound was back (/ga-ga/ or /ka-ka/) and the visible articulation was front (/ba-ba/ or /pa-pa/). Auditory /ga/ with visual /ba/ cannot be interpreted as a middle stop /da/ given that visual /ba/ differs from visual /da/ and auditory /ga/ differs from auditory /da/. Given these stimuli, subjects tended to hear an extra consonant such as /gab-ga/ or /bag-ba/ for the voiced segments and /pak-pa/ or /kap-ka/ for the voiceless segments.

3.5 Mills and Thiem Study

Mills and Thiem (1980) asked German observers to identify bimodal CV syllables consisting of conflicting auditory and visual information. The 15 syllables represented distinctive phonetic categories and the positions of the potentially visible articulatory organs for these consonants are illustrated in Table 4. The table also gives information concerning contextual influences on the visible characteristics. Based on film and X-ray analyses, Lindner (1975, cited in Mills & Thiem, 1980) classified consonants as having obligatory or adaptable positions of the articulators. Adaptable positions can be influenced by context (neighboring segments) whereas obligatory positions cannot. For example, the normally narrow jaw angle of /b/ can be influenced by the following vowel, but the bilabial closure occurs independently of the vowel context. The phoneme /ð/ does not occur in German but was considered to be familiar enough to the subjects, who were native speakers of German but had learned English as a foreign language. Both the auditory and visual components had strong effects on identifying what the speaker had said.

As in previous studies, identification of voicing and manner were usually determined by the auditory component. The visual component was important for identification of place of articulation but the eight visual categories were not equally discriminable. Replicating McGurk and MacDonald (1976),

Table 4. Positions of the potentially visible articulating organs for the consonants used in the Mills and Thiem (1980) study (adapted from Mills & Thiem, 1980).

		b	m	v	ð	f	l	t	z	d	g	n	ŋ	j	h	x
Jaw	wide															
Angle	medium							a			a		a		a	a
	narrow	a	a	o	o	o	a		o	a		a		a		
Tongue	lowered	a	a	a		a			o	a		a	o		a	a
Tip	raised				o		o	o	r	o						
	not involved					a		a	a	a	a	a	a		a	a
	protruded				o											
Lips	rounded															
	spread								a					a		
	labio-dental			o												
	bilabial closure	r	o													

a = adaptable articulatory position
o = obligatory articulatory position
r = obligatory release

combinations were observed; for example, visual /b/ is paired with auditory /l/ and the observer reports /bl/. These combinations also violated phonotactic rules in German as was originally observed in English (McGurk & MacDonald, 1976). In 98 percent of the combinations reported, the first consonant of the pair reported was articulated more forward in the mouth as in /bd/ or /vð/. As the authors point out, these combination responses are reasonably consistent with the visual articulation. For example, a visual /ba/ paired with an auditory /da/ gives a visual articulation that is consistent with the consonant cluster /bd/. When the visual component has a wider lip opening than that appropriate for the auditory component, the visual articulation is inconsistent with a consonant cluster that has the visual component as the first member of the pair. In this case, consonant clusters are not reported as in the case with a visual /d/ and an auditory /b/. This explanation seems to require both that the visual information is available somewhat sooner than the auditory and that the combination response is not very inconsistent with visual articulation.

With respect to identification of the phoneme /ð/, which does not occur in German, a visual /v/ paired with auditory /ð/ never produced the identification of /ð/. A visual /ð/ paired with auditory /v/ gave 33 percent /ð/ responses. This result contrasts with the result for English subjects in which a visual /v/ plus auditory /ð/ gave 17 percent /ð/ responses and a visual /ð/ plus auditory /v/ gave over 80 percent /ð/ responses (Repp et al., 1983, Figure 6). These differences provide a nice demonstration of how the influence of both audible and visible speech is moderated by the perceiver's dominant language.

3.6 Easton and Basala Study

This study serves as the singular exception to the rule of a strong contribution of visible information in face-to-face speech recognition experiments. It is necessary to assess whether this exception weakens or proves the rule. Using single-syllable and two-syllable words, Easton and Basala (1982) asked subjects to lipread the items given just the visual information, or both visual and dubbed auditory information. Discrepant auditory information interfered with lipreading and the judgments were biased towards the auditory information. A subject would report confidence in the lipreading judgment even when it was incorrect because of a bias created by the auditory information. This result parallels the contribution of visual information when subjects report what they hear and reveals that phenomenal experience is directed primarily to the speech event and not to one modality or the other.

In contrast to the studies that have been reviewed, Easton and Basala (1982) also report no influence of the visual information when the subjects reported what they heard. Easton and Basala's (1982) use of real words and the nature of the contradictory auditory and visual information can rationalize the findings. In this study, the discrepant visual place information was not consistent with real words when combined with some of the auditory information signifying place and manner. Subjects knew that only words would be presented as test items in the experiment and would have been highly biased to perceive and report only words. When the visual word *teeth* was dubbed with the auditory word *mouth*, subjects could not report hearing a word beginning with a alveolar nasal because *nouth* is not a word (nor is *neeth* if subjects also used the visual vowel information). The tendency to perceive consonant clusters also would not be observed because these clusters necessarily produce nonwords.

It seems unlikely that the powerful influence of visible speech would be suppressed completely in a meaningful context. McGurk's (1981) demonstration sentence illustrates that the visual information can influence what is heard when the combination of the visual and auditory speech makes meaningful words and even sentences. The visual sentence,

My gag kok me koo grive.

paired with the auditory sentence,

My bab pop me poo brive.

gives the impression of the speaker saying,

My dad taught me to drive.

Although Easton and Basala's skepticism about the functional value of visible speech is not justified, it is necessary to extend the studies to provide boundary conditions on visible speech perception and information about external validity of the findings.

3.7 Speech Memory

By necessity, visual information must play a role in memory for speech if it does in the perception of speech. Memory for speech is nicely demonstrated by the recency effect that is obtained for the last few items in the immediate serial recall of an audible list. This effect is reduced considerably if the auditory list is followed by an auditory suffix (Crowder and Morton, 1969). If it is memory for speech that is being studied, then we might expect a contribution of visible speech. In fact, lipread lists without sound were shown to generate recency effects (Spoehr & Corin, 1978) and this recency could be attenuated by an auditory suffix (Campbell & Dodd, 1980, 1982; Greene & Crowder, 1984). Analogously, a lipread suffix reduces the recency effect in the recall of a list of auditory items (Greene & Crowder, 1984). Regardless of their eventual theoretical importance (Campbell, in press; Crowder, 1983), the demonstrations of audible and visible components in memory for speech offer converging evidence for the importance of these sources of information in speech perception.

4. An Initial Interpretation

The studies with dubbed speech have shown that the visual articulation provides information about place of articulation whereas other distinguishing properties must be conveyed by sound. Campbell's (1974) assumption that a given phonetic feature would be influenced by only the more informative modality anticipated the interpretation offered by MacDonald and McGurk (1978). They proposed the hypothesis that in face-to-face communication manner of articulation is perceived by ear, whereas place of articulation is perceived by eye. Then the information is combined, resulting in an auditory perception. Their hypothesis is unreasonable because it is known that the visual information is rarely sufficient to discriminate all possible places of articulation: for example, middle and back stop consonants. In addition, the present analysis of their results revealed some contribution of the speech sound to perceiving place of articulation when a labial sound was paired with a nonlabial articulation. Therefore, auditory information, as well as visual information, is used to disambiguate place, and it is also necessary to specify how the auditory and visual sources of information about place are combined. One of the central points of this monograph is that the answer to this question requires the independent variation of the values of the auditory and visual sources in factorial designs, using synthetic speech to control the informativeness of the auditory source. Two bimodal tasks using synthetic speech and a study using natural speech have already falsified the proposal that only a single modality contributes to a given phonetic distinction.

4.1 Experimental Tests: Synthetic Speech

Summerfield (1979) synthesized three speech continua from /aba/ to /ada/, /ada/ to /aga/, and /aga/ to /aba/. Subjects identified each synthetic syllable along a given continuum paired with a video display of the syllable from the one end of the continuum, with a video display of the syllable from the other end of the continuum, and with no video display. For example, a synthetic speech syllable from the first continuum would be presented alone, or with the video display of the speaker saying /aba/ or /ada/. The range and variance of different responses to the bimodal stimuli precluded the analysis of the interaction of the auditory and visual variables. Instead, the responses were pooled across the auditory variable and analyzed as a function of the visual condition. For the /aba/-/ada/ continuum, a visual /ada/ increased the number of /ada/ responses, whereas a visual /aba/ only increased the number of /abda/ responses relative to no video condition. For the /ada/-/aga/ continuum, there was very little contribution of the visual source, once again revealing the indistinctiveness of the alveolar and velar articulation. For the /aga/-/aba/ continuum, a video /aga/ increased the number of /aga/ responses, whereas a video /aba/ did not increase the number of /aba/ responses. This pattern of results indicates that visual information does not dominate the identification of place of articulation, but simply contributes an additional source of information for perceptual recognition (Summerfield, in press).

Using the logic and procedures of functional measurement (Anderson, 1974, 1981, 1982), Massaro and Cohen (1983c) determined how auditory and visual sources of information are evaluated and integrated in speech perception. A video recording was dubbed with synthetic speech to vary the auditory and visual sources of information independently of one another. Three levels of visual information (/ba/, /da/, or no articulation) were factorially combined with nine levels of auditory information spanning the place continuum from /ba/ to /da/. College students identified the speech events as /ba/ or /da/ in one task and as one of an open-ended set of alternatives in another task.

Both the visual and auditory variables influenced identification, with the contribution of the visual source larger at the more ambiguous levels of the auditory source. The results were adequately described by the FLMP and could not be accounted for by a categorical model of perception (CMP). These two models are described in more detail in Chapter 5. The CMP assumes that each modality provides only categorical information and, therefore, only a single modality influences a phonetic discrimination on a given trial. Rejection of the CMP also falsifies the hypothesis that only visible speech influences perception of place of articulation. The results provide initial support for the integration of auditory and visual sources of information, as will be discussed in Chapter 3. In addition, the two sources appear to function as continuous and independent cues to speech perception (see Chapters 4 and 6, respectively). In the last study to be reviewed, I illustrate the FLMP and contrast it with the CMP in an informative study factorially combining audible and visible dimensions of four syllables.

4.2 Experimental Test: Natural Speech

Repp, et al. (1983) factorially combined four levels of auditory information with four levels of visual information in a bimodal speech perception task. The visual articulations /ba/, /va/, /ða/, and /da/ were crossed with the natural-speech auditory renditions of these same alternatives. The speaker was a female, which is comforting if similar results are found, because all previous work has been done with male speakers. Subjects were asked to report what they heard and to indicate to what extent the auditory and visual information appeared to conflict. Figure 6 gives the proportion of /ba/, /va/, /ða/, and /da/ responses as a function of the auditory and visual information. The contribution of the visual source is reflected in the differences among the four curves within each of the four panels. The contribution of the auditory source is reflected in the deviations from horizontal curves within each of the four panels. The results reveal strong effects of both the visual and auditory sources.

Both the FLMP and the CMP can be tested against the results. According to the FLMP, each level of visual information gives varying degrees of support for each of the four alternatives and analogously for the auditory information. These feature values are evaluated against prototypes in long-term memory. The feature values are inserted in the prototype definitions and conjoined following a multiplicative rule (see Chapter 5, Section 1.2). The likelihood of a given response is equal to the goodness of match of that alternative relative to the sum of the goodness values of all four alternatives. To test the model against the results, 32 parameters are necessary to predict the 64 data points. The bottom panel of Figure 6 gives the predicted results for the FLMP and Table 5 gives the parameter values. The model does a good job of describing the results with an RMSD of .028. The parameter values are also psychologically meaningful with the feature values decreasing with increases in the differences in place of articulation. As an example, a visual /ba/ has .99 /ba/-ness and .30 /va/-ness and an auditory /va/ has .99 /va/-ness and .33 /ba/-ness, and .36 /ða/-ness.

In the formulation of the CMP it is assumed that each visual level gives rise to the four categorical alternatives with different probabilities and analogously for the auditory level. Thus, the perceiver has discrete information representing each of the two sources. Subjects are assumed to follow the outcomes of both sources when they agree and to follow the outcome of one of the two sources when they conflict. Another parameter is needed to allow some bias to the auditory or visual dimension when the two dimensions conflict. Thus the CMP requires 33 free parameters to predict the 64 data points. The top panel of Figure 6 gives the predicted results. The parameter values are given in Table

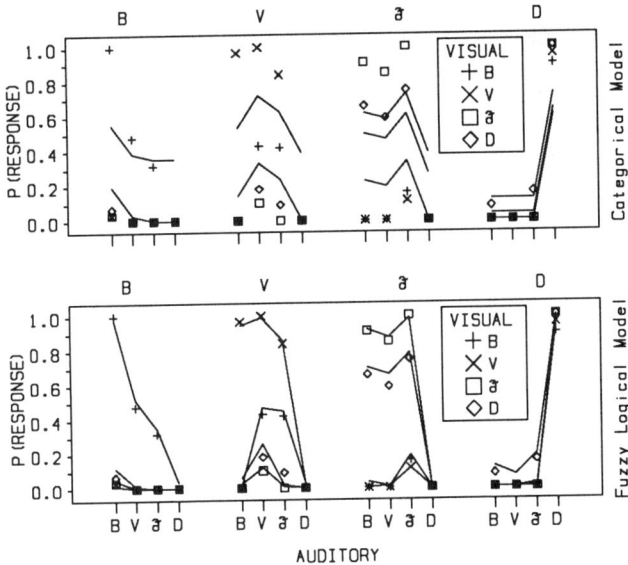

Figure 6. Observed (points) and predicted (lines) probability of identification as a function of the auditory and visual dimensions of the speech syllable. The four panels from left to right correspond to the four response alternatives /b/, /v/ /ð/, and /d/, respectively. The top panel gives the predictions of the categorical model (CMP) and the bottom panel gives the predictions of the fuzzy logical model of perception (FLMP) (observations from Repp, Manuel, Liberman, & Studdert-Kennedy, 1983).

Table 5. Parameter values representing the degree to which a given alternative x is supported, $x-ness$, for the description of the FLMP to the Repp et al. (1983) study. The left-hand entry corresponds to the auditory value (a_i) and the right hand entry to the visual value (v_j).

Stimulus	/ba/-ness a_i	v_j	/va/-ness a_i	v_j	/ða/-ness a_i	v_j	/da/-ness a_i	v_j
/ba/	.99	.99	.06	.30	.10	.02	.01	.01
/va/	.33	.01	.99	.99	.36	.02	.01	.04
/ða/	.03	.01	.16	.04	.99	.98	.09	.04
/da/	.01	.01	.01	.05	.01	.39	.99	.99

6. The categorical model cannot capture the pattern of results with a RMSD value of .191 which is over six times the RMSD given by the FLMP. What is important about the advantage of the FLMP over the CMP is the evidence that integration of the auditory and visual sources must precede categorization,

contrary to the initial interpretation of the McGurk effect.

Table 6. Parameter values representing the probability of a given alternative x, $P(x)$, for the description of the CMP to the Repp et al. (1983) study. The left-hand entry corresponds to the auditory value (a_i) and the right hand entry to the visual value (v_j).

Stimulus	P(/ba/)		P(/va/)		P(/ð a/)		P(/da/)	
	a_i	v_j	a_i	v_j	a_i	v_j	a_i	v_j
/ba/	.32	.91	.24	.00	.37	.00	.00	.09
/va/	.05	.00	.54	1.00	.32	.00	.00	.00
/ð a/	.00	.00	.40	.00	.56	1.00	.00	.00
/da/	.00	.00	.00	.00	.00	.69	1.00	.31

p = probability of responding with auditory decision = .39

5. Conclusion

The state of the art makes it a truism that there are multiple sources of information in speech perception. In addition to multiple auditory sources and top-down (contextual) sources, there is strong evidence for the influence of visible speech. Visible speech has a strong impact even when combined with unambiguous auditory speech. Visible speech is not capable of distinguishing all speech contrasts and, thus, is not a sufficient source. Silent televisions displaying only lip movements are not feasible for communication as are faceless telephones providing only speech sounds. Visible speech supplemented with other information, such as low bandpass auditory speech, tactile speech, or electrical speech delivered to a cochlear implant, offers a potentially viable medium for communication for the hearing-impaired. For our purposes, the contribution of visible speech warrants the study of how it is integrated with audible speech. This is the topic of the next chapter.

Chapter 3: Integration versus Nonintegration of Auditory and Visual Information in Speech Perception

Integration is defined as a process in which perceptual recognition of a bimodal speech event is influenced by both the auditory and visual sources of information. The exact nature of the information and how the two sources are integrated are questions that are relevant once integration is established. The outcome of our first contrast discussed in Chapter 2 indicates that both auditory and visual sources of information are utilized in speech perception. Given this conclusion, the answer to the next question might seem obvious to some because it is only natural to believe that the two contributing sources must be integrated. This belief might be false, however, and demonstrating that two sources are integrated in perceptual recognition is no easy matter.

1. Theoretical Difficulties

There is a popular question in developmental psychology since the time of Piaget. Do young children use only a single property of the environment for making perceptual judgments as, for example, using only height to judge the amount of liquid in a glass? A natural test of this question is to vary two properties of the situation and observe whether both influence the judgment. For our purposes, imagine a hypothetical experiment manipulating two independent properties such as the height and width of rectangles. Children could be tested with rectangular cookies and asked to indicate how happy they would be if they were given each cookie (Anderson & Cuneo, 1978). Average rating judgments of the area of the rectangles might reveal significant effects of both height and width even though these two cues are not integrated in the judgment of area. Some of the subjects may have used one cue, and other subjects may have used the other. This limitation also holds for the analysis of the results of a single subject because the same subject may have used just one cue on some trials and the other cue on other trials. The average performance across subjects or the average performance of a given subject could reveal significant effects of both dimensions even though no integration occurred. Thus, a mixture of trials resulting from judgments using just a single dimension on each trial can give results identical to that expected from a true integration of the two dimensions. Figure 1 illustrates how a mixture of two types of trials, each using only one dimension, can produce average results showing effects of both dimensions.

The two different processes, utilizing just one dimension for a given perceptual judgment versus integrating two dimensions, are even more difficult to distinguish given discrete identification judgments rather than continuous rating responses. With discrete judgments, it might be impossible to eliminate the hypothesis of the single-dimension process if subjects are given only a factorial combination of the dimensions. In some situations, the test of integration versus nonintegration is possible because subjects can be tested on each dimension presented in isolation. By including discrete judgments of the single-dimension conditions, it might be possible to test between the alternative processes.

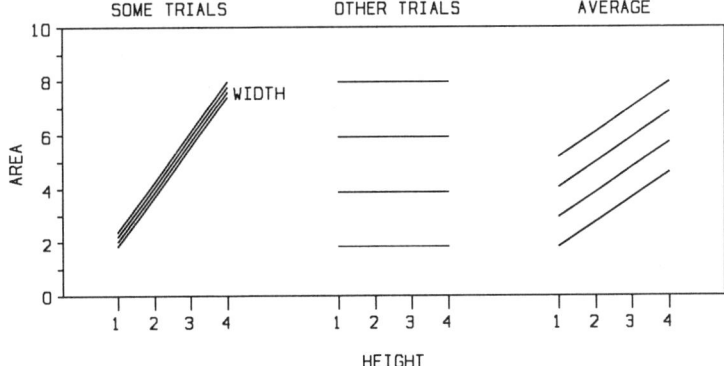

Figure 1. An illustration of how a mixture of two types of trials in which the observer uses only one dimension on some trials and the other dimension on other trials can give average results showing an effect of both dimensions. Thus, main effects of both dimensions do not necessarily imply integration of the two dimensions on any one trial.

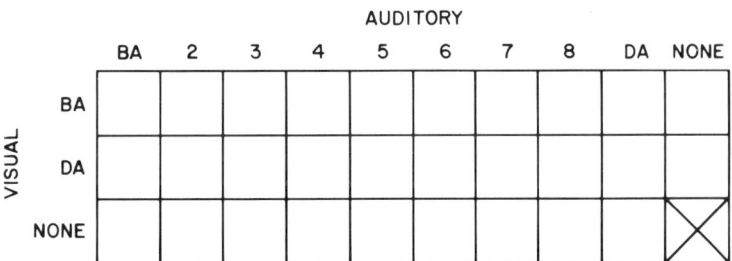

Figure 2. Expansion of a typical factorial design to include auditory and visual conditions presented alone. The nine levels along the auditory continuum represent speech sounds varying in equal steps between /ba/ and /da/.

Consider the perception of bimodal speech events created by the factorial combination of synthetic speech sounds along an auditory /ba/ to /da/ continuum paired with /ba/ or /da/ visual articulations. By also including the auditory and visual conditions as illustrated in Figure 2, it is at least logically possible to reject nonintegration. What is necessary is to find judgments of certain bimodal speech events that cannot be equivalent to some simple mixture of judgments of either the visual or the auditory dimensions presented alone. For example, if a judgment frequently given to a particular bimodal event is seldom given to either the auditory or visual events presented alone, then the results are incompatible with a nonintegration strategy, such as the one described in Figure 1. To make this result possible, it is necessary to allow responses other than /ba/ and /da/. (It is a sobering experience to realize how seldom open-ended alternatives have been used in identification experiments using synthetic speech.) Thus, an expanded factorial design with open-ended response alternatives offers the potential of demonstrating integration of auditory and visual information in speech perception. The novel design illustrated in Figure 2, along with open-ended response alternatives, has not been used previously in speech perception research and it provides a unique method to address the issue of integration versus nonintegration of audible and visible information in speech perception.

2. Expanded Factorial Design with Open-Ended Response Alternatives

2.1 Method

Subjects. Eight college students from the University of California, Santa Cruz, participated for one hour in the experiment.

Test Stimuli. All test stimuli were recorded on videotape. Color videotapes were made of the author seated in front of a wood panel background, illuminated with ordinary fluorescent fixtures in the ceiling. His head was centered in the video field and filled about two-thirds of the screen. On each trial the speaker said either /ba/ or /da/ or nothing, as cued by a video terminal under computer control. When the speaker was cued to say nothing, a computer-controlled tone was recorded on the audio channel of the videotape 400 msec after the onset of the neutral cue.

The original audio track of the videotape was replaced with synthetic speech. A nine-step /ba/ to /da/ auditory continuum was used to replace the original audio. Tokens of the speaker's /ba/ and /da/ were analyzed using linear prediction to derive a set of parameters for driving a software formant serial resonator speech synthesizer (Klatt, 1980). By altering the parametric information specifying the first 80 msec of the consonant-vowel syllable, a set of nine 400 msec syllables covering the range from /ba/ to /da/ was created. Figure 3 gives the spectrograms for five of the nine syllables along the continuum. During the first 80 msec, F1 went from 250 Hz to 700 Hz following a negatively accelerated path. The F2 followed a negatively accelerated path to 1199 Hz, beginning with one of nine values equally spaced between 1000 and 2000 Hz from most /ba/-like to most /da/-like, respectively. The F3 followed a linear transition to 2729 Hz from one of nine values equally spaced between 2200 and 3200 Hz. All other stimulus characteristics were identical for the nine auditory syllables.

The experimental videotapes were made by copying the original tape and replacing the original sound track with the synthetic speech. The presentation of the synthetic speech was synchronized with the original audio track on the

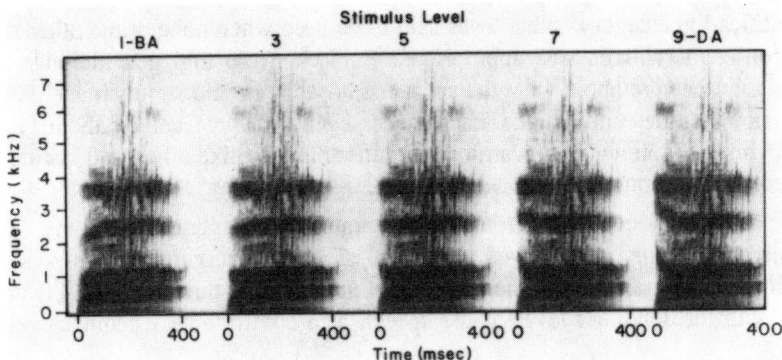

Figure 3. Spectrograms for five of the syllables along the /ba/ to /da/ continuum.

videotape and gave the strong illusion that the synthetic speech was coming from the mouth of the speaker. To accomplish this synchronization, the audio signal was monitored electronically and each syllable was replaced with a synthetic speech syllable or with nothing for visual-alone trials. The tones recorded without lip movements were replaced with synthetic syllables for the auditory-alone trials.

Design and Procedure. Nine levels along an auditory /ba/ to /da/ continuum were factorially combined with two possible visual articulations, /ba/ and /da/. These 18 trials represent the bimodal condition. There were also auditory-alone and visual-alone conditions. In the auditory-alone condition one of the nine auditory stimuli was presented, but the speaker did not move his mouth. In the visual-alone condition the speaker articulated either /ba/ or /da/, but no auditory speech was presented. In every block of 54 trials, there were 18 bimodal conditions, 18 auditory-alone conditions, and 18 visual-alone conditions. Thus, each of the 18 unique bimodal conditions was presented once, each of the nine unique auditory conditions was presented twice, and each of the two unique visual conditions was presented nine times in a block of 54 trials. One session of the experiment consisted of 5-1/2 blocks of trials preceded by 10 practice trials for a total of 307 trials. Subjects served in two sessions with about a 10-min break between sessions.

Subjects were instructed to look at the TV monitor and to listen to a possible speech sound coming from the TV. They were told of the three different kinds of trials: the bimodal trials, the auditory-alone trials, and the visual-alone trials. Subjects were asked to identify the speech event as one of eight alternatives by pressing one of eight buttons on the keyboard in front of them. The eight buttons corresponded to the alternatives /ba/, /da/, /bda/, /dba/, /ga/, /va/, /ða/, and "other." These alternatives were determined on the basis of pilot research and a previous experiment (Massaro & Cohen, 1983c). The identification category "other" was said to be used when none of the other seven response alternatives was appropriate. Subjects were told that although they might not be sure about what the speaker said, they should simply make the best decision that they could make. Each speech event was preceded by about 1175 to 1375 msec by an auditory warning stimulus sounding like a bell and lasting 250 msec. The response interval was 2.75 sec.

The subjects were tested in separate sound-attenuated rooms. Each subject was seated and viewed a NEC 19-in. (.48 m) monitor, which presented both the video and audio. The subjects sat about two to three feet away from the TV with the loudness level of the speech at a comfortable listening level (70 dB-A).

2.2 Results and Discussion

Figure 4 presents the proportion of each of the eight responses for the 29 unique speech events. Three separate analyses of variance were carried out across the three conditions. In all three analyses, the variables of interest were statistically significant. Subjects' judgments, as indicated by the proportion of responses, were influenced by both the visual and the auditory information. The interaction of the visual and auditory information with response was also significant in the bimodal condition.

As can be seen in Figure 4, the response category "other" was used only about five percent of the time. Thus limiting the number of specific alternatives to just seven is probably very similar in principle to giving the subjects a completely open-ended set of alternatives. We limited the number of alternatives for practical reasons; we wanted the subjects to be able to enter a response into the keyboard without undue delay.

The results of the bimodal condition are similar in form to previous findings using bimodal speech (Massaro & Cohen, 1983c) and also provide some new results given the auditory-alone and visual-alone conditions. Figure 4 also shows that visual /da/ produces a dramatic decrease in the likelihood of responding with a /ba/ alternative given an auditory /ba/. Thus, the visual /da/ has a large effect on decreasing the /ba/-ness of a bimodal speech event. For the group results, a visual /da/ decreased a /ba/ response by about 70% relative to the neutral articulation condition. An analogous analysis can be carried out on the stimuli near the /da/ end of the auditory continuum with the different sources of visual information. Of course, a /ba/ articulation dramatically decreases the likelihood of a /da/ response when combined with an auditory syllable at the /da/ end of the auditory continuum. There is some asymmetry in the influence of the visual /ba/ and /da/ syllables. Relative to the auditory-alone condition, a visual /ba/ increases the probability of a /ba/ judgment whereas a visual /da/ does not increase the probability of a /da/ judgment (see Figure 4). In addition, visual /ba/ plus auditory /da/ gives predominantly /bda/ judgments whereas visual /da/ plus

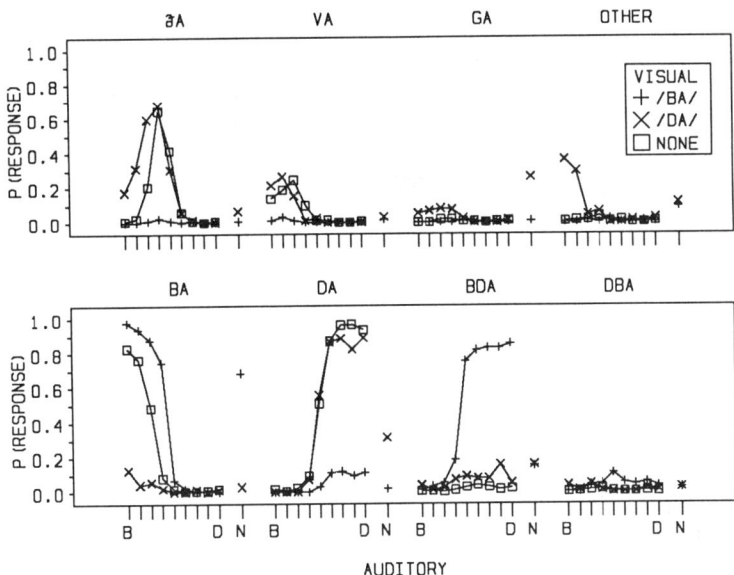

Figure 4. Probability of responding with each of the eight alternatives as a function of the auditory and visual sources under the bimodal and unimodal conditions. The nine levels along the auditory continuum represent speech sounds varying in equal steps between /ba/ and /da/.

auditory /ba/ gives predominantly /ða/, /va/, and "other" responses.

One surprising result is that the speech events at the /da/ end are actually identified as /da/ slightly more often with no visual information relative to having a /da/ visual articulation. This result probably represents, in part, the fact that the speaker was posed with his mouth slightly open during the trials in which no visual articulation was made. Thus, this neutral articulation can be considered to be much more like /da/ than like /ba/ or some other articulation. In addition, it is easy to say /da/ without moving your mouth very much. A /da/ articulation might also dilute the support for the syllable /da/ because a visual /da/ is equivalent to a visual /ga/.

It is somewhat surprising that there were over 30% "other" responses with an auditory /ba/ paired with a visual /da/. We do not know what the subjects are perceiving in this condition. Using an unlimited set of response alternatives, Repp, et al. (1983) found only /da/ and /ða/ responses when a natural auditory /ba/ was paired with a visual /da/. In future studies, it might be more informative to use truly open-ended alternatives where subjects can simply state the alternative on each trial.

This study with open-ended alternatives illustrates some of the differences that are observed when compared with experiments carried out with just /ba/ and

/da/ alternatives (see Massaro & Cohen, 1983c). With two response alternatives, /ba/ and /da/, the bimodal event with conflicting information usually leads to a less extreme probability of response. Thus, a bimodal speech event with an auditory /ba/ paired with a visual /da/ gives about 30 percent /da/ responses and about 70 percent /ba/ responses. With open-ended alternatives, the likelihood of a /ba/ or /da/ response given these conflicting sources decreases dramatically and the responses are replaced with other alternatives. An auditory /ba/ paired with a visual /da/ will be identified as /ð̣a/, /va/, or "other" in many cases with open-ended responses.

The use of open-ended alternatives also has a few surprises concerning perception of the auditory /ba/ to /da/ continuum. The continuum is not symmetric in that the /ba/ half appears to be less robust than the /da/ half. With no visual information, the two syllables at the /ba/ end of the auditory continuum are sometimes identified as /va/ and levels 3 to 5 are identified half the time as /ð̣a/. These confusions are reasonable in terms of the acoustic properties of the syllables. In addition, the syllables /va/, /ð̣a/, and /ba/ are confused for one another in auditory recognition tests (Miller & Nicely, 1955). On the other hand, the syllables at the /da/ end of the continuum are usually identified as /da/, which simultaneously reveals the robustness of auditory /da/ and rationalizes the smaller effect of visible speech given auditory /da/ relative to auditory /ba/ (see Chapter 2, Section 3.4).

2.3 Evidence for Integration.

Following the logic developed in Section 1, the results will be assessed with respect to the integration question. Figure 5 replots the proportion of /bda/ responses for the group and for a typical subject. The occurrence of /bda/ responses in the bimodal condition is good evidence for the integration of auditory and visual information in speech perception. This follows from the fact that very few /bda/ responses are present in either the auditory-alone or the visual-alone conditions. Hence, the large number of /bda/ responses in the bimodal condition cannot simply be a result of a single source of information, but must involve the integration of the two sources on a given trial.

The response /bda/ is found most often when a visual /ba/ is paired with an auditory /da/-like sound. As demonstrated by Cohen (1984), there is evidence that the information representing visual /ba/ is obtained by the perceiver before the auditory /da/. This might occur because the visual /ba/ is processed more quickly and/or the visual articulation information is made available sooner than the auditory speech. Therefore, it could be the case that subjects respond /bda/ to a visual /ba/ and an auditory /da/ because they tend to locate the two sources of information at different points in time and therefore perceive the sequence /bda/. Rather than some combination of the two sources indicating a single articulatory event, it might be argued that this explanation of the /bda/ responses

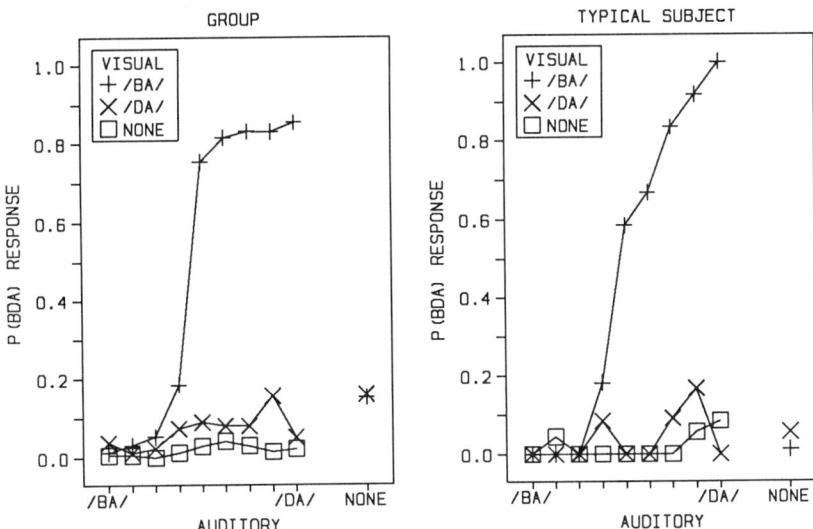

Figure 5. Probability of /bda/ judgments to bimodal, auditory, and visual speech events. The left panel gives the group results, and the right panel gives the results for a typical subject. The nine levels along the auditory continuum represent speech sounds varying in equal steps between /ba/ and /da/.

weakens the case for integration of the auditory and visual sources of information. In a strict sense, no integration is necessary in that the listener only has to perceive /ba/ from the visual source and /da/ from the auditory source as occurring at different points in time. Even with this explanation, however, it is clear that the perceiver is utilizing both sources of information for perceptual interpretation on a given trial. Hence, some process of integration is occurring, although the two sources might not be integrated to perceive a single speech event.

Cohen (1984) found evidence against the idea that /bda/ judgments are solely a function of perceiving a visual /ba/ and auditory /da/ at two successive points in time. By varying the onset times between the two sources, it was possible to present the auditory /da/ well in advance of the visual /ba/. If the time of arrival of the auditory and visual sources is the critical factor, then the proportion of /bda/ judgments should decrease and the proportion of /dba/ judgments should increase. However, very few /dba/ judgments were found even when the auditory /da/ preceded the visual /ba/ by 200 msec. The results are better explained in terms of a true integration of auditory and visual information specifying a single speech event than in terms of the identification of the two sources at two different points in time. Frequent /bda/ judgments and infrequent /dba/ judgments can be interpreted in terms of the compatibility of the visual /ba/ with these two possibilities. A visual /ba/ can be shown to be very similar to a visual /bda/, but not to a visual /dba/. The occurrence of /bda/ and not /dba/ is consistent with integrating the visual and auditory sources and inconsistent with identifying them as separate successive events.

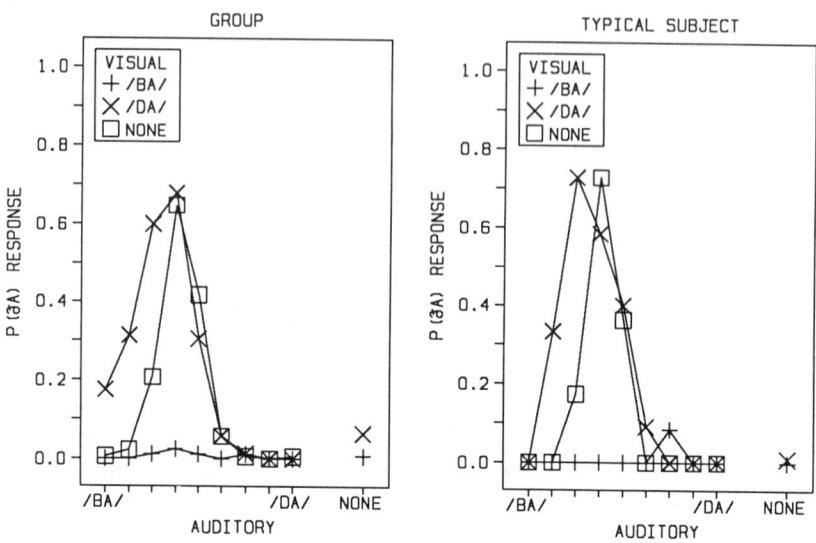

Figure 6. Probability of /ða/ judgments to bimodal, auditory, and visual speech events. The left panel gives the group results, and the right panel gives the results for a typical subject. The nine levels along the auditory continuum represent speech sounds varying in equal steps between /ba/ and /da/.

A good case for integration cannot rest on just a single type of judgment. In addition to the /bda/ responses, there is other evidence supporting the notion of integration of auditory and visual information in speech perception. This evidence comes from the /ða/ and /ba/ judgments. Figure 6 illustrates that an auditory syllable somewhat between the /ba/ and /da/ endpoints is sometimes perceived as /ða/. This perceptual judgment is more frequent when the auditory syllable is paired with a visual /da/ and less frequent when paired with a visual /ba/. These results make good sense in terms of the characteristics of both the auditory and visual dimensions of these syllables. Spectrograms of these sounds are similar to those of a natural /ða/ of the speaker. A /da/ articulation is also similar to a /ða/ articulation in that they both are articulated with a relatively open mouth. A /ba/ articulation is very different from that for /ða/. Relative to the no articulation condition, a visual /da/ combined with this auditory information increases the likelihood of a /ða/ response. On the other hand, the visual information corresponding to /ba/ eliminates a /ða/ response. Visual /da/ provides some support for the alternative /ða/, and visual /ba/ provides no support or negative support for this alternative. Given that the response /ð a/ seldom occurs on visual-alone trials, the increase in /ð a/ responses with visual /da/ probably represents true integration of the auditory and visual information.

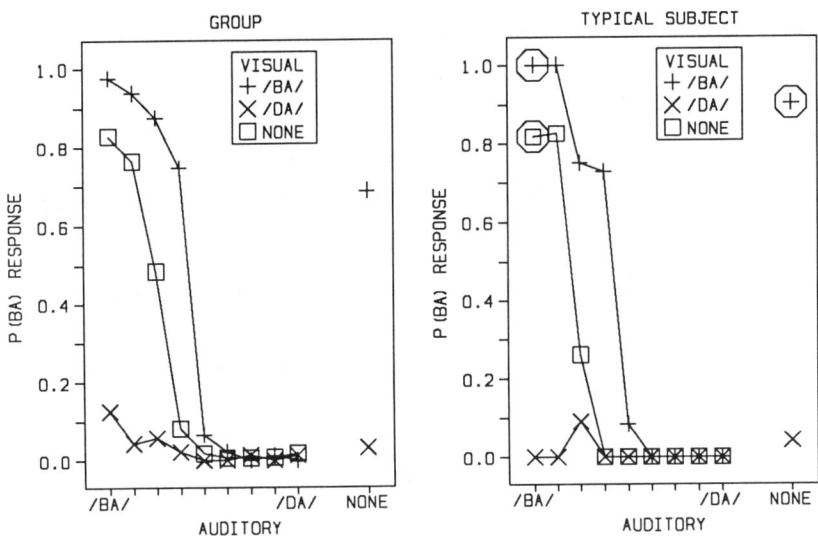

Figure 7. Probability of /ba/ judgments to bimodal, auditory, and visual speech events. The left panel gives the group results, and the right panel gives the results for a typical subject. The nine levels along the auditory continuum represent speech sounds varying in equal steps between /ba/ and /da/. The three circled points in the right panel provide evidence for integration.

The proportion of /ba/ judgments shown in Figure 7 to auditory and visual /ba/ cannot be accounted for by nonintegration or the identification of only the auditory or visual source on a given trial. Consider the three conditions that are circled for a typical subject plotted in the right panel of Figure 7. The speech sound at the /ba/ end of the auditory continuum is heard as /ba/ about 80% of the time when presented alone. A visual /ba/ presented alone is identified as /ba/ about 90% of the time. However, the same speech sound at the /ba/ end of the auditory continuum paired with the same visual /ba/ is identified as /ba/ 100% of the time. Thus, the visual /ba/ adds to the /ba/-ness of a syllable with an auditory /ba/ more than can be predicted by nonintegration.

The results of the experiment with open-ended response alternatives provide strong evidence against the possibility of using just a single dimension on each trial, and for a true integration of the auditory and visual sources. One critical finding is the large proportion of /bda/ judgments given a visual /ba/ and an auditory /da/ when this same judgment is seldom given to either the visual or auditory information presented alone. We find over five times as many /bda/ judgments given to the bimodal events than to the visual-only condition, and the auditory-only condition almost never produces /bda/ judgments. It follows that a /bda/ judgment observed on a bimodal trial could not have resulted from just one of the two sources. Similar findings occurred for /ba/ and /ða/ judgments and accordingly represent the outcome of the integration of both auditory and visual sources of information.

3. Selective Attention to Auditory and Visual Sources

Subjects in the experiment with open-ended responses were told to report what the speaker said. Given bimodal speech, they were free to use either the auditory or visual source or both sources. Our interpretation was that both sources were integrated and influenced judgments given bimodal speech. A strong test of the integration hypothesis is to assess to what extent subjects cannot integrate. That is, can subjects voluntarily identify the speech event on the basis of just a single source of information? If subjects cannot selectively attend to a single source, this result would provide strong evidence for integration of auditory and visual information in speech perception. The following experiment was carried out utilizing the traditional tasks of selective and divided attention (e.g. Massaro & Warner, 1977) to answer the question. Subjects were tested in the bimodal speech recognition task under four different instruction conditions. In the two selective attention conditions, the subjects identified only what they saw or only what they heard. In the divided attention condition, subjects identified both what they saw and what they heard in independent judgments. In the integration condition, subjects identified the speech event on the basis of what they saw and what they heard.

3.1 Method

Subjects. Six subjects were recruited from the University of California, Santa Cruz community and paid $10 for their services.

Test Stimuli. The original video recording and the synthetic speech were identical to those used in the previous experiment (see Section 2.1). The only exception was that the video was viewed in monochrome rather than color on a Sony 11-in. (.3 m) monitor.

Design and Procedure. The design and procedure used in this experiment were the same as in Experiment 2 of the Massaro and Cohen (1983c) study except that four sessions were run over a two-day period with each session introduced by different instructions. There were 27 possible speech stimuli created by a factorial combination of three visual levels (/ba/, neutral, and /da/) with nine auditory levels. The neutral level consisted of a view of the speaker with no mouth movement and the nine auditory levels were identical to the nine synthetic levels used in the previous experiment. In contrast to the previous experiment, there were no visual-alone trials. There were 11 blocks of the 27 unique stimuli preceded by 10 practice tasks for a total of 307 trials per session.

Subjects were tested in the bimodal speech recognition task under four different attention conditions: Selective Visual, Selective Auditory, Divided Attention, and Integration. In the Selective Visual condition, subjects were instructed "to indicate whether you saw the speaker saying /ba/, saying /da/, or saying nothing. You make your decision on the basis of what you saw." Analogous instructions were given in the Selective Auditory condition except that the critical attribute was what the subject heard and the decision alternatives were /ba/ and /da/. In the Divided Attention condition, subjects made separate decisions corresponding to what they saw and what they heard. In the Integration condition, subjects were instructed "to indicate whether the speaker said /ba/ or /da/ using both what you saw and what you heard." Thus, subjects made 1 out of 3 responses in the visual identifications and 1 out of 2 responses in the auditory identifications and in the Integration condition. Subjects were able to make their two separate decisions in the Divided Attention condition by hitting a single 1 out of 6 keys.

3.2 Results

The results were analyzed separately for each of the four sessions with different instructions. In the Selective Visual condition, subjects identified what they saw the speaker say. The three response alternatives were /ba/, /da/, and nothing. The left panel of Figure 8 gives the proportion of correct identifications as a function of the auditory and visual levels of the stimuli. Subjects were fairly accurate in identifying the three types of visual articulations. Even though subjects were instructed to identify only the visual articulation, the proportion of correct responses varied significantly as a function of the level of the auditory stimulus. The reaction times (RTs) shown in the right panel of Figure 8 also show that subjects were not able to completely ignore the auditory information. RTs increased in the cases in which the auditory information was inconsistent with the visual articulation. With no visual articulation, RT was unrelated to the level of the auditory speech. With a visual /da/, RT increased as the auditory syllable moved from the /da/ to the /ba/ end of the speech continuum. The opposite result occurred for a visual /ba/, with the RTs increasing as the auditory syllable changed from the /da/ to /ba/ end of the speech continuum.

In the Selective Auditory condition, subjects identified the speech stimulus as /ba/ or /da/ on the basis of what they heard the speaker say. Because accuracy cannot be meaningfully determined given the auditory speech continuum, the left panel of Figure 9 gives the proportion of /da/ responses as a function of the auditory and visual levels of the stimuli. The proportion of /da/ responses changed systematically as expected with changes with the level of the auditory stimulus. There was also a large effect on the proportion of /da/ responses as a

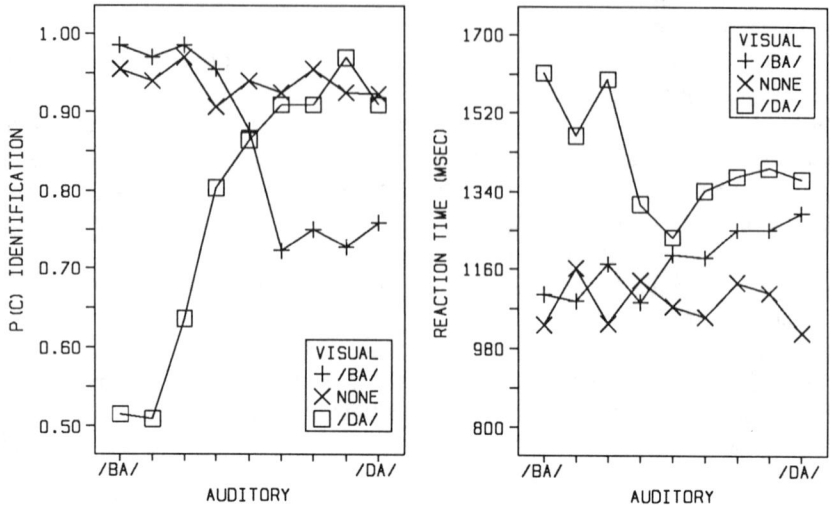

Figure 8. Left panel: The probability of a correct identification of what the subjects saw the speaker say under the Selective Visual condition. Right panel: Reaction times of the identification responses.

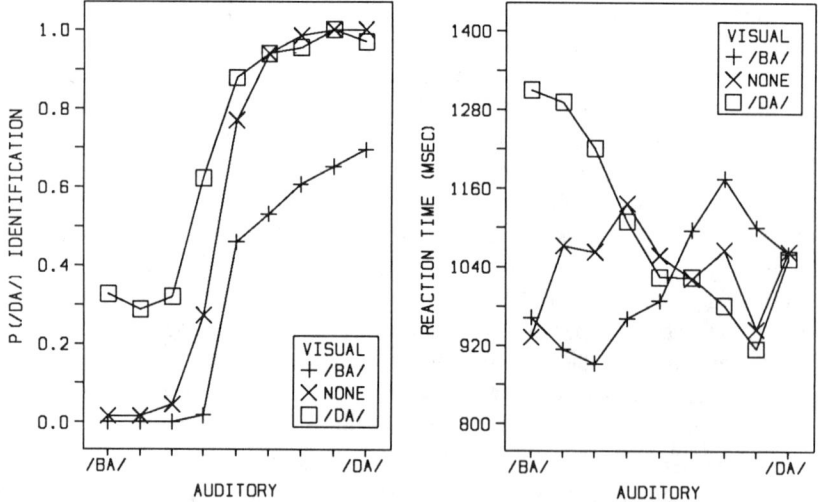

Figure 9. Left panel: Probability of a /da/ identification of what the subjects heard the speaker say as a function of the auditory and visual sources of information under the Selective Auditory condition. Right panel: Reaction times of the identification responses.

function of the visual articulation. The auditory/visual interaction was also significant because the effect of the visual variable is attenuated at the end regions of the auditory dimension. Analogous to the results of the Selective Visual condition, subjects were not able to ignore the visual articulation. The RTs shown in the right panel of Figure 9 also support this conclusion in that the RTs increased when conflicting visual information was present. With no visual articulation, RTs tended to increase toward the middle of the speech continuum. With a visual /da/ RTs decreased as the auditory speech syllable changed from /ba/ to /da/. Similarly, the RT decreased as the auditory syllable changed from /da/ to /ba/ when the auditory speech syllable was paired with a visual /ba/.

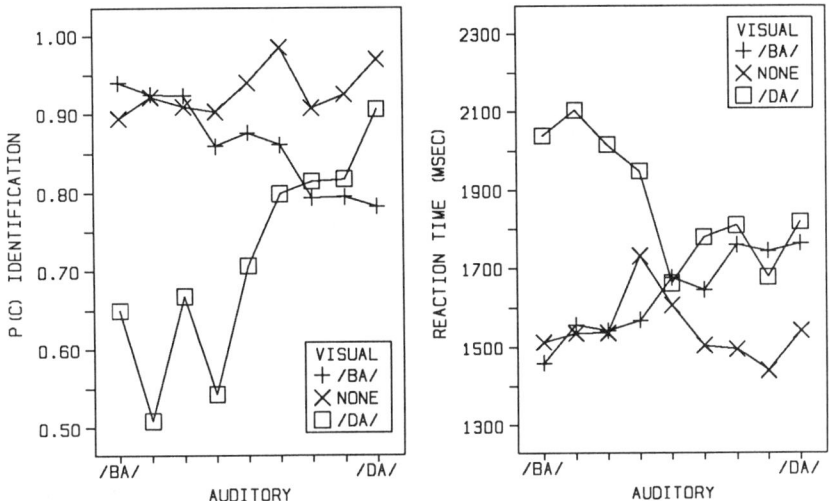

Figure 10. Left panel: The probability of a correct identification of what the subjects saw the speaker say under the Divided Attention condition. Right panel: Reaction times of the identification responses.

In Divided Attention, subjects had to report both what they saw the man say and what they heard the man say. The left panel of Figure 10 gives the proportion of correct identifications for the three visual events: /ba/, none, and /da/. The proportion of correct judgments varied as a function of the auditory stimulus, as a function of the visual stimulus, and as a function of the interaction of these two variables. The results were very similar to those found in Selective Visual attention when subjects only identified what they saw the man say.

When these subjects reported what they heard in Divided Attention, they were highly influenced by the visual information as well as the auditory information. The left panel of Figure 11 shows that the proportion of /da/ identifications changed systematically with changes in the auditory and visual levels. The significant interaction between the auditory and visual sources of

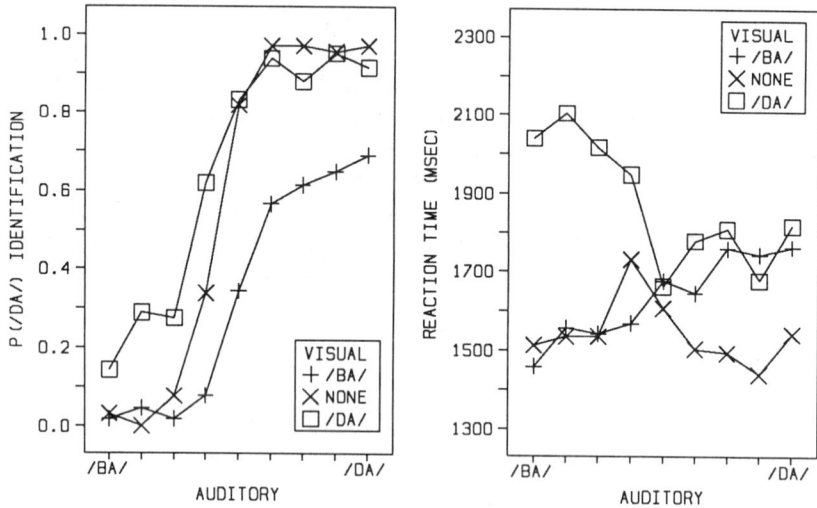

Figure 11. Left panel: Probability of a /da/ identification of what the observer heard the man say as a function of the auditory and visual sources of information under the Divided Attention condition. Right panel: Reaction times of the identification responses.

information is similar in form to that found in the Selective Auditory condition. As expected, the RTs were significantly longer in the Divided Attention relative to the Selective Attention task.

In the Integration condition, subjects identified the speech event on the basis of both what they saw and what they heard. The left panel of Figure 12 gives the proportion of /da/ responses as a function of the auditory and visual levels of the stimuli. The proportion of /da/ responses changed systematically both as a function of the level along the auditory continuum and the visual articulation. The interaction of these two variables was also statistically significant, given that the effect of the visual variable is attenuated at the end regions of the auditory dimension. The RTs for the Integration condition were about the same order of magnitude as for the Selective Auditory condition and significantly longer than for the Divided Attention condition. This result supports the interpretation of the identification judgments. Faced with multiple sources of information, integrating two dimensions appears to be a natural function and this process doesn't take any longer than selectively processing and reporting a single dimension of the speech event.

One assessment of integration involves the ability to selectively process one dimension of the bimodal speech event without influence from the other. We have seen that subjects were not able to identify the speech event on the basis of just a single source without influence of the other. It is instructive to

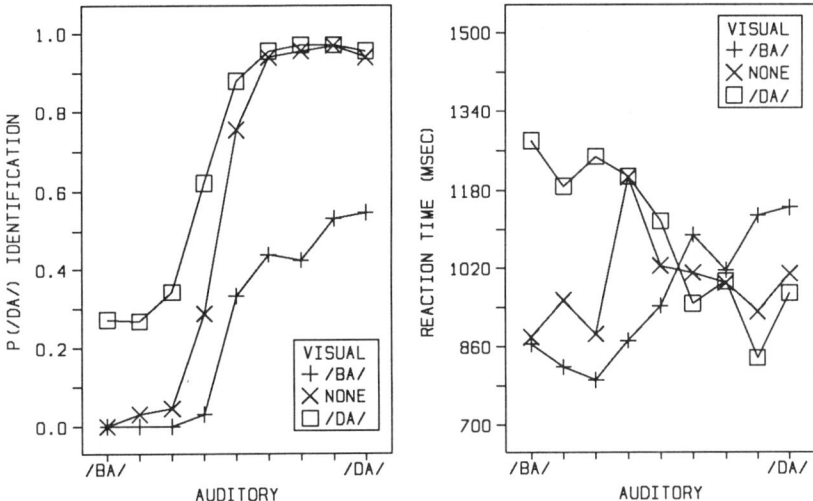

Figure 12. Left panel: Probability of a /da/ identification of what the observer perceived the man say as a function of the auditory and visual sources of information under the Integration condition. Right panel: Reaction times of the identification responses.

assess to what extent the to-be- ignored source can be filtered out relative to the condition in which both sources must be integrated. Thus, we want to compare performance when subjects are instructed to respond on the basis of just one of the dimensions to performance when subjects are instructed to respond on the basis of both dimensions.

Figure 13 contrasts the Selective Auditory condition to the Integration condition. The left panel represents performance in terms of the probability of a /da/ identification as a function of the visual and auditory sources of information when subjects were instructed to make their decision of what was said on the basis of both sources. The right panel corresponds to the results when subjects were instructed to make their decision of what they heard on the basis of only the auditory information. There is only a small difference between these two conditions. Subjects are influenced by the visual information almost as much when they are told to selectively process just the auditory source as opposed to being told to process both sources of information. An analysis of variance contrasting these two indicated main effects of the auditory and visual dimensions but no interaction with the Integration and Selective Auditory conditions.

The right panel in Figure 14 presents the analogous results when subjects were instructed to make their decision of what they saw on the basis of only the visual information. Although the influence of the auditory source seems to be

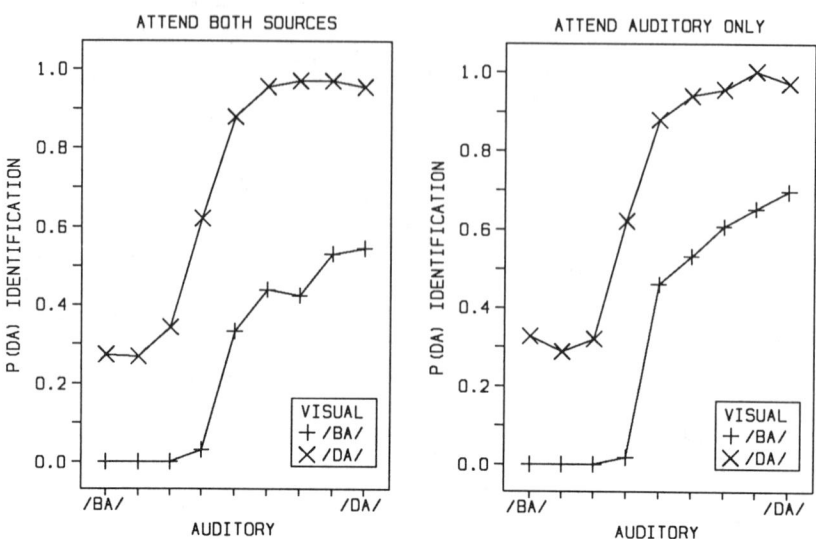

Figure 13. Probability of a /da/ identification as a function of the auditory and visual sources of information under two attention conditions, attending to both sources, or attending to only the auditory source.

somewhat attenuated in the Visual Selective attention condition relative to the Integration condition, there is still a substantial influence of the auditory information on the visual judgments. The auditory and visual conditions did interact with the Integration and Selective Visual conditions, showing that subjects were somewhat successful in decreasing the influence of the auditory source. However, as can be seen in Figure 14, there is still a substantial influence of the auditory dimension when subjects are instructed to respond only on the basis of what they saw. Thus, some integration occurs even though subjects attempt to process selectively only one of the two input dimensions. These results indicate that subjects are not able to selectively process one event independently of influence from the other dimension. At least some integration appears to occur automatically (i.e., without voluntary effort or unintentionally). The to-be-ignored dimension also clearly influences the time it takes to report the relevant dimension in the Selective Attention task. This result provides converging evidence for integration of auditory and visual information in speech perception.

The somewhat better ability to filter our auditory relative to visual speech is consistent with a proposal by Posner (1978). Posner believes that people have an attentional bias toward vision because other modalities such as audition have better alerting properties. An alerting property of a signal is an inducement to respond to a following signal when the first signal is presented. A visual

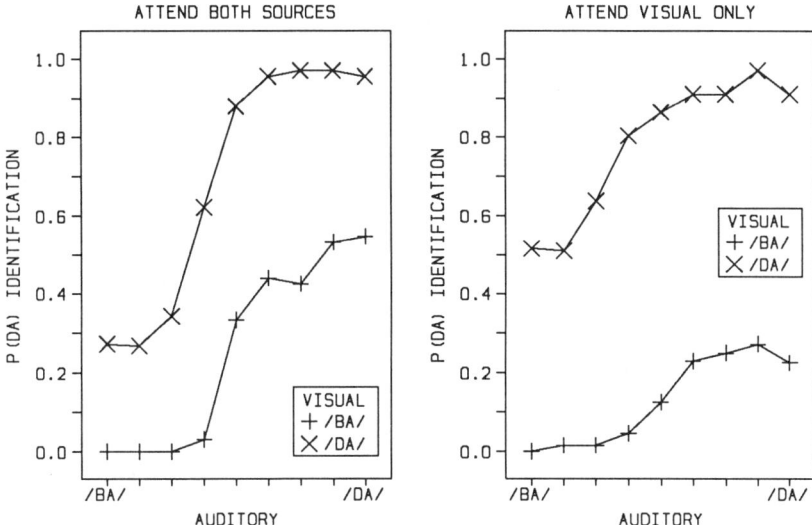

Figure 14. Probability of a /da/ identification as a function of the auditory and visual sources of information under two attention conditions, attending to both sources, or attending to only the visual source.

warning signal only improves processing for visual tasks whereas an auditory warning signal improves processing for both visual and auditory tasks. Posner makes the claim that the visual modality may block information occurring on other modalities from the subject's awareness. In our situation, however, attention to the visual information reduces the influence of the auditory dimension; attention to one modality does not preclude an influence from the other modality. Similarly, there is no loss of resolution of the visual and auditory information in processing bimodal relative unimodal speech (Massaro, 1985a).

3.3 Conflict and Ambiguity

The RTs provided converging evidence for the process of integrating auditory and visual speech. Although the RTs increase with increases in the conflict between the two sources, one should not conclude that the conflict is responsible for the RT increase. Conflict is confounded with other variables such as the ambiguity of the speech event. By ambiguity of the total speech event, we mean the extent to which the speech event supports more than one alternative category. A measure of ambiguity can be determined from the identification judgments (Massaro & Cohen, 1983c). Given the two alternatives /ba/ and /da/, the most ambiguous speech event would correspond to a .5 probability of response and ambiguity would decrease as the probability approaches 0 or 1. Speech events with conflicting auditory and visual information will tend to be more ambiguous than events with nonconflicting sources. Conflicting sources would tend to produce less consistent judgments than nonconflicting sources. One test between the two explanations involves a neutral articulation condition in which no visual articulation is present and, therefore, no differences in conflict are possible. As can be observed in Figures 9-12, RTs increase in the middle of the auditory continuum in which there is ambiguity but no conflict. Thus conflicting sources lengthen RT not because of conflict per se but because of the increased ambiguity of a speech event with conflicting sources of information. This result should be considered as independent evidence for integration, given that RT is a function of a property of the speech event resulting from the contribution of both the auditory and visual sources of information.

4. Integration of Audible and Visible Speech

The experiments reported in this chapter provide convincing evidence for the integration of audible and visible speech in bimodal speech perception. Emergent percepts occur given bimodal speech events that cannot be predicted by only one of the two sources of information. Furthermore, subjects are not able to filter out one source and selectively perceive the other. Not only the identification judgments, but the RTs of these judgments indicate integration of the two sources. Lest the reader conclude that I have taken great pains to demonstrate the obvious, the obvious isn't ubiquitous. For example, the inability to attend selectively to one modality without cross talk from the other could not have been expected from current attention theory (Broadbent, 1982; Massaro, 1985a). Given that integration occurs, we now consider the nature of the integration process. The process cannot be revealed completely at this stage, however, because its properties include answers to some of the binary contrasts discussed in later chapters. We begin with an initial impression of the nature of the integration process to develop our picture of what the process should entail.

4.1 An Initial Impression

Integration seems to be an efficient system for perceiving speech. Given multiple sources of information that are susceptible to random variability, the optimal strategy would be to evaluate and integrate all of the sources, even though they might be ambiguous. One limitation of a system designed in this way would be the relative inability to process selectively a single dimension of the speech event. As illustrated in the selective-attention study, subjects find it difficult to attend to only the auditory speech while looking at the speaker's lips and vice versa. These results demonstrate that integration is a natural process and we find it difficult to process selectively one dimension of the speech event without being influenced by other dimensions.

Some properties of the integration process can be revealed by the types of judgments given conflicting sources of information. Consider the large number of /bda/ judgments given a visual /ba/ and auditory /da/, and the almost nonoccurrence of /dba/ judgments given a visual /da/ and auditory /ba/. These judgments seem to depict a smart process with the following constraints. First, the auditory and visual sources are processed to some level in the system relatively independently of one another (i.e., without cross talk). A second constraint is that some continuous representation is acquired about the auditory and the visual sources in terms of their compatibility with candidate categories.

The large number of /bda/ judgments to a visual /ba/ combined with an auditory /da/ can be described in terms of the visible and audible properties of a /bda/ category. The visible mouth movement for /bda/ is similar to the movement for /ba/. Thus, we can say that visual /ba/ supports both /ba/ and /bda/ alternatives. In addition, auditory /da/ supports the alternative /da/ and might even be considered to support /va/ and /ða/ to some degree. Thus, the system might be faced with auditory information that supports /da/ and visual information that supports /ba/ and /bda/. Thus, /bda/ can be considered the appropriate identification because it maintains the most consistency between two dimensions of the speech input and the perceptual judgment.

The form of the explanation of /bda/ judgments takes on even more meaning because it can explain the rare occurrence of /dba/ judgments. Visual /da/ supports only /da/ (or /ga/) and to some extent /va/ and /ða/ but certainly not /dba/. The latter involves a closing of the vocal tract at the lips which is not contained in the /da/ articulation. The auditory information supports /ba/ and to some extent /va/ and /ða/ (as indexed by the auditory-alone condition). Thus, subjects report /ða/, /va/, and "other" given a visual /da/ and an auditory /ba/. The perceptual system seeks to reach the best compromise between conflicting visual and auditory sources; it will not decide completely in the direction of one source (no matter how unambiguous or invariant) if it flies in the face of another source. We will pursue quantitative analyses of these observations at the appropriate junctures in this research endeavor.

5. Practice Experiment

The perception of bimodal speech exemplifies the joint influence of both sight and sound. One question immediately raised is to what degree subjects can selectively process just one of the dimensions or to what extent this selective processing can be learned. In the previous attention study, we saw that subjects were not able to filter out one source in perceptual recognition. Both sources contribute to perceptual judgment regardless of the intentions of the observer. The present concern is with practice effects and we ask to what extent subjects can learn to identify one dimension independently of the other. To the extent practice and learning are ineffective, we have evidence for integration as a fundamental process in bimodal speech perception.

5.1 Method

Subjects. Four undergraduates were tested for seven days for an hour a day. The subjects were paid $5/hr. for participating.

Stimuli. The stimulus tape was identical to that used in the experiment on open-ended responses (Section 2.1). Subjects served for two sessions a day with 307 trials per session. Within each block of 54 trials, there were 18 auditory-alone, 18 visual-alone, and 18 bimodal speech events. There were five-and-a-half blocks per session plus ten practice trials at the beginning of each session.

Procedure. The task of the subject was to make separate identifications of the auditory and visual events on each trial. Thus, on auditory-alone and visual-alone trials, subjects made just one identification, whereas on the bimodal speech events subjects made two identifications. The design of the response buttons was organized, as illustrated in Table 1, so that subjects hit one button on each trial, even in the bimodal case.

Table 1. Response button layout for practice experiment. Each cell corresponds to a button and the two letters within each cell represent the identification. The first letter corresponds to the visual (v) or auditory (a) modality, and the second letter to a /ba/ (B), /da/ (D), or none (N) event on that modality. The top left hand button, for example, represents the response for a visual /ba/ paired with an auditory /ba/.

vB aB	vB aD	vB aN
vD aB	vD aD	vD aN
vN aB	vN aD	

5.2 Results

Subjects were highly influenced by the other modality in the bimodal speech identification task relative to the single dimension presentations. Figure 15 gives the average probability of a /da/ identification under all of the different conditions of the experiment for the first block and the last block of trials. The left half of the figure corresponds to the auditory identifications and the right half corresponds to the visual identifications. Within each half to the figure, the left portion represents performance under the bimodal condition and the right portion represents performance under the unimodal condition. As can be seen, each dimension had a strong influence on the identification of the other dimension even in the tenth block of trials. Replicating the results of the previous attention study, there is some evidence for learning to filter out the auditory dimension in visual identification by the tenth block of trials.

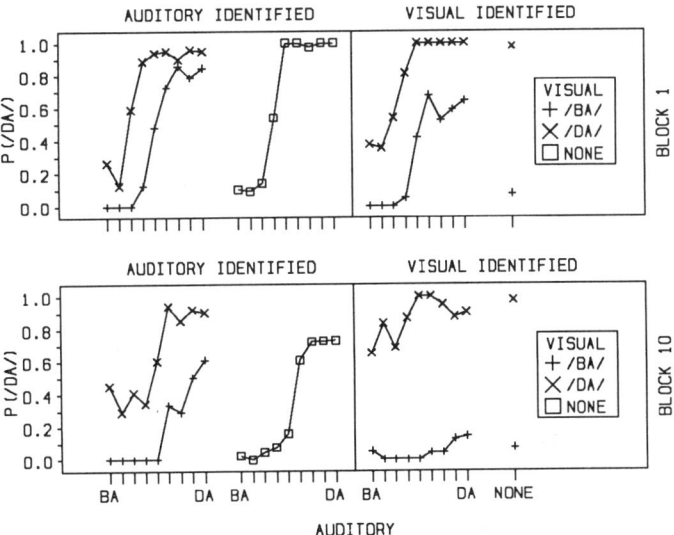

Figure 15. Probability of a /da/ identification of the auditory and visual dimensions of the speech syllable under the bimodal and unimodal conditions of the experiment. The left half of the figure corresponds to the auditory identifications and the right half corresponds to the visual identifications. Within each half to the figure, the left portion represents performance under the bimodal condition and the right portion represents performance under the unimodal condition. The top panel gives performance during the first block of 297 trials and the bottom panel gives performance during the tenth block (group results).

There were significant individual differences and it is instructive to give the individual results for each of the four subjects. Subject 1 shown in the top two panels of Figure 16 was reasonably successful in achieving almost complete independence of processing by the tenth block of trials. Except for a few observations, performance under the bimodal condition was identical to performance under the unimodal conditions during the tenth block. For some unknown reason, Subject 2, shown in the bottom two panels of Figure 16, developed a strong bias to identify the auditory dimension as /ba/. Even with this bias, however, it is readily apparent that this subject was influenced by the one modality in the identification of the other. Subject 3, shown in the top half of Figure 17, was able to achieve less cross talk by the tenth block, but did not achieve anything near independence of processing. The fourth subject shown in the bottom half of Figure 17 developed independence of processing the visual dimension but not the auditory dimension.

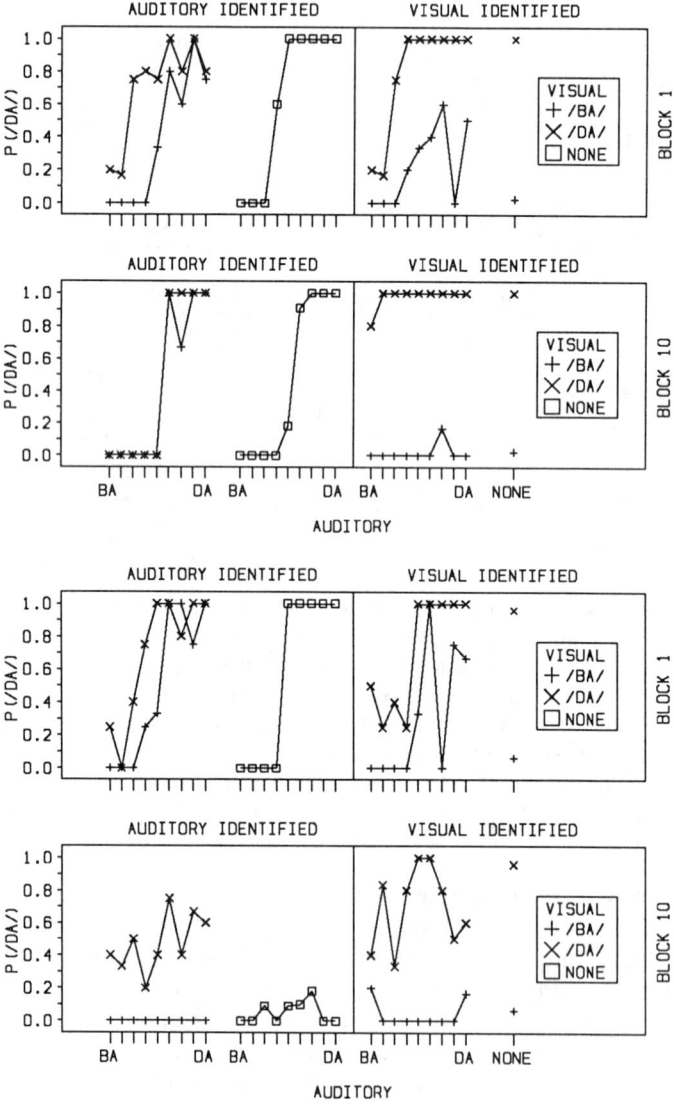

Figure 16. Probability of a /da/ identification of the auditory and visual dimensions of the speech syllable under the bimodal and unimodal conditions of the experiment. The top two panels give the results for Subject 1 and the bottom two panels for Subject 2. For each subject, the top panel gives performance during the first block of 297 trials and the bottom panel gives performance during the tenth block.

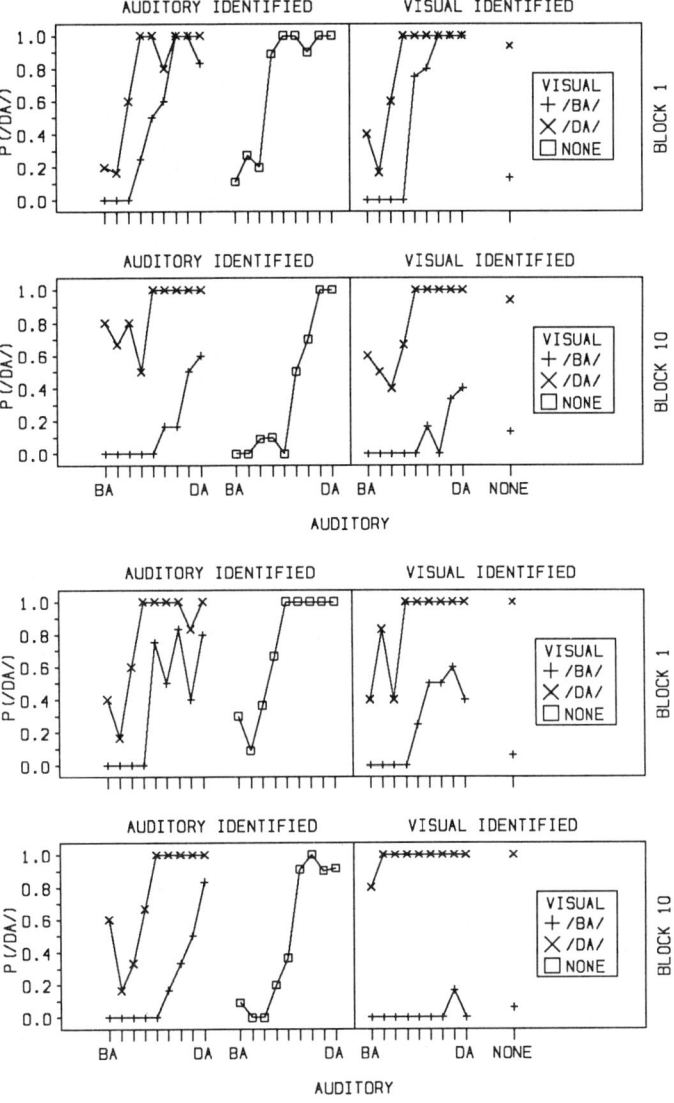

Figure 17. Probability of a /da/ identification of the auditory and visual dimensions of the speech syllable under the bimodal and unimodal conditions of the experiment. The top two panels give the results for Subject 3 and the bottom two panels for Subject 4. For each subject, the top panel gives performance during the first block of 297 trials and the bottom panel gives performance during the tenth block.

As we have seen, the group results camouflage some of the results for individual subjects. As can be seen in the figures, Subjects 1 and 4 learned to process the visual information as efficiently with the presence of the auditory information as without. Only Subject 1 learned to process the auditory information as efficiently with the visual information as without. Subject 4, who had learned to disregard the auditory information in his visual judgments, continued to be influenced by the visual information in his auditory judgments.

The results across all four subjects illustrate the influence of one dimension on the identification of the other, and some decrease in this influence with practice. Subjects are better equipped to process selectively the visual than the auditory dimension and to learn this selective processing with practice.

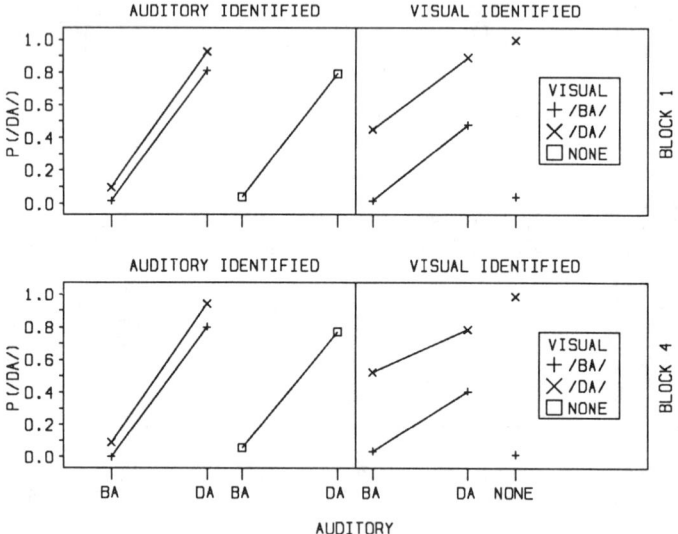

Figure 18. Probability of a /da/ identification of the auditory and visual dimensions of the speech syllable under the bimodal and unimodal conditions of the experiment. The top panel gives performance during the first block of 297 trials and the bottom panel gives performance during the fourth block on the sixth and seventh days of the experiment (group results).

The asymmetry between the influence of the auditory and visual modalities deserves consideration. The result, at first glance, is surprising because speech perception is fundamentally auditory. There is an important experimental difference that must be confronted before we can accept the asymmetry between the two modalities. The experimental design had nine different auditory levels and only two different visual levels. It could be that the advantage of the visual modality was due to this difference in the uncertainty along each dimension rather than to any fundamental difference between the two modalities. To test for this possibility, the experiment was extended an additional two days and the number of auditory levels was reduced to two. The unambiguous levels at the endpoints of the synthesized speech continuum were used as the two auditory levels. Thus, the auditory and visual tasks are now identical in the sense that there are only two auditory levels and only two visual levels of information. Subjects were told of this constraint and were told that they should be responding /da/ to both the auditory and visual information about 50 percent of the time. That is to say, subjects were told that half of the visual events would be /da/ and half of the auditory events would be /da/. All other procedural details were equivalent to the first five days of the experiment.

Figure 18 plots the group results in terms of the probability of a /da/ identification under each condition for blocks 1 (top panel) and 4 (bottom panel) of the additional trials. Subject 1 nearly achieved independence of identification of the two dimensions, although it was not complete. Subjects 2 and 3 continued to show strong influences of one dimension on the identification of the other. Subject 4 attained independence of his visual judgments but not his auditory judgments. Figure 19 gives the results for Subjects 1 and 3 because these subjects give the two extremes of the group results. The advantage of attending to the visual dimension relative to the auditory dimension persists even when the stimulus uncertainty is equated across the two modalities.

The results illustrate that subjects continued to be influenced by the visual information in their auditory judgments even though there were only four unique stimulus events on the bimodal trials. The simplification of the stimulus events on the bimodal trials did not decrease the difficulty of the task. Those subjects who had learned to process the visual information relatively independently of the auditory continued to do so. Those who did not did not learn to do so. Thus, these results demonstrate that it is incredibly difficult for subjects to identify the dimensions independently of one another given the bimodal speech event. Both dimensions influence their judgments, even though they are told to identify the events along each of the dimensions independently of one another. Integration of auditory and visual speech appears to be a robust process, persisting to some extent even when only two visual and two auditory events are possible.

6. Integration of Audible and Visible Nonspeech

The availability of a visual source of information and its integration with auditory information in speech perception generates questions about visual/ auditory perception more generally. Is the recognition of a pattern in one modality influenced by information from another modality? There is a literature concerned with the contribution of visual and auditory signals to perceiving spatial location, but surprisingly little in the domain of pattern recognition. We begin with a recent demonstration of the integration of both modalities in

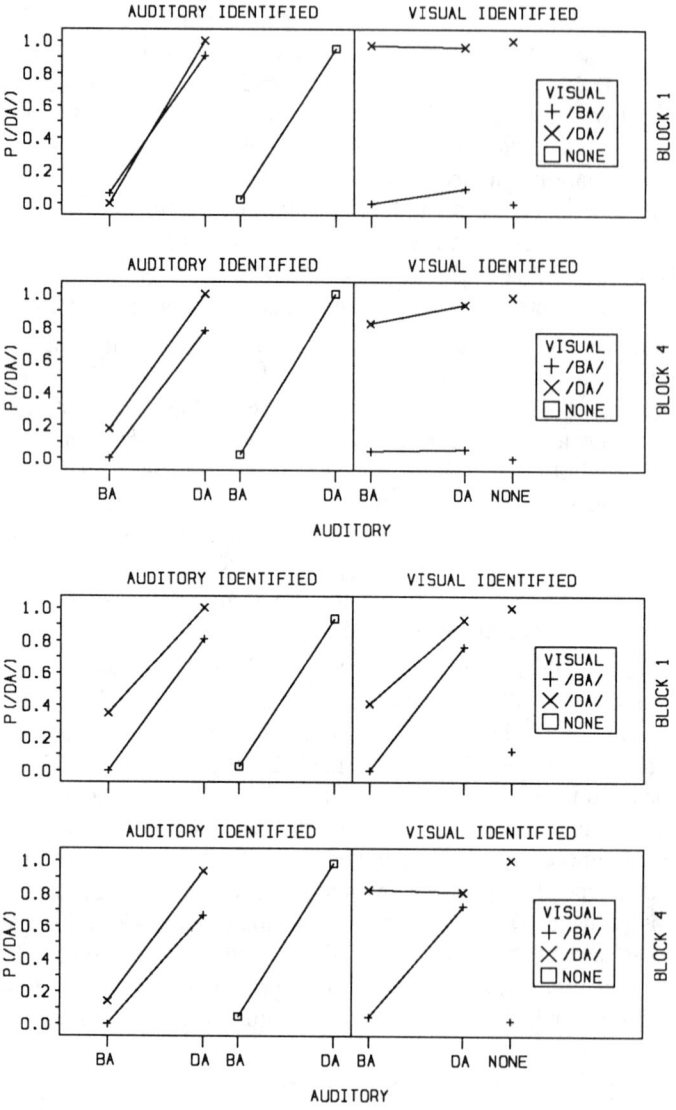

Figure 19. Probability of a /da/ identification of the auditory and visual dimensions of the speech syllable under the bimodal and unimodal conditions of the experiment. The top two panels give the results for Subject 1 and the bottom two panels for Subject 3. For each subject, the top panel gives performance during the first block of 297 trials and the bottom panel gives performance during the fourth block on the sixth and seventh days of the experiment.

perceiving a nonspeech pattern and then discuss findings in perceiving spatial location.

6.1 Pattern Recognition

The paradigm studied by O'Leary and Rhodes (1984) involves the experience of streaming. Consider a sequence of pure tones alternating in frequency at a fairly fast rate. If the successive tones differ by only a few semitones, a single stream of tones is experienced. If the successive tones differ by an octave or so, two streams are experienced (one corresponding to the low tones and one corresponding to the high tones). Similar results can be obtained in the visual modality, with respect to dots varying in height in the visual field. Depending on the relative height of the dots, a single dot appears to move up and down across the screen or two dots appear to follow their high and low paths, respectively. Streaming, or the experience of two streams of events rather than just one, is more likely to occur at shorter durations between the successive onsets of the individual notes or dots in both situations. The duration between the onsets of the successive events is called the stimulus onset asynchrony (SOA).

In the O'Leary and Rhodes study, subjects were tested in unimodal and bimodal conditions. In the unimodal situation, subjects were presented with a sequence in one of the modalities and the SOA for streaming was determined. In the bimodal situation, subjects were required to look at the visual stream and listen to the auditory stream, but to attend to just one of the streams. The sequences in both modalities were presented in synchrony, but the distance between the elements in the nonattended modality was set to give an unambiguous experience of streaming. The SOA for streaming of the attended modality was determined. Integration of the information from the two modalities was apparent in the results. Subjects experienced streaming at longer SOAs in the bimodal than in the unimodal conditions. Streaming along the nonattended modality contributed to streaming along the attended modality. This result is exactly parallel to the findings presented in Section 3. Speech in one modality influenced perception of speech in the other modality. Also consistent with the results in Section 3, the visual modality influenced auditory judgments more than the auditory modality influenced visual judgments.

6.2 Perceiving Spatial Location

Most of the research concerning the interaction of auditory and visual information in perception concerns the contribution of these two modalities to locating objects in space (Warren, McCarthy, & Welch, 1983; Welch & Warren, 1980). The work by Radeau and Bertelson (1976, 1977) has been highly informative about the integration of auditory and visual information in locating events in space. Although the visual dimension appears to be dominant as witnessed in the variety of situations called visual capture, the auditory dimension also contributes to the perceptual judgment. As an example, Radeau and Bertelson (1976) demonstrated auditory capture of a visual point of light presented on a dark background. The auditory source had a negligible effect when the point of light was presented on a textured background. The usual finding that the visual source has the greatest impact on the judgment is compatible with the framework developed here. Resolution of visual space is better than resolution of auditory space and the more informative source will have the largest influence on the perceptual outcome. Analogous to our findings, the visual source seems to be more influential than the auditory source. Other results (Bertelson and Radeau, 1981) are also consistent with the present findings. The degree of influence of a given modality depends on what property subjects report. This result is analogous to the reduced contribution of speech from one modality when subjects are instructed to report the other modality, as shown in Figure 17. Finally, both sources can contribute to a given judgment, even if the two sources are not fused or experienced as emanating from the same event (Bertelson & Radeau, 1981). This result is analogous to the Repp et al. (1983) finding of integration even when subjects rated the bimodal syllable as being dubbed (see Chapter 4, Section 7.4).

Bertelson and Radeau (1976) review convincing evidence that the interaction of auditory and visual information in the perception of spatial location is not simply a postperceptual response bias. This perceptual locus of the effect is exactly parallel to the perceptual locus of the integration of auditory and visual information in speech perception. Bertelson and Radeau (1976) observe that the ventriloquism phenomenon, or the influence of visual information on spatial location, is better viewed as the joint influence of auditory and visual sources of information on spatial location than as visual dominance. These remarkable parallels between speech perception, nonspeech pattern recognition, and perceiving spatial location discredit the notion that speech is special (Liberman and Mattingly, 1985) and add to the negative assessment of the modularity principle (see Chapter 9).

7. Integration and Categorical Perception

We have accumulated evidence for integration and can conclude that the perceptual judgment on a given trial is influenced by both the auditory and visual sources of information. The first of two categorical models developed and tested in Chapter 5 is treated as a true integration model because the perceiver is assumed to have information about both sources on each trial. If the two sources agree, the decision follows their outcome. If the two sources disagree, however, the decision conforms to the auditory source with some probability, and the visual source otherwise. Thus, both sources must be consulted for a perceptual judgment and the concept of integration is a reasonable descriptor. Discouragingly, this categorical model is mathematically equivalent to a single-channel nonintegration model assuming that the observer attends to only one source of information on a given trial (Massaro, 1985a). Attention is probabilistic and the decision is simply based on the information of the source attended. This mathematical equivalence should not preclude us from testing the categorical model, however, given that the categorical model can still be falsified, regardless of its relationship to other interpretations.

8. Sumby and Pollack Study

The Sumby and Pollack (1954) experiment described in the previous chapter is also relevant to the issue of integration. The addition of visual speech improved the recognition of audible speech in noise. The test of integration must evaluate the accuracy of word recognition given bimodal speech against what might be expected given separate recognitions of just auditory and just visual information. Thus, we ask whether recognition accuracy of bimodal speech could be predicted from accuracy of auditory recognition and accuracy of visual recognition. The auditory accuracy could be determined from the auditory-alone condition, and the visual accuracy could be computed from the lowest level of speech-to-noise ratio when auditory recognition is close to chance.

We can evaluate one condition involving the recognition of a test word given 16 possibilities in the vocabulary. Accuracy of identification was at chance (at about 7%) given a -30 dB speech-to-noise ratio. Accuracy increased to 71% when visual information was added to this condition, which gives an estimate of accuracy based on only visual information. Using this as an estimate of the probability of correct identification given just visual information, we can test for integration. With a speech-to-noise ratio of -12 dB, accuracy was 68% given just auditory information and 92% given bimodal information. Although bimodal accuracy was greater than both single-modality conditions, the two sources still might not have been integrated. The performance improvement given both sources might be predicted from separate decisions made on the auditory and visual channels. Subjects might attempt to identify the auditory word and the visual word. Thus, they have two chances to recognize the word in the bimodal relative to the single modality condition. If subjects are correct by recognizing the word on either channel, the percentage of correct recognitions given bimodal speech, $P(C \mid Both)$, would be

$$P(C \mid Both) = P(C \mid A) + P(C \mid V) - P(C \mid A)P(C \mid V) \qquad (1)$$

where $P(C \mid A)$ and $P(C \mid V)$ are the percentages of correct recognitions given just the auditory and just the visual sources, respectively. Given 68% correct and 71% correct for just auditory and just visual information, Equation 1 predicts that the bimodal performance based on independent recognitions of the test word on the auditory and visual channels will be 91% correct.

$$P(C \mid Both) = .68 + .71 - .68 \times .71 = .91$$

Given that this value is close to the observed performance of 92% correct, we have no evidence for integration. Although visible speech clearly facilitated performance, we cannot conclude the two sources are integrated, based on this portion of the Sumby and Pollack (1954) results.

It is surprising that the present experiments and the analysis of the Sumby and Pollack (1954) results should lead to such different conclusions. One explanation might be that there is no valid index of visual information in the Sumby and Pollock study because visible speech was always presented with audible speech. Even if performance with only audible speech is at chance, we cannot assume that bimodal performance reflects only the contribution of visible speech. The pure guessing model must be wrong because it assumes all-or-none rather than partial information from the separate auditory and visual sources (see Chapter 4). We have convincing evidence for partial information in speech and more recent studies allow a rejection of the pure guessing model (Breeuwer & Plomp, 1984, 1985).

9. Relevance to Attention Theory

The findings on perceptual attention to bimodal speech has promising similarities to other developments. Kahneman and Treisman (1984) emphasize the important difference between selection of objects (or inputs) and selection of properties (see also Treisman 1969). In their view, people do not easily ignore properties of an attended object whereas irrelevant objects can be ignored quite easily. For example, Kahneman and Henik (1981) found a decreased Stroop effect when the colored ink and the incompatible name were spatially separated (see also Van der Heijden, Hagenaar, & Bloem, 1984). Treisman, Kahneman, and Burkell (1983) asked subjects to read a word as quickly as possible and to locate the position of a gap in a frame placed either around the word or adjacent to it. Both the reading task and the gap detection task were better when the frame surrounded the word. In the framework presented here, two sources of information are more efficiently processed when they can be integrated with respect to a single event. As stated by Neisser (1976), we pay attention to objects and events, not sensory inputs.

Treisman and Gelade (1980) propose that attention must be directed to an object to integrate its separate features for recognition. This view is compatible with the proposal that multiple sources of information can be integrated efficiently only if they specify a single event (Massaro, 1985a). Two or more events cannot be recognized in parallel without some cost if they each are specified by multiple features. One possible reason is that of cross talk in that the multiple sources of information specifying different events cannot be integrated independently. The important role of cross talk has been acknowledged previously (Broadbent 1982; Neumann, in press), but there is little direct evidence for its role during integration. As an exception, Long

(1975) found cross talk in simultaneous pitch and brightness judgments. Subjects tended to identify the pitch of the test tone as high when the test light was bright. The FLMP provides a specific computational model of the integration process and offers the potential for determining the nature of the cost that is produced when observers are required to recognize two or more events simultaneously.

10. Attention, Consciousness, and Information Integration

The influence of both sources of information regardless of the set of the subject is another instance in which perceivers are not able to selectively process a single aspect of their perceptual world. This result is reminiscent of the Stroop effect (Stroop, 1935) in which a word influences the naming of the color that the word is printed in. With respect to perception and action in the real world, this result at first glance might seem to be an inefficient way to design a perceptual process. One would think that selectivity would be more optimal in the analysis of our perceptual world; however, if the perceptual world contains multiple sources of information, then selectivity can only be damaging to perceptual interpretation.

Given multiple sources of information, the more optimal strategy would be to evaluate and integrate all of the sources of information, even though many of the sources at any one time may be ambiguous. The cost to a system designed as such would be the relative inability to process selectively single aspects or single dimensions of the perceptual world. In natural situations, the difficulty of selectivity is not usually a problem because we have available gross motor movements, such as head and eye movements, that allow us to selectively expose various sources of information. What the present results demonstrate is that within a given view of the perceptual world, we find it difficult to selectively process one dimension independently of the influence of others.

Based on the present research, one view of attention might take the following form. The participant has multiple sources of information available. An intention is generated for the task at hand, and as many sources of information are utilized as possible. In many cases, some sources of information will work against the intended action, such as watching the speaker's lips when the observer intends to report what he heard the speaker say. In this case, the nature of the lip information may bias the judgment relative to what would occur given just the sound. Thus, we have some leakage in that attention or intention cannot be completely focussed. The idea is that integrating and utilizing multiple sources of information is the rule rather than the exception. The exceptions come primarily in experimental tasks that require subjects to do specific things, i.e., have specific intentions. An empirical question is to what extent intentions are consistent with the multiple sources of information in the typical environmental situation.

The results are also relevant to consciousness and phenomenal experience. We seem to be conscious at the highest level possible. We tend to experience a particular speech event, not separate auditory and visual dimensions of that event. As Marcel (1983a, 1983b) proposes, we become conscious of the perceptual hypothesis that is consistent with as much sensory data as possible. The results also imply that there is a rule of parsimony or ecological validity with respect to the perceptual hypotheses. Thus, contradictory auditory and visual events are not a viable interpretation of contradictory auditory and visual sensory information. Rather, the perceptual hypothesis is considered to be a single speech event supported by both auditory and visual sources of information.

Although our findings provide a good example of the phenomenological unity of perception, we must be careful to distinguish between the processes that bring this experience about and the experience itself. The phenomenal experience is influenced by both the auditory and visual sources of information. However, given this experience, it is relatively difficult for the perceiver to tease out the separate auditory and visual contributions. In apparent contrast to the phenomenal experience, the FLMP is based on the assumption that the auditory and visual sources of information are independent before integration. Thus, we have an example in which the process leading to the phenomenal experience treats the auditory and visual sources as independent, but the outcome and phenomenal experience give the impression of dependence (see Chapter 6). In the next two chapters, I address both the information leading to the perceptual experience and the perceptual experience with respect to the issue of continuous versus categorical perception.

Chapter 4: Categorical versus Continuous Information in Speech Perception: The Relationship between Identification and Discrimination

The study of speech perception has been almost synonymous with the study of categorical perception. Categorical perception refers to a mode of perception by which changes along a stimulus continuum are not perceived continuously, but in a discrete manner (Studdert-Kennedy, Liberman, Harris, & Cooper, 1970). For example, listeners might be limited in their ability to discriminate differences between different speech sounds that belong to the same phoneme category. The sounds within a category can be identified only absolutely, and discrimination is possible for only those sounds that are identified as belonging to different categories. The current impression for much of the psychology is that speech is perceived categorically (J. R. Anderson, 1985; Eimas, 1985; Flavell, 1985; Miller, 1981). In this chapter, we examine the evidence for this point of view and find it to be unconvincing. Previous results and more recent studies are better described by the concept of continuous perception. Continuous perception refers to a relatively continuous relationship between changes in a stimulus and changes in the perceptual experience of that stimulus.

In this chapter and the following one, four approaches to testing between categorical and continuous speech perception are presented. One of the two approaches discussed in this chapter is the traditional one used throughout the almost 3 decades of research on this problem in speech perception. The other two approaches discussed in the next chapter are new and capitalize on the development of formal techniques in the areas of psychophysics and mathematical psychology. All four approaches converge on the conclusion of continuous auditory and visual information in speech perception. Thus we must accept the role of continuous information in speech perception.

1. A Seminal Study with Auditory Speech

A seminal study established the experimental paradigm for the study of categorical speech perception. Liberman, Harris, Hoffman and Griffith (1957) used synthetic speech to generate a series of 14 consonant-vowel syllables going from /be/ to /de/ to /ge/ (/e/ as in gate). The onset frequency of the second formant transition of the initial consonant was changed in equal steps to produce the continuum. In the identification task, observers identified random presentations of the sounds as /b/, /d/, or /g/. The discrimination task used the ABX paradigm. Three stimuli were presented in the order ABX; A and B always differed and X was identical to either A or B. Observers were instructed to indicate whether X was equal to A or B. This judgment was supposedly based on auditory discrimination in that observers were instructed to use whatever auditory differences they could perceive.

The Liberman, et al. (1957) experiment was designed to test the hypothesis that listeners can discriminate the syllables only to the extent that they can recognize them as different phoneme categories. The hypothesis was quantified in order to predict discrimination performance from identification judgments. Figure 1 gives the results of a single subject for identification and discrimination reprinted from the Liberman, et al. (1957) article. The authors concluded that discrimination was fairly well predicted by identification. This rough correspondence between identification and discrimination has provided the major source of support for categorical perception. In the most recent review of categorical speech perception, the conclusion from this same study was that "the perception of these syllable-initial stops was invariably quite categorical." (Repp, 1984, p. 282) As pointed out by Macmillan (in press), however, observed discrimination is usually better than that predicted by identification. For some reason, the discrepancy has never been a deterrent for advocates of categorical perception nor a central result for any alternative view.

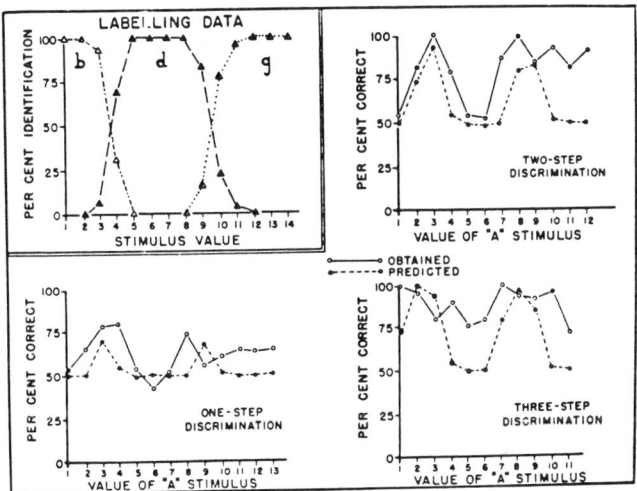

Figure 1. Probability of identification in the labeling task (top left panel) and observed and predicted probability of discrimination in the ABX task (after Liberman et al., 1957).

To provide a proper assessment of the categorical perception model, however, it is necessary to determine how closely the predicted discrimination matches what is observed and to compare the accuracy of this prediction with other possible predictions. The most direct goodness-of-fit measure is the root mean squared deviation (RMSD) which is the square root of the average squared difference between the predicted and observed points. The RMSD can take on values between zero and one if the predicted and observed values lie between zero and one. Hence, a rough measure of goodness-of-fit is simply how close to zero or one is a given RMSD value. In reality, the RMSD value cannot get too close to 1 if the observations cover the range of values between zero and one. The results in Figure 1 give RMSD values of .128, .249, and .253 for the one-, two-, and three-step discrimination tasks, respectively. What is striking is just how poorly the categorical model does in predicting discrimination. Because the discrimination values are between .5 and 1 given the two-alternative task, a model predicting 75 percent correct discrimination across all conditions would have to give RMSD values significantly less than .25. With hindsight, we see that a quantitative test of just about any alternative model would have precluded the authors and others from finding support in these results for categorical perception.

2. A Recent Study with Visible Speech

Using an intelligent graphics system, Walden, Montgomery, Holum-Hardegen, and Prosek (1984) created animations of speech-like articulations of the syllables /ba/, /va/, and /wa/. The animations were two-dimensional vector-based dynamic images representing the lips and teeth. The three syllables were created by videotaping natural productions made with the same neutral starting position. Each syllable was viewed frame by frame, and outlines of the lips and teeth were made during the neutral starting position, the most closed position, the consonant position, and the steady-state vowel position. The images were represented digitally in the computer and an animated syllable was created by linear interpolation between the three articulation positions: starting, consonant closure, and steady- state vowel. To create a continuum of syllables between each pair of the original syllables, the configuration for the consonant closure was determined by linear interpolation between the consonant closures for the pair of original syllables. Three continua of eight syllables each were generated in this manner and used as stimuli in identification, discrimination, and rating experiments. Thus, the investigators were able to replicate a typical synthetic auditory speech experiment with synthetic visible speech.

Using the visible animations, Walden et al. (1984) carried out the traditional identification/discrimination task. Subjects identified the visible syllables in a labeling task and made discriminations in an ABX discrimination task. Figures 2 through 5 give results from observers representing the four patterns of results that were found. The identification function is given in the top panel and discrimination in the bottom panel. Observed discrimination is plotted along with that predicted from identification based on the hypothesis of categorical perception (Liberman et al., 1957; Macmillan, Kaplan, & Creelman, 1977).

Consistent with the notions of categorical perception, the identification functions appear to be fairly discrete in the sense of the syllables being consistently identified as one alternative or the other, except for one or two syllables in the middle of the continuum. Following traditional criteria, it could easily be argued that identification performance gives a fairly good description of discrimination performance. There is a peak in discrimination performance

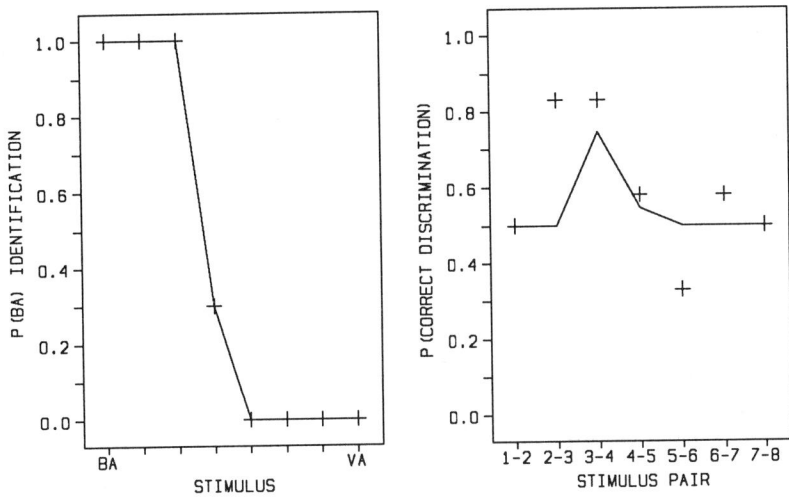

Figure 2. Identification judgments (left panel) and predicted (line) and observed (points) proportion correct discrimination (right panel) for a subject tested on the visible /ba/-/va/ continuum (after Walden et al., 1984).

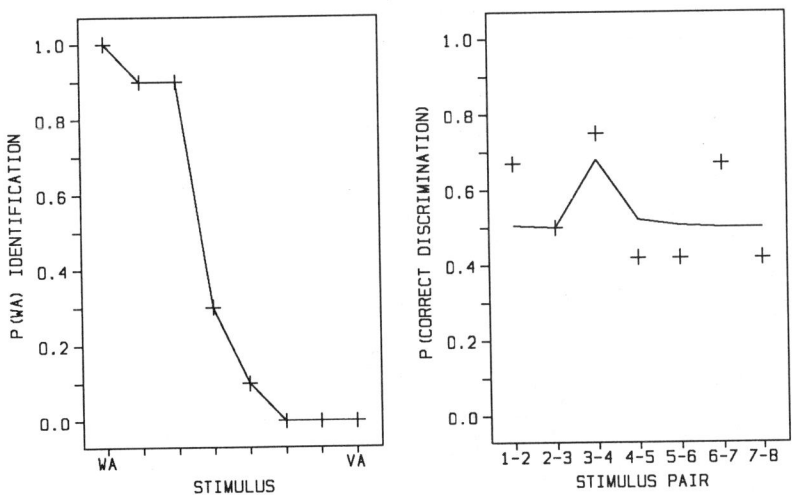

Figure 3. Identification judgments (left panel) and predicted (line) and observed (points) proportion correct discrimination (right panel) for a subject tested on the visible /wa/-/va/ continuum (after Walden et al., 1984).

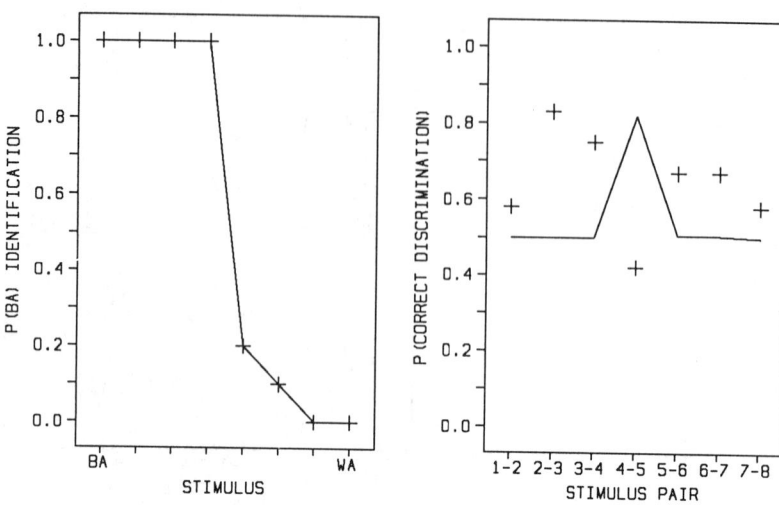

Figure 4. Identification judgments (left panel) and predicted (line) and observed (points) proportion correct discrimination (right panel) for a subject tested on the visible /ba/-/wa/ continuum (after Walden et al., 1984).

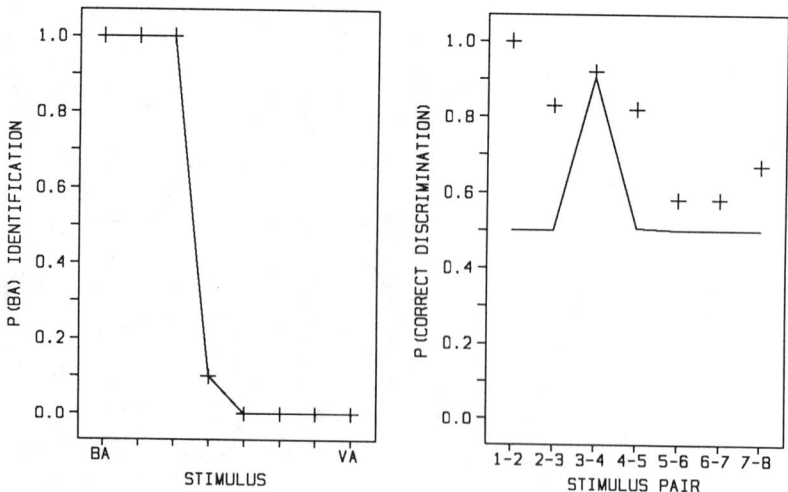

Figure 5. Identification judgments (left panel) and predicted (line) and observed (points) proportion correct discrimination (right panel) for a subject tested on the visible /ba/-/va/ continuum (after Walden et al., 1984).

near the category boundary for 3 of the 4 subjects. Certainly, the RMSD values would be within the same range as that observed for auditory speech. In an absolute sense, however, identification performance gives a poor description of discrimination performance. Two syllables identified equivalently are in some cases easily discriminated from one another, a result clearly counter to the predictions of categorical perception.

3. Identification/Discrimination Tasks with Two Features

As reviewed in Chapter 2, contrasts between auditory speech segments can be cued by several acoustic features in the speech signal. In addition, we have evidence that both visual and auditory features are integrated or combined to achieve perceptual recognition (see Chapters 2 and 3). The issue addressed in this section is to what extent perceivers have access to the values of the different features at some stage of speech perception. One method to answer this question is to synthesize two speech syllables differing by two features in such a way that they are identified equivalently. The question is whether they can be discriminated from one another. If not, then the listener would appear not to have access to the separate cues. The perceptual equivalence between the two different syllables would represent another instance of categorical perception. The observer would have information only about the speech category of the syllable, not the components that made the syllable.

3.1 Fitch, et al. Study

Consider an experiment carried out by Fitch, Halwes, Erickson, and Liberman (1980). The silent closure duration and the vocalic formant transition onsets were independently varied to cue the distinction between the words *slit* and *split*. Silence between the noise of the initial /s/ and the onset of the vocalic portion of the word is a cue for /p/. Rising formant contours at the onset of the vocalic portion is also a cue for /p/. Conversely, little or no silence and flat formants are cues for *slit* rather than *split*. Different values of silence and formant contours can be chosen to produce different stimuli that are identified equivalently in a labeling task. A speech stimulus with a silence of 72 msec and with rising formant contours was identified as *split* about 82 percent of the time. The same identification proportion was found for a speech stimulus with a silence of 104 msec and with flat formant contours. According to Fitch, et al. (1980), these two speech stimuli are perceptually equivalent and difficult to discriminate from one another (see also Best, Morrongiello, & Robson, 1981; Fitch, et al., 1980; Liberman, 1982; Repp, 1982).

Fitch, et al. (1980) claim to have found evidence for perceptual equivalence, based on discrimination performance in an oddity task. The observer in this task chooses which of three syllables differ from the other two. Unfortunately, the oddity task, like the ABX task, encourages the use of abstract encoding or labels (Massaro & Oden, 1980b; Paap, 1975; Pisoni & Lazarus, 1974). That is, subjects find it easier to perform by identifying each stimulus as it is presented. In the oddity task, they can simply pick the alternative that is labeled differently. This strategy leads to a direct match between discrimination performance in the oddity task and that predicted by categorical perception (Massaro, 1976). As pointed out by Hary and Massaro (1982) and Massaro and Hary (1983,1984), categorical results in the identification/discrimination paradigm do not necessarily imply categorical perception.

3.2 Extension to Bimodal Speech

The identification experiments with bimodal speech indicate that the auditory and visual sources of information are available in independent form at the feature evaluation and prototype matching stages. The coverage in Chapter 6 provides converging evidence from a number of domains for independence of the auditory and visual sources. Although these independent sources of information are integrated during the perceptual recognition process to give a perceptual experience of a single event, perceivers should have some access to feature values defining the separate sources of information. An alternative interpretation is that access to the separate cues is not possible. Extending the notion of categorical perception to this new situation, its advocates argue that the cues trade off in such a way that listeners cannot discriminate sounds that are categorized equivalently in identification, even though these sounds differ along two dimensions (Best et al., 1981; Fitch et al., 1980). Liberman (1982) gives a similar view when he offers his introspections of perceiving visual and auditory information in speech perception:

> Surely my percept was unified in the important sense that I could not have decided by introspective analysis that part was visual in origin and part auditory. Even in those cases in which, given conflicting optical and acoustic cues, I experienced two syllables, there was nothing about their quality that would have permitted me to know which I had seen and which I had heard. (Liberman, 1982, p. 162.)

One goal of the experiments reported in this chapter is to test between these two different views of discrimination performance. To test between these continuous and categorical views, we extended the bimodal speech identification task to include discrimination performance. One view states that the perceiver has some access to continuous information from each independent dimension of a speech syllable and the other view states that only categorical information about the complete speech syllable is available. Consider speech events with auditory and visual components A and V. The values of the components are defined by subscripts so that $A_b V_d$ represents an auditory /b/ paired with a visual /d/. Using synthesized speech, we can find $A_b V_d$ and $A_d V_b$ syllables that are identified equally often as /da/. The critical question is whether there is a perceived equivalence between the two syllables. If discrimination has access to the featural information, then listeners should be able to discriminate the different syllables. If listeners are not able to discriminate the syllables, this experiment would provide some evidence for the perceptual equivalence of two different speech syllables that are categorized equivalently. The first result would be consistent with the FLMP, whereas the second result would be consistent with categorical perception.

It should be noted that the FLMP does not insist that information regarding individual features be available for a significant period after recognition, only that continuous featural information is available for integration in speech recognition. On the other hand, if listeners discriminate syllables that are identified equivalently, evidence is provided that identification alone is not a valid measure of perceptual experience, as assumed by categorical perception. Two syllables perceived as different from one another might still be identified identically. In terms of the FLMP, we would expect $A_b V_d$ and $A_d V_b$ to be discriminated from one another even though they are identified equivalently.

4. Identification/Discrimination Tasks with Auditory Instructions

Although not reported in the original paper, the subjects in the Massaro and Cohen (1983c, Experiment 2) study participated in a discrimination task following the identification task. In addition to the standard identification task with bimodal speech events, a same-different discrimination task was carried out with two of the speech sounds from the /ba/ to /da/ continuum. A same-different task overcomes much of the limitation of the oddity or ABX task, even though this task does not guarantee that subjects will not perform using an identification strategy. The sounds chosen (#4 & #7) were from opposite sides of the /ba/-/da/ continuum and gave the closest approximation to chance (50% /da/) responses with conflicting visual information; that is, when level 4 was paired with a visual /da/ and when level 7 was paired with a visual /ba/. These two sounds were chosen on the basis of the first two subjects' labeling performance in the identification task. It should be noted that these two sounds were not exactly balanced for all subjects, but rather gave a proportion of /da/ responses of .524 and .662 with conflicting visual information for levels 4 and 7 respectively. This difference does not compromise the test between continuous and categorical perception, however, because the two theories also made different predictions about the discrimination of these sounds when they are paired with the different levels of visible speech.

We will refer to the levels 4 and 7 along the auditory speech continuum as A_b and A_d, respectively. With respect to the auditory information, there were two kinds of same trials $A_b A_b$ and $A_d A_d$ and two kinds of different trials, $A_b A_d$, $A_d A_b$. Similarly, for the two visual articulations V_b and V_d, there were four kinds of trials $V_b V_b$, $V_b V_d$, $V_d V_b$, and $V_d V_d$. The combination of these four types of auditory and four types of visual trials yielded 16 possible trial types. In addition, the four types of auditory trials were presented without visual articulation. The 20 trial types are shown in Table 1.

Table 1. The five conditions in the same-different discrimination task, providing an index of the discriminability between the two speech sounds as a function of the visual information. Each four-tuple represents the auditory and visual information available for the two successive stimuli in the same different task. For example, $A_b V_d$ - $A_b V_b$ indicates the first stimulus was an auditory /ba/ paired with a visual /da/ followed by a second stimulus that was an auditory /ba/ paired with a visual /ba/.

CONDITION	SAME TRIALS	DIFFERENT TRIALS
Neutral	$A_b V_n$ -$A_b V_n$, $A_d V_n$ -$A_d V_n$	$A_b V_n$ -$A_d V_n$, $A_d V_n$ -$A_b V_n$
Match	$A_b V_b$ -$A_b V_b$, $A_d V_d$ -$A_d V_d$	$A_b V_b$ -$A_d V_d$, $A_d V_d$ -$A_b V_b$
Mismatch	$A_b V_d$ -$A_b V_d$, $A_d V_b$ -$A_d V_b$	$A_b V_d$ -$A_d V_b$, $A_d V_b$ -$A_b V_d$
Mismatch 1	$A_b V_d$ -$A_b V_b$, $A_d V_b$ -$A_d V_d$	$A_b V_d$ -$A_d V_d$, $A_d V_b$ -$A_b V_b$
Mismatch 2	$A_b V_b$ -$A_b V_d$, $A_d V_d$ -$A_d V_b$	$A_b V_b$ -$A_d V_b$, $A_d V_d$ -$A_b V_d$

The data analysis addresses the degree to which the two auditory levels can be discriminated as a function of the available visual information. We can derive measures of observed and predicted discrimination for five types of trials as illustrated in Table 1. First, we have the trials with no visual articulation. These are called "neutral" trials. Second, we have "match" trials in which the visual information agrees with the auditory information. Third, we have the "mismatch" trials in which the visual information conflicts with the auditory. Discrimination of "mismatch" trials should be very poor if the assumption of perceptual equivalence is correct. That is, $A_b V_d$ should be identified as /da/ about the same proportion of time as $A_d V_b$. If identification of the total speech event constrains auditory discrimination, these two speech events should be difficult to discriminate from one another. Finally, we have two conditions of a mismatch, either in the first or second position called "mismatch first" and "mismatch second," respectively.

4.1 Method

Subjects. Seven subjects served in this experiment ten minutes after serving in the identification task reported by Massaro and Cohen (1983c, Experiment 2).

Stimuli. The auditory stimuli were levels 4 and 7, combined with the three visual levels, /ba/, neutral, and /da/.

In creating the videotape, two speech events were recorded for each trial. The speaker was cued separately for each of the two articulations on a given trial. The onsets of the two 500-msec cues were separated by 1500 msec.

Following the two cues there was a 2500 msec period before the next trial. To provide an equivalent interstimulus interval for neutral trials, we randomly varied the time between the two beeps recorded for triggering the synthetic speech during the dubbing of the videotape. By studying a pilot videotape it was determined that the speaker responded with a mean latency of 627 msec and a standard deviation of 51 msec. This distribution was used to randomly determine the beep latency for the visual-neutral trials.

Procedure. On each trial, one of the 20 possible discrimination trials, illustrated in Table 1, occurred. The stimuli were presented in 10 blocks of the 20 possible trial types, and sampled randomly without replacement according to a prearranged order determined at the time of recording. Preceding the experimental trials, a partial block of 10 practice trials was presented for a total of 210 trials in the discrimination task. The subjects were instructed to look at the video monitor and to listen to a sequence of two speech sounds. The subjects were instructed to indicate whether the two *sounds* are exactly the same or differ by a small amount. Subjects were required to make a "same" or "different" response on each trial by hitting one of two keys on the keyboard.

4.2 Test of Perceptual Equivalence

The perceptual equivalence viewpoint predicts that discrimination can be predicted by identification performance. These predictions are identical to the predictions given by categorical perception. The predicted results of categorical perception in a same/different task have been derived by Massaro (1975a, pp. 513-515). Consider two different stimuli defined as x and y. The calculation for the probability of a same response given a same trial, p(s|s), is given by:

$$p(s \mid s) = p(x \mid x1)\, p(x \mid x2) + p(y \mid x1)\, p(y \mid x2) \tag{1}$$

where, for example, $p(x \mid x1)$ and $p(x \mid x2)$ indicates the probability of an x identification given that x was presented as the first $(x1)$ and second $(x2)$ test items in the same-different task. Analogously, $p(y \mid x1)$ and $p(y \mid x2)$ correspond to the probability of a y identification to the first and second test items. A similar equation predicts $p(s \mid s)$ when y is presented as the first $(y1)$ and second $(y2)$ test items.

$$p(s \mid s) = p(y \mid y1)\, p(y \mid y2) + p(x \mid y1)\, p(x \mid y2) \tag{2}$$

The probability of a different response given a different trial, $p(d \mid d)$, is given by:

$$p(d \mid d) = p(x \mid x1)\, p(y \mid y2) + p(y \mid x1)\, p(x \mid y2). \tag{3}$$

when x and y are the first and second test items, respectively. Finally, an identical prediction is made for $p(d \mid d)$ when y and x are the first and second test items, respectively.

$$p(d \mid d) = p(y \mid y1) \, p(x \mid x2) + p(x \mid y1) \, p(y \mid x2)$$

The first product of each equation represents the probability of making a correct decision on the basis of two "accurate" identifications, while the second product represents the probability of a correct decision based on two "inaccurate" identifications.

The observed $p(s \mid s)$ and $p(d \mid d)$ values were computed for each of the seven subjects. For each subject, the predicted proportions of same and different judgments were computed on the basis of the six observed /da/ identification probabilities from the labeling task for the six types of speech events used in the discrimination task (two speech sounds times three articulation conditions).

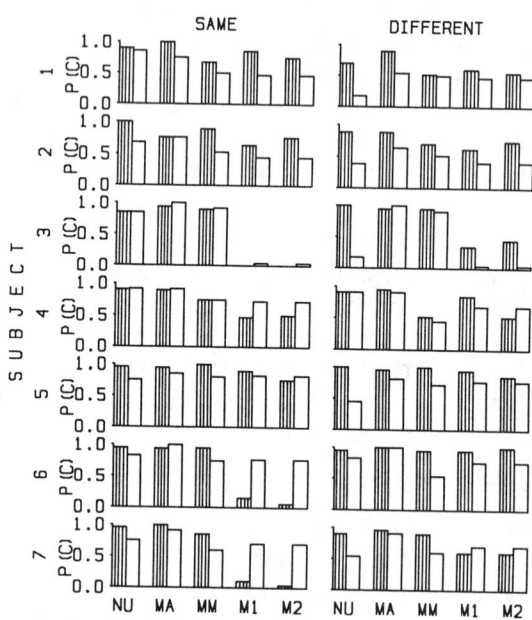

Figure 6. The observed (striped) and predicted (white) proportion of correct judgments for same and different trials for each of the seven subjects for each of the five discrimination conditions (described in Table 1). The predictions are based on the assumptions of perceptual equivalence.

Figure 6 displays the observed and predicted proportion of correct judgments for each of the five discrimination conditions, separately for same and different trials for each subject. The observed proportion is given as the striped histogram for each condition, while the predictions of perceptual equivalence are given by the white histogram. Overall, the predictions given by perceptual equivalence give a very poor description of the observed results. Table 2 gives the RMSD fit for each subject. The average RMSD between the predicted and observed proportion of correct responses is .27.

Table 2. RMSD values between observed and predicted discrimination values for perceptual equivalence and disjunctive difference models. Individual fits, mean of subject fits (X), and fit of mean subject (M) are given.

S	Perceptual Equivalence	Disjunctive Difference
1	.270	.304
2	.294	.317
3	.306	.171
4	.134	.218
5	.229	.130
6	.350	.049
7	.338	.153
X	.275	.192
M	.228	.108

Given the small number of trials per subject, the predictions were also computed on the basis of the mean of the subject identifications and compared with the mean of the subject discrimination data. This test of perceptual equivalence provided only a small improvement in the fit, giving a RMSD of .23. The observed and predicted values for $p(s \mid s)$, $p(d \mid d)$, and overall proportion correct for the mean subject are given in Figure 7.

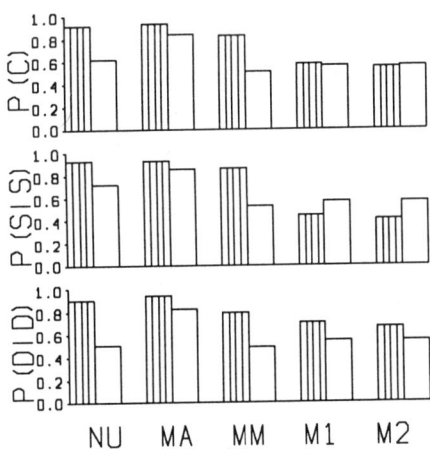

Figure 7. The observed (striped) and predicted (white) proportion of correct judgments for the mean subject for each of the five discrimination conditions (described in Table 1). The predictions are based on the assumptions of perceptual equivalence.

Not only was the observed discrimination better than the predicted, but the predicted results did not capture the variations in the five discrimination conditions. As noted in the introduction to this experiment, perceptual equivalence predicts that discrimination of the "mismatch" trials should be very poor because the identification proportions for the two speech events are similar. However, observed discrimination was much better than that predicted for the "mismatch" trials.

4.2.1 A Potential Limitation

An alternative interpretation of the results might salvage the perceptual equivalence (categorical perception) argument. As pointed out by Repp, Healy, and Crowder (1979), the identification task occurs in a different context than does the discrimination task. If the context influenced identification, then we would not necessarily find a match between the identification and discrimination tasks even if perception is categorical. That is, the probability of identifying a particular stimulus as a particular alternative would differ between the two tasks. Thus, we could not expect the identification results to predict discrimination.

How would identification have to differ between the two tasks to predict the large advantage of observed discrimination relative to that predicted by the identification task? If we assume that contrast occurs in the discrimination task (Healy & Repp, 1982), then the second stimulus will tend to be perceived in a direction away from the first stimulus. In this case, the two successive stimuli will tend to be identified differently. Thus, performance on "different" trials will be very good and performance on "same" trials will be very poor if contrast occurs. Both different and identical stimuli will tend to be identified differently. Although contrast should increase the likelihood of saying "different," it should have very little effect on the overall discrimination as indexed by percentage correct or d'. In fact, the results of the discrimination task do not show a bias for different responses (.544) and, therefore, there is little evidence for contextual influences. It is difficult to see how contextual influences in discrimination would be sufficient to predict the large discrepancy that was observed between predicted and observed discrimination in the present experiment. We expect that observed discrimination would exceed that predicted by identification even if identification judgments are obtained in same context as discrimination.

4.3 Test of Continuous Information

4.3.1 A Discrimination Model Based on the FLMP

As mentioned previously, the FLMP provides the possibility that the information is separately available at the featural level for use in discrimination. This possibility suggests the formulation of a quantitative model for discrimination. In this model, the observer would say "different" to the degree that the speech events differed either in the visual or the auditory features. For each source of information, a difference value Dx would be computed from the absolute difference of the values of that feature for the two speech events. For example, for trials in which the first sound was #4 and the second #7, D_a would equal the absolute difference of auditory /da/-ness of #4 and the auditory /da/-ness of #7. The value D_v would represent the absolute difference in the visual /da/-ness of the first and second speech events. If we assume that the perceived difference between two speech events is equal to the degree to which either the visual or auditory features differ, we have the disjunction of two sources of information. Accordingly, the overall difference D of two speech events is given by:

$$D = D_v \; or \; D_a \qquad (4)$$
$$= D_v + D_a - D_v D_a$$

following the assumption of multiplicative integration (conjunction) given by the FLMP and the definition of disjunction given by DeMorgan's Law.

Given this difference value, the subject must select a same or different response. We assume that the subject evaluates both the degree of difference and degree of sameness (S). In this case, the degree of sameness should be simply one minus the degree of difference:

$$S = 1 - (D_v + D_a - D_v D_a) \qquad (5)$$

Consistent with the logic underlying the pattern classification stage in the FLMP, it is assumed that the subject responds according to the relative magnitude of D and S quantities following Luce's (1959) choice rule:

$$P(d) = \frac{D}{D + S} \qquad (6)$$

where $P(d)$ is the probability of a different response. Given the definitions of D and S, the denominator equals 1, and $P(d)$ is simply given by:

$$P(d) = D_v + D_a - D_v D_a \qquad (7)$$

For the test of this model, the difference values were determined from the appropriate parameter values for the FLMP used to describe the identification data in Massaro and Cohen (1983c, Experiment 2). As an example, the value of D_a was equal to the absolute difference between the parameter values for level 4 and 7 along the auditory continuum. Figure 8 gives the predictions of the disjunctive difference model for the seven individual subjects. The average RMSD fit of this model was .192 across subjects. Table 2 gives the RMSD fits for individual subjects. The assumption of disjunctive difference in the FLMP gives a somewhat better description of the relationship between identification and discrimination than does the assumption of categorical perception. The

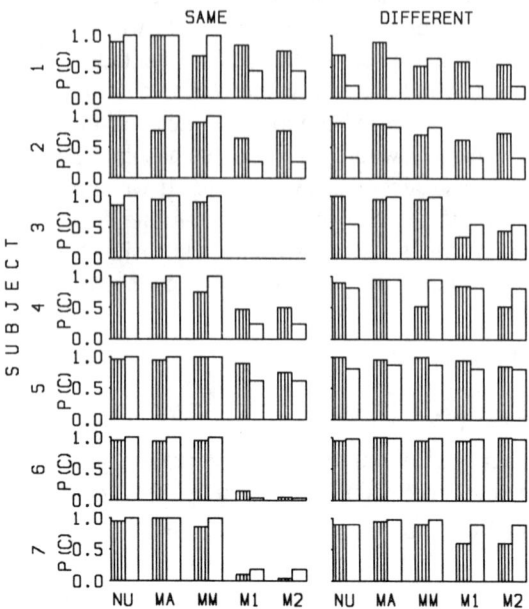

Figure 8. The observed (striped) and predicted (white) proportion of correct judgments for each of the seven subjects for same and different trials for each of the five discrimination conditions (described in Table 1). The predictions are based on the assumptions of the FLMP.

latter model gave a slightly better fit for two of the subjects and a substantially better fit for a third. The FLMP gave a substantially better fit for the other four subjects.

The results for the mean subject give the strongest support for the disjunctive-difference model relative to the perceptual equivalence model. The RMSD values for the two models differed by a factor of two, an impressive difference. It seems that the unambiguous support for the FLMP given by the average results is a function of the increased reliability of the results rather than some quirk that occurs in averaging the results across subjects. Each subject attributed only 20 observations to each of the 10 unique trial types, giving a relatively coarse measure of discrimination performance for the individual subjects. Averaging the results across subjects led to a substantial improvement in the description of the FLMP, decreasing the RMSD value from .192 to .108. Figure 9 gives the observed results for the mean subject and the predictions of FLMP.

It should be noted that the rationale of the disjunctive difference model follows from the assumptions of the FLMP for the description of the identification results. It was assumed that the perceiver has access to featural

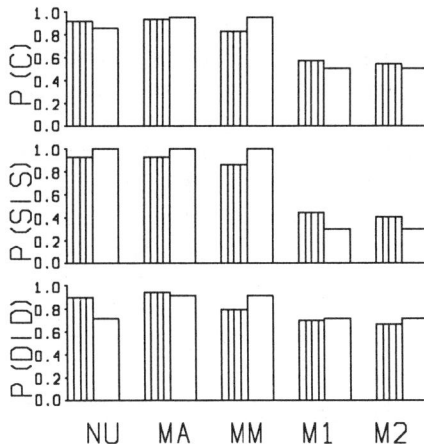

Figure 9. The observed (striped) and predicted (white) proportion of correct judgments for the mean subject for each of the five discrimination conditions (described in Table 1). The predictions are based on the assumptions of the FLMP.

information from the separate visual and auditory sources and that both sources are used in identification. The discrimination results show that subjects cannot disregard one of these sources, the visual, even though they were instructed to discriminate the two events solely on the basis of what they heard. Of course, we already know this from the identification results given by Massaro and Cohen (1983c). In the identification task preceding discrimination, the subjects were strongly influenced by the visual source (Figure 1, Chapter 5) even though they were instructed to identify the sound on the basis of what they heard.

5. Replication with Neutral Instructions

In the previous study, subjects were asked to make both their identification and discrimination decisions on the basis of what they heard. It is important to replicate the study with neutral instructions in which subjects respond on the basis of what the man said. Massaro and Ferguson (1986) tested 20 subjects in identification, rating, and discrimination tasks in the bimodal speech paradigm. Although individual differences in the tasks were the major research question, there were no effects of this variable, and it is appropriate to ignore the question for the present purposes. The videotape used for identification and rating judgments was prepared identically to the stimuli used by Massaro and Cohen (1983c, Experiment 2). On each trial, the videotape showed a speaker saying either /ba/ or /da/ or keeping his mouth closed. The auditory syllables were synthesized from characteristics of the speaker's voice and formed a continuum of nine sounds equally spaced between /ba/ and /da/.

5.1 Method

Procedure. Three subjects could be tested simultaneously in individual rooms. On each trial, one of the nine auditory stimuli on the continuum from /ba/ to /da/ was paired with one of the three possible visual stimuli, /ba/, /da/, or neutral, as synchronized by the computer according to the method described in Massaro and Cohen (1983c). The stimuli were presented in 11 blocks of the 27 possible combinations plus 10 practice trials for a total of 307 trials. Subjects were instructed to "watch a speaker and listen to what is spoken" and simply to "indicate whether the man said /ba/ or /da/." They were warned that "on some trials you will see the speaker say the sound and on other trials the sound will be presented but the speaker will not move his mouth." Subjects had 2750 msec in which to respond by pressing either the "B" or the "D" buttons on a keyboard positioned to the side of the TV monitor.

On each trial in the discrimination task, a pair of stimuli was presented. For each member of the pair one of the three visual levels was synchronized with either level 3 or 7 from the auditory continuum. The stimulus pairs were presented in 10 blocks of the 20 possible combinations described in Table 3. There were about 1250 msec between the onsets of each speech event and subjects had about 2 sec to make a response. Subjects were instructed to respond either "same" or "different" to each pair of stimuli on the basis of both the auditory and visual speech. They were told to answer "same" only if they thought the two members of the pair were identical in both auditory and visual speech. They recorded their judgment by pressing one of two buttons on the keyboard.

Table 3. Stimuli and groupings for the discrimination task. Each four-tuple represents the auditory and visual information available for the two successive stimuli in the same different task. For example, $A_b V_n$-$A_d V_n$ means the first stimulus was an auditory /ba/ with a visual neutral followed by an auditory /da/ with a visual neutral.

Group			
Same	Auditory Different	Visual Different	Both Different
$A_b V_b$-$A_b V_b$	$A_b V_b$-$A_d V_b$	$A_b V_b$-$A_b V_d$	$A_b V_b$-$A_d V_d$
$A_b V_d$-$A_b V_d$	$A_b V_d$-$A_d V_d$	$A_b V_d$-$A_b V_b$	$A_b V_d$-$A_d V_b$
$A_d V_b$-$A_d V_b$	$A_d V_b$-$A_b V_b$	$A_d V_b$-$A_d V_d$	$A_d V_b$-$A_b V_d$
$A_d V_d$-$A_d V_d$	$A_d V_d$-$A_b V_d$	$A_d V_d$-$A_d V_b$	$A_d V_d$-$A_b V_b$
$A_b V_n$-$A_b V_n$	$A_b V_n$-$A_d V_n$		
$A_d V_n$-$A_d V_n$	$A_d V_n$-$A_b V_n$		

5.2 Tests Between the FLMP and CMP

There are six types of identification trials (3 visual x 2 auditory levels) and 20 types of discrimination trials. Six models were tested against the identification and discrimination results. Three pairs of models were tested to contrast the CMP and the FLMP. In the first contrast, the identification results were used to predict the discrimination results, as is standard in the identification/discrimination experiments. These tests used the identification results to predict discrimination and thus no free parameters were used in the test. In the second contrast, free parameters were estimated to predict just the discrimination results. In the third contrast, free parameters were estimated to predict both identification and discrimination.

There were 20 unique trials in the discrimination task as can be seen in Table 3, and 6 relevant identification trials. In the first contrast, the 6 identification probabilities were used to predict discrimination for the CMP, and the feature values estimated to predict identification were used to predict discrimination for the FLMP. Based on the derivations for disjunction for the FLMP, an auditory difference value D_a and a visual difference value D_v were computed by subtracting the two relevant truth values

$$D_a = A_7 - A_3$$
$$D_v = V_D - V_B$$

where A_7 and A_3 are the auditory /da/-ness values for auditory levels 7 and 3 and V_D and V_B are the visual da-ness values for a /da/ and /ba/ visual articulation, respectively.

In the second contrast, 6 identification probabilities were estimated as free parameters to test the CMP and 2 difference values (D_a and D_v) were estimated to test the FLMP. This test allows for some change in the relevant parameters for the two models from the identification to the discrimination task. By allowing for unique identification parameters in the identification task, the plausibility of the Repp et al. (1979) observation that identification might differ in the identification and discrimination contexts (see Section 4.2.1) is tested. In the third contrast, 6 identification probabilities were estimated to test the categorical model simultaneously against both identification and discrimination. For the test of the FLMP, 5 parameters had to be estimated (A_7, A_3, V_D, V_B, and V_N) to predict both identification and discrimination.

The RMSD between predicted and observed values provides a measure of the accuracy of the predictions. The RMSD values for the three contrasts are given in Table 4. These values are based on the fit of the average subject computed for each of the four groups of five subjects. The parameter values are given in Tables 5 and 6. As can be seen from the RMSD values, the description given by the FLMP was superior in every contrast to that given by the CMP.

Table 4. The RMSD values for the CMP and the FLMP for predicted discrimination based on the identification results.

Contrast	Model	
	CMP	FLMP
1	.232	.144
2	.192	.093
3	.180	.090

This result is particularly impressive in contrast 2 in which the CMP requires 3 times as many parameters as the FLMP, and yet the RMSD for the FLMP is less than half of that given by the CMP. Furthermore, the extremely poor description given by the CMP discredits the attempt to salvage it by assuming context-sensitive discrimination (Repp et al., 1979). It is striking that the CMP fairs so poorly relative to its antithesis, the FLMP, as a description of performance in the identification/discrimination task, the central domain traditionally used to support categorical perception (Studdert-Kennedy et al., 1970)

Table 5. The parameter values corresponding to differences or absolute levels of /da/-ness for the fit of the FLMP for contrasts 2 and 3.

Contrast 2		Contrast 3				
D_a	D_v	A_3	A_7	V_B	V_N	V_D
.880	.583	.002	.852	.387	.986	.997

Table 6. Table 6 The parameter values of the implicit identification probabilities of /da/ for the fit of the CMP for contrasts 2 and 3.

Contrast	Speech Stimuli					
	$V_B A_3$	$V_B A_7$	$V_N A_3$	$V_N A_7$	$V_D A_3$	$V_D A_7$
2	.218	.933	.057	.983	.093	.837
3	.303	.957	.062	.985	.049	.782

6. Comparison with the Best et al. Study

Our discrimination results appear to conflict with the conclusions of Best et al. (1981) in their study of trading relations involved in the *say-stay* distinction. The two cues involved in this distinction are the silent gap after the /s/ and the F1 onset frequency at the beginning of voicing. There is a larger gap and the F1 begins at a lower value for *stay* relative to *say*. The investigators varied both the duration of the silent gap and the F1 onset in stimuli presented for identification as *say* or *stay*. The percentage of *stay* responses increased with increases in the silent gap duration. In addition, there were consistently more *stay* responses for the low than for the high F1 onset. The investigators devised a set of stimuli that had either cooperating or conflicting cues by systematically varying the values of the gap duration and F1 onset frequency.

For the discrimination task the investigators found a silent gap of 24 msec to be comparable to the difference between the low and high F1 onsets. The justification for the 24 msec value was the finding that the mean category boundary (50 percent *stay* responses) differed by this amount for the two F1 onset frequencies. According to this logic, a 24 msec difference in the silent gap can compensate for the difference in the F1 onset. For cooperating cues, the two stimuli to be discriminated would have cue values that differed in the same direction. As an example, stimulus one might have a silent gap of 32 msec and a high F1 onset, whereas stimulus two would have a silent gap of 56 msec and a low F1 onset. Thus, both cues are more appropriate for "stay" in stimulus two than in stimulus one. In the conflicting cue condition, the two cues would differ in opposite directions. In this case, the shorter duration cue would be paired with the low F1 onset cue and the longer duration cue would be paired with the high F1 onset frequency cue.

According to Best et al. (1981), discrimination of these stimuli should be predicted by identification performance. To the extent that the stimuli are identified equivalently, they should not be discriminated from one another. Two of the three experiments used an oddity discrimination test and one used a same/different task. The conflicting cues gave poorer discrimination than the single cue condition. The FLMP cannot predict the large difference between the conflicting-cues and the cooperating-cues conditions if discrimination is based on the differences given by feature evaluation. The absolute amount of difference should be the same in the two cases and there should be no difference in discrimination performance.

We can always argue that the separate values of the auditory dimensions of the first stimulus are not available for comparison with the second stimulus. If this is the case, subjects base their discrimination decision on the perceptual categorizations of the two speech events. Thus subjects compare the two stimuli on the basis of the integrated percept indicating the degree to which *say* or *stay* is supported rather than on the basis of the separate auditory dimensions. Even if the separate auditory information sources remain available, it is possible that the subjects interpret the same-different instructions with respect to the percept achieved after integration of the auditory dimensions rather than with respect to their separate values. Although the Best et al. result is consistent with the perceptual equivalence view, it is not necessarily inconsistent with other views of speech perception. As long as subjects discriminate the stimuli on the basis of an integrated percept, rather than in terms of the features responsible for this percept, identification will be reasonably successful in predicting discrimination.

For our purposes, it is important to stress that the ability of identification to predict discrimination is not unique to categorical perception. Continuous perception is also consistent with this result if subjects simply use the integrated continuous percept in the discrimination task. Discrimination of stimuli with cooperating cues would be poorer relative to stimuli with conflicting cues because the percepts will be much more alike in the second case than in the first. The bottom line is that results from the identification/discrimination task cannot be used to support categorical perception even though they are capable of disproving it. (Hary & Massaro, 1982; Massaro, in press b; Massaro & Hary, 1983, 1984).

In fact, obtained discrimination in the Best et al. (1981) study was much better than that predicted by categorical perception. Best et al. argue that this enhancement in discrimination can be explained by within-category distinctions "that are nonetheless phonetic (i.e., relevant to allophonic or articulatory variations)" (Best et al., 1981, p. 204). That is, subjects could hear a *clear* /t/ closure versus a *weak* /t/ closure, and use this information in discrimination. Unfortunately, this posthoc explanation negates the predictive power of the CMP. That is, whenever obtained discrimination exceeds that predicted by identification, one can always postulate additional phonetic categories within the categories being studied. Following this logic, it would no longer be possible to disprove the CMP, and thus the relationship between identification and discrimination cannot be used as evidence for or against categorical perception. The advantage of discrimination over that predicted by identification, as well as the better fit of the disjunctive difference model, weakens the argument for categorical perception.

It remains a possibility that some of the differences between the present results and those of Best et al. (1981) might be due to the different sources of information used in the two studies. For example, it might be the case that the two auditory cues manipulated in the Best et al. (1981) study are more difficult to access independently in discrimination than are the auditory and visual cues manipulated in our bimodal task. Further research should address this issue.

7. Reaction Times

Reaction times (RTs) of identification responses provide an assessment of continuous and categorical models of speech perception. Categorical perception of a speech event implies that the RTs of a given identification response should not change with changes in the speech stimulus. If subjects cannot discriminate differences within a category, then there is no basis for differences in RTs to the different stimuli. A continuous perception model predicts that the RT for identification would depend on the degree to which the sensory information provides unambiguous support for a given category (Norman & Wickelgren, 1969). In addition to the distribution of rating judgments to a particular speech event, RTs of discrete identification judgments can be used to test categorical versus continuous perception. Previous studies have revealed increases in identification RTs near the category boundary between two speech items (Pisoni & Tash, 1974; Repp, 1981). In spite of these results, RTs for identification have not played an important role in the study of the nature of the speech identification process. Analogous to the study of information processing in other domains, RTs have the potential for making transparent perceptual recognition processes and for addressing the issue of categorical versus continuous speech perception.

7.1 Experimental Test

Massaro and Cohen (1983b, Experiment 2) evaluated RTs to assess whether a source of information is continuous or categorical in feature evaluation. By independently varying two sources of bimodal speech, it was possible to provide quantitative tests of the continuous and categorical views of feature evaluation. For the analysis, the RTs of the identification judgments were pooled across /ba/ and /da/ responses before the average RTs were computed. Figure 16 gives the average identification RTs as a function of the auditory and visual levels of the speech event. The RTs varied significantly with the auditory level, decreasing about 100 msec as the auditory level went from /ba/ to /da/. This was probably due to the fact that the auditory continuum was biased toward the sound /da/. The overall response probability for /da/ was higher than for /ba/. It is well known that RTs decrease with increases in response probability (Sternberg, 1969; Theios & Walter, 1974).

The significant interaction shown in the right panel of Figure 10 shows that RTs given a visual /ba/ articulation tend to increase with changes from /ba/ to /da/ along the auditory continuum. An analogous result occurs for the visual /da/ in that RTs tend to decrease with auditory changes from /ba/ to /da/. There are two possible explanations for these results. First, subjects were significantly faster when the auditory and visual information agreed than when they conflicted. A second explanation of the RTs differences is that the processing time is positively related to the ambiguity of the speech event.

Although these two explanations make similar predictions for some of the speech events, conflicting auditory and visual information is not always correlated with the ambiguity of a speech event. Ambiguity can be defined in terms of the degree to which the probability of a /da/ identification differs from .5, and a given probability of a /da/ identification could result from a variety of levels of conflicting information. A very /da/-like sound paired with a good /ba/ articulation could give the same proportion of /da/ identifications as a very ambiguous sound paired with a relatively ambiguous articulation. The first case would have greater conflicting information than the second and yet both would be represented by the same amount of ambiguity.

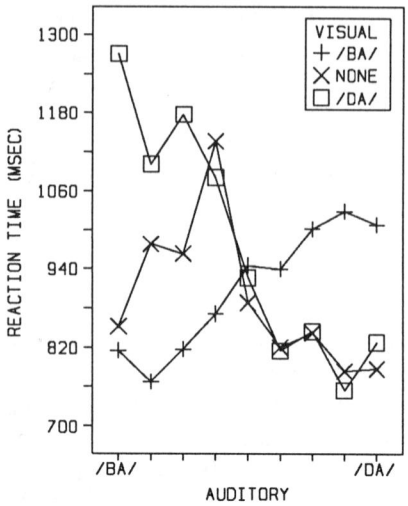

Figure 10. Reaction times as a function of the auditory and visual levels of the speech event (after Massaro & Cohen, 1983b).

7.2 Ambiguity versus Conflict

Continuous perception is consistent with the result that RTs increase with increases in ambiguity of the speech event. To the extent that listeners have ambiguous information, it should take longer to decide on one of the discrete response alternatives at the pattern classification operation (Thomas & Myers, 1972; Norman & Wickelgren, 1969; Smith, 1968). On the other hand, the increase in RTs with increases in conflict of the visual and auditory sources is not necessarily consistent with the FLMP. Given independent sources of information and a multiplicative integration, the time for feature evaluation and prototype matching should not necessarily change with the degree of visual and auditory conflict. Accordingly, determining which explanation best accounts for the RTs provides a new test of the FLMP.

The categorical model has no mechanism to account for an effect of ambiguity, but would seem to predict some effect of conflict. We might expect that different decisions regarding the auditory and visual sources would lead to longer identification times than the same decision regarding the two sources. Accordingly, conflict should be related to the likelihood that the two sources give different decisions. To quantify the idea of conflicting information, we used the parameter values for the auditory and visual sources of information given by the FLMP. The degree of conflict was taken to be the absolute difference between the parameter values specifying the auditory a_i and visual v_j sources of information:

$$C_{ij} = |a_i - v_j|$$

where C_{ij} is the conflict given by the i th level along the auditory continuum and the j th level of visual information.

Ambiguity A_{ij} was defined as one minus the absolute difference between $P(/da/)$, the probability of a /da/ identification, and .5

$$A_{ij} = 1 - |P(/da/) - .5|$$

That is, the most direct index of nonambiguity is the extent to which a given speech event is always identified as the same speech category. In this conceptualization, the smallest amount of ambiguity possible would be zero, while the highest would be .5.

7.3 Results

To evaluate the conflict and ambiguity explanations, the critical result is the performance on neutral trials in which no articulation is given. In this case, the ambiguity of the auditory source of information will vary without a concomitant variation in the conflict between it and the visual source. If RTs increase with increases in ambiguity along the auditory dimension, the result cannot be accounted for by conflict. In fact, the RTs to neutral trials increased toward the middle of the auditory continuum. This result replicates previous studies that evaluated identification RTs as a function of only a single source of information (Pisoni & Tash, 1974; Repp, 1981; Studdert-Kennedy, Liberman, & Stevens, 1963). Accordingly, RTs increased with increases in the ambiguity of the auditory stimulus even though there was no change in conflict between the auditory and visual sources.

For a quantitative test between the conflict and ambiguity explanations, correlations between conflict and ambiguity with RT were carried out on the results of individual subjects in the Massaro and Cohen (1983b, Experiment 2) study. Partial correlations across the seven subjects revealed that ambiguity accounted for 26 percent of the RT variance that could not be accounted for by ambiguity. Conflict accounted for only 3 percent of the variance that could not be accounted for by ambiguity. This result seems to resolve the question in favor of continuous perception of the auditory and visual sources of information, with identification RT a direct function of the ambiguity of the speech event.

7.4 Ratings of Conflict

The effectiveness of ambiguity over conflict in accounting for the RTs of the identification judgments should not be interpreted to mean that perceivers have no information about the individual featural values. As assumed in the FLMP, feature values are available in independent form at the feature evaluation operation. Some access to this information appears to be possible, as illustrated in another finding of the Repp et al. (1983) study discussed in Chapter 2 (Section

4.2). Subjects were presented with visual articulations of /ba/, /va/, /ða/, and /da/ factorially combined with auditory renditions of the same syllables. In addition to identifying what they heard, subjects rated the degree to which the two modalities appeared to conflict.

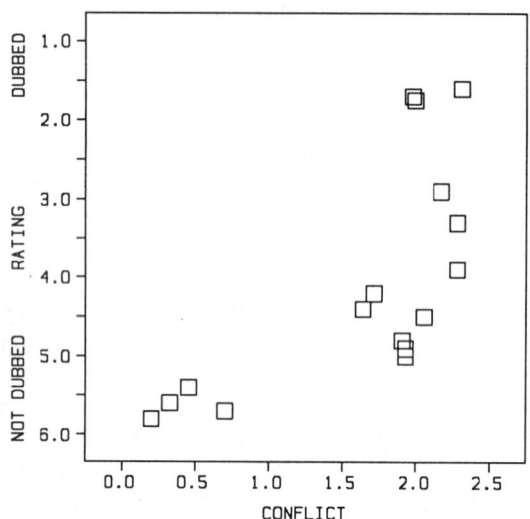

Figure 11. Plot of the ratings indicating the degree to which the subjects felt the stimulus had been dubbed as a function of the conflict values derived from the FLMP description of the identification judgments (observations from Repp, Manuel, Liberman, & Studdert-Kennedy, 1983).

The FLMP can be formalized to account for the ratings of conflict between the auditory and visual sources. Subjects rated on a scale from 1 (dubbed) to 6 (not dubbed) the degree to which they felt a stimulus had not been dubbed. In terms of the FLMP, we can define conflict as the degree to which the auditory and visual sources support different alternatives with respect to the four alternatives /ba/, /va/, /ða/, and /da/

$$C = |VB{-}AB| + |VV{-}AV| + |V\eth{-}A\eth| + |VD{-}AD|$$

where VB is visual /ba/-ness, AB is auditory /ba/-ness, VV is visual /va/-ness, and so on. The sum of these four absolute quantities give a conflict value C reflecting the degree of conflicting information given by the auditory and visual sources. These C values were computed for each of the 16 bimodal speech events using the same parameter values given by the FLMP in the description of the identification judgments. As can be determined from Table 4 in Chapter 2, the conflict for an auditory /ba/ paired with a visual /va/ is

$$C = |.01{-}.99| + |.99{-}.06| + |.02{-}.10| + |.04{-}.01| = 2.02$$

The conflict for consistent auditory and visual information should be much less, for example, the value of C for an auditory /ba/ with a visual /ba/ is

$$C = |.99-.99| + |.06-.30| + |.10-.02| + |.01-.01| = .32$$

The relationship between these C values and the rating responses is shown in Figure 11. The significant correlation of -.696, p < .001, is encouraging given that the model is predicting the rating judgments based on parameters derived from the identification judgments. The rating judgments provide a source of converging evidence for the FLMP, in addition to that provided by the identification judgments.

8. Categorical Partition

I cannot understand why categorization behavior was (and continues to be) interpreted as evidence for categorical perception. It is only natural that continuous perception should lead to sharp category boundaries along a stimulus continuum. Given a stimulus continuum from A to *not* A that is perceived continuously, GOODNESS(A) is an index of the degree to which the information represents the category A. The left panel of Figure 12 shows GOODNESS(A) as a linear function of Variable A.

An optimal decision rule in a discrete judgment task would set the criterion value at .5 and classify the pattern as A for any value greater than this value. Otherwise, the pattern is classified as *not* A. Given this decision rule, the probability of an A response would take the step-function form shown in the right panel of Figure 12. That is, with a fixed criterion value and no variability, the decision operation changes the continuous linear function given by the perceptual operation into a step function. Although based on continuous perception, this function is identical to the idealized form of categorical perception in a speech identification task (Studdert-Kennedy et al., 1970). It follows that a step function for identification is **not** evidence for categorical perception because it can occur given continuous information.

If there is noise in the mapping from stimulus to identification, a given level of Variable A cannot be expected to produce the same identification judgment on each presentation. It is reasonable to assume that a given level of Variable A produces a normally distributed range of GOODNESS(A) values with a mean directly related to the level of Variable A and a variance equal across all levels of Variable A. If this is the case, noise will influence the identification judgment for the levels of Variable A near the criterion value more than it will influence the levels away from the criterion value. Figure 13 illustrates the expected outcome for identification if there is normally distributed noise with the same criterion value assumed in Figure 12.

If the noise is normal and has the same mean and variance across the continuum, a stimulus whose mean goodness is at the criterion value will

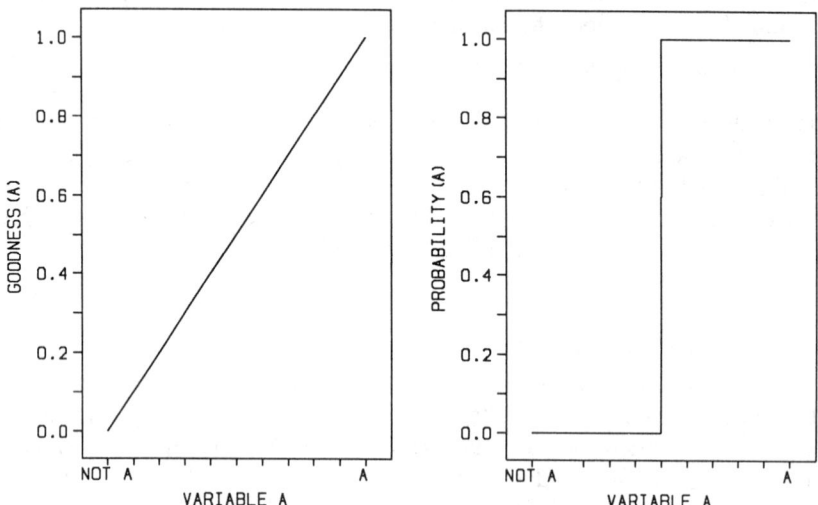

Figure 12. Left Panel: The degree to which a stimulus represents the category *A*, called GOODNESS(A) as a function of the level along a stimulus continuum between *not A* and *A*. Right Panel: The probability of an *A* response, Probability(*A*), as a function of the stimulus continuum if the subject maintains a decision criterion at a particular value of GOODNESS(A) and responds *A* if and only if the GOODNESS(A) exceeds the decision criterion.

produce random classifications. The goodness value will be above the criterion on half of the trials and below the criterion on the other half. As the goodness value moves away from the criterion value, the noise will have a diminishing effect on the identification judgments. Noise has a larger influence on identification in the middle of the range of goodness values than at the extremes because variability goes in both directions in the middle and only inward at the extremes.

This example shows that categorical decisions made on the basis of continuous information produce identification functions with sharp boundaries, previously taken to represent categorical perception. Strictly speaking, of course, categorical perception was considered present only if discrimination behavior did not exceed that predicted from categorization (Studdert-Kennedy et al., 1970). However, one should not have been impressed with the failure of discrimination to exceed that predicted by categorization if the discrimination task resembled something more akin to categorization than discrimination (Fujisaki & Kawashima, 1970, Paap, 1975).

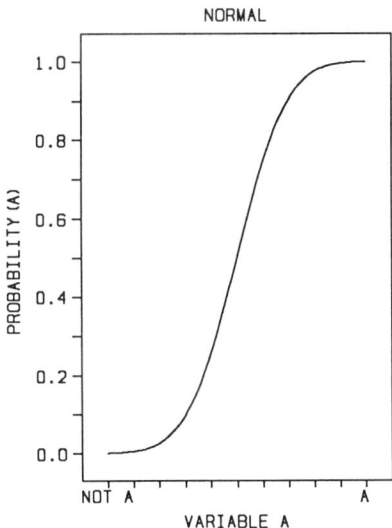

Figure 13. Probability(A) as a function of Variable A given the linear relationship between GOODNESS(A) and Variable A and the decision criterion represented in Figure 12, but with normally distributed noise added to the mapping of Variable A to GOODNESS(A).

9. Conclusion

Drawing upon a broad range of methodological, theoretical, and experimental issues, I have tried to disprove the theory of categorical perception. At the methodological level, we have learned that the relation between identification and discrimination provides no support for categorical perception. First, the categorical model usually provides an inadequate description of the results, and it has not been shown to provide a better description than alternative models. Second, even if the results provided unequivocal support for the categorical model, other explanations than categorical perception are possible.

At the theoretical level, it is necessary to distinguish between sensory and decision processes in the categorization task. What is central for our purposes is that decision processes can transform continuous sensory information into results usually taken to reflect categorical perception. Finding relatively categorical partitioning of a set of stimuli in no manner implies that these stimuli were perceived categorically. Tapping into the process in others ways than simply measuring the identification response reveals the continuous nature of speech perception. Perceivers can rate the degree to which a speech event represents a category and they can easily discriminate among different exemplars of the same speech category. In addition, RTs of identification judgments illustrate that members within a speech category vary in ambiguity or the degree to which they represent the category.

Although speech perception is continuous, there may be a few speech contrasts that qualify for a weak form of categorical perception. This weak form of categorical perception would be reflected in somewhat better discrimination between instances from different categories than between instances within the same category. As an example, consider an auditory /ba/ to /da/ continuum similar to one used in the current experiments. The F2 and F3 transitions were varied in linear steps between the two endpoints of the continuum. The syllable /ba/ is characterized by rising transitions and /da/ by falling transitions. Subjects might discriminate a rising from a falling transition more easily than discriminate two rising or two falling transitions even though the frequency difference is identical in the two cases. Direction of pitch change is more discriminable than the exact magnitude of change. This weak form of categorical perception would be due to a fundamental characteristic of auditory processing and would not be a result of having speech categories. Thus similar results would be found in humans, chinchillas, and monkeys and for nonspeech analogs. However it is important to note that discrimination between instances within a category is still possible. Although a weak form of categorical perception might exist for a few distinctions, most distinctions do not appear to have this property, and we are left with explaining continuous rather than categorical speech perception. The next chapter continues the demise of categorical perception in two new paradigms.

Chapter 5: Categorical versus Continuous Information in Speech Perception: Model Tests and Ratings

Our phenomenal experience in speech perception is that of categorical perception. Playing an auditory continuum between /ba/ and /pa/ by varying voice-onset time is an impressive demonstration. Students and colleagues usually agree that their percept changed from one category to the other in a single step or two with very little fuzziness in between. This author has a similar experience and, during an extended period of writing this book, heard certain German phonological categories in terms of similar English ones. Our phenomenal experience, however, is not sufficient to accept the notion of categorical perception. As noted by Marcel (1983b), phenomenal experience might be dependent on linking current hypotheses with sensory information. If the sensory information is lost very quickly, continuous information could participate in the perceptual process but might not be readily accessible for introspective reports. Reading a brief visual display of a word might lead to its recognition even though the reader is unable to report certain properties of the type font or even a misspelling of the word (McClelland, 1976). Yet the particular visual characteristics that subjects cannot report could have been functional in word recognition. Analogously, continuous information might have been functional in speech perception even though retrospective inquiry might imply the opposite. As in most matters of psychological inquiry, we must have methods to tap the processes involved in cognition without depending on only introspective reports.

In most studies of categorical perception, only a single property of a speech syllable is varied and theorists have not addressed whether it is the property or the syllable that is perceived categorically. Given the independent variation of two properties, it is necessary to make a distinction between these two forms of categorical perception. To clarify this distinction, we consider two different categorical models of bimodal speech perception. In the first model, the information obtained from each modality is assumed to be categorical. In the second model, the information from each modality need not be categorical. What is categorical is the percept resulting from the integration of the information from the separate modalities. Previous advocates of categorical perception have not been clear about which alternative they support and it would be negligent on our part to test only one of these. The first model, but not the second, can be formalized to give quantitative predictions of identification judgments. Rating judgments can be used to test the predictions of the second categorical model. We begin with tests of the first categorical model and contrast its predictions with those of a model assuming continuous information from the auditory and visual sources.

1. Model Tests in Factorial Designs

The model assuming categorical information from the auditory and visual sources can be formalized and tested against identification judgments in factorial designs. Categorical information implies that only discrete (e.g., phonetic) information is obtained from each source before the sources of information are integrated. Continuous information implies that continuous information from each source is made available for the integration process. Although these two hypotheses might seem to be easily distinguished, in reality, they are not. If only a single source of information is varied, it is always possible that a given property was perceived continuously even though the results indicated categorical perception of the syllable. Taking a new tack, Massaro and Cohen (1983c) formulated mathematical models of categorical and continuous perception of bimodal speech and tested these against the identification results of a factorial design. The design involved a visual /ba/, visual /da/, or no visual articulation crossed with nine synthesized speech sounds equally spaced along a /ba/-/da/ continuum. Subjects watched and listened to presentations of the 27 aural-visual events and identified the events as /ba/ or /da/ on each trial. We now derive the predictions of the two models for this experimental task.

1.1 Categorical Model

Following the logic of previous views of categorical perception, it is reasonable to assume that each dimension of the speech event is categorically perceived. There have been many conclusions that the auditory place continuum between /b/ and /d/ is perceived categorically (Eimas, 1963; Liberman et al., 1957). A similar logic might apply to the visual information (MacDonald & McGurk, 1978). According to a categorical model based on this logic, the listener has only categorical information representing the auditory and visual dimensions of the speech event. This model implies that separate categorical decisions are made with regard to the auditory and visual sources and that these decisions are subsequently integrated (MacDonald and McGurk, 1978).

In the identification task, separate /da/ or /ba/ decisions would be made to both the auditory and visual sources and the identification response would be based on these separate decisions. Given categorical information from each dimension, there are only four possible outcomes for a particular combination of auditory and visual information: /da/- /da/, /da/-/ba/, /ba/-/da/, or /ba/-/ba/. If the two decisions to a given speech event agree, the identification response can follow either source. If the two decisions disagree, it is reasonable to assume that the subject responds with the decision of the auditory source on some proportion p of the trials, and responds with the decision of the visual source on the remainder $(1-p)$ of the trials. In this conceptualization, the magnitude of p relative to $(1-p)$ reflects the relative dominance of the auditory source.

The probability of a /da/ identification response, P (/da/), given a particular auditory/visual speech event, $A_i V_j$, would be:

$$P (/da/ | A_i V_j) = (1)a_i v_j + (p)a_i(1-v_j) \qquad (1)$$
$$+ (1-p)(1-a_i)v_j + (0)(1-a_i)(1-v_j)$$
$$= pa_i + (1-p)v_j$$

where i and j index the levels of the auditory and visual modalities, respectively. The a_i value represents the probability of a /da/ decision given the auditory level i, and v_j is the probability of a /da/ decision given the visual level j. Each of the four terms in the equation represents the likelihood of one of the four possible outcomes of the separate decisions multiplied by the probability of a /da/ identification response given that outcome. In the experiment, nine auditory levels are factorially combined with three visual levels. In this model, each unique level of the auditory stimulus would require a unique parameter a_i, and analogously for v_j. Given that p reflects a decision variable, its value also requires a unique parameter that would be constant across all stimulus conditions. Thus, a total of 9+3+1=13 parameters must be estimated for predicting identifications in the 27 independent conditions.

1.2 Continuous Model

The continuous model will be formulated in terms of the FLMP (Oden & Massaro, 1978; Massaro & Cohen, 1983c). Applying the model to the present task using auditory and visual speech, both sources are assumed to provide continuous and independent evidence for the alternatives /ba/ and /da/. Defining the onsets of the second (F2) and third (F3) formants as the important auditory cues and the degree of initial opening of the lips as the important visual cue, the prototypes are

/da/   :   Slightly falling F2-F3 & Open lips
/ba/   :   Rising F2-F3 & Closed lips

Given a prototype's independent specifications for the auditory and visual sources, the value of one source cannot change the value of the other source at the prototype matching stage. In addition, the negation of a feature is defined as the additive complement. That is, we can represent Rising F2-F3 as (1-Slightly falling F2-F3) and Closed Lips as (1-Open lips),

/da/   :   Slightly falling F2-F3 & Open lips
/ba/   :   (1 - Slightly falling F2-F3) & (1 - Open lips).

The integration of the features defining each prototype is evaluated according to the product of the feature values. If a_i represents the degree to which the auditory stimulus A_i has Slightly falling F2-F3 and v_j represents the degree to which the visual stimulus V_j has Open lips, the outcome of prototype matching would be:

/da/   : $a_i v_j$
/ba/   : $(1-a_i)(1-v_j)$.

If these two prototypes are the only valid response alternatives, the pattern classification operation would determine their relative merit leading to the prediction that

$$P(/da/ \mid A_i V_j) = \frac{a_i v_j}{a_i v_j + (1-a_i)(1-v_j)} \qquad (2)$$

Given nine levels of A_i and three levels of V_j in the present task, the predictions of the model require 9+3=12 parameters, one less than the categorical model.

1.3 Experimental Test

The results used to test between the models are from Massaro and Cohen (1983c, Experiment 2). Three levels of visual information were factorially combined with nine levels of auditory information and subjects identified the bimodal events as /ba/ or /da/. The points in Figure 1 give the average proportion of /da/ identifications as a function of the auditory level; the curve parameter is the visual condition. Both the auditory and visual sources influenced identification, with the contribution of visual source larger at the middle range of the auditory continuum. The lines in the left panel of Figure 1 give the average predictions of the continuous model applied to the individual results of each of seven subjects. The right panel gives the same results along with the predictions of the categorical model. As can be seen in the figure, the continuous model gave a significantly better account of the identification judgments than did the categorical model (Massaro & Cohen, 1983c). The average RMSD for the individual-subject fits of the seven subjects was .058 for the continuous model and .128 for the categorical model.

In the fit of the categorical model to the trials containing no visual articulation, we maintained the assumption that the subject based the identification decision on the auditory source with the same probability p used when an articulation actually occurred. It might be argued, however, that this probability should be one for visual-none trials. These trials might be considered to be qualitatively different from the other bimodal trials and there is no reason for the subjects to base their judgment on the visual information. Thus, it is possible that the fit of the model would be greatly improved if the judgment on

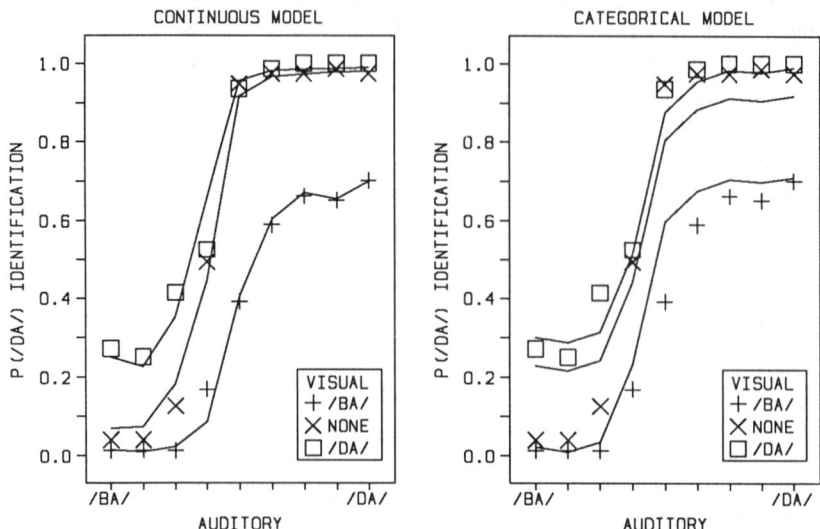

Figure 1. Proportion (points) of /da/ identifications as a function of the auditory and visual levels of bimodal speech. The lines in the left panel give the predictions based on continuous perception of each source, whereas the predictions for categorical perception of each source are given in the right panel.

visual-none trials was based on just the auditory information. When the categorical model was refit to the results with this revision, the fit was improved but not significantly. The average RMSD was .097 and was not statistically different from the average RMSD value of .128 of the original categorical model.

1.4 Categorical/Continuous Model

An obvious compromise between the assumption of either categorical or continuous information is to assume that one dimension is continuous and the other is categorical. There are two possibilities for a model assuming one continuous and one categorical dimension. In one, the auditory information would be continuous and the visual information categorical. The other would be the reverse. There is significant controversy concerning the perception of the auditory dimension (Repp, 1984; Macmillan, in press) even though there has been a plethora of experimental studies. In contrast, very little empirical work has been carried out on the visual dimension. As we will see in Section 2.4, Walden, et al. (1984) used an intelligent graphics system to create a continuum between different visible articulations. They interpreted their results as strong evidence for a continuous perceptual mode in lipreading and contrasted this with the supposedly categorical mode in auditory speech perception. Thus, it might be suggested that the advantage of the continuous model over the categorical model is solely a function of the continuous nature of the visual dimension.

There are two tacks for dealing with this possibility. The first is to isolate the auditory dimension and to assess categorical versus continuous perception within that dimension. Although the FLMP has been tested successfully against the results of a number of experiments manipulating multiple auditory dimensions, a categorical model of perception (CMP) has not been previously tested against these same studies. Therefore, it might seem worthwhile to compare the two models in terms of some representative experiments using auditory speech. However, it is possible that the multiple auditory properties are perceived continuously even though the auditory syllable is perceived categorically. With respect to the auditory syllable, Massaro & Cohen (1983a) found strong support for continuous perception of the syllable varying in voice onset time, F2-F3 transitions, and vowel quality (see Section 2.3).

The second tack involves the derivation of a model assuming one categorical and one continuous dimension. The question is whether this model can describe performance as well as the FLMP. Two different models can be derived, one a modification of the CMP and one a modification of the FLMP. A possible modification of the CMP would assume categorical auditory and continuous visual information. Some auditory level A_i elicits the /da/ category with probability a_i. In contrast, some visual level V_j gives rise to some continuous amount of /da/-ness v_j. The value v_j lies between 0 and 1 and can be considered to be the amount of support for the category /da/. One minus this value would be the support for the category /ba/.

The important challenge facing such a hybrid model is how to combine the two sources of information: one categorical and the other continuous. There may be too many alternatives to make the derivation of any particular model meaningful, especially for one with no vested interest in the success of such a model. One reasonable interpretation is that the continuous visual information can be assumed to compromise the categorical auditory information. However, these formulations ought to make very similar predictions to the following modification of the FLMP and therefore they will not be explored further.

The modification of the FLMP seems the most straightforward approach because categorical perception might be interpreted as limiting the number of different feature values to just two along a given dimension. One unique feature value would describe all of the stimulus levels within one category and the other feature value would describe all of the stimulus levels that fall within the other category. For example, the first 4 levels along a 9-step auditory /ba/ to /da/ continuum might correspond to .15 /da/-ness and the last 5 levels might correspond to .95 /da/-ness. A generalization of this model would allow determination of the ideal number of unique truth values for any continuum along some dimension of speech. Although perception may not be completely categorical, fewer truth values than the number of the unique stimulus levels might be sufficient to describe most situations.

To test the notion of continuous visual information and categorical auditory information, we constrained the FLMP to have just 2 levels of auditory information while maintaining 3 levels of visual information. In this case, the parameter value for each of the nine auditory levels can take on only one of two values. Of course, these values are estimated to give the best fit between the predicted and observed values. This two-state model was fit to the Massaro and Cohen (1983c, Experiment 2) results and gave an extremely poor description of the results, with an average RMSD of .134. To assess whether only these levels of auditory information were available, a three-state model gave an average RMSD of .096, still significantly poorer than the average RMSD of .058 of the standard FLMP with 9 levels of auditory information.

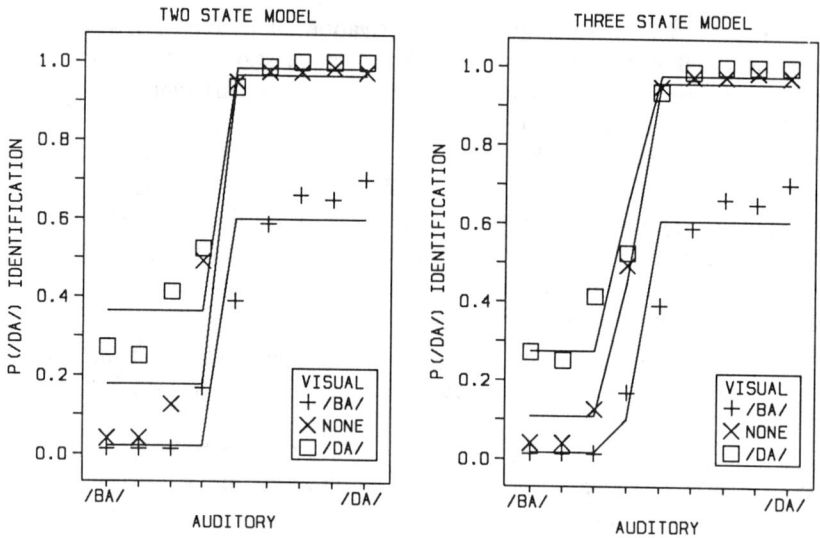

Figure 2. Proportion (points) of /da/ identifications as a function of the auditory and visual levels of bimodal speech. The lines give the predictions based on two (left panel) and three (right panel) levels of auditory information.

Figure 2 gives the observed proportion of /da/ identifications in the bimodal speech perception task. The predictions in the left panel assume two levels of auditory information. The predictions in the right panel are based on three levels of auditory information. As can be seen in the figure, the idea of continuous visual information and discrete auditory information cannot describe the results adequately. Although there is probably some finite-state model with less than nine auditory states that gives a reasonable description of the results, the point is clear. A model assuming one continuous and one categorical dimension cannot capture the results: it is necessary to assume that continuous information is available from both of the separate sources.

We cannot provide a strong test of the notion of categorical visual information because we have only three levels of visual information in the Massaro and Cohen (1983c) experiment. To do so would require a larger number of levels of visual information. As will be noted in our review of the Walden et al. (1984) experiment, the visual information appears to be continuous rather than categorical. There is very little hope for explaining bimodal speech perception in terms of one categorical and one continuous dimension. Both sources appear to make available continuous rather than only categorical information.

1.5 Open-Ended Response Alternatives

The tests between the continuous and categorical models have been limited to situations with just two response alternatives. It is important to test between the models in a situation with a greater number of response alternatives. Massaro and Cohen (1983c, Experiment 3) replicated the experiment described in the previous section but now permitted eight response alternatives. The alternatives, determined on the basis of a pilot study, were /ba/, /da/, /bda/, /ð̃a/, /dba/, /va/, /ga/, and "other." Subjects watched and listened to the speech event and identified it as one of the eight alternatives.

The identification data from this experiment were evaluated with respect to the two models of interest: the CMP and the FLMP. Only the responses /ba/, /da/, /bda/, /ð̃a/, are predicted because these four alternatives accounted for 93% of the identifications, and no other alternative accounted for more than 3.5% of the responses. Four possible responses at each of 27 experimental conditions gives 108 points to be predicted. Before presenting the outcome, the predictions of the models for situations with multiple response alternatives are derived.

1.5.1 Categorical Model

The derivation of the CMP for four responses closely follows the derivation for the two choice data. The CMP assumes that categorical decisions regarding the alternative percepts are made separately to the auditory and visual sources and that the identification judgment is based on some integration of these separate decisions. Given four response alternatives, there are four possible outcomes for a particular combination of auditory and visual information. Considering the /ba/ identification, the visual and auditory decisions could be /ba/-/ba/, /ba/-not /ba/, not /ba/-/ba/, or not /ba/-not /ba/. If the two decisions to a given speech event agree, the identification response can follow either source. When the two decisions disagree, it is assumed that the subject will respond with the decision to the auditory source on some proportion p of the trials, and with the decision to the visual source on the remainder $(1-p)$ of the trials. The weight p reflects the relative dominance of the auditory source.

The probability of a /ba/ identification response, P(/ba/), given a particular auditory/visual speech event, $A_i V_j$, would be:

$$P(/ba//A_i V_j) = (1)\ aB_i\ vB_j + (p)\ aB_i\ (1-vB_j) \qquad (2)$$
$$+ (1-p)(1-aB_i)vB_j + (0)(1-aB_i)(1-vB_j)$$

where i and j index the levels of the auditory and visual modalities, respectively. The aB_i value represents the probability of a /ba/ decision given the auditory level i, and vB_j is the probability of a /ba/ decision given the visual level j. As in the CMP for two alternatives, the value p reflects the bias to follow the auditory source. Each of the four terms in the equation represents the likelihood of one of the four possible outcomes multiplied by the probability of a /ba/ identification response given that outcome. To fit this model to the results, each unique level of the auditory stimulus requires a unique parameter aB_i, and analogously for vB_j. The modeling of /ba/ responses thus requires 9 auditory parameters plus 3 visual parameters. Each of the other three response alternatives needs an analogous equation to Equation 2 and an additional 12 parameters, thus requiring a total of 48 visual and auditory parameters. An additional p value would be fixed across all conditions for a total of 49 parameters. For any particular auditory-visual combination, the sum of the four decision probabilities to a given source also has to be constrained to be less than or equal to one; the assumption is that a given source is categorized as only a single category on any given presentation.

1.5.2 Continuous Model

In the FLMP description of the experiment, each of the response alternatives requires a prototype defined as the conjunction of some visual information and some auditory information. For example, the prototype for /da/ is defined as in the case with two response alternatives. The prototype for /ba/ would have ideal values for the auditory and visual information, but these would no longer have the complementary relationship to the ideal values for /da/. And similarly for the prototypes for /ða/ and /bda/.

The important assumption of the FLMP is that the auditory source supports each alternative to some degree and analogously for the visual source. Each alternative is defined by ideal values of the auditory and visual information. Each level of a source supports each alternative to differing degrees represented by feature values. The feature values representing the degree of support from the auditory and visual information for a given alternative are integrated following the multiplicative rule given by the FLMP. The model requires 3 parameters for the visual feature values and 9 parameters for the auditory feature values, for each of the 4 response alternatives, for a total of 48 parameters.

Thus, we have a fair comparison to the CMP which requires 49 parameters.

1.5.3 Experimental Contrast

Figures 3 and 4 give the average observed results and the average predicted results of the FLMP and CMP. As can be seen in the figures, the CMP gave a poor description of the observed results. The FLMP, on the other hand, provides a very good fit. The FLMP gave a mean RMSD of .052 averaged across the individual subject fits of the 8 subjects compared to an average RMSD of .193 for the CMP. Once again, we can reject the CMP in favor of the FLMP. This analysis reveals that the same processes of information evaluation and integration which account for two-choice identification performance can account for essentially open-ended identifications.

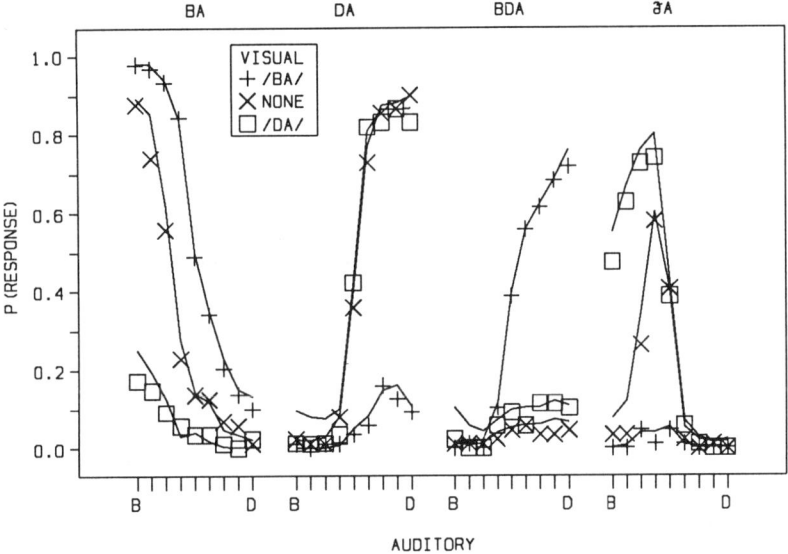

Figure 3. Proportion (points) of identifications as a function of the auditory and visual levels of bimodal speech. The lines give the predictions based on continuous perception of each source.

Table 1 gives the average best fitting parameters of the FLMP. The values of these parameters are of some interest and support the conclusions reached about integration in Chapter 3. Consider, for example, the degree to which the visual feature for each percept is supported by a visual /ba/ articulation. Although the prototype /ba/ is supported to degree .999 by a visual /ba/ articulation, the prototype for /bda/ also is supported .331. Thus, a visual /ba/ is fairly consistent with the alternative /bda/. Similarly, a visual /da/ supports not only /da/ .937, but also /ða/ to degree .535. The fourth level along the auditory

Table 1. Average best fitting parameters of the FLMP model for four response alternatives. Each parameter represents the degree of support of the stimulus level for the response alternatives.

	Response Alternative			
Stimulus Level	/ba/	/da/	/bda/	/ðˑa/
Visual				
/ba/	.999	.029	.331	.032
neutral	.425	.784	.116	.420
/da/	.037	.937	.207	.535
Auditory				
/ba/	.998	.011	.063	.081
2	.998	.010	.046	.151
3	.899	.026	.061	.513
4	.412	.066	.169	.931
5	.199	.458	.351	.740
6	.156	.896	.519	.116
7	.051	.975	.442	.045
8	.025	.971	.516	.026
/da/	.015	.962	.570	.056

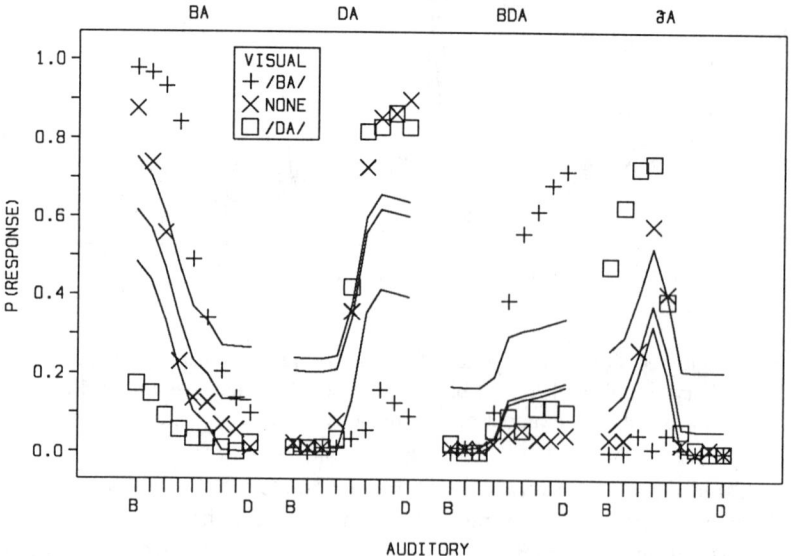

Figure 4. Proportion (points) of identifications as a function of the auditory and visual levels of bimodal speech. The lines give the predictions based on categorical perception of each source.

continuum supports /ð'a/ to degree .931. Given the support for /ð'a/ by both the auditory and the visual information, the high probability of a /ð'a/ identification given a visual /da/ paired with the fourth level along the auditory continuum is to be expected. The FLMP not only gives a good description of the results, the parameter values are psychologically meaningful.

1.6 Summary

The model tests against identifications of speech events generated by factorial combination of audible and visible speech overwhelmingly support the idea of continuous rather than categorical information. This conclusion is true for the situation with just two response alternatives and with an open-ended set of alternatives. In addition, evidence was provided that neither the audible nor the visible dimension could be considered to be categorical. We now address the issue of whether the bimodal syllable is perceived categorically even though its component modalities are not. That is, is the perceptual experience of the total speech event best described as continuous or categorical? An answer to the question can be provided by an analysis of continuous rating judgments of speech.

2. Continuous Rating Judgments

Massaro and Cohen (1983a) offered a new approach to the question of categorical speech perception. The distinguishing feature of this approach is the use of continuous rather than discrete perceptual judgments (Watson, Rilling, & Bourbon, 1964). Although rating judgments had been used in a number of previous studies (Elman, 1979; Sawusch, 1977) they had not been analyzed in such a way as to test definitively between categorical and continuous models of speech perception. Relative to discrete judgments, continuous judgments may provide a more direct measure of the listener's perceptual experience. For example, McNabb (1974) found that a binary response proved insensitive to the manipulation of an independent variable whereas confidence ratings revealed significant effects of this variable. In the Massaro and Cohen (1983a) study, subjects were asked to rate the degree to which they felt that the speech stimulus represented one alternative or the other, rather than simply indicating which alternative was presented. Categorical and continuous models of speech perception were formalized and evaluated against the distribution of repeated rating responses to each test stimulus along a synthetic speech continuum.

2.1. Categorical Model

Consider the assumptions of the categorical perception model illustrated in Figure 5. The assumption is that the percept resulting from the integration of the auditory and visual information is categorical. Given a stimulus continuum between two alternative categories *A* and *B*, it is assumed that the subject has only two perceptual states, *a* or *b*, along a continuum of five levels. At stimulus level 1, the likelihood of an *a* percept is very high whereas the likelihood of a *b* percept is very low. As the levels increase, the relative likelihood of the two percepts changes, so that *b* is the most likely percept at level 5. But in all cases, the stimulus is perceived as either *a* or *b*. If perception is truly categorical, any stimulus along the continuum can be perceived only as *a* or *b* and nothing in between.

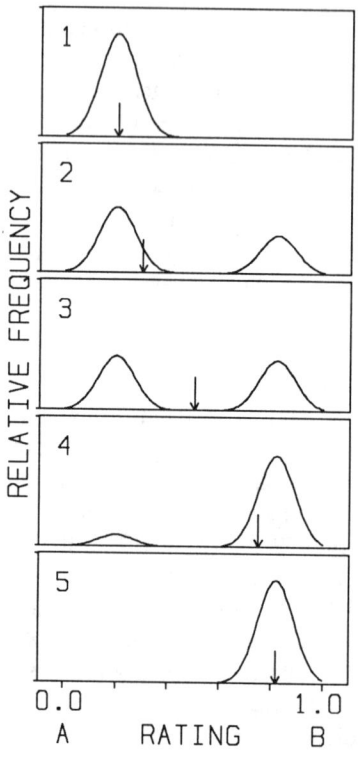

Figure 5. The left and right distributions depict the likelihood of an *a* or *b* percept given each of five levels along a stimulus continuum. According to the categorical perception model, the rating responses are drawn from these two distributions and the downward pointing arrows give the mean ratings for each of the five levels along the stimulus continuum.

What do categorical-perception subjects do when asked to make continuous rating judgments? They might note the foolishness of the request, but most probably would attempt to comply in a reasonable manner. The subject would choose a rating toward the *A* end of the response scale for the perception of *a* and toward the *B* end for the perception of *b*. If there is variability in memory and response, however, the subject would generate a distribution of rating responses for each of the two percepts. That is, subjects may not remember where they last rated the *a* category and they may also only approximate the intended rating because of response variability. Furthermore, given the demand characteristics of the task, subjects might actually generate additional variability in their ratings if their percepts are categorical and they feel that they are expected to make a range of rating responses. A safe assumption is that the rating responses given the percept *a* would be normally distributed, with a mean *Xa* and a variance *Sa*, and similarly for the *b* percept.

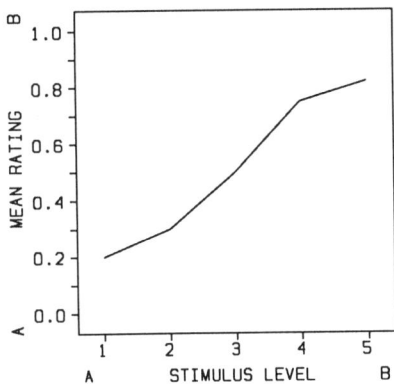

Figure 6. Hypothetical mean rating responses predicted by both the categorical and continuous models as derived from the representations in Figures 5 and 7.

The important question is how the mean rating responses are expected to differ as a function of the different stimulus levels along the speech continuum. Consider the speech continuum of five levels as illustrated in Figure 5. Although perception is categorical, a stimulus is more likely to produce the percept *a* to the extent that it is away from the category boundary and towards the *A* end of the continuum. Variation in the category boundary, or variation in the perceptual system, or both, allows the percept to have only a probabilistic relationship to a given stimulus. A given stimulus produces the percept *a* with probability *Pa* and the percept *b* with probability 1-*Pa*. Therefore, the distribution of rating responses to a given stimulus will actually be a mixture of ratings generated by the two percepts. The proportion of ratings generated from the percept *a* will increase with increases in *Pa*. Similarly, the proportion of ratings generated from the percept *b* will decrease with increases in *Pa*. The arrows in Figure 5 give the mean rating responses resulting from the mixture of the two distributions over trials. Figure 6 gives the mean ratings based on the analysis in Figure 5 and illustrates that continuous changes in the mean rating response with continuous changes in the stimulus can be predicted by the categorical model.

2.2. Continuous Model

The continuous model is illustrated in Figure 7. In this model, the rating given to a stimulus is a direct function of the percept generated by that stimulus. This model is similar to Thurstone's (1927) law of comparative judgment in which it is assumed that each stimulus gives a normal distribution of percepts along an internal dimension. In the continuous model, the percepts of two adjacent stimuli will usually differ from each other and the rating responses will reflect this fact.

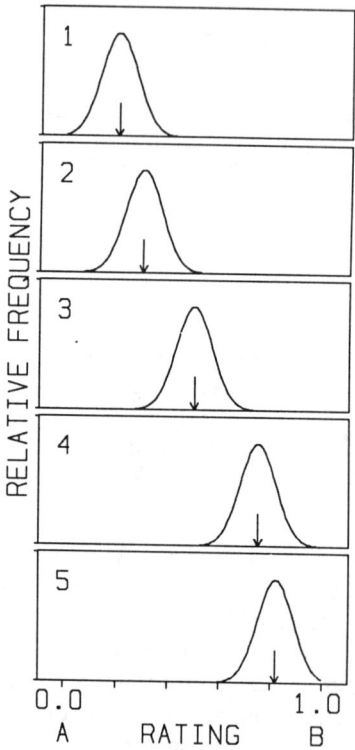

Figure 7. According to the continuous perception model, the percept can be represented by just one unique distribution for each of the five levels along the stimulus continuum. The rating responses are drawn from these distributions and the downward pointing arrows give the mean ratings for each of the five levels along the stimulus continuum.

The percept of a stimulus towards the *A* end of the continuum will be more *A*-like than that of a neighboring stimulus towards the *B* side of the continuum. Random variability in the perceptual, memory, or response systems will also result in a distribution of rating responses to any given stimulus. Figure 7 shows how the continuous model predicts a systematic and continuous change in mean rating responses with changes in stimulus level. The continuous model, therefore, makes the same predictions as the categorical model with respect to the mean rating responses.

Given that the categorical and continuous perception models make similar predictions about the mean rating judgments, they are not capable of testing between the two models. The models, however, can be distinguished on the basis of the distribution of rating responses. The final distribution of rating responses is predicted to differ for the two models. Figures 5 and 7 illustrate the overall form of the predicted distribution of rating responses for each of the the two models. As can be seen in the figures, although the average rating function (indicated by the arrows) is identical for the two models, the distribution of rating responses is not. For example, at level 3 on the stimulus continuum, the continuous model would predict a distribution with a single peak, whereas the categorical model would predict a bimodal distribution with a central trough.

2.3. Experimental Test: Auditory Source

To gather data for the model tests, Massaro and Cohen (1983a) had three groups of subjects rate continua of synthetic speech stimuli. One group of subjects rated consonants differing in place of articulation from /bæ/ (as in bat) to /dæ/, a second group rated consonants differing in voicing from /bæ/ to /pæ/, and a third group rated vowels on a continuum from /i/ (as in heat) to /I/ (as in hit). The three continua gave similar results and only the voicing and place data will be presented here. The place continuum consisted of seven syllables with the second and third formant transitions varying in equal steps. The voicing continuum consisted of seven stops with voice onset times varying from 0 to 60 msec. in steps of 10 msec. Subjects were instructed to rate each stimulus on a continuum between the two alternatives by adjusting a pointer on a 5 cm linear scale. A given subject provided 128 ratings to each of the seven test sounds, and all analyses were carried out at the single-subject level.

The ratings were represented as values between 0 and 1 by treating the distance between the end points as an interval scale. Figure 8 gives the mean ratings for 3 of the 12 subjects. As expected from both models, the mean ratings changed relatively continuously as a function of the stimulus level. The critical feature of our analysis is not the examination of the mean ratings, however, but rather the exact nature of their distribution of occurrence. In order to determine whether the observed distributions of ratings were best fit by the continuous or categorical models, two models were formulated to predict the distributions of ratings for each subject. Analogous to our model tests using identification judgments, we can discriminate between competing models on the basis of the overall goodness of fit. The categorical model requires 11 free parameters which includes 2 means and 2 standard deviations for the 2 normal distributions and 7 sampling probabilities for the 7 stimulus levels. For the continuous model, 14

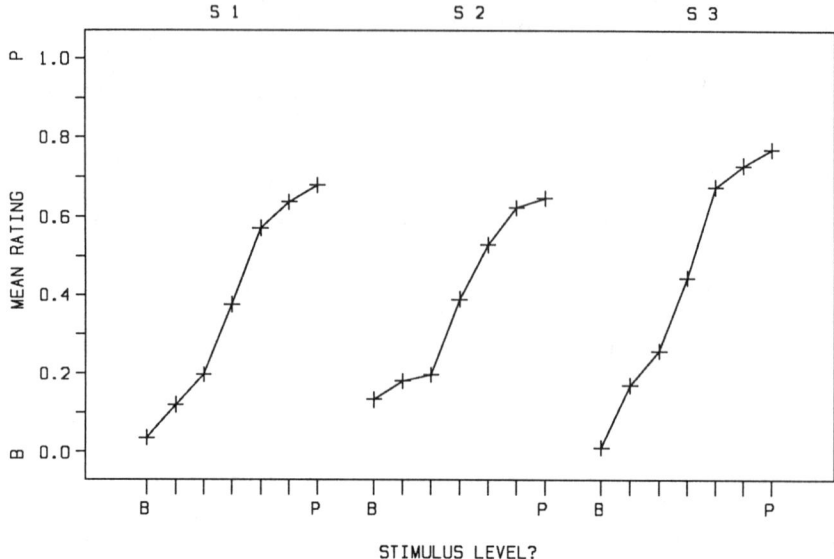

Figure 8. Mean rating judgments for 3 subjects across the voice onset continuum (after Massaro & Cohen, 1983a).

parameters are required which include 7 means and 7 standard deviations for the 7 normal distributions corresponding to the 7 stimuli.

Figure 9 gives the distributions of the rating judgments for a typical subject, along with the predicted distributions of the continuous and categorical models. The continuous model does a better job of fitting the observed data. What is most noticeable in the figure is how much better the continuous model does for the intermediate stimulus level. The figure also reveals how much better the continuous model does for the other levels of the distributions. We can see that the continuous model more accurately captures and reproduces the different number of observations occurring in the tails of the distributions corresponding to the endpoint stimulus levels. The observed data appear to result from a single, central distribution rather than from a mixture of two peripheral distributions.

The continuous model also gave a better description of the results when contrasted with a categorical model which included a guessing state. This model is the same as the categorical model but with an additional assumption: for each level of the stimulus there is a certain probability that the rating response is generated from a guessing distribution. One way of viewing the guessing model is in terms of a threshold or criterion for making a particular response. In this conceptualization, if the strength of the evidence for one or the other alternative does not exceed the criterion, then a guessing response would be made.

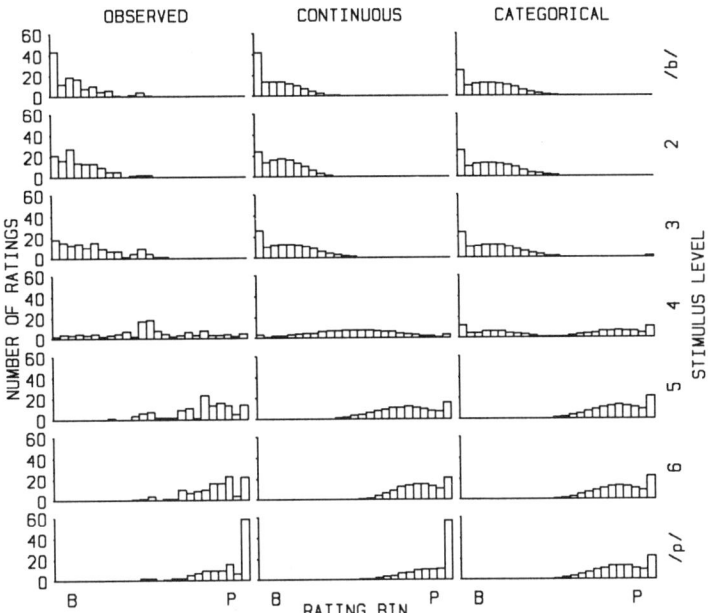

Figure 9. Observed and predicted distributions of rating responses along the voice-onset-time continuum for a typical subject (after Massaro & Cohen, 1983a).

Naturally, it would be expected that the guessing response would occur most frequently for the more central, ambiguous levels of the stimulus dimension. This model has 20 parameters: 3 means and 3 standard deviations for the /bæ/, /pæ/, and the guessing distribution, and 2 sampling probabilities for each of the 7 levels along the continuum. Each of the 7 stimulus levels needs only 2 free probability parameters because the 3 probabilities must sum to 1. Figure 10 gives the observed and predicted results for another subject tested on the place continuum, contrasting the guessing model with the continuous model. The continuous model gave the better description of the results, even with the disadvantage of having 6 fewer free parameters than the categorical guessing model.

   To summarize, the distribution of rating judgments to auditory speech is better described by continuous than by categorical two-state or three-state models. Subjects appear to have continuous information about the degree to which a particular speech sound represents a speech category.

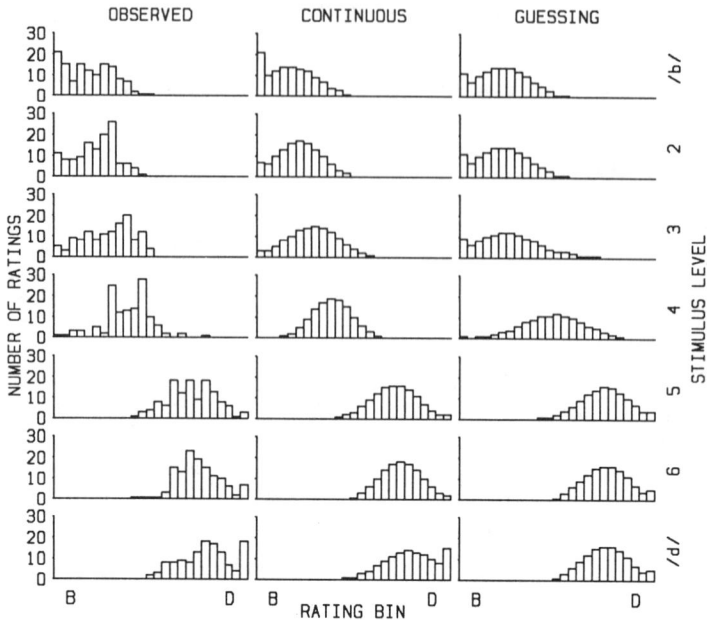

Figure 10. Observed and predicted distributions of rating responses along the place continuum for a typical subject (after Massaro & Cohen, 1983a).

2.4 Experimental Test: Visual Source

Analogous to auditory speech, there are constraints on the use of natural visual speech in speech perception experiments. Given two contrasting categories, such as /ba/ and /da/, only three levels of visual information can be reasonably made with natural articulations: /ba/, neutral or no articulation, and /da/. A rating experiment with only three stimulus levels cannot provide a good assessment of categorical versus continuous perception. A larger number of levels is necessary to create a situation in which the two models are more easily distinguished. Analogous to the utilization of synthetic speech, however, visible speech synthesis is being developed and offers the potential given by synthetic audible speech.

As described in Chapter 4 (Section 2), Walden et al. (1984) created animations of speech-like articulations of the syllables /ba/, /va/, and /wa/. Three continua of eight syllables each were generated and used as stimuli in a rating experiment. The results of primary interest are the rating responses to the stimuli along each continuum. Subjects rated on a scale from 1 to 9, indicating the degree to which each stimulus was like one syllable or the other of a pair. Given the /ba/-/va/ continuum, for example, subjects rated on a scale from "most-/ba/-

like" to "most-/va/-like." Following the logic that the distribution of ratings can be informative even if the mean ratings are not, we can assess the rating distributions to see if they are better described by categorical or continuous perception. The authors presented only the group results of 13 subjects consisting of 10 ratings per stimulus for each subject. The distributions of rating judgments for the three continua are shown as the points in Figures 11, 12, and 13.

It is not always valid to test continuous and categorical models against group results. In some situations, group results bias the outcome in favor of the prediction of continuous models (Massaro, 1975a, Chapter 29). In the present test, however, the bias seems to favor the categorical model. In general, the categorical model should have the advantage to the extent that there is large variability in the rating judgments because it predicts two underlying distributions as opposed to a single distribution predicted by the continuous model (see Figures 5 and 7). Group results might resemble what might be expected from categorical perception if there are large subject differences in the mean ratings given each stimulus; large differences in the mean ratings would give distributions of ratings more easily described by a mixture of two distributions rather than just one. In addition, the reverse does not seem to be true. It is less likely that the distribution of group ratings can look continuous when the individual subject ratings are generated by a categorical model. Given this asymmetry, group results rejecting categorical perception would appear to be more valid than group results rejecting continuous perception. The distribution of rating judgments pooled across subjects must be evaluated with caution, especially if there is large variability between subjects. The group ratings will be most informative when there are small differences in the subjects' mean ratings of each stimulus along the continuum.

Given the outcomes shown in Figures 11, 12, and 13, the group results appear to be highly informative. All of the distributions are clearly unimodal and none are bimodal as might be expected from categorical perception. Consider the distribution of ratings of stimulus level 4 along the /ba/- /va/ continuum shown in Figure 11. The mean rating is about in the middle of the rating scale and the categorical model must describe this mean rating in terms of a mixture of two ratings, one given the categorization /ba/ and the other given the categorization /va/. However, the distribution of ratings is clearly unimodal with relatively little variance, especially considering the fact that the ratings are pooled across subjects. It follows that the distribution of ratings provides strong evidence against the categorical model. Confirming this graphical interpretation, quantitative tests of the two models against the results provide unequivocal support for the continuous model and against the categorical model. A summary of these tests is given in Table 2. The fits of the continuous model are between 4 and 7 times better than the fits of the categorical model. Thus we can conclude that visible speech (at least as represented in animated form) is perceived

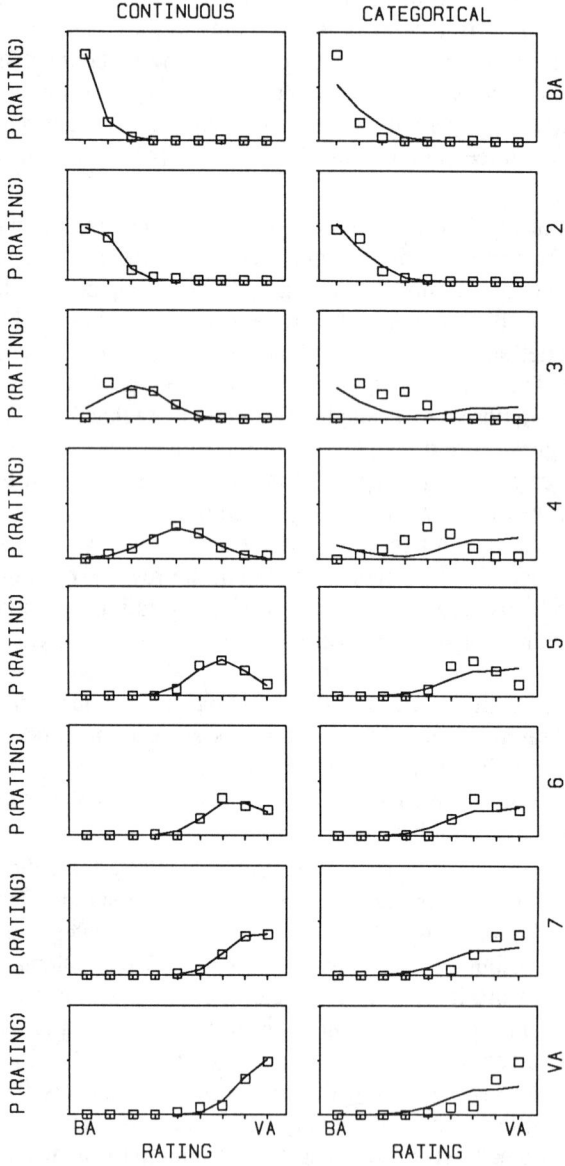

Figure 11. Observed (points) and predicted (lines) distributions of rating responses for 13 subjects for the /ba/-/va/ continuum. The left and right panels give the predictions of the continuous and categorical models, respectively (after Walden, Montgomery, Holum-Hardegen, & Prosek, 1984).

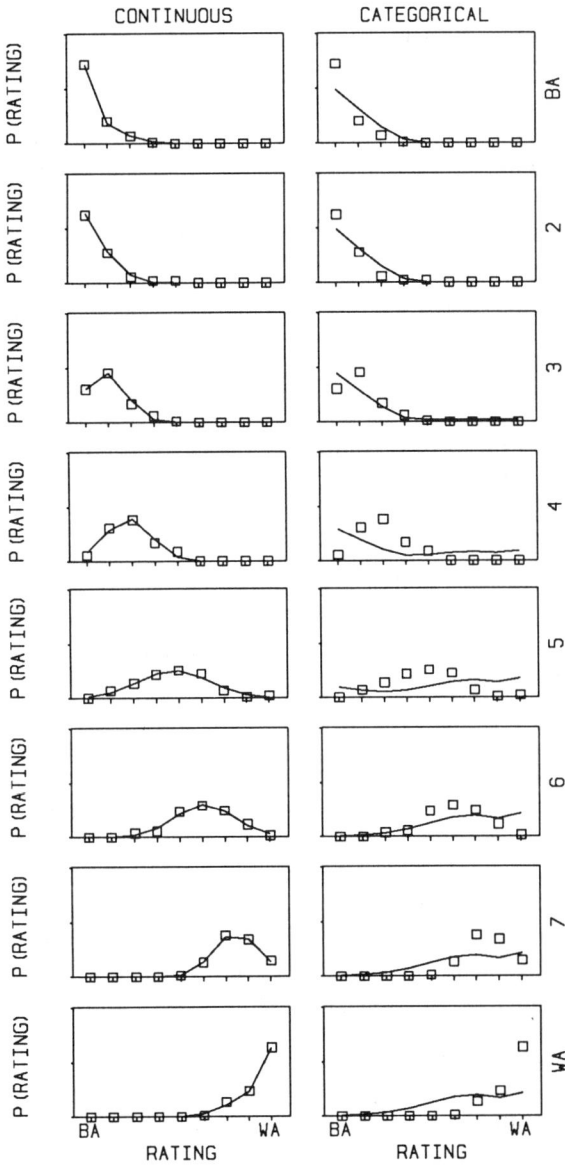

Figure 12. Observed (points) and predicted (lines) distributions of rating responses for 13 subjects for the /ba/-/wa/ continuum. The left and right panels give the predictions of the continuous and categorical models, respectively (after Walden, Montgomery, Holum-Hardegen, & Prosek, 1984).

continuously rather than categorically.

One potential limitation in the Walden et al. (1984) study must be overcome in future studies of animated visible speech. The time course of the synthetic syllables was several times the duration found in natural speech. Although the results might change if this difference is eliminated, the results with synthetic auditory speech that maintain a natural duration also produce continuous perception. There is the potential for much gold to be mined using synthetic visual speech, especially when combined with synthetic auditory speech.

Table 2. The RMSD values for Continuous and Categorical fits of Walden, Montgomery, Holum-Hardegen, & Prosek (1984) study.

	Continuum		
Model	/ba/-/va/	/ba/-/wa/	/wa/-/va/
Continuous	.025	.015	.024
Categorical	.100	.109	.103

2.5 Experimental Test: Bimodal Speech

Rating judgments can be used to assess the issue whether the percept resulting from a speech event contains continuous or only categorical information. We have seen that both audible speech and visible speech, when presented alone, provide continuous information. It is possible that a speech event composed of both audible and visible speech is perceived categorically, even though the two components presented alone are not. It is necessary, therefore, to test the two models against the distribution of rating responses to repeated presentations of bimodal speech events. Consider the bimodal speech events created by the orthogonal variation of audible and visible speech. Nine levels along a synthetic auditory /ba/ to /da/ continuum are crossed with the three visual levels /ba/, neutral, and /da/. The task of the subject is to rate each of the 27 speech events along a nine-point /ba/ to /da/ continuum. Categorical information predicts that the ratings to repeated presentations of a single event will come from two kinds of trials: those trials on which the event was categorically identified as one alternative /ba/ and those on which the event was categorically identified as the other alternative /da/. Thus, categorical perception predicts that the distribution of ratings to a given stimulus is a result of two different phonetic categorizations or a mixture of /ba/ identification and /da/ identification trials. On the other hand, continuous perception predicts that perceivers have information about the degree to which the bimodal speech event represents one category or the other. If follows that the rating judgment should contain continuous information. Hence, the ratings to a given speech event should be represented by a single distribution.

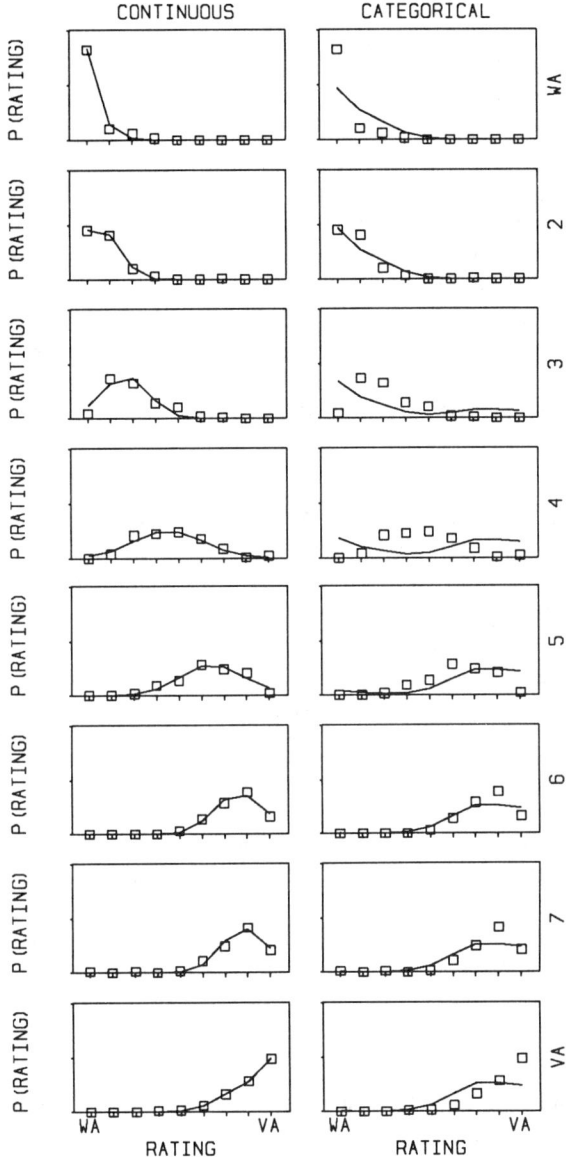

Figure 13. Observed (points) and predicted (lines) distributions of rating responses for 13 subjects for the /wa/-/va/ continuum. The left and right panels give the predictions of the continuous and categorical models, respectively (after Walden, Montgomery, Holum-Hardegen, & Prosek, 1984).

2.5.1 Method

Massaro and Ferguson (1986) asked 20 subjects to rate the bimodal syllables on a continuum from 1 to 9. The value 1 was the best possible /ba/ and the value 9 was the best possible /da/. The value 5 would be ambiguous, 7 would be more /da/-like than /ba/-like, and so on. On each trial, the monitor showed a speaker saying either /ba/ or /da/ or keeping his lips closed (the neutral condition). The auditory stimuli were synthesized from characteristics of the speaker's voice and formed a continuum of nine sounds equally spaced between /ba/ and /da/. One of the nine auditory stimuli on the continuum from /ba/ to /da/ was synchronized with one of the three possible visual stimuli, /ba/, /da/, or neutral. The stimuli were presented in 11 blocks of the 27 possible combinations plus 10 practice trials for a total of 307 trials per session. Subjects had 2750 msec in which to make their rating response. Each subject made 11 ratings of each of the 27 bimodal syllables.

2.5.2 Results

The proportion of rating judgments given each of the nine rating values was computed for each subject for each test syllable. The ratings changed systematically with changes in the auditory and visual properties of the bimodal syllables. The mean rating judgments are analyzed in Chapter 7 (Section 2.3).

Analogous to our previous tests, an analysis of the distribution of ratings can test between categorical and continuous models of bimodal speech perception. The categorical and continuous models were quantified to predict the distribution of ratings under the 27 stimulus conditions. For the test of the categorical model, a unique parameter value is needed for each of the 27 different speech events, representing the probability that the event is perceived as /ba/. One minus this probability represents the probability that the speech event is perceived as /da/. In addition, one mean and one standard deviation must be estimated for each of the two hypothetical rating distributions corresponding to the /ba/ and /da/ alternatives respectively. Implemented in this manner, the test of the categorical model requires 31 parameter values.

A test of a continuous model would normally require 27 means and 27 standard deviations to predict the ratings to the 27 stimulus conditions. To reduce the number of free parameters, the integration rule of the FLMP was used to combine the auditory and visual information to predict the distribution of ratings to the 27 bimodal speech events. The FLMP rating model assumes that there is a distribution of truth values for each modality and this generates the range of rating judgments because the combination gives a range of truth values. In this formulation, there are nine unique means for the nine levels along the auditory continuum and three unique means for the three visual levels. An additional twelve parameters are necessary for the standard deviations. Given these values, the 27 rating distributions corresponding to the 27 speech events

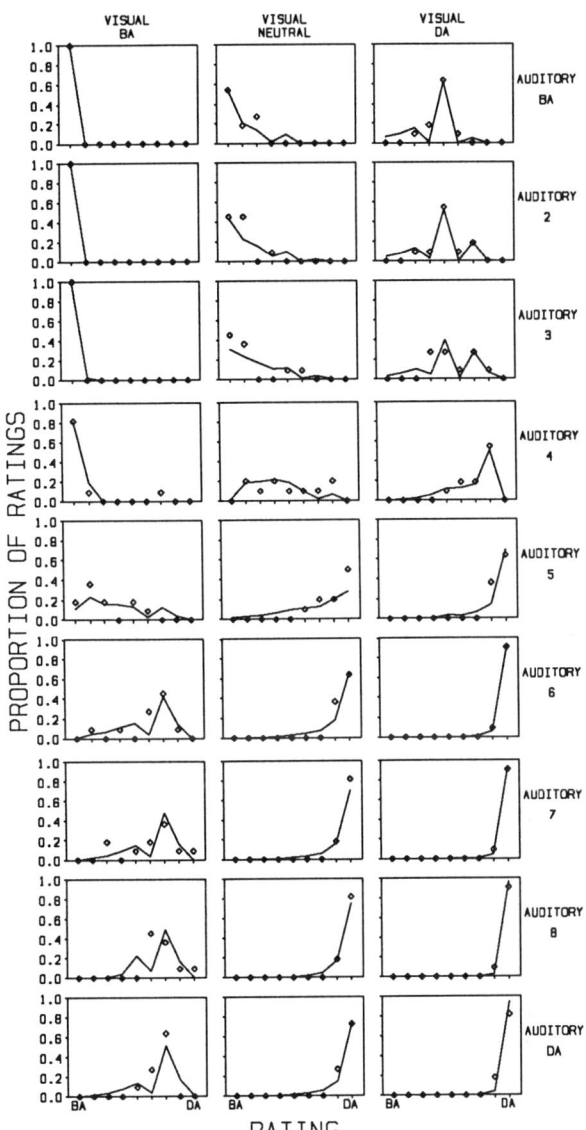

Figure 14. Observed (points) distributions of ratings and predictions (lines) of the continuous model as a function of the auditory and visual levels of the speech event for a typical subject.

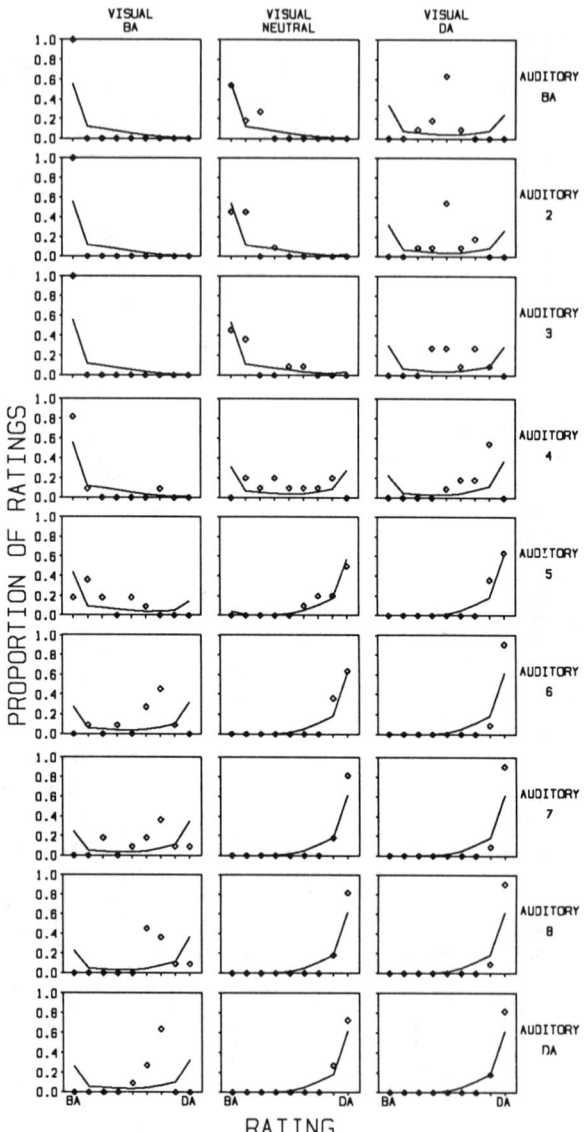

Figure 15. Observed (points) distributions of ratings and predictions (lines) of the categorical model as a function of the auditory and visual levels of the speech event for a typical subject.

can be computed directly by convolving the two unimodal distributions through the integration rule of the FLMP. Therefore, the implementation of the continuous model requires only 24 parameters relative to the 31 required by the categorical model.

The computation of the fuzzy logical combination of two feature distributions A and B is done as follows: First, each feature distribution is divided into n bins. A resultant distribution of n bins is also constructed and each bin set to 0. Now we consider all possible joint occurrences of feature A falling in bin j and feature B falling in bin k. For each jk combination, we take the center values of the bins and combine them according to the FLMP. The resulting value tells us in which bin of the resultant distribution the identification will fall. To that bin we then add the product of the areas of the two bins j and k, which gives the probability of the joint occurrence of feature A falling in bin j and feature B falling in bin k. This entire process is repeated for each possible combination of stimulus levels for the two features.

Figure 14 gives the observed distributions of ratings for a typical subject in the experiment. Figure 14 also gives the predictions of the continuous model and Figure 15 gives the same observations plotted against the results of the categorical model. The results are highly informative with respect to the question of continuous versus categorical information. Consider the top right hand panel corresponding to a visual /da/ paired with an auditory /ba/. All of the ratings to this syllable were between 3 and 6, with the majority at 5. This result is nicely predicted by the continuous model because integration of visual /da/ and auditory /ba/ should produce an ambiguous percept (see Figure 14). The categorical model cannot predict this same result because the syllable should be heard as /da/ some of the time and as /ba/ the rest of the time. The ratings should be divided between low and high ratings, as illustrated in the predictions of the categorical model in Figure 15. A similar conclusion is reached in the other conditions. Although not obvious in a single glance, the continuous model captures the trends in the results whereas the categorical model does not. The average RMSD across the 20 subjects was .089 for the continuous model and .132 for the categorical model. The continuous model gave a better fit for each of the 20 subjects, which was statistically significant, $F(1,19) = 65$, $p < .001$. Thus we have evidence based on the distribution of ratings that bimodal speech is perceived continuously rather than categorically.

It is also possible to test the categorical model by computing the probabilities for the bimodal speech event on the basis of the probabilities of categorizing the auditory and visual dimensions. In this case, nine parameter values are needed for categorizing the nine levels along the auditory continuum as /ba/; and three parameter values for the three visual levels. These twelve parameters can be used to generate the 27 unique probabilities of a /ba/ rating. One minus these values gives the probabilities of a /da/ rating. Four additional parameters are needed for the means and standard deviations of the /ba/ and /da/ rating distributions, respectively. This 16-parameter model did only slightly poorer than the 31-parameter categorical model with an average RMSD of .141. For all subjects, the continuous model gave a much better description of the results than did the categorical model.

2.6 Summary

Building on the developments in psychophysics, it is important to distinguish between sensory and decision stages of processing (Massaro, in press b). Categorical and continuous models of speech perception make different predictions about the distribution of repeated rating judgments to a given stimulus along some speech continuum. The results of both synthetic auditory and synthetic visual speech studies provide conclusive evidence that there is continuous information available in speech perception. In agreement with these observations, bimodal speech appears to be perceived continuously rather than categorically.

3. Implications for Theories of Speech Perception

The prevailing view has been that speech perception is special (Liberman, Cooper, Shankweiler, & Studdert-Kennedy, 1967). Although several phenomena have been brought to bear on this speciality, the most popular has been categorical perception. During the last decade in which categorical perception has been challenged (Pisoni, 1973; Samuel, 1977), it has made its appearance in various disguises (Best et al., 1981). The demise of the theory of categorical perception pulls the rug from under many of the arguments for speech being special. Without categorical perception, there is little evidence to support the uniqueness of speech perception relative to other domains of perceptual recognition. Other lines of support for speciality of speech such as duplex perception, trading relations, and the McGurk effect are better described by nonspecialized mechanisms (Macmillan, in press; Massaro, in press d).

A strong assumption of cohort theory (Marslen-Wilson, 1984) is that lexical access is achieved phoneme by phoneme in strict serial order. A candidate is eliminated from a cohort set when the incoming phoneme disagrees with the appropriate phoneme in the representation of the word. Although cohort theory has several worthwhile assumptions, the assumption of categorical information at the phoneme level is wrong (McClelland & Elman, 1986; Norris, 1982). Once continuous information is acknowledged, many of the processing assumptions will have to be made more complicated. By incorporating continuous information in cohort theory and utilizing integration algorithms analogous to the FLMP, the theory can be brought in line with recent results taken as evidence against the theory (Frauenfelder & Marcus, 1985).

The demise of the assumption of categorical perception also poses a serious problem for the Trace model of speech perception (McClelland & Elman, 1986). This model is one of a class of models in which information processing occurs through excitatory and inhibitory interactions among a large number of simple processing units. These units are meant to represent the functional properties of neurons or neural networks. Three levels or sizes of units are used in TRACE: feature, phoneme, and word. Features activate phonemes which activate words, and activation of some units at a particular level inhibits other units at the same level. In addition, an important assumption of interactive-activation models is that activation of higher-order units activates their lower-order units; for example, activation of the /b/ phoneme would activate the features that are consistent with that phoneme. Given that multiple units at one level simultaneously activate units at a higher level, the model provides a natural account for the integration of auditory and visual information in speech perception. In addition, the model also predicts that integration can be enhancing, not just compromising. These two properties of the model agree with the outcomes of the binary contrasts. The model makes some of the same predictions as the FLMP, and quantitative tests between the models are difficult, if not impossible.

Notwithstanding the similarity in the predictions of the TRACE and FLMP models, the two models make very different predictions about categorical perception. As described in Chapter 4 (Section 8), categorization in the FLMP occurs as a consequence of pattern classification and not at the featural evaluation or integration operations. In contrast, the TRACE model produces categorical-like behavior at the sensory (featural) level rather than at simply the decision stage. In this model, a stimulus pattern is presented and activation of the corresponding features sends more excitation to some phoneme units than others. Given the assumption of feedback from the phoneme to the feature level, the activation of a particular phoneme feeds down and activates the features corresponding to that phoneme (McClelland & Elman, 1986, p. 47). This effect of feedback produces enhanced sensitivity around a category boundary, exactly as predicted by categorical perception. Given the falsification of categorical perception, an important weakness in a powerful and comprehensive model of speech perception has been documented. It appears that the TRACE model will have to be modified significantly because the evidence points to continuous rather than categorical perception. This modification will not be easy to implement because of the large amount of activation assumed to exist from the phoneme level down to the feature level. It will be interesting to determine if the power of the TRACE model can be maintained without top-down activation of feature evaluation.

4. Conclusion

The most convincing evidence against the hypothesis of categorical perception comes from direct experimental tests between categorical and continuous models of perception. Two new results were brought to bear on the issue of categorical versus continuous perception. First, subjects asked to classify speech events independently varying along two dimensions produce identification results consistent with the assumption of continuous information along each of the two dimensions. A model based on categorical information along each dimension gives a very poor description of the identification judgments. Second, subjects were asked to make repeated ratings of the degree to which a stimulus represents a given category. The distribution of the rating judgments to a given stimulus is more adequately described by a continuous rather than a categorical model of perception. The best conclusion is to reject all reference to categorical perception of speech and to concentrate instead on the structures and processes responsible for categorizing the world of speech.

Notwithstanding the three decades of misinterpreting the relationship between identification and discrimination of auditory speech, we must conclude that it is perceived continuously and not categorically (Massaro, in press b). The current work reveals that visible and bimodal speech also are perceived continuously. Parenthetically, this observation pulls the carpet from under current views of language acquisition that attribute to the infant and child discrete speech categories (Eimas, 1985, Gleitman & Wanner, 1982). Most importantly, the case for the specialization of speech is weakened considerably because of the central role that the assumption of categorical perception has played. We are now faced with a more challenging situation in that we must address how multiple continuous sources of information are evaluated and integrated to achieve a percept with continuous information. This challenge is the topic of the next two chapters.

Chapter 6: Independent versus Dependent Evaluation of Sources

Having obtained evidence for the integration of continuous sources of information in bimodal speech perception, the current branch of the binary-opposition tree involves the issue of whether the two sources of information are dependent or independent. As also somewhat apparent in the other contrasts, the question of independence is to some extent model dependent (Ashby & Townsend, 1986). Assuming separate evaluation and integration operations, independent sources of information imply that the information value determined in the evaluation of one source remains independent of the information value of the other. Dependent sources imply a violation of this principle.

The distinction between independence and dependence is more easily made if it is assumed (as in the FLMP) that three operation—feature evaluation, integration, and pattern classification—are involved in perceptual recognition. It is claimed that almost any model of recognition would have to assume stages functionally equivalent to these three operations of evaluation, integration, and decision. Although not stated explicitly, the CMP also has these three operations. Recall that the CMP derives discrete categorizations for the visual and auditory sources (feature evaluation), chooses one of the two categorizations with some probability (integration), and always responds with the alternative corresponding to the chosen categorization (decision). The primary distinction between the CMP and the FLMP is that the CMP has binary outputs from the feature evaluation stage, whereas the FLMP has continuous outputs.

In our representation of the contrast of independence versus dependence, the differences are assumed to exist also at feature evaluation. In the independence model, the feature value assigned to one source of information remains independent of the value assigned to another source of information. In the dependence view, the feature assigned to one source is some function of the feature value or the level of information of the other source.

The difference between independence and dependence is best represented in terms of the two different models illustrated graphically in Figure 1. In the independence model, the auditory feature value is dependent on only the level of the auditory source. In the dependence model, the auditory feature value is dependent upon both the auditory and visual sources. The feature value is represented as a_i in the independence model because the feature a is a function of level i of the auditory source. The feature a is dependent on both the auditory level i and visual level j in the dependence model. Thus the feature value is called a_{ij} in the dependence model.

The dependence model in Figure 1 illustrates dependence in both dimensions. It is also possible to have dependence in just a single direction. For example, the visual level would influence the feature value assigned to the auditory source but the auditory level would not influence the feature value assigned to the visual source. Unfortunately a model based on dependence in a single direction is not much easier to formalize and test than is a model based on

Dependent Evaluation

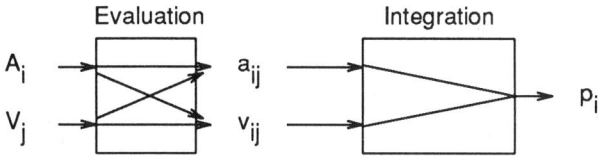

Independent Evaluation

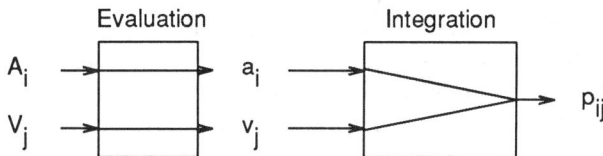

Figure 1. Illustration of dependent evaluation and independent evaluation. In dependent evaluation, the evaluation of one dimension is influenced by the value of the other whereas the evaluation of a dimension remains independent of the other in independent evaluation.

dependence in two directions.

It should be stressed that the idea of independence at the feature evaluation stage in no way implies statistical independence between the two sources of information; the integration operation and the pattern classification operation can introduce statistical dependence even though the featural values remain independent of one another at the feature evaluation stage. Researchers (e.g. Miller, 1977; Port & Dalby, 1982) who have claimed dependence based on a result of statistical dependence are not necessarily correct in their conclusions. In our factorial experiments, we consistently observe that the magnitude of the effect of one source on identification depends on the level of the other source. This statistical dependence between the auditory and visual sources does not reject the class of independence models.

We have taken three approaches to address the issue of independence-dependence. One of them is model-free and two are model-dependent. (Strictly speaking, no test can be completely model-independent; what is meant is less dependence on specific models of performance). In the model-free test (Cohen, 1984), RTs to the single-dimension and bimodal events are assessed to determine whether the two dimensions show some form of dependent interaction. If they do, it should not be possible to account for the RTs to a bimodal /ba/ in terms of simply the RTs to a visual /ba/ and to an auditory /ba/.

If the two dimensions are independent, we might expect RTs to the bimodal event to be somewhat faster than those to the single-dimension events, but the advantage should be completely accounted for by the statistical facilitation of having two horses in the race rather than just one.

For the model-dependent tests, independence and dependence models are tested against the perceptual judgments of speech by ear and eye. The previous discovery of a particular kind of dependence between two auditory dimensions serves as the basis for the development and testing of a dependence model of bimodal speech perception. We also ask whether a model assuming independence of auditory and visual information provides an adequate account of bimodal speech perception. The hypothesis of dependence must predict a failure of any model assuming independence (unless for some strange reason the independence model is mathematically equivalent to the dependence that exists). Independence models must assume that the information obtained along one source is independent of the information obtained along the other source. The models described in the test between categorical and continuous sources of information are independence models. Both models must fail if the auditory and visual sources are dependent. However, the adequate description of the FLMP provides evidence for independence and against dependence of auditory and visual information in speech perception.

In the third approach, the independence model will be extended to account for identification judgments obtained using an expanded factorial design that includes conditions in which the sources of information are presented alone. As will be demonstrated in the derivation of the model, very strong predictions are made about the relationship between classification of the single sources of information and classification of speech events composed of both auditory and visual sources of information. The model predicts that the information available given just a single source of information is identical to the information from that source when both sources of information are available. This assumption illustrates complete independence in that the feature value of a given level of a source is identical when presented alone and when presented in the context of an additional source of information. If the model is able to describe identification of speech events composed of single sources and composed of both sources given this constraint, it provides very strong evidence for the idea of independence. Evidence in favor of independence, as stated previously, automatically infirms the idea of dependence. It is logically possible that dependence exists but that an independence model is able to capture that particular form of dependence. Until an adequate dependence model is presented, however, the most parsimonious description is that of independence.

1. Model-Free Test

The first test between independence and dependence involves the use of RTs to the unimodal and bimodal events. The question is whether the time to respond to a bimodal event can be predicted from the RTs to the unimodal events. If it can, this means that the two sources of information were processed independently. Subjects identify as quickly and accurately as possible six unambiguous speech syllables (Cohen, 1984). The syllables /ba/ and /da/ are presented auditorily, visually, or bimodally and the subject's task is to identify the syllable as /ba/ or /da/. Performance accuracy is near perfect and RTs are the primary dependent variable of interest. Independence at the evaluation stage means that the time to evaluate one source is independent of the presence or absence of the other source. Given that the two sources never conflict, subjects always have unambiguous information from each source and can respond as soon as one of the sources is evaluated. Because of variability in the time for evaluation of either source, there should be some advantage for bimodal trials when subjects can initiate a response to the source that is evaluated first. This advantage is known as statistical facilitation (Raab, 1962) and is a general prediction of horse-race models assuming independence between the different input sources. The assumption of independence makes exact predictions about the relationship between the RTs to the unimodal and bimodal sources and the independence-dependence test asks whether these predictions are correct.

The reader might have realized that the predictions of independence appear to contradict those of integration. The independence prediction implies that subjects respond to the auditory or visual source that is processed first, without waiting to integrate the two sources. Although this implication is correct, it does not necessarily mean that the two sources are not integrated. Integration of auditory and visual information might always occur even if a response can be initiated before both sources are integrated. In the present task, the auditory and visual sources are completely unambiguous and they always agree with one another in the bimodal condition. Subjects are also instructed to respond as quickly as possible. Thus, although integration may still have occurred, it might not be observed in the RTs because subjects could initiate a response based on evaluation of just a single dimension whether or not integration of the two dimensions was complete.

1.1 Statistical Facilitation

Our question is whether the auditory and visual sources are evaluated independently of one another. A central concept for the present test is that of statistical facilitation, and it is informative to trace quickly the discovery of this concept. Hershenson (1962) measured detection RTs to simple visual and auditory stimuli. He found that subjects averaged 120 msec to the visual and 160 msec to the auditory signal. Earlier, Todd (1912) found that when a combined visual-auditory stimulus was presented, the latency was equal to the latency for the faster of the two. Hershenson confirmed this result and also presented observers with a combined stimulus event in which the auditory signal followed the visual signal after various intervals. He reasoned that in the absence of any auditory-visual interaction, the RT should be an increasing linear function of the delay of the auditory signal. The RT should asymptote at 160 msec, when the auditory signal lagged the visual by 40 msec. As can be seen in Figure 2, the RT was faster than predicted. Thus it seemed that when the two sources were brought into physiological synchrony (Hilgard, 1933) some sort of intersensory facilitation was taking place. This finding was in agreement with another by Todd (1912), who found that the latency to a joint auditory-shock stimulus was faster than the approximately equal RTs for the two component stimuli.

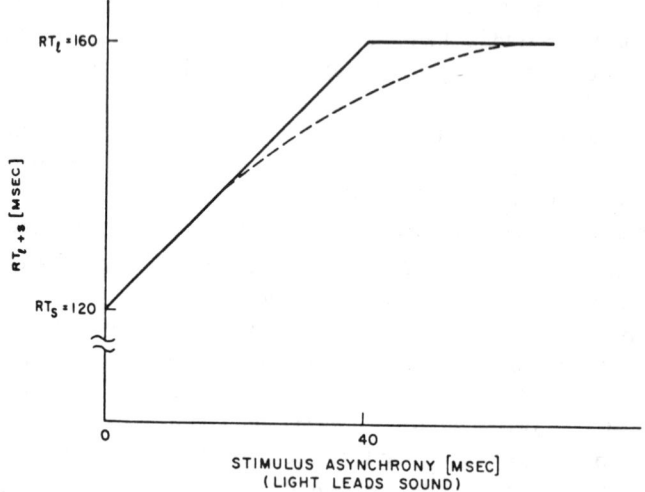

Figure 2. Observed (dashed line) RT to an auditory-visual signal as a function of the stimulus onset asynchrony between the light and sound. The solid line gives the predicted RT given independence and if no variance in the RTs is assumed (after Raab, 1962).

A number of studies have shown that this facilitation effect occurs for both simple-RT (did something occur?) and choice-RT (identify the stimulus as one of several possible events) paradigms (Bernstein, Clark, & Edelstein, 1969a, 1969b; Bernstein & Edelstein, 1971; Morrell, 1968). Although these results seem to indicate some kind of dependence between the two channels, Raab (1962) illustrated that the facilitation might be only statistical and not sensory. His proposal was the first horse-race model that acknowledged variability in the finishing times of the independent horses in the race. The empirical basis for this idea is the simple fact that the mean RT to a given stimulus is based on a distribution of RTs. Given both auditory and visual signals on a given trial, the subject can respond as soon as either of them is detected. There will be a distribution of RTs corresponding to the visual signal and an independent distribution corresponding to the auditory signal. If the two distributions overlap, the mean RT to the bimodal trials with both auditory and visual signals will necessarily be faster than the mean RT to either the auditory or visual trials. On bimodal trials, some of the longer auditory RTs will be replaced by some of the shorter visual RTs, and analogously for the longer visual RTs. Using a vacuum tube analog with normal latency distributions, Raab showed that the degree of facilitation is directly related to the degree of overlap of the two distributions, as illustrated in Figure 3.

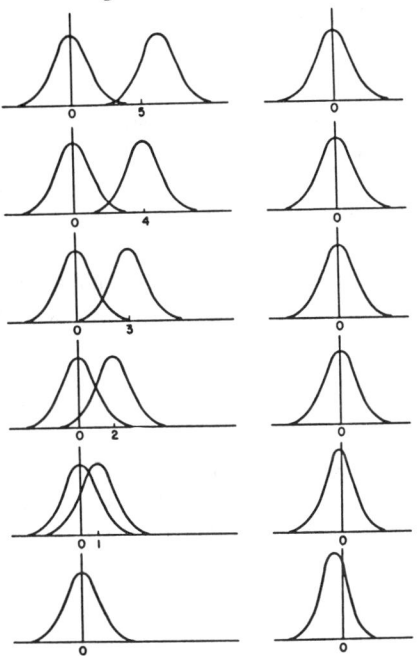

Figure 3. Illustration of horse-race model in which the degree of facilitation predicted for the RT to the joint occurrence of two stimuli is positively related to the overlap in the two distributions of RTs to the stimuli presented separately (after Raab, 1962).

Mathematically, the predicted minima distribution resulting from auditory and visual distributions is given by

$$M(t) = a(t) \int_t^\infty v(t)dt + v(t) \int_t^\infty a(t)dt \qquad (1)$$

$M(t)$ defines the predicted probability density at time t. The values $a(t)$ and

$v(t)$ correspond to the probability densities at the time t for the auditory and visual distributions, respectively. What this equation says is that the subject responds according to the auditory distribution to the extent that the visual takes longer, and to the visual to the extent that the auditory takes longer. This model provided a nice fit to the Hershenson (1962) data.

Given that actual latency distributions do not exactly follow a normal distribution, a modification of the minima formula has been suggested by Gielen, Schmidt, and Van den Heuvel (1983). Rather than using theoretical normal distributions, Gielen et al. used the actual distributions of the component latencies to the individual signals to compute the minima function:

$$M(t) = a(t)\sum_{j=t}^{\infty} v(j) + v(t)\sum_{j=t}^{\infty} a(j) \qquad (2)$$

In their experiments, Gielen et al. found some very small but significant facilitation effects not accounted for by statistical facilitation. The advantage of the RT to bimodal stimuli over that predicted by statistical facilitation was 12 msec for visual-auditory stimuli and 13 msec for visual-kinesthetic stimuli. A modification of the calculation of Gielen et al. will be used to evaluate whether statistical facilitation can account for any facilitation effects found with speech. The modification of the Gielen et al. (1983) formulation is necessary because the discrete form requires that the cross product of the two terms $a(t)$ and $v(t)$ be subtracted in the computation of $M(t)$

$$M(t) = a(t)\sum_{j=t}^{\infty} v(j) + v(t)\sum_{j=t}^{\infty} a(j) - a(t)v(t) \qquad (3)$$

If this prediction cannot account for the results, we must look to explanations which assume some form of interaction in the perceptual processing of auditory and visual information in speech perception. If statistical facilitation is sufficient, we cannot reject the independence of the auditory and visual sources at feature evaluation.

1.2 Experimental Test

To implement the test of independence, the observed distribution of RTs to auditory, visual, and bimodal test signals will be computed. The test will determine whether the visual and auditory RTs can predict the bimodal RT, as given by Equation 3. Consider a t value of 200 msec in the computation of the predicted $M(t)$. The first term of Equation 3 is equal to the probability of an auditory RT of 200 msec times the probability of a visual RT equal to or greater than 200 msec. The second term is exactly analogous to the first except that the visual and auditory components are reversed. The third term is the cross product of the probabilities of visual and auditory RTs of 200 msec. To clarify the equation, assume that

$$a(t) = .1, \quad \sum_{j=t}^{\infty} v(j) = .7, \quad v(t) = .2, \quad \sum_{j=t}^{\infty} a(j) = .8$$

Equation 3 would give

$$M(t) = .1 \times .7 + .2 \times .8 - .1 \times .2 = .07 + .16 - .02 = .21$$

The predicted probability density for this value of t is greater than the values of .1 and .2 given by the two component distributions. Given this result, the predicted mean RT computed from $M(t)$ can differ from the mean RTs of the two component distributions. The question for the test of independence is whether the mean RT computed from $M(t)$ using the RTs from the auditory and visual trials will differ from the observed mean RT on bimodal trials.

1.2.1 Method

Subjects. Ten subjects were recruited from an introductory psychology class. They were given extra course credit for their participation. One subject was excluded from the data analysis due to excessively long RTs.

Stimuli. Prior to the experiment, a videotape was prepared for presentation of the visual speech information and synchronization of the auditory information. The videotape was identical to that used in the Massaro and Cohen (1983c, Experiment 2) study. This videotape is identical to that described in the experiment on open-ended responses in Chapter 3 except that it is monochromatic rather than color. The two auditory stimuli for the experiment were the endpoints of the synthetic /ba/ to /da/ continuum. For the auditory /ba/, the F2 started at 1000 Hz and followed a negatively accelerated path to 1199 Hz. The F2 started at 2000 Hz for /da/. The F3 followed a linear transition to 2729 Hz for /ba/ and 3200 Hz for /da/. The resulting stimuli, quantized at a 10000 sample per second rate were stored on the computer disk for later presentation.

Procedure. All experimental events were controlled by a DEC PDP-11/34a computer. The synthetic speech was filtered 20-4900 Hz, amplified (McIntosh MC50), and presented over Grason Stadler TDH-50 headphones at a comfortable listening level (77 dB-A measured with a B & K 4134 microphone in B & K 4153 artificial ear). SONY 11 in monitors were used for presentation of the visual portion of the videotape.

Each trial of the experiment was either a visual (V), auditory (A), or visual plus auditory (VA) trial. On V trials, no auditory stimulus was presented. Type A trials were those for which no visual articulation was recorded on the videotape. On VA trials both a visual articulation and a consistent auditory stimulus were presented. The type of trial (A, V, or VA) was selected randomly with replacement, and there were about 99 of each type out of 297 total experimental trials. For each type of trial about half were /ba/ and half /da/. Preceding the experimental trials, a partial block of 10 practice trials was presented, for a total of 307 stimuli.

The presentation of the synthetic speech was synchronized with the original audio track on the videotape by schmidt trigger (Chapter 3, Section 2.1). When the original audio channel on the videotape exceeded a preset threshold, one of the 400 msec CV syllables was played. The subjects had 1000 msec to make their response by pressing adjacent buttons labeled "B" or "D" on their keyboards followed by a 1.75 sec inter-trial interval. For half of the subjects, the "B" button was to the left of the "D" button. For the other half of the subjects, the position of the two buttons was reversed. The subjects were instructed to rest their right index finger on the right button and their left index finger on the left button, and to respond with these fingers.

Each subject was instructed in part: "On some trials, you will see and hear the speaker say the sound, on some trials you will see the speaker say a sound but no audio will be presented, and on some other trials, a sound will be presented but the speaker will not move his mouth. On all types of trials, you are simply to indicate whether the speaker said /ba/ or /da/. Please respond as quickly as possible, without making too many errors."

1.2.2 Results

The mean RT for the 9 subjects was 598 msec and the mean accuracy was 97.1% correct. As expected, the bimodal condition was significantly faster than either of the unimodal conditions. RTs averaged 626, 612, and 555 msec for V, A, and VA trials, respectively. Accuracy also varied significantly as a function of presentation condition, with averages of 94.7, 98.1, and 98.4% correct responses for V, A, and VA trials, respectively.

Table 1. Mean RT (msec) as a function of presentation condition and stimulus identity with the F statistic and significance level (p) for stimulus identity comparisons within presentation condition. Also given are the mean predictions (Min) of the minima formula of statistical facilitation (Equation 3).

Condition	/b/	/d/	$F(1,8)$	p
V	578	673	78.4	<.001
A	623	601	1.9	ns
VA	537	573	6.1	.038
Min	526	557	8.4	.019

The mean RTs for /ba/ responses (580 msec) were faster than those for /da/ responses (616 msec). Identification accuracy of /b/ stimuli (98.0%) was higher than for /d/ stimuli (96.1%). For both RT and accuracy, the interaction of presentation condition with stimulus identity was statistically significant. Table 1 gives the mean RT as a function of presentation condition and stimulus identity. The largest difference as a function of stimulus identity was in the V presentation condition. For the V condition, the responses to a /ba/ were significantly faster than to /da/, and more accurate (97.6 vs. 91.7%). In contrast, RT and accuracy to /ba/ and /da/ were not significantly different in the A condition. In VA condition, the response to a /ba/ was faster than to a /da/.

1.2.3 Test of Statistical Facilitation

Given the interaction of stimulus identity (/ba/ vs /da/) with presentation condition (A, V, or AV) it is necessary to test for statistical facilitation separately for /ba/ and /da/ responses. For each subject and for each response alternative, the unimodal RTs were used to derive the predicted minima distribution using Equation 3. The correct RTs were ordered in msec steps for the analysis to obtain the highest resolution in the predictions. The mean predicted bimodal RTs computed from the predicted minima distribution given Equation 3 are given in Table 1. Figure 4 gives the predicted and observed distributions for one of the 9 subjects for the two response alternatives.

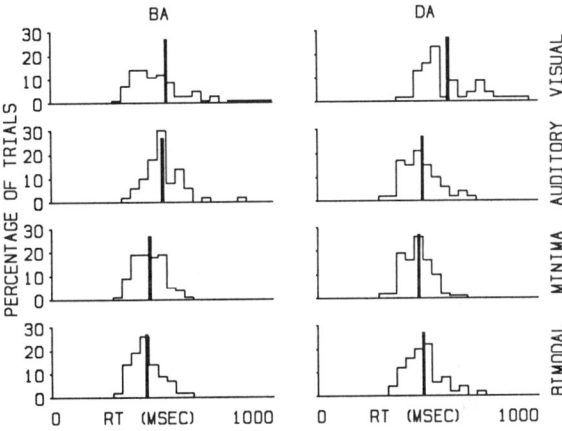

Figure 4. Distribution of RTs for a typical subject for the /ba/ and /da/ response alternatives to visual alone, auditory alone, and bimodal speech events. The minima distribution is that predicted by Equation 3 for bimodal trials based on the auditory alone and visual alone trials. The vertical bar gives the mean RT.

An analysis of variance was carried out on the predicted versus observed values with the response alternatives /ba/ and /da/ included as a factor in the design. The analysis revealed no significant differences between the predicted and observed values (555 vs 542 msec) and no interaction with the two response alternatives. Thus, we have strong evidence that subjects evaluated the two sources independently of one another and were able to initiate a response as soon as one of the sources was evaluated. There is no evidence for dependence (either facilitatory or inhibitory) in the processing of a bimodal speech event relative to the corresponding unimodal speech events.

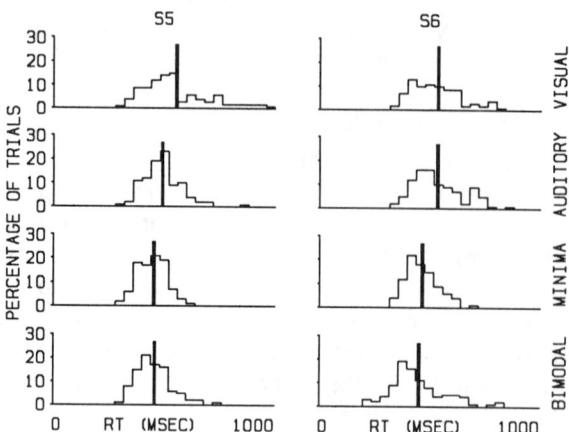

Figure 5. Distribution of RTs for two subjects to visual alone, auditory alone, and bimodal speech events. The minima distribution is that predicted by Equation 3 for bimodal trials based on the auditory alone and visual alone trials. The vertical bar gives the mean RT.

Figure 5 gives the distributions of RTs for two subjects pooled across the two response alternatives. As can be seen in the figure, the subjects are somewhat faster to the bimodal relative to the auditory and visual speech events but no faster than expected if the subject simply begins to initiate a response when either the auditory or visual dimension is evaluated. The advantage of bimodal trials can be accounted for simply in terms of the variability of the processing times along each dimension allowing the average RT to bimodal events to be shorter than to either dimension presented alone. These results also do not contradict the earlier conclusion that the two sources of information are integrated for perceptual recognition.

A recent analysis of Ulrich and Giray (1986) indicates that variance in some process that follows evaluation of the two sources makes it more difficult to reject the assumption of dependence. Independence might still be the case even if the RTs to the bimodal speech events are somewhat slower than the RTs predicted by statistical facilitation. Even with this possibility, however, the RT paradigm offers a potentially powerful technique to assess the independence or dependence of sources of information in perception.

2. Testing Independence and Dependence Models

Massaro and Cohen (1983c) formulated independence and dependence models of the perception of bimodal speech. The independence model was formalized in terms of the FLMP, because a central assumption of the model is the independent evaluations of the auditory and visual sources. In addition, we now have provided additional evidence for integration and the continuous nature of the sources, two other important assumptions of the model. We have a more valid test of the independence assumption to the extent that the other assumptions of the model are correct.

2.1 A Dependence Model

The test of the independence assumption can be viewed as equivalent to a test of the FLMP. On the other hand, it is very difficult to formalize and test a dependence model unless a particular type of dependence between the sources is specified exactly. If no type of dependence is assumed, it is necessary to estimate a unique parameter for each unique set of experimental conditions. In this case, the dependence model would require as many parameters as there are independent conditions. This violation of parsimony might be sufficient for some to reject the dependence model as a meaningful description of performance. Rather than rejecting it without test, however, two tests of the dependence hypothesis are considered. If the contribution of one source is dependent on the value of the other, any model assuming independent contributions of each source must fail. To the extent that the independence model gives an adequate description of the results, we have evidence against the hypothesis.

A second test is to assume a particular form of dependence. Massaro and Cohen (1977) manipulated two dimensions that would not seem to qualify as independent sources of information in speech perception. The duration and intensity of the fundamental frequency during the onset of fricative-vowel syllables were varied, and subjects judged the test syllables along a /zi/ to /si/ continuum. Five levels of intensity were combined with five levels of duration giving a set of 25 test syllables. We might expect that both intensity and duration would combine before feature evaluation to give a higher-order feature representing the degree to which energy is present at the fundamental.

Following the summation of duration and intensity in hearing, we might expect that the two properties would combine multiplicatively. In this case, we would be able to describe quantitatively the effect of the two dimensions even though they are dependent. The feature value v_{ij}, representing the degree of voicing, would be a multiplicative function of both duration d_i and intensity i_j,

$$v_{ij} = d_i i_j \tag{4}$$

where v_{ij} reflects dependence on both duration level i and intensity level j. We allow the estimation of subjective values of duration and intensity for the test of dependence model and represent them by the lowercase d and i.

The dependence model was fit to the Massaro and Cohen (1977, Experiment 1) study. As can be seen in Figure 6, the model gave a good description of the individual judgments of fricative voicing. The description given by dependence was better than the predictions given by the independence FLMP. It is encouraging that we are able to reject the independence model in a situation in which dependence seems more appropriate.

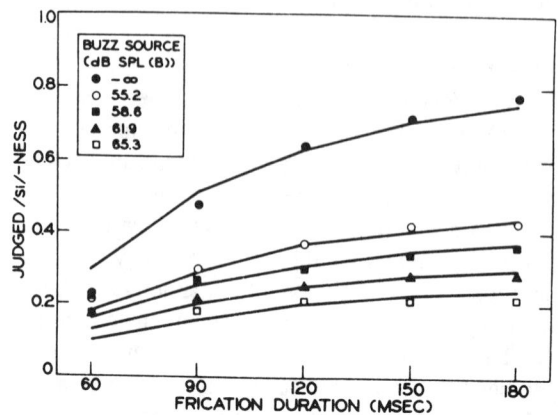

Figure 6. Observed judged /si/-ness (points) as a function of the duration of the frication period and the intensity of the buzz source simulating vocal cord vibration during the frication period. The lines give the predictions of the dependence model.

The multiplicative dependence relationship found for duration and intensity might be appropriate to describe a dependence relationship between the auditory and visual sources. This dependence relationship can be viewed within the context of the FLMP. In contrast to the independence assumption of separate auditory and visual values defining a prototype in memory, the prototype is defined in terms of a single global feature defined by the dependence relationship between the auditory and visual sources. The prototype for /da/ is

/da/ : (Slightly falling F2-F3 x Open Lips) = (a_{ij})

where a_{ij} is the product of the auditory and visual sources:

$a_{ij} = a_i \, v_j$.

Given one integral source, the prototype description for /ba/ is equal to one minus the prototype for /da/

/ba/ : 1 - (Slightly falling F2-F3 x Open Lips) = 1 - (a_{ij})

This dependence formalization assumes that only a single, multiplicatively combined (dependent) feature is available for prototype matching. It is important that this model has the same potential predictive power as does the independence FLMP, because the same number of free parameters are estimated for each model.

Massaro and Cohen (1983c, Experiment 2) tested the dependence model against the individual results of the seven subjects. The experiment involved identification of bimodal syllables generated by the factorial combination of visual /ba/, neutral, or /da/ with nine levels along an auditory synthetic speech /ba/ - /da/ continuum. The results in Figure 7 permit an unqualified rejection of this form of dependence in the perception of bimodal speech. The average RMSD value was .112, significantly larger than the RMSD value of .058 for the independence FLMP. Until some other form of dependence is demonstrated to give an adequate description of the results, we reject dependence in favor of independent evaluation of auditory and visual dimensions in perception of bimodal speech.

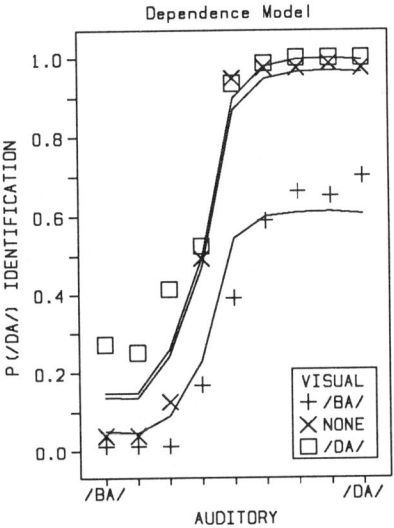

Figure 7. Observed proportion of /da/ identifications (points) as a function of the auditory and visual dimensions of the speech syllable. The lines give the predictions of the dependence model (after Massaro & Cohen, 1983c, Experiment 2).

2.2 Understanding Categorization

The issue of independence is central to how one hopes to understand categorization as a function of multiple sources of information. If the sources of information can be considered to be independently available at some stage of processing, then describing the perceptual judgment in terms of some combination of the separate sources is a possible goal. If the sources are not independently available, then such a description might not be feasible; dependence implies that each combination of sources is unique and is not easily described in terms of values from the separate sources. Some description might be possible if the exact form of dependence were known as, for example, in the Purkinje effect. Our perception of hue as a function of wavelength changes with overall illumination and thus wavelength and illumination cannot be considered independent dimensions to color perception. Given that the Purkinje effect is probably a direct result of sensory processes, the dependence might be relatively easy to formalize. Therefore, a parsimonious description of perception of color as a function of wavelength and illumination would be possible. For more complicated domains, it appears that it will be easier to describe the necessary integration process if the two sources are independent at some stage of processing.

3. Expanded Factorial Design

A strong prediction of independence is that the information provided by a source of information remains invariant with the addition or deletion of other sources of information. A direct test of this prediction can be made by employing the expanded factorial design illustrated in Figure 2 in Chapter 3. Subjects are asked to identify speech events consisting of just sound, just sight, or both audible and visible speech dimensions. The auditory event is chosen from a synthetic speech continuum between /ba/ and /da/. The visual event is a view of the speaker articulating /ba/ or /da/. The bimodal speech events are made by a factorial combination of the auditory and visual events. The FLMP assumes that the auditory and visual dimensions are evaluated independently of one another in parallel as long as attention is directed at the complete speech event. Identification judgments of both unimodal and bimodal speech can provide a much stronger test of independence than a test based on only bimodal speech. The reason for this can be illustrated in the derivation of the predicted judgments for the auditory-alone and visual-alone trials and how these predictions relate to those given for bimodal speech.

The predictions will be derived for the situation with /ba/ and /da/ response alternatives. Given an auditory speech event, the featural evaluation stage determines the degree to which /ba/ is supported and analogously for /da/. Using fuzzy truth values, a value between zero and one is assigned indicating the degree to which the auditory information supports /da/. The support for /ba/ would simply be one minus the support for /da/ given the definition for negation in fuzzy logic. Given the pattern classification operation based on relative truth values (Luce, 1959: Oden & Massaro, 1978), the probability of a /da/ decision given an auditory event A_i is equal to

$$P(/da/ \mid A_i) = \frac{a_i}{a_i + (1 - a_i)} = a_i \tag{5}$$

Following the same logic, we derive an exactly analogous description for the recognition of a visual speech event V_j

$$P(/da/ \mid V_j) = \frac{v_j}{v_j + (1 - v_j)} = v_j \qquad (6)$$

In both cases, the probability of a given decision is predicted to be equal to the truth value of the relevant variable.

Applying the model to the bimodal task with both auditory and visual speech, both sources are assumed to provide independent evidence for the alternatives /ba/ and /da/. Defining the important auditory cue as the onsets of the second and third formants and the important visual cue as lip closure, the prototypes for /da/ and /ba/ are defined as

/da/:   Slightly falling F2-F3 & Open lips
/ba/:   Rising F2-F3 & Closed lips

where F2-F3 represent the onsets of the second and third formants. Given a prototype's independent specifications for the auditory and visual sources, the value of one source cannot change the value of the other source at the prototype matching stage. Using the definition of negation, we can represent Rising F2-F3 as (1 - Slightly falling F2-F3) and Closed lips as (1 - Open lips).

/da/:   Slightly falling F2-F3 & Open lips
/ba/:   (1 - Slightly falling F2-F3) & (1 - Open lips)

The integration of the features defining each prototype can be represented by the product of the feature values. If a_i represents the degree to which the auditory source A_i has Slightly falling F2-F3 and v_j represents the degree to which the visual source V_j has Open lips, the outcome of prototype matching would be

/da/: $a_i \, v_j$
/ba/: $(1 - a_i)\,(1 - v_j)$.

If these two prototypes are the only valid response alternatives, the pattern classification operation determines their relative merit leading to the prediction that

$$P(/da/ \mid A_i V_j) = \frac{a_i \, v_j}{a_i \, v_j + (1 - a_i)(1 - v_j)} \qquad (7)$$

It should be noted that identical predictions are made for the unimodal conditions if auditory and visual information is integrated with respect to prototypes as in the bimodal condition. It is reasonable that the missing source of information would be assigned the ambiguous truth value of .5. Inserting .5 for either a_i or v_j in Equation 7 gives predictions identical to Equations 5 and 6, respectively.

In terms of the independence assumption of the model, the featural value given a particular level of one source is identical in the unimodal and bimodal conditions. That is, the degree of /da/-ness given by a visual /da/ is identical when the visual information is presented alone for lipreading and when it is combined with auditory speech. This assumption also provides a more challenging test of the model, given that a larger number of observations is predicted with the same number of parameters relative to just the bimodal speech task. Given 2 visual levels crossed with 9 auditory levels, we have 18 stimulus conditions with just bimodal speech and 29 stimulus conditions when the auditory-alone and visual-alone conditions are included. In both cases, 11 parameters would be required, giving an observations-to-parameters ratio of 29 to 11 in the expanded factorial design, compared to only 18 to 11 in the simple factorial design.

3.1 Experimental Test

To test the independence assumption of the FLMP, subjects identified auditory-alone, visual-alone, and bimodal speech events as described in the experiment on open-ended responses (Chapter 3, Section 2). Recall that the subjects were instructed to look at the television monitor, listen to the speaker and decide what the speaker said on each trial. Given nine levels along the auditory continuum and two levels long the visual continuum, the predictions of the FLMP require eleven parameters (nine a_i values and two v_j values). Thus, the model predicts the nine auditory-alone conditions, the two visual-alone conditions, and the eighteen bimodal conditions for a total of twenty-nine independent observations with eleven free parameters for each response alternative.

There were eight valid response alternatives /ba/, /da/, /bda/, /dba/, /va/, /ða/, /ga/, and "other". Thus we have 29 times 8 minus 29 or 203 independent observations predicted by 11 times 8 or 88 parameters. The reason that the number of independent observations is reduced by 29 is that the response probabilities must add to one. Given seven response probabilities to a particular stimulus, the eighth is completely determined. What is most relevant for independence is that the same truth value is given a particular level of a dimension at the feature evaluation stage in both the unimodal and bimodal condition.

3.1.1 Results

Figure 8 gives the observed results averaged across subjects. For the predictions of the model, the number of prototypes was increased from two to eight, one for each response alternative. Also, there were no constraints among the estimated truth values so, for example, auditory /ba/-ness was not necessarily equal to one minus auditory /da/-ness. Each of the seven phonetic prototypes was permitted a unique truth value representing the auditory support for that alternative and a unique truth value representing the visual support for that alternative. For example, the prototypes for /bda/ and /ga/ would be

/bda/: auditory /bda/-ness & visual /bda/-ness
/ga/: auditory /ga/-ness & visual /ga/-ness

and so on for all eight alternatives.

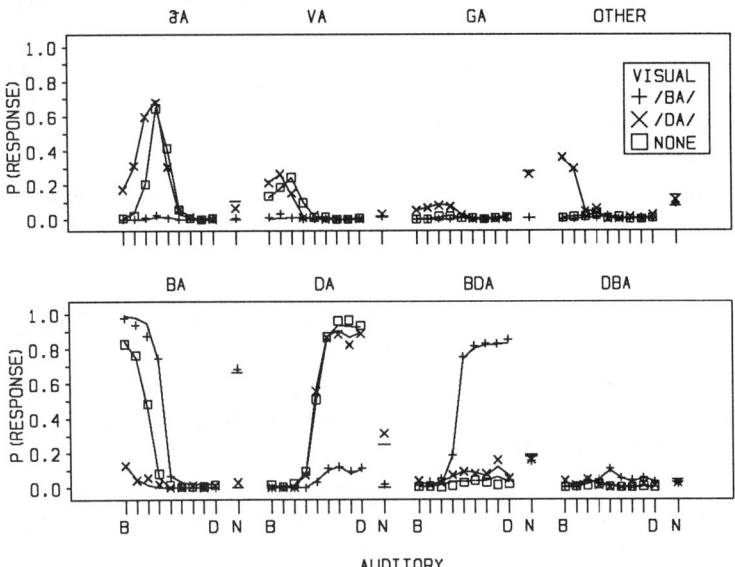

Figure 8. Observed (points) and predicted (lines) proportion of identifications for the eight response alternatives as a function of the auditory and visual dimensions for the auditory, visual, and bimodal syllables. The predictions are for the FLMP assuming independence between the auditory and visual sources.

The model was fit to the results of each of the individual subjects. Figure 8 also gives the predicted results averaged across subjects. As can be seen in the figure, the model provides a good description of the results. This result is probably the most impressive model fit to date because it is predicting an essentially open ended set of response alternatives with the assumption of identical information for the unimodal and bimodal speech events.

4. Adaptation to Unimodal and Bimodal Syllables

Converging evidence for the independence of auditory and visual information in speech perception comes from something completely different. The Roberts and Summerfield (1981) study was formalized in terms of whether selective adaptation in auditory speech perception is purely auditory, but their results also speak to the issue of independence of the auditory and visual information. The authors performed an ingenious marriage between the selective adaptation paradigm and the McGurk effect. Selective adaptation was the focus of much research in speech perception for the decade or so after its introduction to the speech community by Eimas and Corbit (1973). Listeners are exposed to a number of repetitions of an adapting syllable and are tested on a speech continuum between two speech categories (Ades, 1977). Relative to the baseline condition of no adaptation, the identification judgments of syllables along the speech continuum are pushed in the opposite direction of the adapting syllable. As an example, adaptation with the syllable /be/ (rhymes with say) decreases the number of /be/ judgments and increases the number of /de/ judgments along a /be/-/de/ synthetic speech continuum.

Roberts and Summerfield (1981) employed 7 different adaptors to evaluate the contribution of auditory and visual information to auditory adaptation along a /be/ to /de/ continuum. The adaptors were auditory /be/ and /de/, visual /be/ and /de/, audiovisual /be/ and /de/, and an auditory /be/ paired with a visual /ge/. (It should be noted that visual /ge/ and /de/ are essentially indistinguishable and similar results would be found with visual /de/ or visual /ge/.) If auditory and visual speech make available independent sources of information, then auditory adaptation should be only a function of the auditory characteristics of the adaptor and independent of its visual characteristics.

This is exactly the result that obtained when subjects were tested on an auditory continuum between /be/ and /de/. Equivalent levels of adaptation were found for an auditory adaptor and a bimodal adaptor with the same phonetic information. The visual adaptors presented alone produced no adaptation along the auditory continuum. The most impressive result, however, was the adaptation obtained with the conflicting bimodal adaptor. The adaptor auditory /be/ paired with visual /ge/ produced adaptation equivalent to the auditory adaptor /be/. This result occurred even though the subjects usually experienced the bimodal adaptor as /de/. Thus, the adaptation followed the auditory information and was not influenced by the visual information and the phenomenal experience of the bimodal syllable. Although the experiment is very convincing, it would be informative to provide a similar assessment of adaptation along a visual continuum as a function of the auditory, visual, and phenomenal properties of the adapting stimuli. The requirement for such a study is to generate a visual continuum between two contrasting speech categories, given that adaptation occurs primarily in the ambiguous range of a continuum. Perhaps visual animations similar to those used by Walden et al. (1984) would be sufficient for this test.

Interactive-Activation Models

The outcome of the binary contrast assessing independence at the evaluation of audible and visible sources of information in speech perception contradicts a fundamental assumption of TRACE, an interactive-activation model of speech perception (McClelland & Elman, 1986). Three levels of units are used in TRACE: feature, phoneme, and word. The interaction among the units involves both activation and inhibition. Features activate phonemes which activate words, and activation of some units at a particular level inhibits other units at the same level. In terms of the present contrast, dependence is assumed in that activation of higher-order units activates their lower-order units; for example, activation of the /b/ phoneme would activate the feature voiced. Given bimodal speech, the model predicts that visible speech activating /b/ would result in top-down activation of the audible features of /b/, contrary to our observations of the independence of the features of audible and visible speech. This falsification of the TRACE model appears to be significant and not easily remedied because top-down activation from phoneme to feature played one of the essential roles in predicting a variety of results in speech perception (McClelland & Elman, 1986).

6. Introspective Reports

Analogous to the perceiver's incorrect impression of categorical perception (see Chapters 4 and 5), we experience a dependence between the auditory and visual dimensions of speech. Liberman's (1982) quote in Chapter 5 best captures the impression that sight and sound are mutually dependent upon one another and we do not evaluate one property independently of the other. The experience can be misleading, however, because we might not have introspective access to the result of feature evaluation, but only to the outcome of integration. It might be instructive to consider the relation between processing and introspection in another domain to convince the reader that the current discrepancy between underlying process and phenomenal experience is not unique to the perception of speech by eye and ear.

6.1 Person Impression

Independent evidence exposing the limits of introspective reports involves verbal protocols given during impression formation. When subjects form impressions of persons described by lists of personality traits, they report that their interpretation of the meaning of a particular adjective depends on its interrelations with the other adjectives (Asch, 1946). After a review of research, Anderson (1981, p. 218) concludes: "Evidently, conscious report is not a reliable guide to psychological truth." The reason for this conclusion is that the person impression judgments are described adequately without any need to assume a change of meaning of the adjectives. In a seminal experiment, for example,

Anderson (1962) illustrated that adjectives have fixed, constant meanings regardless of the other adjectives with which they are combined. Judgments of likeableness can be described by a simple combination of the likeableness values of each of the adjectives in the list. It is not necessary to assume that the value given the adjective *intelligent* will change when paired with *polite* rather than *blunt*.

It is also of interest to ask why the introspections are what they are, even though they are unreliable. Nisbett and Wilson (1977) claim that people have implicit causal theories about how stimuli influence responses and these theories are incorrect. It is only coincidental when introspections are found to agree with the actual processes involved. Introspective reports are more appropriately evaluated as behavioral data to be explained rather than as explanations or theories of psychological processes. Given two decades of ingenious research supporting meaning-constancy, it is disconcerting to find social scientists ignoring or forgetting the empirical results and falling back on their introspections when they discuss person impression and social cognition. A similar observation and caveat applies to speech perception.

Chapter 7: Additive, Minimization, or Multiplicative Integration

The binary contrasts up to this point have provided evidence for the integration of independent and continuous sources of information in bimodal speech perception. The issue addressed in the current chapter concerns the nature of the integration process. Without a doubt, this question is the most difficult to answer primarily because of its intricate dependence on quantitative models and tests (Falmagne, 1985). Background on the nature of testing integration rules is provided because the question is a relatively novel one, not only for speech perception, but pattern identification in any domain. Our goal is to provide a reasonable foundation for testing various integration rules given multiple sources of continuous information. We consider three classes of integration rules: additive, minimization, and multiplication. The first class has been most successfully applied in the area of person impression. The latter two classes are based on theoretical work in the field of fuzzy sets.

Another important issue in the present chapter involves the pattern classification operation assumed by the FLMP. It is a fact of life that integration rules usually are not directly observable. If they were, the solution to the integration-rule question would be much easier to obtain. After information is integrated, the outcome must be transformed to some judgment demanded by the experimental or natural situation. This transformation is described by the relative goodness rule of the pattern classification operation in the FLMP. We will evaluate some evidence relevant to both the nature of the integration rule and the pattern classification operation from situations in which supposedly only one of the processes is functional. These situations offer a potential insight into each of the processes without the potential confounding of the other.

1. Integration in Person Perception

In a seminal study, Anderson (1962) initiated a methodological and theoretical framework for the study of person impression. Methodologically, a factorial design was used to vary independently descriptive adjectives of a hypothetical person. Anderson used 3 factors with three levels along each factor, giving a total of 3^3 or 27 unique combinations. A subject was tested repeatedly on each of the 27 unique descriptions presented in a random order. The three levels along each factor contained adjectives of high, medium, and low "likeableness" value. On a given trial, a subject might judge a hypothetical person who was *good-natured*, *unsophisticated*, and *tactful*. The judgments involved a 20-point rating along a scale between likeable and dislikeable. Analysis of variance was performed on the judgments of individual subjects to assess the contribution of each factor and any interaction among the factors. As expected, there were large effects of "likeableness" value for each factor but, surprisingly, there was no interaction among the factors for nine of the twelve subjects. The interaction for the other three subjects was relatively small and accounted for very little of the variance.

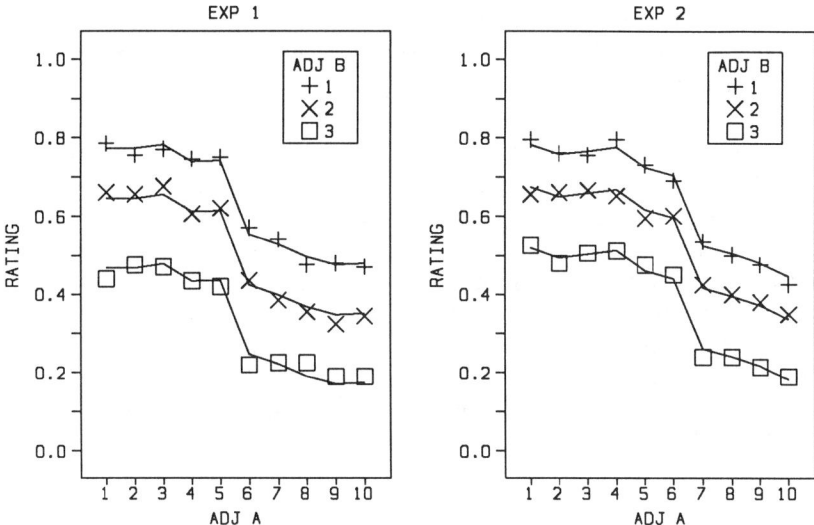

Figure 1. Rating judgments of social desirability of hypothetical persons described by two adjectives (after Anderson, 1973). The observations are given by the points and the lines give the predictions of an additive (or averaging) model.

Figure 1 gives the results of a later experiment involving judgments of social desirability of hypothetical persons described by two adjectives (Anderson, 1973). The combination of two factors with 3 and 10 levels, respectively, gives 30 unique judgments. Subjects made their judgments on a 20-cm. rating scale between desirable and undesirable. The ratings were transformed into values between zero and one, assuming distance as an interval measure between desirable and undesirable. As can be seen in the figure, the two variables have significant effects but do not interact. The parallel curves provide evidence consistent with the idea of an additive combination of the evaluations of the two adjectives. In addition, the evaluation of one adjective remains independent of the evaluation of the other.

Theoretically, Anderson's work made viable a highly parsimonious description of personality impression. Contrary to previous descriptions within the Gestalt tradition (Asch, 1946), each adjective appeared to make a consistent contribution to the overall impression. The contribution of an adjective to the judgment could be considered to be independent of the other adjectives in the description. *Good-natured* contributes to the likeableness of a person by the same amount regardless of whether the person is also described as *unsophisticated* or as *tactful*. There is no contextual change of meaning of the adjectives, as had been assumed since the studies of Asch (1946). The value of *good-natured* in no manner depends on the other adjectives defining the hypothetical person. Furthermore, the additive results imply that the likeableness value of an adjective does not change the weight given that adjective during the integration process.

1.1 Adding versus Averaging

The additive results, such as those shown in Figure 1, are consistent with two alternative integration rules. Subjects might simply add the likeableness of each adjective, or they might average them. In the many experiments to follow, Anderson was able to distinguish between adding and averaging rules for the integration of the component adjectives. By varying the number of adjectives forming the description, Anderson (1965) demonstrated that averaging rather than adding seems to be the rule. The adding rule predicts that providing additional medium positive adjectives should increase the likeableness of a very likeable person, whereas averaging predicts a neutralizing effect of the additional adjectives. This latter result has been obtained (Anderson, 1965).

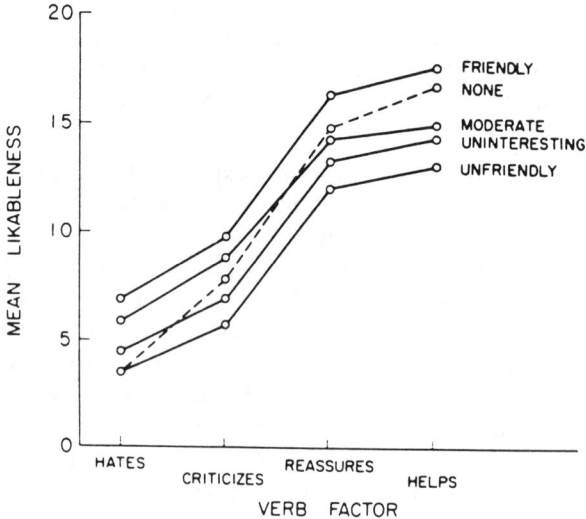

Figure 2. The average likeableness of a man described by a personality trait (curve parameter) and a characteristic behavior (verb factor) toward other people (after Anderson, 1981).

Anderson (1974) provided a second critical test between adding and averaging by adding another condition to the standard factorial design. Subjects judged the likeableness of a man described by a personality trait and a characteristic behavior toward other people. The results of the two-factor design gave roughly parallel curves as predicted by either adding or averaging (see Figure 2). A test between these two possibilities was devised by also asking the same subjects to judge the man's likeableness given only a characteristic behavior toward other people. The judgments in this condition are given by the points labeled "none" in Figure 2. As reasoned by Anderson (1974), the relationship between the "none" curve and the "moderate" curve eliminates the adding model. If adding were the rule, then the "moderate" curve should lie above the "none" curve at all levels of the verb factor. Providing additional positive information should increase likeableness given an adding rule. However, adding only moderate positive information to a very positive trait lowered likeableness, which is consistent with an averaging rule. The advice to job candidates, given this result and interpretation, is that padding a vita with mediocre contributions might tarnish an otherwise positive record.

Anderson's research paradigm in the hands of Anderson, colleagues, and students led to the development of a substantial body of literature on the cognitive algebra of information integration (Anderson, 1981; 1982). The foundation of all of the work is the important assumption that the final judgment is some combination of the individual components made available by the stimulus set. Various combination rules have been demonstrated in a variety of domains. Anderson and Shanteau (1970) found that a multiplying rule best described the judgments of the personal value of lottery tickets, given the likelihood of winning and the amount to be won. Lopes (1976) discovered that subjects estimated the probability of a poker hand beating two opponent hands to be roughly equal to the multiplication of the separate estimates of beating each of the two hands. In situations involving multiple sources of information defining some attribute such as likeableness, social desirability, or preference, however, an averaging rule has received the most support (Anderson, 1981).

2. Averaging Integration Rule

The averaging rule derived from the domain of personality impression is a viable and intuitively plausible candidate for bimodal speech perception. Given continuous and independent evidence from the auditory and visual sources, the perceiver might simply average the two sources of evidence and classify or rate the speech event on the basis of the computed average. The averaging rule can be implemented either directly (relatively atheoretically) or within the context of the three operations assumed by the FLMP. We begin with a discussion of the atheoretical application of the averaging rule.

2.1 Direct Implementation

For the direct implementation, the /da/-ness of a bimodal speech event $A_i V_j$ can be assumed to be an average of its visual /da/-ness v_j and its auditory /da/-ness a_i

$$/da/-ness\,(A_i\,V_j) = \frac{a_i + v_j}{2} \tag{1}$$

Thus, averaging is easily derived for the case of bimodal speech perception in a relatively atheoretical manner—a property that some may consider to be positive, but others may see as negative. For the latter group, we develop averaging within the theoretical framework of our general model of pattern recognition.

In Anderson's theory of averaging, no pattern classification stage was deemed to be necessary given that the judgment was taken to be a direct reflection of outcome of the integration process. At first glance, this assumption seems reasonable when continuous rating judgments are used; a discrete judgment would necessarily demand a pattern classification operation. Once the operation is admitted for discrete judgments, it might be argued that it is also involved in continuous rating judgments. What is revealing in this regard is how the pattern classification operation in the FLMP changes the interpretation of the averaging results observed by Anderson and others. We will see that averaging results imply an additive integration rule when interpreted in terms of the three operations of the FLMP.

2.2 Averaging in the FLMP

Averaging results can also be obtained in the context of the FLMP by assuming the addition of truth values representing the different sources of information. To implement the averaging integration rule in the FLMP, it is instructive to consider how this model differs from the assumptions underlying previous treatments. The central difference in the FLMP conceptualization of the person impression task is the role of prototypes in long-term memory. The idea is that it is difficult to judge how likeable a person is without evaluating the information that is presented with respect to prototypes (or schemas) of likeable and dislikeable people. In the FLMP, prototype matching involves integrating the information by assessing the features with respect to the relevant prototypes. It should be noted that these prototypes could be generated and modified for the task at hand. They should not be considered to be immutable templates in memory.

In the person impression task, it is assumed that the adjectives on a given trial define the relevant descriptors in the likeable and dislikeable prototypes. Thus, *meek* and *well-mannered* would be evaluated and given truth values defining the likeableness of each adjective. The prototypes in memory can be conceptualized as

Likeable Person: t(Adjective A is Likeable)
     and t(Adjective B is likeable)
     and ....
Dislikeable Person: 1 - t(Adjective A is Likeable)
     and 1 - t(Adjective B is Likeable)
     and ....

Thus, the adjectives in some sense define the prototypes, and the remaining question is how conjunction (and) is implemented to derive the overall likeableness and dislikeableness of the hypothetical person being rated.

Prototype representations as defined in the FLMP offer a unique interpretation of judgment by distinguishing information at the prototype matching stage and information at the pattern classification stage. During person impression, the outcome of prototype matching is a truth value defining how true it is the person is likeable and how true it is that the person is dislikeable. An important assumption of the FLMP is that the rating or categorization judgment reflects the truth values of both propositions. The decision is assumed to follow the relative-strength assumption given by Luce's (1959) choice rule. The rated likeableness of a person, R, would be

$$R = \frac{Likeableness}{Likeableness + Dislikeableness} \qquad (2)$$

We now develop additive integration in the FLMP description of bimodal speech perception. Both sources are assumed to provide independent evidence for the alternatives /ba/ and /da/. Defining the onsets of the second (F2) and third (F3) formants as the important auditory cues and the degree of initial opening of the lips as the important visual cue, the prototypes are

/da/ :   Slightly falling F2-F3 & Open lips
/ba/ :   Rising F2-F3 & Closed lips

Given a prototype's specifications for the auditory and visual sources, the value of one source cannot change the value of the other source at the prototype matching stage. In addition, the negation of a feature is defined as the additive complement. That is, we can represent Rising F2-F3 as (1 - Slightly falling F2-F3) and Closed Lips as (1 - Open lips),

/da/ :   Slightly falling F2-F3 & Open lips
/ba/ :   (1 - Slightly falling F2-F3) & (1 - Open lips).

The integration of the features defining each prototype is computed by the addition of the feature values. If a_i represents the degree to which the auditory stimulus A_i has Slightly falling F2-F3 and v_j represents the degree to which the visual stimulus V_j has Open lips, the outcome of prototype matching would be:

/da/ : $a_i + v_j$

/ba/ : $(1 - a_i) + (1 - v_j)$.

If these two prototypes are the only valid response alternatives, the pattern classification operation would determine their relative merit, leading to the prediction that both the two-choice classification judgments and the rating judgments would be equal to

$$P(/da/ \mid A_i V_j) = \frac{a_i + v_j}{a_i + v_j + ((1-a_i)+(1-v_j))} = \frac{a_i + v_j}{2} \ , \qquad (3)$$

where $P(/da/ \mid A_i V_j)$ would be the proportion of /da/ judgments or the /da/-ness rating scaled between 0 and 1.

2.3 Experimental Test

Massaro and Ferguson (1986) tested 20 subjects in the bimodal speech perception task. The major question of interest was individual differences in the task. Because there were no differences, it is appropriate to ignore this variable for the present purposes. The videotape used for identification and rating judgments was prepared identically to the stimuli used by Massaro and Cohen (1983c, Experiment 2). On each trial, the videotape showed a speaker saying either /ba/ or /da/ or keeping his lips closed (the neutral condition). The auditory stimuli were synthesized from characteristics of the speaker's voice and formed a continuum of nine sounds equally spaced between /ba/ and /da/. One of the nine auditory stimuli on the continuum from /ba/ to /da/ was synchronized with one of the three possible visual stimuli, /ba/, /da/, or neutral. The stimuli were presented in 11 blocks of the 27 possible combinations plus 10 practice trials for a total of 307 trials per session. Subjects had 2750 msec in which to respond by pressing either the "B" or the "D" buttons on a keyboard positioned to the side of the TV monitor.

In the identification task, subjects were instructed to "watch a speaker and listen to what is spoken" and simply to "indicate whether the man said /ba/ or /da/." They were warned that "on some trials you will see the speaker say the sound and on other trials the sound will be presented but the speaker will not move his mouth."

A rating task was carried out in the second experimental session. Subjects were instructed that, because they had probably noticed that some of the trials in the first session had been difficult to classify as either /ba/ or /da/, they were going to have a chance to make finer distinctions among the stimuli. They were to "identify what the man said on a continuum from 1 to 9 with 1 being the best possible /ba/ and 9 being the best possible /da/." The stimuli and testing conditions were identical to those used in the two-choice task except for the fact that subjects responded to each trial by pressing one of the numbered buttons

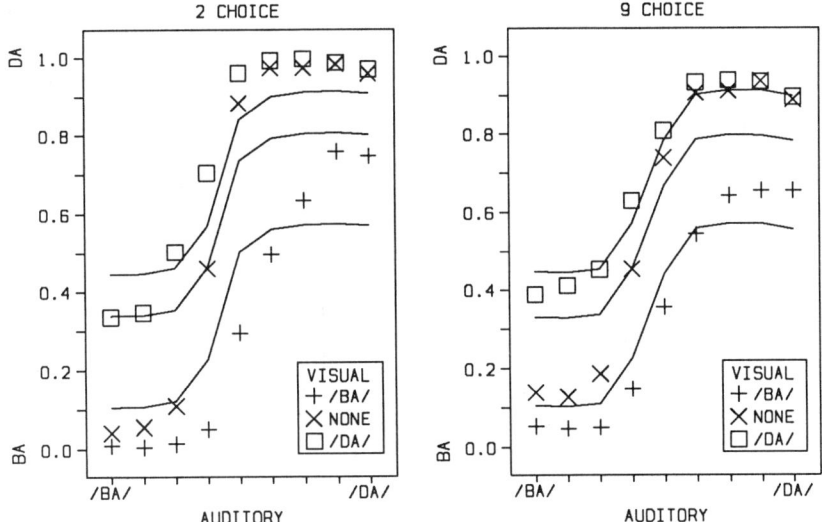

Figure 3. The average probability of a /da/ identification (left panel) given the alternatives /ba/ and /da/ and the average rating along a nine point scale (right panel). The lines give the average predictions of an averaging rule for the conjunction of the two sources of information (average results of 20 subjects after Massaro & Ferguson, 1986).

from "1" to "9" on the keyboard.

The averaging prediction given by both the atheoretical formalization and the implementation of the additive rule in the FLMP was fit to the results of both the two-choice and the rating judgments. Given nine levels of A_i and three levels of V_j in the present task, the predictions of the model require 9+3=12 parameters. Different parameters were estimated for the different tasks. Figure 3 gives the averaged observed and average predicted results for both the two-choice identification judgments (/ba/ or /da/) and the rating judgments. The average RMSD of the individual subject fits was .205 for the two-choice and .119 for the nine-choice task.

Figure 4 gives the results of a typical subject in the experiment along with the predictions of additive integration rule. Given the illusion of seeing nonparallel lines as parallel (Cleveland, 1985), the differences between the curves are plotted in Figure 5. As can be seen in the figures, the pattern of the results contradicts the parallelism prediction of the additive rule. The results indicate instead that the contribution of one source has more of an impact to the extent that the other source is ambiguous. As can be seen in Figure 5, the effect of the visual variable is larger in the middle of the auditory continuum. In addition, Figure 5 shows that a visual /da/ has a larger effect paired with an

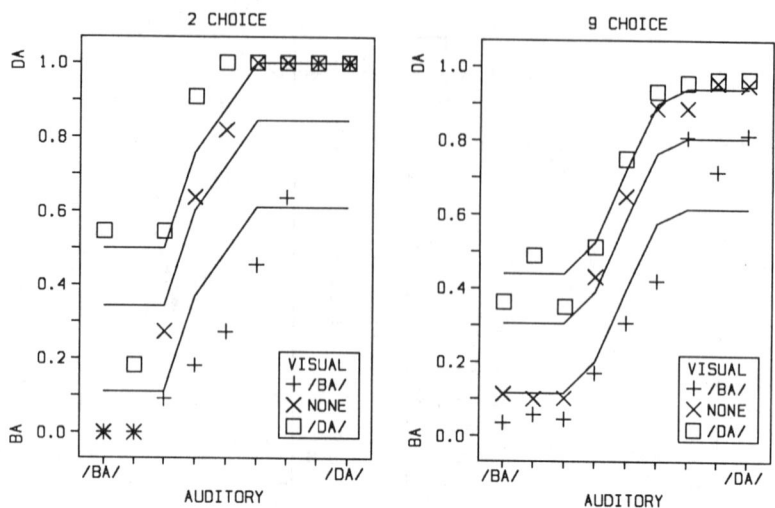

Figure 4. The average probability of a /da/ identification (left panel) given the alternatives /ba/ and /da/ and the average rating along a nine point scale (right panel). The lines give the prediction of an averaging rule for the conjunction of the two sources of information (results of a typical subject after Massaro & Ferguson, 1986).

auditory /ba/ than with an auditory /da/. Similarly, a visual /ba/ has a larger effect paired with an auditory /da/ than with an auditory /ba/. This result occurs because consistent visual information cannot add much to auditory information that is already fairly unambiguous.

2.4 Weighted Averaging Rule

An extension of the averaging rule is a weighted averaging rule in which one of the modalities would receive more weight than the other. A weighted adding model gives the following prototypes

/da/ : $wa_i + (1-w)v_j$
/ba/ : $w(1-a_i) + (1-w)(1-v_j)$

where w is the weight given the auditory dimension and $(1-w)$ is the weight given the visual dimension. Given the relative merit rule of the pattern classification operation, the additive model predicts that

$$P(/da/|A_iV_j) = wa_i + (1-w)v_j \qquad (4)$$

which is equivalent to the prediction of the CMP described in Chapter 4 when p is set equal to w. The weighted averaging model was fit to the results and the predictions are shown in Figure 6. The average RMSD of the individual subject

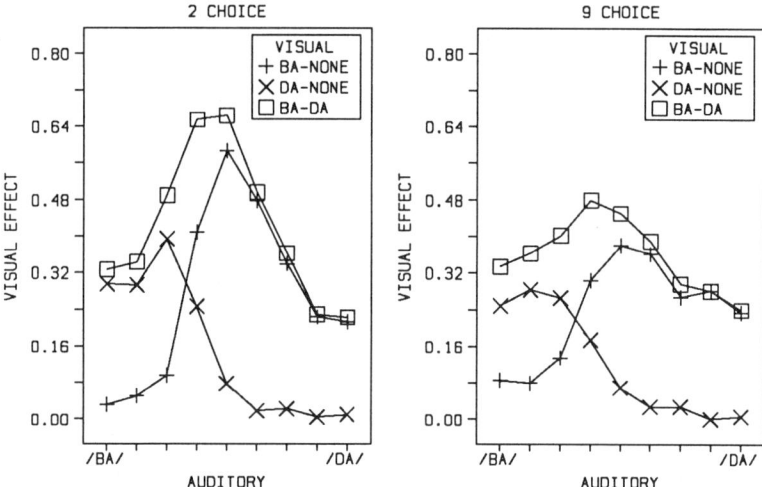

Figure 5. Visual effect for visual /ba/ versus none, visual /da/ versus none, and visual /ba/ versus visual /da/ comparisons as a function of the auditory level of the syllable. The results are based on the single subject shown in Figure 4.

fits was .156 for the two-choice and .088 for the nine-choice task. The model does almost as poorly as the unweighted additive model, again casting doubt on an additive (or averaging) combination of the features. Thus, we can also reject a weighted averaging model for evaluating and integrating sources of information in speech perception.

2.5 Expanded Factorial Designs

Including single-factor judgments in the typical two-factor design is a powerful extension of the paradigm typicality used to test different models of information integration. The correct integration rule should describe judgments in both the single-factor and two-factor conditions, with the constraint that the scale values of the factors be identical in the two conditions. The value of the description *hates* should be identical if this is the only information provided about the man or if it is also stated that the man is *uninteresting*. An analogous argument was made in the previous chapter concerning the test between independence and dependence. Although Anderson (1965, 1974) and others have included presentation of one of the factors in a two-factor design , we are unaware of any studies including both factors presented alone. In a 4 x 4 design, for example, the eight traits presented alone, as well as the sixteen possible combinations of the two factors, would be judged. Thus, twenty-four, rather than sixteen, independent data points would be available to test various integration rules, ideally with the same number of free parameters.

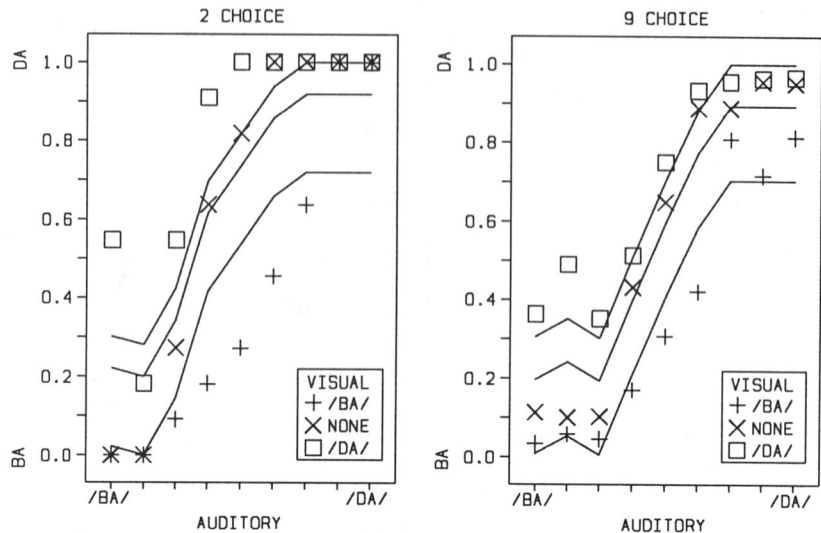

Figure 6. The probability of a /da/ identification (left panel) and the average rating along a nine point scale (right panel). The lines give the prediction of a weighted averaging rule for the conjunction of the two sources of information (results of a typical subject after Massaro & Ferguson, 1986).

2.5.1 Model-Free Test

A model-free test of the nature of the integration process can be performed on identifications of the single modality and bimodal speech syllables. Most tests of the integration rule are based on only bimodal trials. Extending the test to include the single-modality conditions permits new contrasts and more powerful tests. Consider identifications of an auditory syllable A_i and a visual syllable V_j and the relationship of these two identifications to the identification of the bimodal speech syllable $A_i V_j$ composed of the same auditory and visual levels. An averaging of the component dimensions predicts that the identification of the bimodal syllable must be less extreme than the identifications of either unimodal syllable.

Experiments including single modality and bimodal conditions have been carried out and are described in detail in Chapters 3 and 8. In one set of studies, subjects identified as /ba/ or /da/ auditory, visual, and bimodal speech syllables composed of five levels along an auditory /ba/ to /da/ continuum and the visual articulation /ba/ and /da/ (see Chapter 8). Figure 7 gives results from a typical three-year-old tested in the study. The three conditions involving the second auditory level and the /ba/ articulation are circled. As noted previously, the averaging rule predicts that the judgment of the bimodal syllable cannot be more extreme than either of the single modality conditions. However, the likelihood of a /da/ judgment to the bimodal syllable is less than the likelihood of a /da/ judgment to either of the unimodal syllables making it up. The 0% /da/ judgment to the bimodal syllable is more extreme than both the 20% /da/ judgment to the visual dimension and the 25% /da/ judgment to the auditory dimension when these dimensions are presented alone.

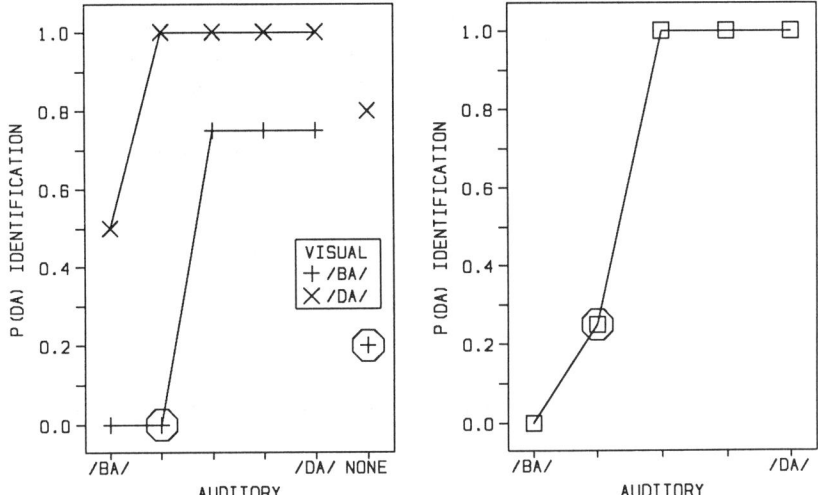

Figure 7. Observed proportion of /da/ identifications as a function of the auditory and visual levels of the speech event for the bimodal and visual conditions (left panel) and auditory condition (right panel) for one of the three-year-old children. The three circled points provide a disproof of averaging.

The results might also be considered in light of two more general integration rules: compromising and enhancing. Averaging would be an example of the former and the FLMP an example of the latter. In compromising integration, integrating additional sources of information can never lead to a more extreme judgment relative to any of the sources presented alone. Enhancing integration, on the other hand, can lead to a more extreme judgment relative to that given the single sources. The evidence for enhancing integration supports the search for nonadditive combination rules for bimodal speech perception. Two candidates have been proposed in the context of fuzzy logic.

3. Fuzzy Logic and Fuzzy Sets

The discussion of minimization and multiplication integration rules requires an initial presentation of fuzzy logic and fuzzy sets. In fuzzy logic, propositions are neither entirely true nor false but rather can be represented by continuous truth values. For example, we might say that a team is having a relatively good season or that a meal is somewhat spicy. Ordinary logical quantification would require that the team be performing well or not and that the meal is either spicy or it isn't. The theory of fuzzy logic (Zadeh, 1965; Goguen, 1969), on the other hand, allows us to represent the continuous nature of things. In fuzzy logic, we can construct a membership function: for example, short(x) that is true to the extent that item x is a member of the set short. It should be noted that fuzzy truth is different from probability. If we say that a whale is a fish to degree .2, that does not mean that there is a .2 probability that a particular whale is a fish. Rather, it is true that the whale is a fish to degree .2.

It is unfortunate for psychological theory that Zadeh (1965) dubbed this view of continuous truth as fuzzy, because continuous representation in no manner implies fuzziness. When we say a whale is a fish to degree .2, we are not necessarily any less confident of this proposition than we are of the proposition that a robin is a bird to degree .99. The difference between discrete versus continuous truth values might be a more descriptive contrast than that between standard logic and fuzzy logic. We will see that the principles of fuzzy set theory are direct generalizations of standard set theory and once again the descriptor "fuzziness" misses the contrast between the two logics. In related work on concepts and categorization, the representation of the concept does not have to be fuzzy even though any instance only fits the concept to some degree (Mervis & Rosch, 1981).

Fuzzy logic uses graded or qualified statements rather than those that are strictly true or false as in traditional bivalent logic. Fuzzy sets do not have crisply defined membership, but rather permit objects to have grades of membership from 0 to 1. Even if the number of continuous values of psychological truth is limited to a much smaller number such as 7 ± 2, the generalization from bivalent to a form of multivalent logic is very significant. The principles of fuzzy set theory were developed as direct generalizations of standard set theory. Given a domain of discourse D, and A a subset of D, the characteristic function for A in standard set theory is defined as

$$C_A : D \rightarrow \{0,1\}$$

such that

$$(\forall x \in D) \, C_A(x) = 1 \text{ if } x \in A;$$
$$= 0 \text{ if } x \notin A$$

According to the standard theory, an object is either in or out of the set A; there is no permissible fuzziness. The German idiom, "Alles klar," signifying complete clarity in a transaction, perfectly captures standard theory's lack of fuzziness.

Standard set theory also provides definitions for complements, intersections, and unions of two sets A and B. For the complement,

$$(\forall x \in D) \, C_{\neg A}(x) = 1 - C_A(x)$$

For the intersection and union of two sets,

$$(\forall x \in D) \, C_{A \cap B}(x) = min \, (C_A(x), C_B(x))$$

$$(\forall x \in D) \, C_{A \cup B}(x) = max \, (C_A(x), C_B(x))$$

The standard set theory definitions make sense when applied to various domains such as identification of bimodal speech. Define set A as the auditory information and set V as the visual information and assume that

$$C_A(/ba/) = 1; \quad C_V(/da/) = 0$$

which is a bimodal syllable evaluated as having auditory /ba/ and visual /da/. It follows that

$$C_V(/ba/) = 1 - C_A(/da/) = 1 - 1 = 0$$

$$C_{V \text{ and } A}(/ba/) = min \, (C_V(/ba/), C_A(/ba/)) = min \, (1,0) = 0$$

$$C_{V \text{ or } A}(/ba/) = max \, (C_V(/ba/), C_A(/ba/)) = max \, (1,0) = 1$$

Fuzzy set theory enlarges the number of values defined by the characteristic function from 0 and 1 to also include all values between 0 and 1. Set membership now becomes continuously graded so that an element x belongs to a set A to the extent $C_A(x)$ is close to one. The appealing property of Zadeh's (1965) fuzzy set theory was that the definitions of standard set theory did not have to be changed because they readily accommodated fuzzy values between 0 and 1. In our speech example, assume that

$$C_A(/ba/) = .8 \quad \text{and} \quad C_V(/da/) = .9$$

In words, the auditory dimension is evaluated as having a fairly high degree of /ba/-ness and the visual dimension as having very strong /da/-ness. It follows that

$$C_V(/ba/) = 1 - C_A(/da/) = 1 - .9 = .1$$

$$C_{V \text{ and } A}(/ba/) = min \, (C_V(/ba/), C_A(/ba/)) = min \, (.1, .8) = .1$$

$$C_{V \text{ or } A}(/ba/) = max \, (C_V(/ba/), C_A(/ba/)) = max \, (.1, .8) = .8$$

4. Minimization Rule for Conjunction

The minimization rule for conjunction is reasonable in standard logic because an object cannot be an exemplar of a category if it does not have all of the properties of that category. A mismatch on just a single property will disqualify the object as an exemplar of the category, With the introduction of graded membership as assumed by fuzzy set theory, minimization says that the attribute with the most minimum truth value is the important one and determines the truth value of the object belonging to the intersection of the attributes in question.

An apparent limitation of the minimization rule is that the value of the larger truth value cannot influence the outcome of conjunction. The multiplicative rule allows each source of information to influence the outcome of conjunction. Consider two different bimodal speech events that both have auditory /ba/ equal to .3. In one case, visual /ba/ is .35 and in the other case visual /ba/ is .95. The minimization rule would give the same value for the conjunction of auditory /ba/ and visual /ba/.

t(/ba/-ness) = min (t(auditory /ba/), t(visual /ba/))
Case 1 = min (.3, .35) = .3
Case 2 = min (.3, .95) = .3

The computed /ba/-ness is the same for both speech events even though the visual /ba/-ness is much greater in one case than in the other.

The multiplicative rule for conjunction is

$$C_{A \wedge B}(x) = C_A(x) \wedge C_B(x))$$

In this case, we would get different values for conjunction in the example

$$C_{A \wedge B}(x) = C_A(x) \times C_B(x)) = .3 \times .35 = .105$$
$$C_{A \wedge B}(x) = C_A(x) \times C_B(x)) = .3 \times .95 = .285$$

Using a multiplying rule, the truth value that the syllable is /ba/ is much greater in the second case than the first. This makes good sense given that the visual /ba/ is so much greater in the second case than the first. Given a meal composed of two courses, we would choose the meal with the better dessert even though the entree was equally terrible in both. Strictly speaking, the minimization rule does not appear to involve integration and thus we would expect it to give a poor description of the perception of bimodal speech. Sometimes our expectations prove to be incorrect, however, as we will see in experimental tests of minimization.

4.1 Experimental Tests

The minimization rule can be formalized within the context of the FLMP and tested against various results. All aspects of the minimization model are identical to the FLMP except that the conjunction of the features at prototype matching is implemented as minimization rather than as multiplication. The first test involved judgments of bimodal speech in the Massaro and Cohen (1983c, Experiment 2) study. This experiment and the application of the FLMP to the results were presented in Chapter 4 (Sections 1, 1.2, and 1.3). Figure 8 gives the results along with the predictions of the model based on the minimization rule. It turns out that this model gives a equivalently good description of the results, with an average RMSD value of .056 (compared to .058 for the FLMP).

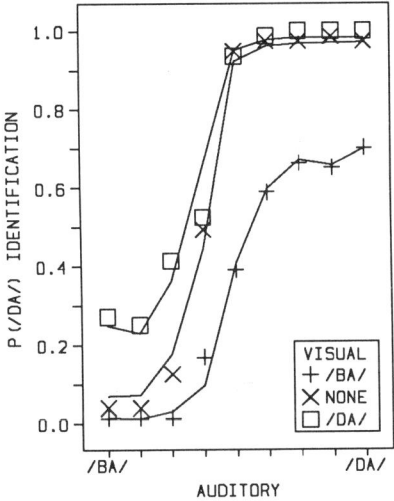

Figure 8. Observed (points) and Predicted (lines) probability of a /da/ identification as a function of the auditory and visual levels of the speech syllable. The predictions are for the minimization rule formulated in the FLMP (results after Massaro & Cohen, Experiment 2, 1983c).

The minimization model was also tested against the results of an experiment with open-ended response alternatives (Massaro & Cohen, 1983c, Experiment 3) described in Chapter 4 (Section 1.5). Once again, the FLMP and the minimization model provided similar descriptions of the results. The RMSD values were .052 and .061, respectively.

The minimization rule was also tested against the experiment using an expanded factorial design with opened-ended responses described in Chapter 3. This experiment provides a more stringent test of the minimization rule because it includes both unimodal and bimodal speech syllables and allows an open-ended set of response alternatives. Figure 9 gives the observed and predicted results. Once again the results are well described by the minimization rule used for integration with an average RMSD of .026.

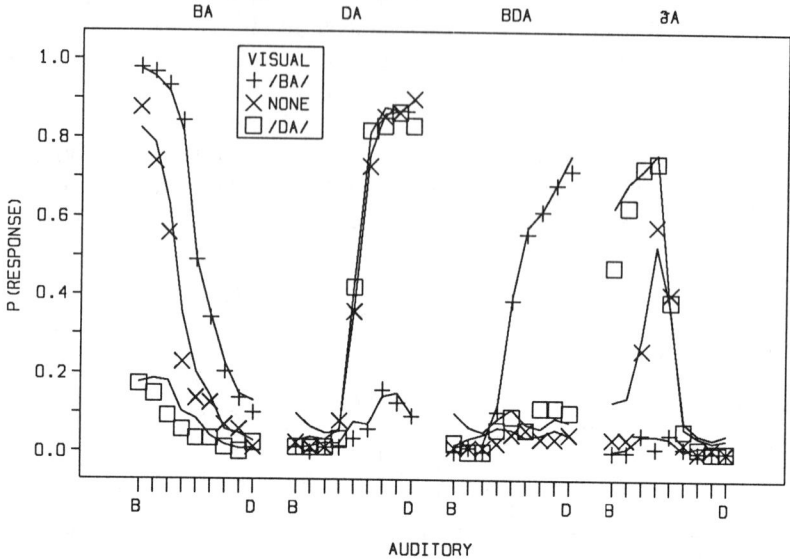

Figure 9. Observed (points) and Predicted (lines) probability of an identification as a function of the auditory and visual levels of the speech syllable. The predictions are for the minimization rule formulated in the FLMP (results after Massaro & Cohen, Experiment 3, 1983c).

4.2 Integration and Minimization

It is surprising that the minimization model gave a good description of the results because the minimization rule, by definition, does not involve an integration of the auditory and visual features. Minimization seems to contradict the concept of integration because the outcome of a given conjunction is determined by just a single attribute rather than some algebraic combination of all of the attributes. That is, the outcome of minimization is determined only by the most minimum truth value in the conjunction process. Consider the concept *good student*. Two students with equally poor grades might still be distinguished on the basis of their contribution to class discussions. Given the minimization rule, the student with very good class participation would *not* be considered a better example of *good student* than would the student with only good class participation. If subjects integrate both sources of information, the minimization rule seems inadequate to account for conjunction of component attributes in conceptual classification.

The resolution of this paradox is that the minimization rule becomes a form of integration when the minimization rule is implemented in the FLMP with evaluation, integration, and pattern classification operations. To return to the categorization of *good student*, a prototype for *poor student* would also be functional when minimization is implemented in the FLMP. In this case, the two students in the example would differ with respect to the concept *poor student.* The student with very good class participation would be a poorer match to *poor student* than would the student with only good class participation. Given that the pattern classification operation is based on relative goodness of match, the student with very good class participation would, in fact, be determined to be the better student, even though both students give an equally poor match to the prototype good student.

The minimization rule is, therefore, consistent with the concept of integration when the conjunction occurs within the context of the FLMP. All attributes have an impact on the outcome because each attribute is considered at the prototype matching stage and the attribute with the minimum truth value can differ for different prototypes. Consider a syllable with auditory and visual speech supporting the alternative /ba/ to degree .8 and .1 respectively. Given the definition of negation, the auditory and visual support for the alternative /da/ would be .2 and .9, respectively. At the prototype matching operation, conjunction of the two attributes following the minimization rule would give .1 for /ba/ and .2 for /da/. What is interesting is that the conjunction was determined by the visual speech for /ba/ and by the auditory speech for /da/. It turns out that both attributes contribute to a single perceptual judgment of the syllable in contrast to what might be expected from the minimization definition of conjunction.

4.3 Test between Minimization and Multiplication

We have favored the multiplicative form over the minimization form of conjunction because of a study carried out by Oden (1977b). The attributes were statements about class membership such as

> *a bat is a bird*
> *a refrigerator is a piece of furniture.*

Subjects were given pairs of these statements and asked three different types of questions.

> *1. What is the average truth value of the two statements?*
> *2. How true is it that both statements are true (conjunction)?*
> *3. How true is it that either statement is true (disjunction)?*

Subjects made a rating response along a linear scale with one end labeled absolutely false and the other end labeled absolutely true. The judgments in this situation were taken as direct reflections of the integration process, without passing through the pattern classification operation. If this assumption is correct, then it is possible to test between minimization and multiplicative forms of conjunction. The results support the averaging rule for the averaging task and the multiplying rule for the conjunction task. The results are shown in Figure 10. Subjects appear to average when told to average but appear to multiply when conjoining two sources of information. Given the linear fan results, it appears that the multiplicative rule is a better description of conjunction than is minimization. It should be noted that the disjunction task also could be used to test between minimization and multiplication because disjunction can be derived from these rules using DeMorgan's Law (see Chapter 5, Section 4.3.1). The results of the disjunction task also provided evidence for multiplying over the minimization rule.

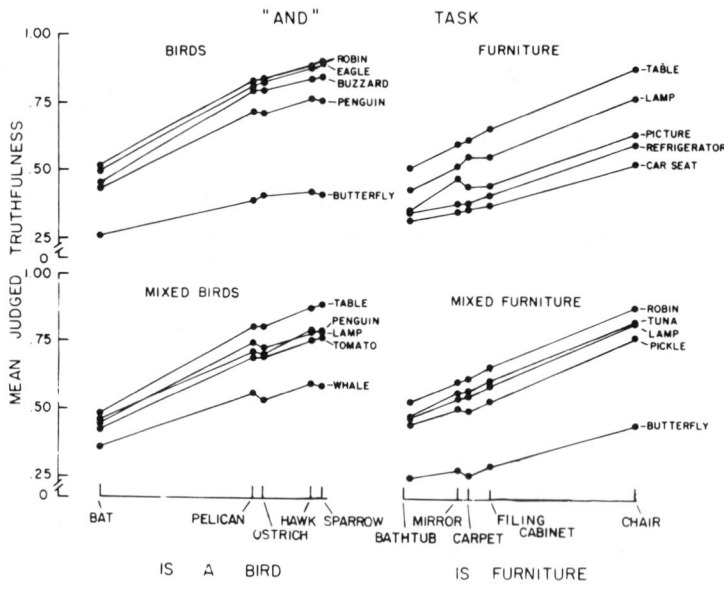

Figure 10. Mean judged truthfulness of the conjunction of two independent statements such as *A butterfly is a bird* and *A chair is furniture*. The spacing along the x axis is proportional to the the marginal mean judgments at each level along the x axis. The roughly linear spread between the different curves within each panel is evidence for multiplication and against minimization (after Oden, 1977b).

5. Multiplicative Rule

Goguen (1969) and Oden (1977b) rationalize the multiplying rule by referring to a paradox created by Eubulides, a Greek philosopher. A man with lots of hair loses only one hair a day. This man would not be bald tomorrow because he is not bald today. Yet with the passage of time, he will eventually become bald. This paradox is partially dependent on treating baldness as a all-or-none property as in standard logic. Even with a fuzzy-logical interpretation, however, the minimum conjunction rule cannot eliminate the paradox. Adding terms corresponding to the decrease in hair with each day will not change the outcome of the minimum rule. On the other hand, multiplying the terms will decrease the truth value of having hair with the addition of each day in the man's life. The conjunctive statement

"A man has lots of hair and (losing a hair does not make him bald)
and (losing a hair does not make him bald) and..."

will not become less true given a minimization rule but will become less true given a multiplying rule with the passage of time (adding terms to the statement). The truth value of the man having hair can be represented by the conjunctive statement

$$t\,(not\ bald) = min\,(t\,(has\ hair), t\,(losing\ hair)) =$$

$$= \min(.95, .95) = .95$$

With each day, another term, $t\,(losing\ hair)$, would be added to the proposition. The truth value of $t\,(not\ bald)$ would remain at .95, however, because the minimization would always be .95. It should be noted that adding another prototype **bald** would not overcome Eubulides' paradox because *t(bald)* would stay at .05 with each loss of hair. A multiplying rule for conjunction, however, would allow the truth value to decrease with each additional loss of a hair.

The multiplying rule has been assumed to describe integration in the FLMP. We do not assume that humans actually carry out the process of multiplication, just that multiplication closely represents the processes involved in conjoining or integrating different sources of information. A model mimics the behavior of the phenomenon of interest. A mathematical model doesn't necessarily attribute the mathematical processes to the entities involved; it simply describes the outcome of the processes. By assuming that the feature values are multiplied, we do not mean that the perceiver actually multiplies feature values. We simply mean that the features are combined in such a way to produce an outcome that is equivalent to a multiplication of the feature values. As acknowledged by Rumelhart and Norman (1983), modeling a bouncing ball with differential equations does not imply that the ball itself understands or uses these equations. Modeling human performance with various formalisms should not be taken to mean the human understands or uses these formalisms.

5.1 Nonidentifiability

Although we have emphasized evidence (Oden, 1977b) and rational arguments to favor a multiplicative rule for conjunction over the minimization rule, it is not an easy matter to reject the latter rule in favor of the former. When implemented in the FLMP, minimization and multiplication forms of integration cannot always be differentiated from one another. The two rules are often nonidentifiable because their predictions are essentially mathematically isomorphic for some situations (Greeno & Steiner, 1964). To demonstrate this isomorphism, we generated hypothetical data from a multiplicative FLMP and fit these results with a minimization FLMP. We also generated hypothetical results from a minimization FLMP and fit them with a multiplicative FLMP. Figure 11 gives the hypothetical results from one model and the description of these results by the other model. As can be seen in the Figure, each model is capable of adequately describing the results produced by the other model. The RMSD values were less than .01, much less than we can expect to find with actual results containing random variation.

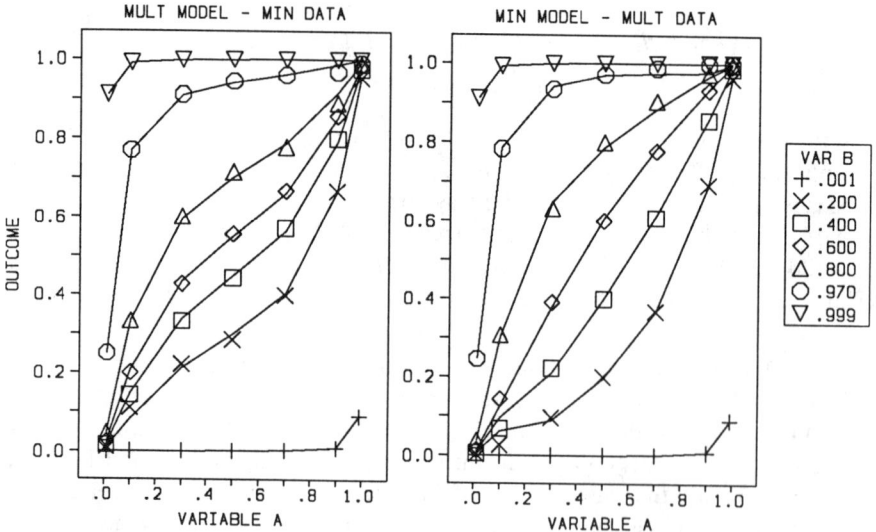

Figure 11. Left panel - Predictions (lines) given by the multiplicative model to results (points) generated by the minimization model. Right panel - Predictions (lines) given by the minimization model to results (points) generated by the multiplicative model (simple two factor design).

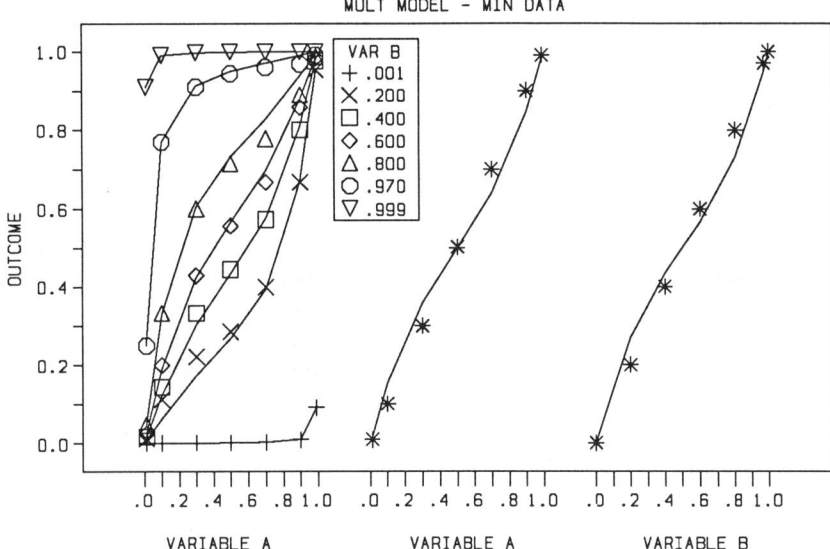

Figure 12. Predictions (lines) given by the multiplicative model to results (points) generated by the minimization model. Similar results are obtained for predictions given by the minimization model to results generated by the multiplicative model (expanded two factor design).

With an expanded factorial design of two independent variables, the two conjunction rules do not mimic each other completely. Repeating the generation and fit of hypothetical data, we observed that the RMSD was .025 for the fit of one model to the hypothetical data of the other. Figure 12 gives the predicted and observed results for one of these two situations. The other situation is very similar in form. Finally, given the logic of the minimization rule, we expected that three independent variables with two response alternatives might differentiate the models even more, because the minimization rule for conjunction will give a goodness value for each prototype based on just one of the three variables. With two prototypes, one of the variables will play no role in determining the judgment on any given trial. The two models make reasonably different predictions given two response alternatives and three independent variables, especially with an expanded factorial design. The RMSD values were .058 and .065 for the simple and expanded factorial design for the fit of the multiplicative model to data generated by the minimization model. The RMSD values were .122 and .122 for the simple and expanded factorial design for the fit of the minimization model to data generated by the multiplicative model. In this case, there is some asymmetry between the two models in that multiplication is better able to mimic minimization than the reverse. It follows that it should be easier to reject minimization if it is incorrect than to reject multiplication if it is incorrect. In any event, we will need much larger designs than those currently being used to test between the minimization and multiplicative conjunction rules. To test between the two rules, visible speech synthesis will be needed to increase the number of visual levels. It will also be necessary to increase the number of independent variables within a modality such as by varying place and voicing auditory cues (Oden & Massaro, 1978).

5.2 Integration Rules and Optimal Performance

In addition to the experimental evidence, a theoretical reason to question the applicability of adding or averaging the evaluations of the separate sources of information is that this combination rule is non-optimal. If perceptual systems evolved to integrate multiple sources of information, we might expect that the integration would be highly efficient and productive (i.e., optimal). Averaging an ambiguous source of information with an informative source will tend to neutralize the judgment relative to the informative dimension being presented alone. Optimal integration would seem to require that more ambiguous sources be given less of a say in the decision. Some time after the development of the FLMP, it was determined that it corresponded to an optimal integration rule. Multiplying the sources of information within the context of the FLMP (Massaro, 1984a; Oden & Massaro, 1978) is mathematically identical to Bayes Theorem and the Likelihood Ratio (Massaro, in press a).

The multiplicative rule formalized in the context of the FLMP turns out to be an optimal decision strategy for classifying objects given multiple sources of information. The FLMP with multiplicative integration is mathematically equivalent to an optimal decision theory based on probabilities. The heart of the probability model is Bayes Theorem, which is an optimal decision rule for obtaining and revising probabilities. Bayes Theorem states that

$$P(H_1|E) = \frac{P(E|H_1) \times P(H_1)}{\sum_i P(E|H_i) \times P(H_i)} \tag{5}$$

where $P(H_i|E)$ is the probability that some hypothesis H_i is true given that some evidence E is observed; $P(E|H_i)$ is the probability of the evidence E, given the hypothesis H_i is true, and $P(H_i)$ is the a priori probability of the hypothesis H_i. The likelihood of hypothesis H_1 given some evidence E is equal to the likelihood of the evidence given the hypothesis times the a priori likelihood of the hypothesis divided by the sum of analogous likelihoods for all possible hypotheses. If the a priori probabilities of all possible hypotheses are equal, Bayes Theorem reduces to:

$$P(H_1|E) = \frac{P(E|H_1)}{\sum_i P(E|H_i)} \tag{6}$$

If each hypothesis corresponds to a particular response alternative, Equation 6 is similar in form to the pattern classification operation in the FLMP. The pattern classification operation in the FLMP is based on Luce's choice rule (Luce, 1959, 1977) and is of the form

$$P(H_1|E) = \frac{t(E|H_1)}{\sum_i t(E|H_i)} \tag{7}$$

which gives the probability of choosing a particular response alternative as equal to the truth value of that alternative divided by the sum of the truth values for all relevant alternatives.

The important question that remains is how different sources of evidence are combined according to Bayes Theorem. Given two pieces of evidence E_1 and E_2, the likelihood of a hypothesis H_1 is equal to

$$P(H_1|E_1 \text{ and } E_2) = \frac{P(E_1 \text{ and } E_2|H_1)}{\sum_i P(E_1 \text{ and } E_2|H_i)} \tag{8}$$

$$= \frac{P(E_1|H_1) \times P(E_2|H_1)}{\sum_i P(E_1|H_i) \times P(E_2|H_i)}$$

The equation with two sources of evidence follows from probability theory in which the likelihood of the joint occurrence of two independent events is the multiplicative combination of the likelihoods of the separate events. The likelihood of two heads in two tosses of a coin is the multiplicative combination of the likelihood of a head on each toss. A psychological model on Bayes Theorem could simply assume that the probability of a response corresponding to hypothesis H_i is equal to Equation 8. In this case, a multiplicative combination of independent sources of evidence in the FLMP is identical in form to a probability model based on Bayes Theorem. The two models would also be applied to experimental results in the same manner. In the FLMP, a parameter is estimated for each level of each source of evidence. The same would be true with respect to the probabilities assumed by Bayes Theorem.

The mathematical equivalence of the FLMP and Bayes Theorem poses a new dilemma for the FLMP. Given that previous research has rejected Bayes Theorem in a variety of judgmental situations, why has the mathematically-equivalent FLMP been so successful? Two possibilities must be considered. The first is that the rejections of the Baysean model have been premature and the second is that the models have been tested in very different domains. Both possibilities appear to be true to some extent. The rejection of Bayes Theorem in many experiments has been a rejection of the normative form of the model rather than a psychological form of the model. Predictions have been derived on the basis of the objective rather than the subjective sources of information. In contrast, tests of the FLMP allow for subjective values for the various objective sources of information. Consider the test of the model in situations in which subjective base rates are assumed to be equal to objective base rates. In these cases, performance falls short of the predictions of Bayes Theorem (Leon & Anderson, 1974). Central to the FLMP, however, is the evaluation stage that transforms the objective source of information into some subjective value. Thus, performance could still fall short of the optimally objective prediction but be described by the same algorithm if subjective values are assumed.

The second possibility also exists to some extent because most tests of Bayes Theorem have focused on estimates of probability in some variant of the two urn task. Subjects see two urns and are told the proportion of red and blue beads in each urn. One urn is picked with some probability and a sample of beads is drawn. Given the sample, the subject estimates what urn was, in fact, picked. Probability of picking a urn, the relative proportion of beads in each urn, the sample size, and the sample makeup can be varied. Even in these situations, however, it has been the normative Baysean model that has been rejected. It remains an empirical question whether the FLMP can survive in situations in which the Baysean model has supposedly failed.

5.3 Probabilities versus Truth Values

Given the mathematical equivalence between a probability model and the FLMP based on fuzzy truth values, it is important to determine whether one can be justified over the other. Traditionally, the use of probabilities in psychology has been associated with threshold or categorical models (Massaro, 1975a). Thus, the use of fuzzy truth values represents a shift away from these models to continuously-valued states of information. In a strict sense, however, the Baysean probability theory makes use of continuous information if the evidence is continuous. Both representations are thus also equivalent in the assumption of continuous rather than categorical states of information. Given the formal identity of the FLMP to a decision model based on Bayes Theorem, either of these two models is adequate to account for the results. As noted in Chapter 5, however, probabilistic models usually represent discrete rather than continuous processes. In this case, Bayes Theorem could easily be interpreted as the subject having only categorical information about a given hypothesis (response alternative). Given the pattern recognizer's ability to transmit continuous information about the alternatives, the representation in terms of truth values appears more reasonable than a representation in terms of probabilities.

6. Pattern Classification Operation

An important operation of the FLMP is the pattern classification stage formalized in terms of Luce's Choice rule. There is an abundance of evidence that decisions tend to follow relative rather than absolute criteria. In addition to the mathematical tests within the context of choice experiments (Luce, 1977), this notion is supported by research with natural categories revealing the context-sensitivity of our categorizations. The category *TALL* differs for describing fourth-graders and professional basketball players. In both cases, it is relative tallness with respect to the appropriate cohort of alternatives. Analogously in pattern recognition, it is the degree to which the stimulus pattern matches one alternative relative to the set of relevant alternatives.

6.1 Luce's Choice Rule

The pattern classification operation is assumed to follow Luce's choice rule which captures a possible measurement constraint proposed by Clarke (1957). Although most of the subsequent research has been in the domain of visual letter confusions (e.g., Townsend & Landon, 1982), Clarke (1957) actually proposed the rule for confusion matrices in speech perception. Consider a master confusion matrix M of n stimuli and m responses and $P_M(j \mid i)$ representing the probability that response j is given to stimulus i. Similarly, a subset confusion matrix S represents a subset of s stimuli and s responses from the master confusion matrix M. The probability that response j is given to stimulus i for the subset matrix, $P_S(j \mid i)$, is claimed by the constant-ratio rule of Clarke to be equal to

$$P_S(j \mid i) = \frac{P_M(j \mid i)}{\sum_{K \in S} P_M(k \mid i)} \tag{9}$$

In words, the probability that response j is given stimulus i in the subset confusion matrix is equal to $P_M(j \mid i)$ divided by the sum of all *relevant* response probabilities to stimulus i in the master confusion set. The relevant response probabilities are based on those responses that are members of the subset confusion matrix S. For example, consider a master confusion matrix with the stimuli and responses /ba/, /va/, /ð͡a/, and /da/. The probability of a /ba/ response given stimulus /da/ in a subset confusion matrix with just the alternatives /ba/ and /da/, $P_S(/ba/ \mid /da/)$, is assumed to be equal to

$$P_S(/ba/ \mid /da/) = \frac{P_M(/ba/ \mid /da/)}{P_M(/ba/ \mid /da/) + P_M(/da/ \mid /da/)} \tag{10}$$

That is, the proportion of /ba/ judgments with just two alternatives in the subset matrix is equal to the ratio of the corresponding entries in the master confusion matrix.

Luce (1959) proved that the critical-ratio rule can be derived from a general theory of choice behavior. The critical assumption is that alternatives that are defined as irrelevant to the choice task play no role in the decision. This general theory can be expressed as

$$P_S(i) = \frac{V(i)}{\sum_{K \in S} V(j)} \tag{11}$$

or the probability of an i response in any subset matrix S is equal to the constant scale value, $V(i)$, of that alternative divided by the sum of the constant scale values of all of the alternatives in the subset matrix S. The response probability of an alternative is predicted to be equal to the ratio of the response strength of that alternative to the sum of the response strengths of all relevant alternatives (including the alternative of interest).

The major problem with using Luce's choice rule to describe pattern classification is that a process model is not defined to allow a choice on each trial. The model only predicts response probabilities. Townsend and Landon (1983) provide a few alternative process interpretations that are consistent with the choice rule, but there have been no tests among these alternatives. Thus, it is premature to consider different process alternatives. For our purposes, it is encouraging that the choice rule is mathematically equivalent to the choice rule given by signal detection theory in which the observer adopts a criterion and responds relative to the criterion on each trial. The response is probabilistic because of noise influencing the strength values on each trial. We discuss just one experimental test of the pattern classification operation and refer the reader to Luce (1977) for additional evidence and considerations.

6.2 Experimental Test

Oden (1977a) provided a direct test of Luce's relative-goodness choice rule in the same domain of semantic memory used in his integration tasks. Subjects were given two statements such as

> *An eagle is a bird*
> *A pelican is a bird*

and asked: "Which of the following statements is truer and how much more true is it?" The judgments provided support for the relative strength or goodness assumption and violated predictions that might be made from a simple subtractive model

$$J(A) = t(A) - t(B) \tag{12}$$

where $J(A)$ would be equal to the truthfulness of statement A minus statement B and $t(A)$ and $t(B)$ represent the truth values of the individual statements. The results were more adequately described by

$$J(A) = \frac{t(A)}{t(A) + t(B)} \tag{13}$$

where the statement A is judged to be more true in terms of the truthfulness of A relative to the sum of the truthfulness values of A and B. As noted in the discussion of prototypes in Section 2.2, any judgment appears to have a relative aspect to it. In the person impression task, the likeableness of a person is assumed to be determined by assessing the likeableness relative to the sum of the likeableness and dislikeableness values. Implicit in the judgment task is the existence of contrasting prototypes which contribute to the judgment in the manner of the relative goodness described by the pattern classification operation of the FLMP.

7. Criticisms of Fuzzy Set Theory

Recently, fuzzy logic has come under heavy fire as a psychological description of the integration of information in categorization (Osherson & Smith, 1981, 1982). These criticisms have been addressed in some ways (Oden, 1984; Zadeh, 1982), but the central issue of whether the use of fuzzy logic is adequate to describe the combination of concepts remains unresolved. The important deficiency in all of the criticisms and replies has been the failure to account for all of the operations involved in categorization behavior. As in most instances, a subject's behavior cannot be taken as a direct measure of a single underlying process. Thus, some categorization behavior does not necessarily reflect directly a process of conceptual integration or combination. Other processes contribute to the behavior and these must be accounted for before a true index of integration can be obtained. The evidence used to criticize fuzzy logic can be described within the framework of the FLMP which provides a more complete account of the processes involved in the categorization task.

7.1 Conjunction of Attributes

Consider the criticism that the truth value of a conjunction of two concepts as defined in fuzzy logic must always be less than the truth value of either concept alone (Osherson & Smith, 1981). For example, an apple with stripes can never be a better exemplar of striped apple than it is an exemplar of apple. Applying this logic to the speech domain, the argument would be that an auditory-visual /da/ could never be a better exemplar of /da/ than is either an auditory /da/ or a visual /da/. In both the fruit and speech domains we might expect instances in which the conjunction would be a better exemplar than either dimension alone, and these instances have been interpreted as evidence against fuzzy logic. The role of the prototype matching and pattern classification operations are central to understanding the observations in these situations. One can expect prototypes to be formed dynamically as a function of the dimensions present in the stimulus and the categorization alternatives. In addition, the viable alternatives entering into the determination of relative goodness will differ across different categorization tasks.

To illustrate the feature evaluation, integration and prototype matching, and pattern classification operations with a single source relative to two sources of information, assume a bimodal speech event consisting of .8 visual /da/-ness and .9 auditory /da/-ness. Feature integration would give .8 × .9 = .72 /da/-ness for the bimodal event, which is less than the /da/-ness given by either of the single dimensions. However, this does not mean that the categorization of the bimodal event as /da/ would be less likely than categorization of either of the single events as /da/. Pattern classification is based on the relative truthfulness of the alternatives, and the goodness-of-match with all other alternatives must be considered. If /da/ and /ba/ are the response alternatives in the task, the /ba/-ness of the bimodal event is also computed, giving (1-.8) (1-.9) = .02. The likelihood of a /da/ classification would be

$$P(/da/) = \frac{.8 \times .9}{.8 \times .9 + (1-.8) \times (1-.9)} = \frac{.72}{.74} = .973 \qquad (14)$$

Given a single dimension with just two choice alternatives, the likelihood of a classification is simply equal to the truth value because the denominator of the relative goodness equation always sums to one. As an example, the probability of a /da/ identification in a lipreading task given .8 visual /da/-ness would be

$$P(/da/) = \frac{.8}{.8 + (1-.8)} = .8 \qquad (15)$$

Actually, this strategy is mathematically equivalent to assigning completely neutral (.5) truth values to all missing sources of information. The same predictions would be derived if missing dimensions were assigned completely neutral truth values of .5 given that the choice response is not influenced by .5 truth values. If the visual /da/-ness is .8 and the auditory dimension is not present, then

$$P(/da/) = \frac{.8 \times .5}{.8 \times .5 + (1-.8) \times (1-.5)} = \frac{.4}{.5} = .80 \qquad (16)$$

which is equivalent to the truth value of visual /da/-ness. Similarly, $P(/da/)$ given only the auditory dimension would be .9, (the truth value of auditory /da/-ness). The FLMP can predict that classifying the bimodal event as /da/ is greater than the likelihood of classifying either of the single dimensions as /da/. Analogously, the FLMP can predict that the likelihood of classifying some instance as a conjunction of two dimensions is greater than the likelihood of classifying it as an instance of either single dimension. Put differently, the model can describe how an instance with two properties is more representative of the conjunction of the properties than it is representative of either property (see Chapter 9, Section 6).

The natural alternative to striped is not striped and the natural alternative to striped apple is a category defined by not striped and not apple. Consider an object .8 striped and .6 apple. The judged truth values of striped predicted by the FLMP would be

$$J(striped) = \frac{t(striped)}{t(striped) + t(not\ striped)} = t(striped) = .80$$

because not striped is the natural contrasting category for judging stripedness. The analogous prediction holds for the attribute apple

$$J(apple) = \frac{t(apple)}{t(apple) + t(not\ apple)} = t(apple) = .60$$

For striped apple, the appropriate contrasting category would be an object that is both not striped and not apple

$$J(striped\ apple) = \frac{t(striped)t(apple)}{t(striped)t(apple) + (1-t(striped))(1-t(apple))}$$

$$= \frac{.8 \times .6}{.8 \times .6 + (1-.8) \times (1-.6)} = \frac{.48}{.56} = .857$$

Here it can be seen that counter to the opinion of Osherson and Smith, a pattern recognition schema using fuzzy set theory can predict that a person's categorization judgment based on the conjunction of two attributes can be larger in truth value than either of the component truth values. Hence, we have an object being a better example of striped apple than either striped or apple when fuzzy logic is incorporated into a process model of categorization. The FLMP can describe conceptual combination because it can predict the observation that an instance might be a better exemplar of a concept defined by the conjunction of two dimensions than it is an exemplar of a concept of either of the single dimensions.

7.2 Fuzziness is Not Vagueness

Johnson-Laird (1983) argues against the use of fuzzy set theory to cope with vagueness of assertions about set membership; for example, *John is a tall man*. The author distinguishes three kinds of vagueness and observes that fuzzy logic is ill-equipped to represent them. The first is an uncertainty about something that is intrinsically determining. If you are uncertain about whether Homer existed, this is an example of the first type of vagueness. The second type of vagueness is a certainty of the exact indeterminability of something that is intrinsically indeterminate. Knowing the probability that an unbiased coin coming up heads is .5 is an example. Third is an inability to decide an issue because it is outside the rules of the system. If you do not know the permissible size of a baseball bat, because there is nothing in the rules of the game defining the size of the baseball bat, then you are in this third state of mind.

Although none of the three examples captures the need for fuzzy truth values, the scenarios can be easily extended to illustrate how fuzzy logic can be used to describe mental representations. If the matter of Homer's existence can be determined unambiguously, we might expect that there is no need for fuzzy truth. However, a historian's knowledge about Homer's existence might well be represented by fuzzy logic. At any point in time, she has information about the degree to which Homer existed and this information can change. New information might be integrated with the old following one of the integration algorithms discussed here. If I know the probability of a coin coming up heads is .5, there is no fuzziness to be represented. If I am faced with a biased coin and observe a series of tosses, however, my knowledge about its bias can be fuzzy and can be changed with each new toss. The third situation might exist, but an individual might believe that there is a rule of the game defining the size of the bat. This individual's representation of this "rule" might be described by fuzzy truth values and could easily change with experience with the game. In all three examples, the proposition does not seem to require fuzzy logic but the representation of the proposition does. Fuzzy logic captures the multiple states of continuous information as opposed to having only categorical information. As an example, you know that a penguin is less representative of the class of birds than is a bluejay.

I claim that none of the three types of vagueness as described by Johnson-Laird corresponds to the use of fuzzy logic in the FLMP. In terms of mental representation, the representation of continuous information is not uncertain, nor it is intrinsically indeterminate, nor it is undecided. It is simply the representation of continuous or grades of knowledge about set membership. The differences in typicality can be represented very easily in terms of fuzzy truth values between 0 and 1. Thus, we can say that it is .4 true that a penguin is a bird and .8 true that a bluejay is a bird. Penguin is less representative of the concept bird than is bluejay. There is not any less uncertainty in one case than the other in the same way that there is no uncertainty in my liking fresh figs more than dried ones.

7.3 All Concepts are Fuzzy

Armstrong, Gleitman and Gleitman (1983) challenge the idea that concepts are non-definitional in character, that is, cannot be described by necessary and sufficient attributes. If concepts are definitional, we have evidence against the use of fuzzy logic to describe the processing of concepts. Previous work by Rosch and her followers has shown that judgments of most natural concepts produce graded responses representing the degree to which instances represent the concepts. These results have led some theorists to conclude that most natural concepts are non-definitional, fuzzy, or ambiguous. If this conclusion is correct, Armstrong et al. propose that categories that are well-defined should not produce graded responses because graded responses have been interpreted to mean that the concepts being judged are not well defined. A strong prediction, they reason, is that well-defined concepts, with necessary and sufficient descriptions, should not yield graded responses in terms of the degree to which an instance of the concept represents the category.

Armstrong et al. (1983) chose well-defined categories such as odd number, geometric figure, and female. An odd number seems to have a clear definition, namely an integer not divisible by two without a remainder. Analogously, geometric figure and female seem to be well-defined. What may come as a surprise to some of the readers is that instances of these categories were not rated as equally good members or exemplars of the category. Subjects rated 7 as a more typical odd number than 731. Analogously, a square is viewed as a much more prototypical geometrical figure than is a trapezoid or an ellipse. And finally, a police-woman is seen as less typical of the category female than is a mother.

What do these results imply for a theory of concepts? Must we reject the recent theoretical work utilizing fuzzy logic as a description of concepts and categorization? The answer to the two questions is "very little" and "no". I do not see any qualitative difference between the concepts odd number and female and those of bird and furniture. Consider the concept female, employed by the authors because they believe that this concept is well-defined. This interpretation contrasts sharply with our impression of the concept. No one would argue with the idea that some people are more representative of the category female than are others. The value of a continuous measure of androgeny, which can be measured both psychologically and physiologically, provides support for the idea of the gradedness of the property female. By these criteria, it is a mistake to consider female as a well-defined concept that should not give graded responses in terms of judgments of category membership.

In the FLMP we view concepts as having well-defined descriptions in memory. Concepts are considered to be well-defined, not in the sense of necessary and sufficient conditions for an instance to be a member of the category, but in terms of the psychological representation of a summary description of the concept. The degree to which any instance fits this description will vary depending on the difference between the summary description and the perception of the instance. Conceptual classification will also be influenced by other exemplars or members of the category and it is probably realistic to assume both exemplar-based and prototype-based representations of concepts (see Chapter 9, Section 2.3).

Conclusion

The exact form of the integration of multiple , independent and continuous sources of information has not been resolved. It is difficult to assess the integration process independently of prototype matching and pattern classification. Although the exact mathematical form could not be determined, the integration is certainly enhancing. Two relatively ambiguous sources of information decrease a perceiver's uncertainty relative to just one of the sources. Either the multiplicative or minimization form of integration can describe this result. Finally, previous criticisms of fuzzy set theory were shown to be unjustified, primarily because they did not address how fuzziness is implemented in a process model of categorization. Having traversed the tree of binary contrasts in bimodal speech perception by college students, the next chapter addresses how these contrasts interact with development and aging.

Chapter 8: Lifespan Changes in Speech Perception by Ear and Eye

Any theory of language processing must eventually confront the acquisition of the processes involved in this skill. It is surprising how little research on speech perception across development has been carried out relative to the large number of studies of infants and young adults. Lifespan studies are central to evaluating theories of the processes responsible for observed differences and similarities in language processing with age. The experiments discussed in this chapter were designed to assess the evaluation and integration of audible and visible speech across a broad range of ages. The question of interest is whether the differences and similarities could be accounted for in a reasonable way within the framework of this investigation.

1. Binary Oppositions Across Development

The framework guiding the present investigation is also ideal for the study of developmental and aging changes in processing audible and visible speech. A developmental study implies that all of the questions that can be tested within the framework can also be tested in terms of interactions with development. Thus the binary oppositions generated in the present paradigm can now be asked as a function of developmental level. The potential interaction of each binary opposition with development will now be proposed before assessing previous and new experimental evidence.

1.1 Single versus Multiple Sources

With respect to our first contrast, we can inquire whether children also have both visible and audible sources of information available in their spoken discourse. At first blush, a positive answer seems the only likely alternative but we should consider any possible sensory/perceptual differences as well as differences in the ecological contact with audible and visible speech. The studies described in the literature review in Section 5.1 make it apparent that infants are recognizing correspondences between audible and visible speech. The development of auditory and visual processing might not coincide exactly, however, which would lead to an advantage of one source of information over the other. In addition, children might not have the same access to the sources as do adults. For example, children are short and adults are tall and this difference in height might be expected to limit visible relative to audible speech. With respect to ecological validity, the muppets and other cartoon characters would seem to destroy the potential visible information given by place of articulation while leaving intact the audible domain. At the other end of the developmental continuum, high-frequency hearing loss with age might degrade the audible information relative to the easily-correctable loss of visual acuity with age. These observations lead to the impression that multiple sources of information are available regardless of age, but the relative quality of the various sources might vary systematically with age.

1.2 Integration versus Nonintegration

On the heels of the decision of multiple sources of information for both children and adults, we can ask whether children also integrate the sources in perceptual recognition. There is a tradition in developmental theory, best represented by Piaget, to postulate an early stage of development in which integration does not occur. In the classic failure of conservation of mass, the young child attends only to height and not width of a glass of liquid (Anderson & Cuneo, 1978; Piaget, 1970). If perceiving speech is viewed as an analogous function, we might expect relatively young children to utilize just one of the available sources in perceptual judgment. The obvious candidate would be the audible source, given that it distinguishes all speech contrasts whereas the visual source does not. In addition, the observations made with respect to the question of single versus multiple sources revealed more ecological validity for audible relative to visible speech.

As in the test of this opposition with adults, children can be asked to recognize auditory, visual, and bimodal speech events. Although we have not performed this exact study, McGurk and MacDonald (1976) found fairly convincing support for integration for children as young as three years. Children were presented with auditory and bimodal speech events and asked to report what they heard the speaker saying. The bimodal speech events were dubbed articulations in that the two sources were in conflict. Performance was highly accurate (over 90% correct) given the auditory speech, but not given bimodal speech in the sense that the judgments did not correspond to the auditory domain. The authors noted two types of errors. Fusion errors involve a response not contained in either of the modalities, such as the response /da/ to an auditory /ba/ and a visual /ga/. Combination errors represent responses including the components from both modalities, such as the response /bda/ given an auditory /da/ and a visual /ba/. What is important for the opposition under question is that the young children produced a significant number of both fusion and combination responses, which are difficult to explain in terms of just a single source of information.

One might still argue that the lack of a visual condition precludes concluding that integration occurred. However, unambiguous support was obtained for integration in our study with adults (discussed in Chapter 3), and the children behaved very much like the adults in the McGurk and MacDonald (1976) study. The children's identification responses were similar to those given by adults, although somewhat fewer in number. It is unlikely that either the visual or the auditory source alone can account for the judgments given by both children and adults, permitting us to continue down the right side (no pun intended) of the binary tree illustrated in Chapter 1 but now crossed with development.

1.3 Categorical versus Continuous Sources of Information

The next question concerns whether a stimulus variable is perceived categorically or continuously. Much of the speech research with infants has been interpreted as supporting the categorical perception of certain phonetic contrasts (Eimas, Siqueland, Jusczyk, and Vigorito, 1971; Gleitman and Wanner, 1982). In contrast, recent research with adult subjects has demonstrated that listeners have available continuous information corresponding to the degree to which a speech event represents a given perceptual category (Carney, Widin, and Viemeister, 1977; Massaro and Cohen, 1983a, 1983c; Pisoni and Lazarus, 1974; Samuel, 1977). For example, Massaro and Cohen (1983a, 1983c) demonstrated that the auditory /ba/-/da/ continuum was perceived continuously rather than categorically (see also Chapter 4). In contrast, this same dimension is supposedly perceived categorically by infants (Eimas, 1974). Thus, it is possible that young children would tend to produce categorical results, whereas adults would not, given a /ba/-/da/ auditory continuum paired with visible speech. We will address this question in Sections 2.1 and 2.2.

1.4 Independent versus Dependent Sources

This binary contrast concerns the independence of the two sources of information. According to the independence view, the auditory and visual inputs provide independent sources of information about the speech event. A contrasting assumption claims that the visual and auditory sources are not evaluated independently, but that the stimulus event is perceived holistically. According to this view (Shepp, 1978; Smith and Kemler, 1978), independent dimensions might be present in the stimulus environment but not in the processing of the subject. Shepp (1978) and his colleagues (Shepp, Burns, & McDonough, 1980) and Smith and Kemler (1977, 1978) have proposed that there is a developmental trend from holistic processing to dimensional processing. Preschool children supposedly process some stimuli holistically, whereas adults do not. If this hypothesis is correct for visual and auditory speech events, then holistic (dependent) processing should be found for preschool children but not for adult subjects. This question is addressed in Sections 2.1 and 2.2.

1.5 Integration Rule Across Development

The final question to be addressed involves the integration rule used by children relative to that used by adults. There is now a body of work in information integration that finds less optimal integration rules for young children than for adults. The judgment of the area of rectangles has been shown to follow a height times width rule for children older than 7 and to follow either a height + width rule or a maximum linear extent rule for children between 3 and 5 years old (Anderson & Cuneo, 1978; Leon, 1982. The integration of the audible and visible sources of information in young adults is better described by a multiplying rule than an adding rule. It is conceivable, given the developmental differences in the perceptual domains of area and number, that younger children will utilize something more akin to an adding rather than a multiplying rule. We now turn to the experimental investigation of these and additional oppositions.

2. Children versus Adults

In an inaugural developmental study, Massaro (1984b) independently varied auditory and visual information in a speech perception task. Subjects identified as /ba/ or /da/ speech events consisting of synthetic speech syllables ranging from /ba/ to /da/ combined with a videotaped /ba/ or /da/ or no articulation. Children averaging about six years of age were tested and compared to adults in the speech identification task. Subjects were asked to view a male speaker on a TV monitor and to indicate whether he said /ba/ or /da/. Five levels of auditory information going from /ba/ to /da/ were factorially combined with three levels of visual information: /ba/, no articulation, and /da/.

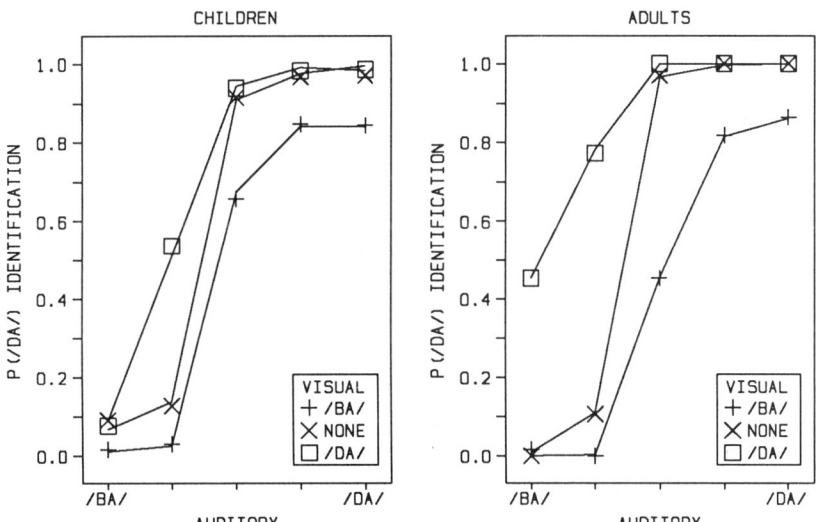

Figure 1. Observed (points) and predicted (lines) proportion of /da/ identifications as a function of the auditory and visual levels of the speech event. The predictions are for the FLMP (from Massaro, 1984b).

The proportion of /da/ responses was computed for each subject for each of the 15 conditions. The left and right panels of Figure 1 give the average results for the children and adult subjects, respectively. The proportion of /da/

responses as a function of the five levels along the auditory speech continuum is shown for the visual /ba/, /da/, and no articulation conditions. The average proportion of /da/ responses increased significantly as the level of the auditory speech was changed from /ba/ to /da/. There was also a large effect of the visual speech on the proportion of /da/ identifications. The interaction of these two variables was also significant, because the effect of visual speech was smaller at the less ambiguous regions of auditory speech.

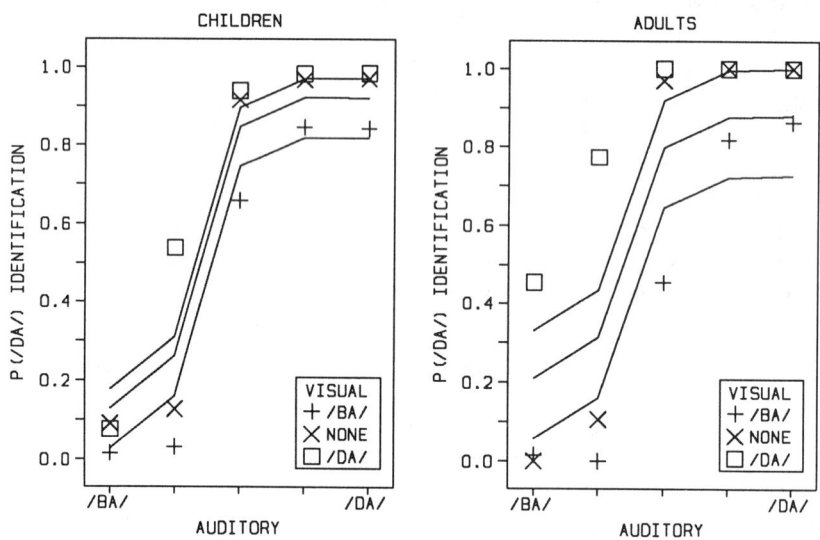

Figure 2. Observed (points) and predicted (lines) proportion of /da/ identifications as a function of the auditory and visual levels of the speech event. The predictions are for the CMP (from Massaro, 1984b).

The design of this study does not permit model-free tests of the questions of integration versus nonintegration, categorical versus continuous perception, and dependent versus independent sources with children as we did for adults (see Chapters 4 and 6). The model-free tests require a relatively large number of observations from an individual subject, which make them difficult to do with young children. Without these tests, we are left with model-dependent tests involving the contrasts of categorical versus continuous models and dependence versus independence models. These models have been derived in Chapters 4 and 6.

2.1 Model Analyses

The CMP, the dependence model, and the FLMP were tested against the results of the 15 independent experimental conditions. The models were tested against the results of individual subjects to preclude any distortion of performance by averaging across subjects. It can be demonstrated, for example, that averaging results across individual subjects will tend to improve the description given by the CMP, even if the actual model generating the results is not categorical.

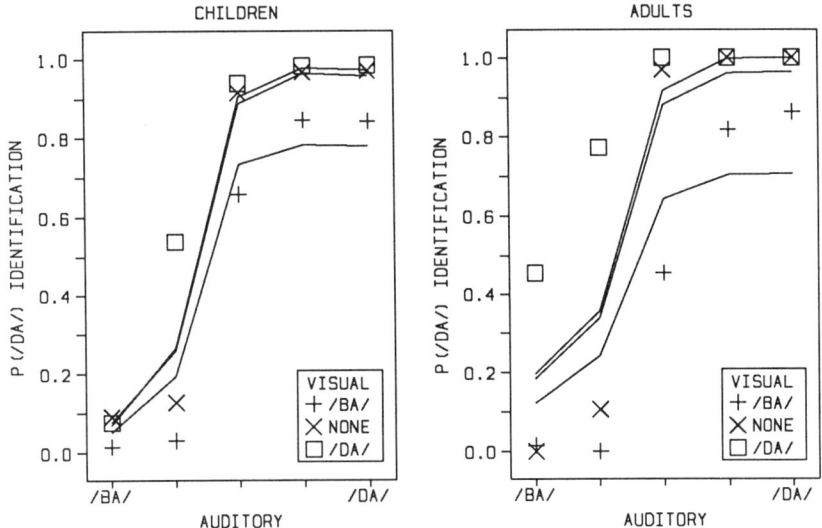

Figure 3. Observed (points) and predicted (lines) proportion of /da/ identifications as a function of the auditory and visual levels of the speech event. The predictions are for the dependence model (from Massaro, 1984b).

Figure 1 gives the observed and average predicted results of the FLMP for the children and adults. As can be seen in the figure, the model gave a good description of the observed results for both groups of subjects. Figures 2 and 3 give the same results with the predictions of the CMP and dependence models. These two models failed to capture the pattern of results for both age groups. The FLMP provided a much better description than the CMP and dependence models. The average RMSDs across the fit of the individual children were .026, .130, and .123 for the FLMP, CMP, and dependence models, respectively. The corresponding value for the adults were .010, .195, and .206.

The results of the Massaro (1984b) study also allow the rejection of an addition or averaging of the separate sources of information. A weighted adding model gives the following prototypes

$$/da/ : wa_i + (1-w)v_j$$

$$/ba/ : w(1-a_i) + (1-w)(1-v_j)$$

where w is the weight given the auditory dimension and $(1-w)$ is the weight given the visual dimension. Given the relative merit rule of the pattern classification operation, the additive model predicts that

$$P(/da/\mid A_i V_j) = wa_i + (1-w)v_j \tag{1}$$

which is equivalent to the prediction of the CMP when p is set equal to w. Thus, we can reject the adding-type model for evaluating and integrating sources of information in speech perception. In contrast to results in other domains (Anderson and Cuneo, 1978), there is no evidence for different integration rules for six-year-olds and young adults in the perceptual categorization of speech.

It should be stressed that the good description of the FLMP cannot be simply due to a large number of free parameters. The CMP and dependence model required as many or more parameters and gave significantly poorer descriptions of the results. We reject the categorical, averaging, and dependence models in favor of the FLMP model for both adults and children.

2.2 Developmental Differences in Information Value

With respect to the processes involved in the evaluation and integration of audible and visible information in speech perception, children behave similarly to adults. The FLMP model gave equally good descriptions of the individual performance of children and adult subjects. This result provides evidence consistent with the integration of continuous and independent featural information for both children and adults. Although the children and adults appear to give similar answers to the binary contrasts, it would have been unusual and disappointing to find no differences between the two age groups.

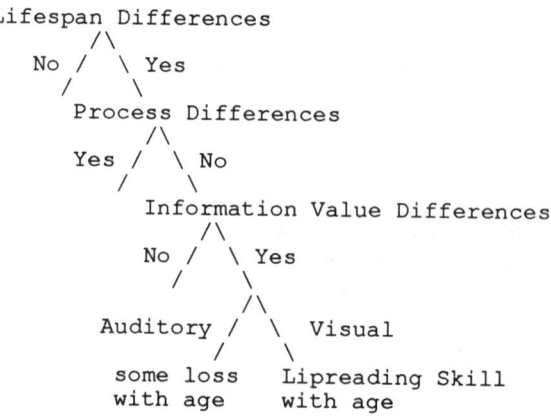

Figure 4. Binary contrasts in terms of developmental differences in processes and/or information value.

Within the framework of the FLMP we are able to distinguish between processing and information. Figure 4 gives a binary tree for developmental differences with respect to the processes involved in bimodal speech perception and the information utilized by these processes. As we will see, there are developmental differences, but not with respect to the fundamental processes involved in pattern classification. As illustrated in the binary tree, the information values representing the two sources might differ for children and adults even though the fundamental processes do not.

Differences in information value would be reflected in quantitative differences between the children and adult subjects. There was no group main effect and group did not interact with the auditory variable. This means that the auditory source was as effective for children as for adult subjects. This result may be relatively unique to this age group and the contrast under study, because other results have revealed less sensitivity for children relative to adults. Zlatin and Koeningsknecht (1975) found increasing sensitivity to voice onset time differences with aging, and Krause (1982) reported similar results for vowel duration differences. In our more recent studies, we have found large differences in the influence of the auditory source of information across development in both /va/-/ða/ and /ba/-/da/ contrasts (see Sections 3 and 4).

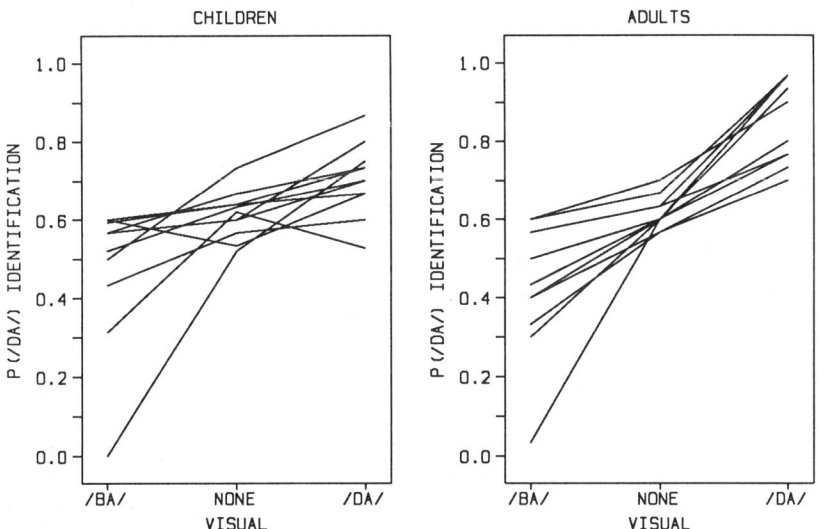

Figure 5. The proportion of /da/ identifications for individual subjects as a function of the visual level of the speech event, averaged across the five auditory levels (from Massaro, 1984b).

With regard to the visual source, however, the children were influenced by the visual variable only about half as much as were the adults. Figure 5 gives the effect of the visual variable for each subject in the two groups. Larger changes in the proportion of /da/ identifications across the three visual conditions indicate a larger influence of the visual variable. The smaller influence of the visual variable for the children was highly consistent. Eight of the 11 children showed a smaller effect of the visual variable than ten of the 11 adults.

Given the good description of the results by the FLMP, it is reasonable to evaluate the parameter values as indices of performance in the task. The parameter values a_i and v_j represent the degree of /da/-ness corresponding to the auditory and visual dimensions of stimulus A_{ij}. The values corresponding to the auditory variable were very similar for the two groups, showing a significant effect of the auditory level, but no interaction with age. An analogous analysis on the visual parameter values gave both a significant effect of the visual level, and a significant interaction of visual level with age. The parameter values for the /ba/ and /da/ levels of the visual variable were less extreme for the children than for the adults, reflecting the smaller effect of this variable for the children. When the model was fit to the average results of each of the two groups simultaneously with the restriction that the five auditory parameters be identical for the two groups, the RMSD increased from .018 to only .030. This represents a stronger test of the model by predicting 30 independent data points with just 11 free parameters. Accordingly, the model accurately describes the results in the same way for the two groups, allowing only for differences in the influence of the visual source of information.

2.2.1 Attentional Explanation

One possible explanation of the smaller visual effect for children is an attentional one. It has been proposed that the influence of a modality in perceptual judgment is related to the attention given to that modality (Welch & Warren, 1980). Some support for this proposition was found for bimodal speech perception (Chapter 3, Section 3.2). If children attend less to the visual than to the auditory source they should be less influenced by the visual source. The attention explanation predicts that the influence of a source will be positively related to the attention given the source. To increase the attentional demands of the visual source, the children in the Massaro (1984b) study were also required to indicate whether or not the speaker's lips moved during the speech event. We might expect that this requirement would increase the amount of attention given the visual source. To the extent that differences in attention are responsible for the smaller effect of the visual variable, the children should show a larger visual influence in this dual task relative to the single identification task.

However, the additional task of identifying whether or not the speaker's mouth moved had no influence on the identification of the speech event as /ba/ or /da/. The relative influence of the visual source and the integration of this source with the auditory information was identical in the two conditions. It is unlikely that the children show less of a visual influence because the visual dimension receives less attention.

2.2.2 Developmental Differences in Lipreading

To pursue the differences between children and adults, Massaro, Thompson, Barron, and Laren (1986) tested the idea that children are less sophisticated lipreaders than adults. The cues children use to distinguish a visual /ba/ from a /da/ may be less complete. Thus, children should be poorer at lipreading than are adults. If the visual variable is less informative for young children than for adults, its influence in bimodal speech perception will be smaller. More generally, we might expect a positive correlation between lipreading ability and the visual influence given bimodal speech.

Adults and preschool children were tested in a bimodal condition and a visual-only condition (Massaro et al., 1986). The results provided a comparison between the size of the visual effect in the presence of auditory speech and the subject's ability to identify accurately the two types of visual articulation when no sound is present. Replicating the previous experiment, the visual variable had a much larger influence on the adults' than on the children's judgments given bimodal speech. The proportion of /da/ identifications given a visual /da/ minus the proportion of /da/ identifications given a visual /ba/ was taken as a measure of the visual influence. Adults showed much more visual influence than the children. (.82 for adults and .35 for children).

The adult subjects were much better at lipreading than children. The average correct responses ranged from .86 to 1.0 (mean = .96) for the adults and from .57 to .95 (mean = .79) for the children. A correlation between subjects' proportion correct in the visual-only condition and the size of their visual influence in the bimodal condition was significant for each subject group and for the combined results of both groups. This finding lends credence to the supposition that the developmental difference in the size of the visual effect given bimodal speech is due to children's poorer ability to lipread, as compared to adults.

2.2.3 Model Analyses

If children do not lipread as well as adults, then the visible speech must be less informative in the bimodal condition. In terms of the FLMP, the amount of visual /da/-ness given by a /da/ articulation would be less for children than for adults. If poorer lipreading performance is totally responsible for the reduced size of the effect of the visible speech, then the information available in lipreading should be identical to that used for the visual source in the bimodal condition. In the most parsimonious form of the FLMP, a single value of visual /da/-ness should represent a given articulation in both the visual-alone and bimodal conditions (see Chapter 4, Section 2.5).

Another experiment was carried out by Massaro et al. (1986) with preschool children to assess more formally whether lipreading performance could predict the influence of the visual variable in the bimodal condition. Figure 6 presents the proportion of /da/ responses in the bimodal condition with auditory and visual speech and in the lipreading condition with just visual speech. We asked whether the visual /da/-ness values computed from the lipreading condition could be used as the visual parameters in the bimodal condition. Applying the FLMP to the lipreading task, the subject derives visual information and evaluates the degree to which that information supports the alternative /ba/, and similarly for the alternative /da/. The amount of /ba/-ness is equal to one minus the amount of /da/-ness. The probability of responding /da/ in the lipreading task can be thought of as corresponding to the amount of /da/-ness (given by the lips) divided by the sum of the /da/-ness and /ba/-ness values. If v_j is the visual /da/-ness, then the probability of a /da/ response given a particular visible lip movement (V_j) would be

$$P\,(/da\,/\,|\,V_j) = \frac{v_j}{v_j - (1 - v_j)} = v_j \qquad (2)$$

The equation shows that the lipreading accuracy can be taken as a direct index of visual information. The probability of a /da/ identification corresponds to the visual /da/-ness, whereas the probability of a /ba/ identification corresponds to the visual /ba/-ness.

Two versions of the FLMP were fit to the results of each of the children and to the average results. In one version, two visual and five auditory parameters were estimated to describe the ten response probabilities in the bimodal speech condition. In the other, five auditory and two visual parameters were estimated to predict 12 identification probabilities (10 from the bimodal task and 2 from the lipreading task). If lipreading can predict the effect of visible speech, then there should be no difference in the goodness of fits in the two conditions. This outcome occurred for the fit of the individual children and the fit of the average results. Figure 6 gives the average fit of the FLMP to the individual children assuming identical visual parameters in the two tasks.

In summary, the answer to the question of why the size of the visual effect is smaller for children than for adults reflects a developmental difference in the cue value of the visual source. The poorer quality of the visual information for children can be illustrated by their poorer lipreading. In contrast, the processes children employ to evaluate and combine both sources of information do not appear to differ from that used by adults.

3. /va/-/ðʲa/ Experiments

Previous experiments have used the syllables /ba/ and /da/ to assess the contribution of auditory and visual information to speech perception. It is

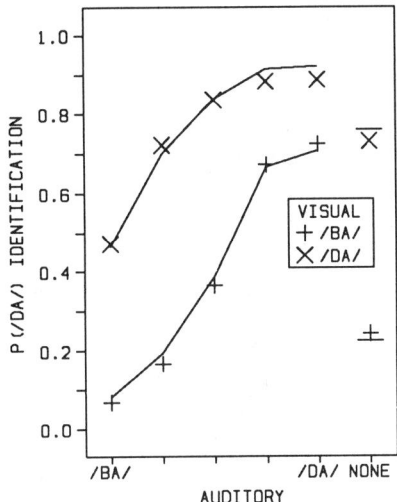

Figure 6. Observed (points) and predicted (lines) proportion of /da/ identifications for children as a function of the auditory and visual levels of the speech event in the bimodal condition and the lipreading condition (auditory none). The predictions are for the FLMP (after Massaro et al., 1986).

important to test their relative contribution within the context of other distinctions. The next set of experiments studied the contrast /va/-/ð̃a/. With respect to place of articulation, /va/ and /ð̃a/ are intermediate to /ba/ and /da/ articulations. Thus, it might be argued that /va/ and ð̃a/ are psychophysically more similar to each other than are /ba/ and /da/. This result is apparent in the experiment by Repp et al. (1983), who independently varied these four places of articulation along the auditory and visual dimensions (see Chapter 2, Section 3.9). Confusions among the stimuli always consisted of neighboring identifications along the place continuum; that is, a /va/ might be identified as /ð̃a/ or /ba/, but never as /da/, and so on. Synder and Pope (1970) found that about 70% of their first-graders failed to discriminate /v/ and /ð̃/ in both initial and final position in the contrasts *vow-thou* and *clothe-clove*. It is not apparent from their description whether the tester provided visual as well as auditory information during the presentation of the test words. Phatate & Umano (1981) found similar results for /fa/ and /θa/, the voiceless cognates of /va/ and /ð̃a/.

A second reason for these experiments is to better determine the improvement in lipreading with age. Although Massaro et al. (1986) found large differences between preschool and adult subjects, no differences were observed within an age range from 3 to 6 years. In the present studies, preschool children are tested and contrasted with adolescents in speech perception by ear and eye.

In addition, we will be able to provide some assessment of the development of lipreading skill with experience in the task.

3.1 General Method

Stimuli. Prior to the experiment, a video-audio master tape was recorded as described in Chapter 3, Section 2.1. On each trial the speaker said either /va/, or /ð̃a/ as cued by a video terminal under control of a DEC PDP-11/34a computer. Each recording trial started with a 400 msec warning tone presented by the emitter in the terminal keyboard base. Following 280 msec after the offset of the warning tone, the computer cued the speaker by displaying either a large "V", or "TH" on the screen for 320 msec. Following the offset of the cue, there was a 4000 msec period before the next warning tone. During the videotape recording, only the visual level of information was communicated to the speaker as a cue. The tape was reviewed to insure that the stimuli were created correctly according to the visual cues.

Table 1. Speech synthesis parameters for five sounds on continuum between /va/ and /ð̃a/.

	F1(Hz)		F2(Hz)		F3(Hz)		B3	A6
	0-100	120	0-100	120	0-100	120	(Hz)	(dB)
/va/ 1	220	532	1080	1110	2080	2425	130	0
2	225	493	1117	1148	2210	2473	147	6
3	230	454	1155	1187	2340	2521	165	13
4	235	415	1192	1225	2470	2569	182	20
/ð̃a/ 5	240	376	1230	1264	2600	2618	200	27

Five auditory fricative-vowel syllables between /va/ and /ð̃a/ were created using a software formant serial resonator speech synthesizer (Klatt, 1980). The following properties were identical for all five syllables. Their duration was 420 msec. Voicing amplitude, AV, rose from 44 dB at 0 msec to 47 dB at 105 msec, to 53 dB at 110 msec, to 56 dB at 160, to 58 dB at 405 msec and then fell to 40 dB at 415 msec. The amplitude of sinusoidal voicing, AVS, was set to 40 dB at time 0. It then rose to 50 dB at 120 msec, then fell to 40 dB at 140 msec. After 140 msec, AVS was shut off entirely. Frication amplitude, AF, rose from 40 dB at 0 msec to 48 dB at 10 msec, to 50 dB at 30 msec, and then fell to 48 dB at 100 msec and then 0 dB at 150 msec. Fundamental frequency, F0, was 130 Hz from 0 to 100 msec, then rose to 150 Hz at 130 msec and then fell to 120 Hz at 415 msec. The first formant bandwidth, B1, went from 55 Hz at 0 msec to 60 Hz at 90 msec, and then to 130 Hz at 160 msec, where it remained for the duration of the vowel. Similarly, the second formant bandwidth, B2, went from 100 Hz for the first 100 msec to 70 Hz at 175 msec, remaining at that value thereafter. The

F4, F5, and F6 frequencies were fixed at 3300, 3850, and 4900 Hz, respectively.

The synthesis parameters that differed for the 5 levels between /va/ and /ða/ are given in Table 1. The F1 frequency for the first 100 msec and the value at 120 msec is given in the table. After 120 msec the F1 value rose to 700 Hz where it stayed during the vowel. Similarly, F2 and F3 changed to 1220 and 2600 Hz, respectively, at 180 msec from the values given in the table. The third formant bandwidth, B3, for the first 100 msec is given in the table. This value was changed to 160 Hz by 160 msec where it stayed for the remainder of the vowel. The sixth formant amplitude, A6, was set to one of the five values given in Table 1 during the first 160 msec of the syllable. The resulting stimuli, quantized at a 10000 sample per second rate, were stored on the computer disk for later use.

An experimental tape was created from the 3/4" master tape on a Panasonic NV-8200 1/2" VHS video tape recorder according to the following design. Each trial on the tape consisted of one of the five auditory stimuli on the continuum from /va/ to /ða/ paired with one of the two possible visual stimuli, /va/ or /ða/. The dubbing of the experimental tape was synchronized with the original audio track on the videotape by a schmidt trigger circuit. When the original audio channel on the videotape exceeded a preset threshold, one of the 420 msec stimuli was played. Similarly, the original warning tones were replaced by a 250-msec tone. The auditory stimuli were played at a rate of 10000 samples per second and filtered 20-4900 Hz (KHRON-HITE 3500R).

Procedure. During the experiment, the experimental tape described above was played to the subjects over a NEC model C12-202A 12" in. (.31 m) color monitor. The audio portion of the experimental tape was presented to the subjects over the built-in speaker of the monitor at a comfortable listening level of about 67 dB-A, measured at the approximate position of the observers head using a B&K 2203 sound level meter with a 4134 microphone. All subjects were tested in a research van (Mayer, 1982).

3.2 Preschool Subjects

Subjects. Nineteen preschool children were tested; most of the subjects had participated in previous experiments. The age range was 42 to 75 months, with a mean of 61.5 months.

Procedure. On any trial, a bimodal, auditory-alone, or visual-alone trial could be presented. Seven auditory levels and two visual levels were varied in an expanded factorial design (see Chapter 3, Section 1, Figure 2). Five of the auditory levels were the synthesized speech levels on the /va/ to /ða/ continuum. The two other auditory levels were natural speech tokens, one natural /va/ and one natural /ða/. Subjects were tested for 84 trials on a single day. Each subject was tested 14 times under each of the two visual-alone conditions, 4 times under each of the 7 auditory-alone conditions, and 2 times under each of the 14 bimodal conditions. All trial types were completely randomized within a block of 42 trials. The children were instructed to listen and to watch the TV monitor, and to identify the speech event on each trial as /va/ or /ða/.

Results. Figure 7 presents the average proportion of /ða/ identifications as a function of the experimental conditions. As can be seen in the figure, subjects showed a monotonically increasing identification function in the auditory-alone condition. The proportion of /ða/ responses increased from .13 to .91 along the /va/-/ða/ continuum. Lipreading accuracy in the lipreading condition indicated that subjects correctly identified the /va/ articulation about 82 percent of the time and the /ða/ articulation about 85 percent of the time. In the bimodal condition, the main effects of the two independent variables and their interaction were highly significant. The auditory variable showed an increase in /ða/ articulations from .32 to .83 along the /va/-/ða/ continuum. The visual variable indicated that the children responded 23 percent of the time with a /ða/ response to a /va/ articulation, whereas they responded 74 percent of the time with a /ða/ articulation to the articulation /ða/. The interaction was also highly significant, indicating a larger effect of the visual variable in the middle of the auditory continuum relative to the extreme.

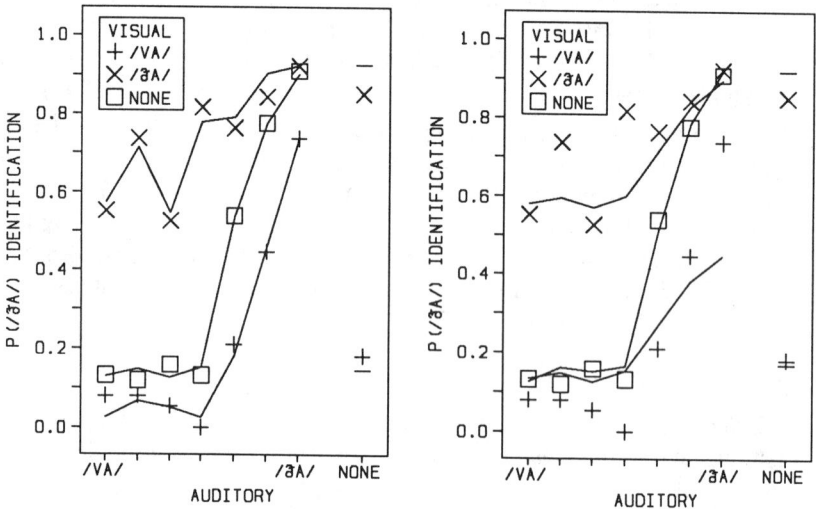

Figure 7. Observed (points) and predicted (lines) proportion of /ða/ identifications as a function of the auditory and visual levels of the speech event for the bimodal, visual, and auditory conditions for the preschool children. The predictions for the FLMP are given in the left panel and the predictions for the CMP in the right panel.

The FLMP and the CMP were fit to the individual subjects and to the average results. Figure 7 presents the results of these fits. As can be seen in the figure and the RMSD values in Table 2, the FLMP does a much more adequate job of describing the trends in the data than does the CMP.

Table 2. The RMSD values for the fit of the average subject and the average RMSD values of the individual fits for the FLMP and the CMP for the /va/-/ðˀa/ experiments.

	RMSD for Average Subject		Average RMSD	
Group	FLMP	CMP	FLMP	CMP
preschool	.058	.090	.100	.175
adolescents	.020	.068	.058	.101

3.3 Adolescent Subjects

Subjects and Procedure. Six fourth and fifth graders with an average age of 150 months were tested for 126 trials. All other procedural details were equivalent to the study with preschool children.

Results. The results are shown in Figure 8. Subjects showed good discrimination of the auditory continuum in the auditory-alone condition. The proportion of /ðˀa/ responses increased from .25 to .94 along the /va/-/ðˀa/ continuum. Lipreading performance in the visual-alone condition was near perfect at 98 percent correct. In the bimodal condition, there were significant effects of the auditory source, the visual source, and an interaction between these two variables. The auditory variable showed an increase in /ðˀa/ articulations from .50 to .72 along the /va/-/ðˀa/ continuum. The visual variable indicated that the adolescents responded 9 percent of the time with a /ðˀa/ response to a /va/ articulation, whereas they responded 93 percent of the time with a /ðˀa/ articulation to the articulation /ðˀa/. The interaction indicated a larger effect of the visual variable in the middle of the auditory continuum relative to the extreme.

The fits of the FLMP and CMP to the results are also shown in Figure 8. As can be seen in the figure and Table 2, the FLMP gave a significantly better description of performance than did the CMP.

3.4 Developmental Contrast

To assess the developmental trends, the results with preschool children were contrasted with the results for adolescents. Although it might be argued that the additional experience of the preschoolers in the experimental task relative to the adolescents might invalidate such a comparison, an analysis of the preschool subjects showed no significant changes in their performance with experience.

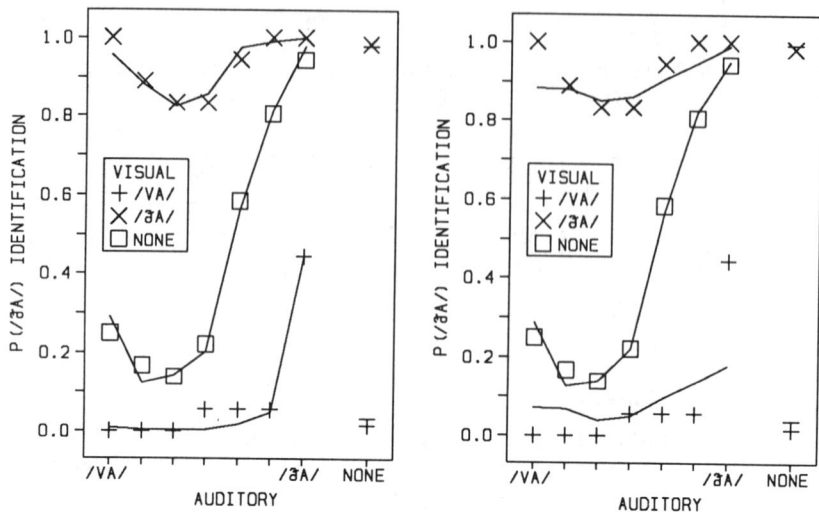

Figure 8. Observed (points) and predicted (lines) proportion of /ð'a/ identifications as a function of the auditory and visual levels of the speech event for the bimodal, visual, and auditory conditions for the adolescents. The predictions for the FLMP are given in the left panel and the predictions for the CMP in the right panel.

Six preschoolers were randomly selected and compared with the six adolescent children. The group comparisons reveal an advantage in lipreading for the adolescents but not in auditory discrimination of synthetic speech. This advantage can be seen in the larger spread between the visual /va/ and /ð'a/ curves for the adolescents in Figure 8 relative to that found for the preschool children in Figure 7.

4. Lifespan Study

The present experiment extends the study of bimodal speech perception to children and senior citizens covering an age range of 3 to 84 years. In addition to testing the role of auditory and visual information in bimodal speech perception across development and aging, the expanded factorial design adds two tasks. The subjects identify speech sounds presented alone in an auditory condition and identify speech articulations (read lips) in a visual condition. The three tasks taken in combination provide an informative assessment of the role of auditory and visual information in speech perception.

The central question is whether bimodal speech perception can be described by some combination of its auditory and visual sources of information. If the two sources are independent, then it should be possible to describe the three tasks in terms of the same information and processing operations. Given that the FLMP and the CMP make clear predictions about performance across the three tasks, the results will be tested against the predictions of the two models. The wide age range of the subjects also addresses the issue of whether either model can account for performance across most of development and aging. Analogous to the finding of poorer visual information for children than for adults, we might expect to find poorer auditory information for senior citizens. Even with degraded auditory information, however, older subjects may utilize the same processes for evaluation, integration, and pattern classification.

4.1 Method

Subjects. There were six groups of subjects with 10 to 16 subjects per group. The age range and average age of each of the six groups are given in Table 3. Ten children, three females and seven males, composed the inexperienced preschool group. Sixteen children, four males and twelve females, served as subjects in the experienced preschool group. The preschool children were recruited from the University Child Care Center. There were seven females and nine males in the kindergarten group. The sixteen fourth-grade children consisted of seven males and nine females. The kindergarten and fourth-grade children were tested during their school day. The college-student group was composed of seven males and eight females. They were recruited from an introductory psychology class. Finally, there were thirteen senior citizens with five males and eight females. The children received a small toy, the senior citizens a meal gift certificate, and the college students class credit for participating in the experiment. All subjects except the experienced preschool children and the senior citizens were new to the experimental situation. The preschool children had considerable experience in previous experiments lipreading /ba/ and /da/ and identifying bimodal speech. The senior citizens had participated in an experiment identical to the present one except that the auditory continuum was somewhat more ambiguous in the earlier experiment.

Table 3. The age (years-months) range and average age of the six groups of subjects.

Group	Age Range	Average Age
Inexperienced Preschool	2-6 to 4-0	3-5
Experienced Preschool	2-9 to 6-8	4-9
Kindergarten	5-0 to 6-1	5-4
Fourth Grade	8-11 to 10-4	9-7
College Students	19 to 33	22
Senior Citizens	60 to 84	72

Stimuli. The speech events were recorded on a videotape as described in Chapter 3, Section 3.1. The five synthetic speech syllables, equally spaced along a /ba/ to /da/ continuum, were identical to those used in the Massaro (1984b) experiment.

All subjects except the college students were tested individually in a research van (Mayer, 1982). The college students were tested in a sound-attenuated room. All subjects viewed a 12-in. (.31 m) color TV monitor, which presented both the audio and the video. The loudness of the audio was at comfortable listening level (70 dB-A). The subjects sat two to three feet from the monitor.

Procedure. There were three experimental conditions tested between blocks of trials: bimodal, visual, and auditory. During each trial of the bimodal condition, one of the five auditory stimuli on the continuum from /ba/ to /da/ was paired with one of the two visual stimuli, a /ba/ or a /da/ articulation. Trials in the visual condition used the same video tape but without the speech sounds. In the auditory condition, the TV screen was covered so that only the auditory information was presented.

A 250-msec bell preceded each trial in all conditions. The silent interval between the bell and the onset of the speech event ranged from 1175 to 1375 msec. The subjects had about four sec to make a response before the next trial.

In the bimodal condition, subjects were instructed to watch and to listen to the "man on the TV" and to tell the experimenter whether the man said /ba/ or /da/. Before the visual condition, each child watched the experimenter's mouth as she demonstrated silent articulations of the two alternatives. In this condition, children were instructed to report whether the speaker's mouth made /ba/ or /da/. The adults were simply told to lipread. In the auditory condition, the subjects were instructed to listen to each test sound to indicate whether the man said /ba/ or /da/. For all but the college students, the experimenter watched the subjects to insure that they were watching the screen at the time of the speech event. If this criteria was not met, the trial was disregarded. The college students made their responses by hitting one of two keys connected to a computer. All of the other subjects made their response by verbally reporting what they heard. All subjects, except the preschool children, were tested for a single session of forty trials under each of the three experimental conditions. The preschoolers were tested for two sessions of twenty trials each. The order of the three conditions was counterbalanced across subjects. Except for discarded trials, each subject contributed four responses to each of ten bimodal conditions, eight responses to each of the five auditory conditions, and twenty responses to each of the two visual conditions.

4.2 Results

Given that the task required a two-alternative forced-choice judgment, a single dependent variable, the proportion of /da/ responses, provides all of the information about choice performance. This proportion was computed for each subject in each of the seventeen experimental conditions. Separate analyses of variance were carried out for each of the six groups on the bimodal, visual, and auditory conditions. In all cases, the auditory and visual variables produced significant differences as did the interaction between these two variables in the bimodal condition. Figures 9 through 14 give the results for the three conditions for each of the six groups of subjects.

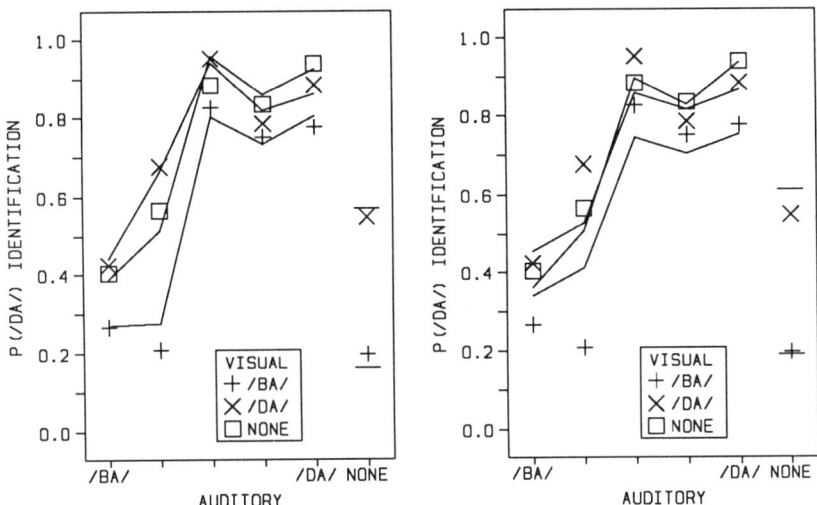

Figure 9. Observed (points) and predicted (lines) proportion of /da/ identifications as a function of the auditory and visual levels of the speech event for the inexperienced preschool children. The predictions are for the FLMP (left panel) and CMP (right panel).

Table 4. Average parameter values indicating degree of /da/-ness given the auditory and visual sources for the FLMP for the six groups of subjects.

Group	Auditory (a_i)					Visual (v_j)	
	/ba/	2	3	4	/da/	/ba/	/da/
Inexperienced Preschool	.389	.514	.57	.858	.923	.161	.570
Experienced Preschool	.114	.237	.959	.980	.992	.087	.885
Kindergarten	.037	.162	.876	.992	.992	.064	.668
Fourth Grade	.001	.017	.862	.999	.998	.014	.949
College Students	.015	.037	.786	.983	.990	.004	.976
Senior Citizens	.089	.172	.723	.961	.980	.002	.971

Rather than overwhelming the reader with the plethora of large F ratios and significant differences that were found, we focus on two aspects of the

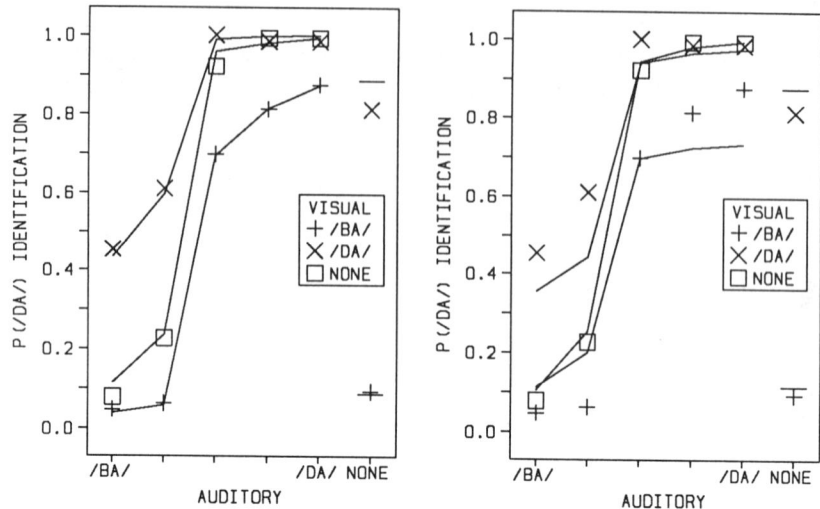

Figure 10. Observed (points) and predicted (lines) proportion of /da/ identifications as a function of the auditory and visual levels of the speech event for the experienced preschool children. The predictions are for the FLMP (left panel) and CMP (right panel).

Table 5. Average parameter values indicating the probability of a /da/ decision to the auditory and visual sources and the bias parameter indicating the probability of responding with the decision of the auditory source for the CMP for the six groups of subjects.

Group	Auditory (a_i)					Visual (v_j)		Bias
	/ba/	2	3	4	/da/	/ba/	/da/	
Inexperienced Preschool	.362	.508	.894	.827	.935	.192	.612	.698
Experienced Preschool	.105	.254	.942	.980	.994	.114	.874	.297
Kindergarten	.036	.135	.802	.983	.981	.056	.677	.175
Fourth Grade	.006	.093	.800	.995	.988	.019	.952	.264
College Students	.019	.028	.759	.972	.989	.054	.955	.759
Senior Citizens	.107	.169	.127	.966	.988	.058	.979	.796

results. First, to what extent do the FLMP and the CMP describe performance for the six groups of subjects? Second, what is the contribution of the auditory and visual sources of information when they are presented alone and together for each group of subjects? The two models were fit to the results of individual subjects and to the average results. Figures 9 through 14 give the fits of the FLMP in the left panel and the fits for the CMP in the right panel for the six groups of subjects. Tables 4 and 5 give the average parameter values for each model for each group of subjects. The average RMSDs between the predicted

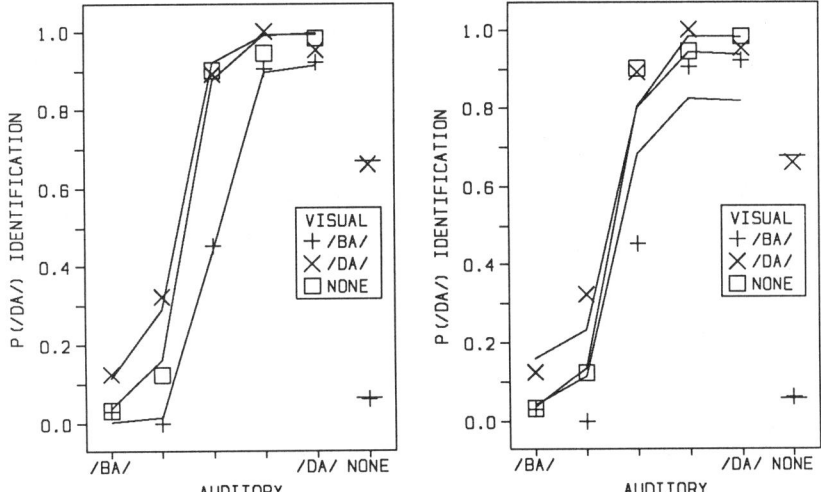

Figure 11. Observed (points) and predicted (lines) proportion of /da/ identifications as a function of the auditory and visual levels of the speech event for the kindergarten children. The predictions are for the FLMP (left panel) and CMP (right panel).

and observed values and the RMSDs for the fit of the average subjects are given in Table 6.

As can be seen in Table 6, the FLMP gave a much better description of performance than did the CMP for each of the six groups of subjects. This advantage of the FLMP held for both the results of individual subjects and for the results of the average subject. The fit of the CMP to the average subject was about three or four times poorer than was the description given by the FLMP. The much better description given by the FLMP is especially impressive given that this model required one fewer free parameter than did the CMP. The CMP seemed to give an equally poor description for all groups of subjects. The FLMP gave a somewhat poorer description for the preschool and kindergarten children relative to the older three groups.

The test of the two models makes the assumption that the auditory and visual information is identical in the unimodal and bimodal conditions. Any fatigue, learning, or practice effects across the three tasks carried out in separate sessions would work against this assumption of identical parameters across the three tasks. One question is to what extent the descriptions given by the two models change without this assumption. Relaxing the assumption is equivalent to analyzing only the bimodal task. Table 7 presents the RMSD values for the two models for the description of just the bimodal task. As can be seen in the table, the fit of the FLMP is improved considerably, whereas no improvement is

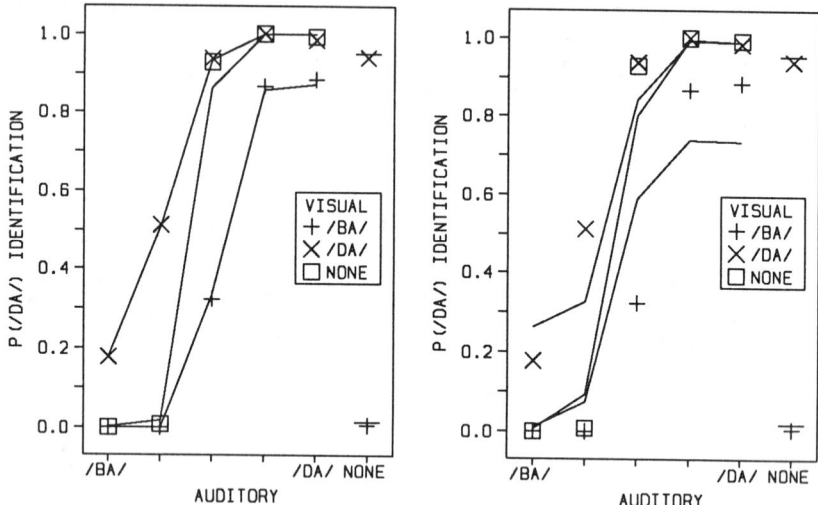

Figure 12. Observed (points) and predicted (lines) proportion of /da/ identifications as a function of the auditory and visual levels of the speech event for the fourth-grade children. The predictions are for the FLMP (left panel) and CMP (right panel).

Table 6. Average RMSD values and the RMSD value for the average subject for the FLMP and the CMP for the six groups of subjects for all experimental conditions.

Group	FLMP		CMP	
	Average	Average Subject	Average	Average Subject
Inexperienced Preschool	.091	.051	.144	.076
Experienced Preschool	.051	.020	.122	.078
Kindergarten	.077	.027	.133	.080
Fourth Grade	.027	.018	.141	.105
College Students	.039	.021	.113	.067
Senior Citizens	.022	.015	.105	.063
Average	.043	.020	.121	.079

observed for the CMP. Thus, the extremely poor fit of the CMP cannot be due to a change in parameter values across the three conditions, whereas the improved fit of the FLMP of just the bimodal condition indicates that small changes in the parameters may have taken place across the three test sessions. Future work could assess this question by comparing performance differences across the three conditions varied within and between blocks of trials.

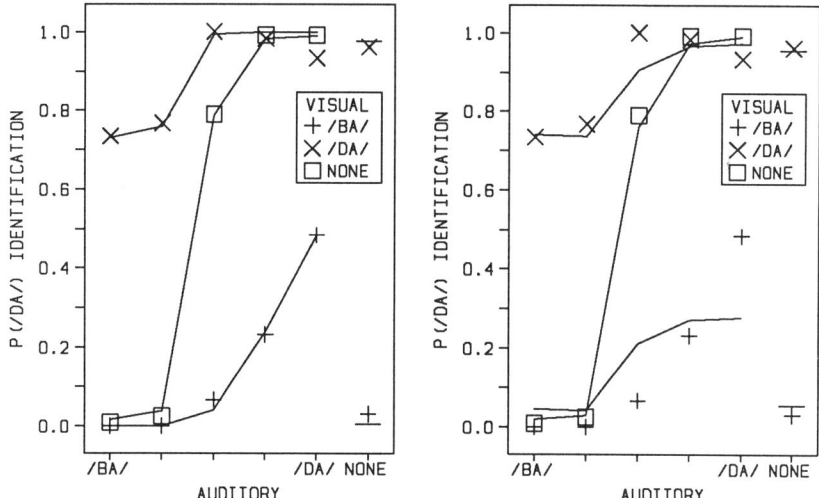

Figure 13. Observed (points) and predicted (lines) proportion of /da/ identifications as a function of the auditory and visual levels of the speech event for the college students. The predictions are for the FLMP (left panel) and CMP (right panel).

4.3 Lifespan Differences

The results for different groups of subjects allow the assessment of lifespan differences. We ask whether the information values for the auditory and visual sources change with age and whether the processes involved in perceptual recognition of speech differ with age. The first question might be easier to address if the answer to the second question was negative. We found that the FLMP consistently gave a better description of performance for all six age groups than did CMP. This observation argues against any change from one type of process to another in perceptual recognition of speech. At every age, performance is more appropriately described as following the operations of the FLMP.

It is also of interest whether the description given by the FLMP differed as a function of age. At first glance, this question might appear to be answered simply by comparing the RMSD values across the six groups. This analysis is reasonable but the fit of the FLMP, or any other model, is biased in favor of subjects who give more extreme judgments. Every judgment has some error of measurement associated with it and this variability is related to the probability of the judgment. Both the binomial variance (Green & Swets, 1966) and the actual variance in a psychophysical task (Mayer, unpublished) decreases as response probability moves either higher or lower than .5. If variances of judgments in the present experiment have this same property, subjects with less extreme

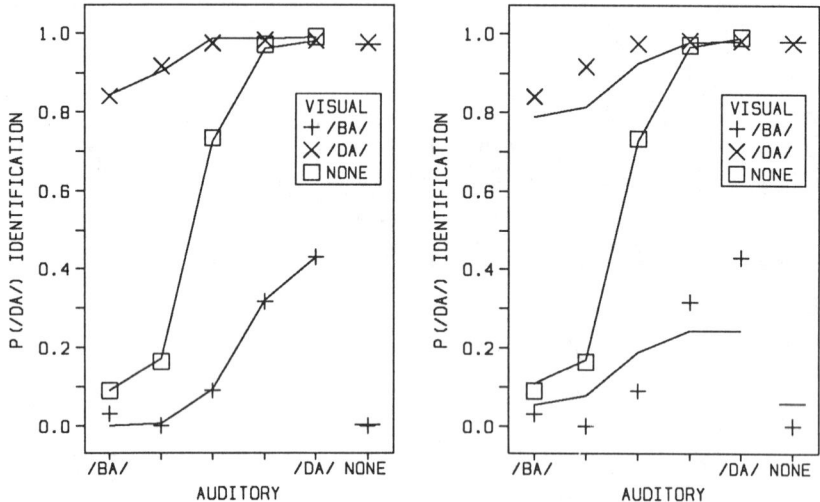

Figure 14. Observed (points) and predicted (lines) proportion of /da/ identifications as a function of the auditory and visual levels of the speech event for the senior citizens. The predictions are for the FLMP (left panel) and CMP (right panel).

Table 7. Average RMSD values and RMSD values for the average subject for the FLMP and the CMP for the six groups of subjects for just the bimodal condition.

	FLMP		CMP	
Group	Average	Average Subject	Average	Average Subject
Inexperienced Preschool	.059	.036	.132	.075
Experienced Preschool	.013	.007	.137	.087
Kindergarten	.024	.019	.132	.081
Fourth Grade	.007	.010	.159	.117
College Students	.016	.021	.132	.083
Senior Citizens	.001	.011	.123	.078
Average	.012	.014	.137	.089

response probabilities will tend to have higher RMSDs, everything else held constant. Consistent with this observation. the preschool and kindergarten children tended to have less extreme response probabilities and somewhat higher RMSD values. Thus, we can *not* use the absolute RMSD values to conclude that the description of the FLMP differed across development. The safest measure appears to be a relative one and the better description given by the FLMP relative to the CMP is evidence for the conclusion that the processes involved in speech perception are identical across the age span studied here. These processes are best described by the FLMP, which then provides a framework for assessing lifespan differences in information value.

A reasonable measure of information value is the degree to which a subject discriminated the different levels of the speech dimensions. An index of discrimination can be determined by taking the difference in parameter values for two different levels of a speech dimension. Thus, visual discrimination is given by the degree of /da/-ness given a visual /da/ minus the degree of /da/-ness given a visual /ba/. As an example, visual discrimination for the inexperienced preschoolers would be .570 minus .161 or .409. The auditory discrimination is given by the degree of /da/-ness given the most /da/-like auditory syllable minus the degree of /da/-ness given the most /ba/-like auditory syllable (that is, the two end points along the auditory continuum). This discrimination value is .923 minus .389 or .534 for the inexperienced preschoolers.

Utilizing the FLMP as a reasonable description of performance, it is possible to address the question of how the information value of the sources changes with age. To assess differences in information value, an analysis of variance was carried out on the auditory and the visual discrimination values with the six different groups as a factor. To assess how the information from auditory and visual speech changes across the lifespan, we carried out an analysis on the parameter values determined in the fit of the FLMP. Separate analyses were carried out on the auditory and visual parameters. Table 4 gives the average parameter values for the six groups of subjects. Given 5 degrees of freedom, we performed five specific contrasts as shown in Table 8. The question is whether the left (L), right (R), or neither (N) group has more information from the auditory and visual sources.

Table 8. Comparison of experimental groups in terms of whether the left (L), right (R), or neither (N) group has more information from the auditory and from the visual source.

Groups Compared	Auditory	Visual
College Students vs. Senior Citizens	N	N
Inexperienced Preschool vs. Experienced Preschool	N	R
Kindergarten vs. Fourth Grade	R	R
Fourth Grade vs. College Student	N	N
Experienced Preschool vs. Kindergarten	N	N

Although no significant differences were found between the college students and senior citizens, this was probably due to the task being too easy. Massaro (1985a) found that senior citizens showed poorer discrimination than fourth graders when tested on a more difficult version of the same auditory continuum. Given a high-frequency hearing loss with aging, there can be no question of poorer auditory speech perception with aging. On the other hand, there is no convincing evidence for a decrease in lipreading with aging. The experienced preschool children revealed some advantage in lipreading relative to the inexperienced children. Given our previous findings (Massaro, 1984b; Massaro et al., 1986) and unpublished results, some of the advantage is probably due to experience and not just the age difference. Fourth graders are superior to Kindergartners in both audible and visible speech perception and performed as well as the college students. The experienced preschoolers did not differ from the kindergartners in either audible or visible speech perception.

4.4 /va/-/ðⁱa/ versus /ba/-/da/ Contrast

It is of interest to compare the /va/-/ðⁱa/ results with the /ba/-/da/ results. This comparison can provide a measure of the relative contribution of the auditory and visual information in the two situations. The preschool children were tested in both situations and, therefore, the comparison will have to be limited to this single contrast. Fifteen preschool children participating in the /va/-/ðⁱa/ experiment were compared with fifteen of the experienced preschoolers in the /ba/-/da/ experiment. The first group had participated in an earlier /va/-/ðⁱa/ experiment. The natural speech trials were discarded from the /va/-/ðⁱa/ results to make the two contrasts directly comparable. By pooling the /va/-/ðⁱa/ results across the two experiments, each child has the same number of observations as the children participating in the /ba/-/da/ experiment. It turns out that some children participated in both experiments but for simplicity the contrast will be treated as between groups in the statistical analysis.

As in the analysis of the lifespan differences, the index of discrimination of a given modality was the difference in parameter values for the two extreme levels of that dimension. The results revealed an interesting interaction between the contrast being tested and the contribution of a given source of information. The auditory source was more informative for the /ba/-/da/ contrast than for the /va/-/ðⁱa/ contrast. On the other hand, the visual source was more informative for the /va/-/ðⁱa/ contrast than for the /ba/-/da/ contrast. These results agree with the psychophysical properties of the syllables. For auditory presentation, /ba/ and /da/ are less likely to be confused with one another than are /va/ and /ðⁱa/ (Miller & Nicely, 1955). Visual presentation gives just the opposite results (Walden et al., 1977) in that the two fricatives are less likely to be confused with one another than the two stops. There is no dominant source of information in bimodal speech perception: the contribution of a given source depends on its relative ambiguity with respect to the distinction of interest.

4.5 Summary

One challenge to any theory is its ability to describe constancy and change in the phenomena with development and aging. The theoretical framework for the present investigation has been previously tested with only college students. Accordingly, there has been little concern for how similarities and differences across development and aging might be explained. Extending the experimental paradigm to include individuals across the lifespan revealed positive aspects of the theoretical framework not previously apparent. The distinction between information and information processing is central to understanding changes across the lifespan.

There were significant differences in the information value of audible and visible speech as a function of age, but no differences in information processing. Acquisition of the visible speech distinctions occurs gradually across development, as does the acquisition of audible distinctions. Experience with speech enhances the quality of the information but does not appear to influence how the information is evaluated, integrated, and utilized for decision. Aging, on the other hand, can decrease the resolution of the sensory systems and limit the information that is available. There was no evidence that the decrease in resolution with aging is accompanied by modifications of how the information is processed. As a cautionary note, differences in information processing might eventually be found when additional speech contrasts, experimental tasks, and theoretical analyses are used. The current developmental and aging research has only scratched the surface of a rich mine of interesting research.

5. Relevance to Developmental Research and Theory

The developmental and lifespan study of speech perception by ear and eye revealed remarkable similarities and yet some reasonable differences across age. The major finding is that the fundamental processes involved in pattern recognition as described by the FLMP appear to exist at age 3 and to remain constant for the next seven decades. Needless to say, we have not reduced uncertainty about the first three years of language perception. Other experimental paradigms, such as habituation and preferential looking, will be needed to address this question. With respect to the information value of auditory and visual speech, there are substantial changes with age. These changes are readily explained by increased experience with age and changes in the sensory systems with aging. Preschool children are still acquiring speech-perception skills. The change that is observed appears to be best described in terms of the feature evaluation stage of the FLMP. A given source of information is less informative for preschool children than for adults. This is not surprising given that it is experience with speech that permits speech data to be treated as information. We can except that the prototype descriptions of the distinguishing characteristics of speech will increase in resolution with experience.

Aging, on the other hand, can decrease the resolution of the sensory systems resulting in less accurate speech perception. Luckily, the availability of multiple sources of information should preclude a catastrophic breakdown even with a fairly severe loss of a given source. For example, visible speech from the speaker's lips appears to compensate for a high-frequency hearing loss with age. The value of the FLMP is that it not only describes how speech perception might be accomplished, it provides a framework for understanding how it changes with development and aging. These findings have implications for developmental study both within and outside the field of speech perception. Five different areas of research will be discussed and related to the present results.

5.1 Infant Auditory/Visual Perception

To perceive speech bimodally means that the auditory and visual information can be related to the same event. Integrating sight and sound appears to be a natural function even for infants. Lawson (1980) explored the perception of auditory and visual signals for 6-month-old infants as a function of spatial and temporal contiguity. Infants were first exposed to an object moved periodically in synchrony with a periodic sound emanating from the object. In a later test, the infants looked longer at the familiar object in the presence of the sound than at the same object in the presence of a novel sound. Similar results were found with continuous movement of the object with a periodic sound, but not with periodic movement and continuous sound. If the sound was not spatially congruent with the object, infants did not reveal any learning of the association of the object and sound.

In a series of experiments, Spelke (1979a, 1979b) demonstrated the infant's ability to detect the correlation between the audible and visible dimensions of an object. In the first study (Spelke, 1976), the infants watched two films presented side by side. One film showed a woman playing "peekaboo," and the other film showed percussion instruments being played. An audio speaker located between the two films played a sound track appropriate to one film or to the other. Infants tended to watch the film corresponding to the appropriate sound track (see also Bahrick, Walker, & Neisser, 1978). Other studies have revealed that infants can detect both simultaneity of sound and sight and the overall tempo of the two modalities. In addition, infants detect correlations based on previously remembered events, such as remembering the nature of a parent's voice. Infants averaging about five months of age, given the two parents sitting motionless, will look at the parent whose voice they can hear (Spelke and Owsley, 1979). These results illustrate that infants have the ability to process auditory and visual attributes somewhat independently and to associate them when the attributes are ecologically related. A holistic interpretation would be strained to account for the different results as a function of spatial and temporal contiguity.

There is evidence that visual information about articulation is available very early developmentally. Trevarthen (1977) reported that infants watch their mother and mimic the movements of her mouth during pre-speech oral play. Meltzoff and Moore (1977) persuaded two and three week-old infants to imitate facial and finger gestures of the experimenter. The infants were able to imitate a tongue protrusion or a mouth opening, even when they had to delay their imitation until after the experimenter's gesture was finished. Even though it might be argued that the delayed imitation was really just a continued imitation that began with the experimenter's gesture and continued for a long period, the demonstrations of imitation illustrate the infant's ability to differentiate articulatory gestures and to modify their behavior. Other failures to replicate imitation might be explained by the fact that the investigators measured only the first movement of the infant, and imitation can have a long latency and continue for a long period after the model has stopped gesturing.

It has also been demonstrated that young infants can discriminate when a voice is displaced from a visual image of the face in either time or space. O'Connor and Hermelin (1981) had infants of 10 weeks look at the mirror image of the experimenter's face as she spoke nursery rhymes. Infants attended more in the condition in which sounds and lips were in synchrony than in the condition in which the speech sounds were delayed 400 msec relative to the lip movements. Dodd (1979) presented two to four month-old infants with nursery rhymes with the lip movements in synchrony with the spoken text or with the lip movements presented 400 msec before the sound. The infants attended to the normal presentation about 85% of the time, whereas the out-of-synchrony presentation was attended to 66% of the time.

Early studies reported that infants become distressed when sound and sight are made incompatible. Aronson and Rosenbloom (1971) had mothers speak to their one to two-month old infants. After 2 or 5 minutes of congruent stimulation, the mother's voice was displaced 90 degrees away from the infant's view of the mother. The infants became visibly distressed and they would refuse to look at the mother even after spatial congruity was restored. Other results showed that the infants were upset over the visual/auditory discrepancy and not simply a shift in voice location. Although McGurk and Lewis (1974) and Condry, Haltom, and Neisser (1977) failed to replicate these results, these latter studies had significantly shorter congruent episodes and the disturbance may depend on the intraexperimental experience (Butterworth, 1981). Even more damaging to the conclusion that can be reached is the possibility that the distress observed by Aronson and Rosenbloom (1971) was due to the presence of two separate events. The infant's distress may simply reflect the conflict between the tendencies to orient to both events present in different locations (Lawson, 1980). Infants might not expect sight and sound of mother speaking to come from the same place; they are simply upset when sight and sound come from two different places and when only one of the two can be oriented to. More recent research has shown that one-month-olds show visual capture and are not distressed, whereas four-month-olds orient back and forth between the auditory and visual inputs presented at different locations (Vinter, De Nobili, Pellegrinetti, & Cioni, 1982, 1984).

Following the paradigm used by Spelke and her colleagues, Kuhl and Meltzoff (1982) demonstrated that 5-month old infants recognize cross-modal correspondences of the vowels [i] and [a]. A film showing two side-by-side views of the same speaker, one articulating [i] and the other articulating [a] was played in synchrony with the sound [i] or the sound [a]. A significant proportion of infants looked longer at the view of the speaker matching the sound than at the nonmatching view. Given a control condition, the results appear to be due to the structural rather than temporal properties of the speech events.

Kuhl and Meltzoff tested an intriguing explanation of the ability of infants to perceive some relationship between the auditory and visual concomitants of the speech syllables. Rather than being due to the correlation of visible and audible properties of these syllables in speech, our sensory systems might be tuned to detecting certain relationships between sound and sight. For whatever reason, the sound properties of a /a/ might be related to an open mouth whereas the sound properties of /i/ might be related to spread lips. In this scenario, our sensory systems would have evolved to perceive not only the properties individually but also to perceive the relationship between the two. To test this idea, the authors repeated the experiment with pure-tone analogs of the vowel sounds. These analogs have energy at the appropriate three formant frequencies but do not have the fundamental and harmonic structure of auditory speech. Infants showed no preference in looking at the lip movements associated with the pure tone analog, falsifying this nonspeech explanation. It might also be worthwhile to repeat the experiment using natural auditory speech and nonspeech visual analogs corresponding to the visible syllables. Given that it appears to be the experience with speech that is critical, infants should show no preference in looking at a nonspeech visual analog of the mouth corresponding to the auditory speech being heard.

The infant's ability to spot the relationship between visible and audible speech complements the present findings of a substantial contribution of lip reading to children's speech perception. The integration of auditory and visual speech demands that they be evaluated and integrated with respect to the same event. Noticing the correspondence between these two modalities allows the infant and child to learn about both characteristics. In terms of the FLMP, the prototypes corresponding to speech would contain visual as well as auditory information, and the resolution of these prototypes will increase with experience.

5.2 Infant Speech Perception

The present results of continuous perception for young children stand in sharp contrast to conclusions reached in previous speech research with infants. Infant speech perception has been interpreted as being categorical (Eimas et al.,

1971; Gleitman and Wanner, 1982). One can always resolve the apparent contradiction by assuming that speech perception develops from categorical to continuous and is continuous by age three. However, some of the infant research might be interpreted in terms of possible irregularities in the discrimination of some speech dimensions rather than in terms of categorical perception (Massaro and Oden, 1980b). By irregularity is meant that the same amount of stimulus change gives rise to different amounts of perceptual change at different places along the stimulus continuum. Thus, infants might be better at discriminating some changes than others, but this does not mean that they have only categorical information available. Perception would still be continuous in that changes along the stimulus dimension produce noticeable changes in perception, even when these changes occur within a speech category. Evidence for this view comes from more recent studies that have found within-category discriminations with infants. There is now evidence that infants can make within-category discriminations along nasal-stop (Eimas & Miller, 1980), voiced-voiceless (Aslin, Pisoni, Hennessy, and Perey, 1981) and stop-glide (Miller & Eimas, 1983) continua. Continuous perception appears to describe infant, child, and adult speech perception.

5.3 Language Acquisition

The problem of language acquisition is nicely introduced by the classic example of the ambiguity of translation between different languages (Quine, 1960). A linguist and a native watch a rabbit scurrying by, and the native says *Gavagai*. Does the utterance refer to rabbit, white, animal, running, or a multitude of other possibilities and conjunctions of these words. The child is faced with a similar scenario when she has available the form of the linguistic utterance and the meaning of the context. How does the child learn to project or pair these two entities? That is, how does the child learn to pair the perceptual experience of an utterance and the meaning involved in the environmental situation? As an example, when an adult points to a cat and says "The cat is on the mat," the child supposedly has some perception of an utterance and some perception of a cat on a mat. How does the child project the appropriate interpretation on the perceptual form of the utterance?

I do not plan to solve this problem, but simply point out that the problem might differ significantly from what has been assumed. Given the belief in categorical perception, it has been usually assumed that the perception of the utterance contains ordered categories bracketed by stress into words and by intonation into phrases (Gleitman & Wanner, 1982). In this case, the projection problem involves only pairing the appropriate semantic interpretation of the environmental event with the specific surface form being heard. If categorical perception does not exist, however, and there is little reason to believe that it does, the problem is that the perceived utterance is also somewhat ambiguous. Experience with language must reduce ambiguity about both the utterance, the environment, and their pairing. This does not appear to be a formidable task. Analogous to Premack's (1986) faith in the power of behavioral methods in the study of animal communication, the child's experience will allow the code to be broken.

I view language acquisition as highly interactive in that the meaning of the situation can help disambiguate what is being heard, not simply the interpretation of the categories being heard. For example, if the child hears an utterance that narrows down the speech alternatives to *ball* and *doll*, the presence of one or the other object can inform the child about what is being heard. In this case, the child can obtain feedback about the auditory properties of the words and can build prototype descriptions that differentiate them. Analogous to development in other domains (Kendler, 1983), language acquisition at all levels (even the feature and segmental levels) is continuous and gradual. The overthrow of categorical perception offers a new outlook and a new challenge for theories of language acquisition.

5.4 Classifying Multidimensional Objects

There is a long tradition in developmental theory centered around the idea that the child progresses from holistic to dimensional processing (James, 1890; Shepp, 1978; Smith & Kemler, 1978; Werner, 1957). Holistic processing is a loaded term; somehow the child perceives the whole but not by way of the components. Preschool children are claimed to process certain objects holistically whereas adults process the same objects analytically (Shepp, 1983; Smith and Kemler, 1977, 1978). Given this view, there should be some fundamental change in perceptual processing with development. To accommodate the present negative results, one can always claim that preschool children only perceive some stimulus events holistically; other events would be perceived in terms of independent attributes, features, or dimensions. As an alternative to this easy tack, it is possible to reinterpret the previous studies used to support holistic perception. Consider the perceptual categorization of objects varying in size and brightness (Smith and Kemler, 1978). Older children and adults will tend to group two objects together if they have the same size even if they differ greatly in brightness. Younger children, on the other hand, will group two objects together if they differ by relatively small amounts on both dimensions. Rather than accepting these results as implying holistic perception for young children, however, the dimensions of size and brightness might be evaluated independently at all developmental levels. The different results may simply reflect different strategies in the grouping task at the different developmental levels. Consistent with this interpretation, Kemler and Smith (1978) found that young children could treat size and brightness as independent dimensions to learn a higher-order conceptual rule. Contrary to what might be expected from holistic perception, Ward (1980) found that five-year olds had no difficulty making dimensional judgments given length and density.

Ward (1983) and his colleagues (Ward, Foley, and Cole, 1986) have offered an alternative to the developmental explanation. The central assumption is that the processing of the test stimulus makes available the overall similarity of the items earlier than the information on specific levels of component dimensions. This interpretation can be formalized within the general framework developed in this book. In the FLMP, featural evaluation occurs before integration but the evaluation process extends over time and increases in resolution with increases in processing time (Massaro, 1972). Early in featural evaluation, therefore, the perceiver would have some information about each feature (dimension) but the information would not be of sufficient resolution to inform the perceiver about the identity of two stimuli on a given dimension. Because integration occurs on the tail of evaluation, integration could be completed before the identity along one of the dimensions is resolved at the featural level. If the response is made at this point in processing, the observer would be more likely to group the two items with the largest overall similarity than the two items that are equivalent on one of the dimensions.

With additional processing time, however, the perceiver would eventually resolve the features sufficiently to make available the identity information along one of the dimensions. In this case, subjects may decide to respond on the basis of this identity rather than on the overall similarity resulting from the integration of the different dimensions. Notice that this explanation in no way assumes holistic processing in one case and analytic processing in the other. The same processes occur in both cases: evaluation of independent features. The pattern classification operation of the FLMP would be responsible for the different results that are observed. In the case of grouping by overall similarity, the decision is based on the integration of information along both dimensions. In the case of grouping by identity on a given dimension, the decision is based on the identity information made available at the level of feature analysis. No loaded terms such as holistic and analytic are necessary to describe the processing.

It should be noted that saturation and brightness, or chroma and value in Munsell terminology, would not be expected to be processed in the same manner as the independent dimensions of size and brightness, length and density, or circle area and radius orientation. The former dimensions of light appear to exemplify dependence as defined in the present framework. The evaluation of one color dimension is influenced by the level of the other dimension. Our evaluation of degree of redness is necessarily influenced by the value of the color and our color terms reflect this fact. Our color (chroma) terms are a function of intensity in addition to varying with wavelength.

5.5 Processing Deficits with Aging

One popular explanation of declines in perceptual and cognitive functions with aging is based on the notion of processing capacity. The assumption is that age-related changes in performance result from reduced processing capacity or resources with aging (Salthouse, 1985). In addition to the well-founded scepticism about the resources concept (Navon, 1984; Neumann, in press), it appears to offer little insight into understanding performance differences across the life span. The present results illustrate that a process model is essential to understand aging differences in bimodal speech perception. With such a model, the fundamental differences are revealed to be a result of the information available rather than a result of the processing of the information. What is important is that information differences can lead to performance differences that could easily be mistaken for processing differences. Having less information available would only naturally lead to an increase in the time to perform various tasks. As an example, having both auditory and visual sources of information speeded up speech recognition relative to having just one of these sources (Chapter 6, Section 1). Investigators of life span changes will have to tease apart information differences and information-processing differences in order to arrive at a better understanding of development and aging. Having successfully applied the current framework to development and aging, we address the specificity versus generality of the approach in the final chapter.

Chapter 9: Specificity versus Generality of the Findings

The problem of speech perception by ear and by eye has been studied within the framework of falsification and strong inference. The issues that we have addressed seem fundamental to developing a psychological understanding of the phenomenon. The methods of information integration and mathematical model testing appear to be ideally suited for addressing many issues. Although the experiments have been reasonably successful in providing answers to some of the questions, future work will be necessary in order to resolve other questions. On the basis of the research, perceiving speech by ear and by eye is described within the context of a model representing a general theory of perceptual recognition. This model provides an algorithm for evaluating and integrating multiple sources of information in pattern classification.

The contribution of the current approach has to do with the question of the uniqueness of the processes that have been uncovered in bimodal speech perception. We offer the possibility that the processes involved in bimodal speech perception are similar to those involved in a number of other domains of perceptual and cognitive functioning. We explore five domains and ask whether similar or analogous processes occur across these domains. The domains include person impression, learning of arbitrary categories, sentence interpretation, probability judgments of possible events, and judgments of category membership. To the extent that we can provide a unified account of this broad range of phenomena, modularity is not a reasonable guideline for psychological inquiry. Following Fodor's (1983) classification, these five domains include both input modules and central systems. It should not be possible to provide the same process description across these domains, especially a description developed from another unique input domain of bimodal speech perception.

In person impression, subjects are given descriptions of a hypothetical person and asked how likeable (or extroverted, etc.) the person is. If the bimodal speech framework can be generalized to this domain, then the judgments should reflect the integration of multiple, continuous, and independent attributes and the integration should be enhancing rather than compromising. In the learning of arbitrary categories, subjects are given examples of the categories along with their category status. The exemplars are composed of a set of features that are independently varied. After the learning phase of the experiment, subjects are asked to categorize these exemplars and other new exemplars. By testing the FLMP against the results of these experiments, we can determine to what extent categorization of arbitrary object categories resembles categorization of speech. In the sentence-interpretation domain, subjects are asked to interpret sentences that are varied along a number of dimensions. The experimental question is how the various syntactic and semantic properties of the sentence, such as word order and animacy, influence its interpretation. The fourth domain involves the judged probability of some event given hypothetical descriptions of the situation. Does this cognitive decision making fall outside the regularity we have observed in speech perception by ear and eye? Finally, subjects judge the degree to which a pictured object represents a given category. For example, to what degree does a picture of a colored object represent the categories as apple, red, and red apple? Are these judgments consistent with the general framework developed here?

1. Person Impression

As described in Chapter 7, there is a substantial body of research in person impression and social judgment. Subjects are given descriptive adjectives of a hypothetical person and judge some characteristic such as likeableness. Our contention is that social judgment might follow the algorithm of the FLMP that has proven appropriate for speech perception. That is, subjects would establish prototypes for likeable and dislikeable persons and evaluate and integrate the adjectives with respect to these prototypes. The likeableness judgment would directly reflect the relative goodness of the match to the likeable prototype. Our interpretation is similar, in principle, to those offered by Anderson (1981) and other contenders (e.g. Birnbaum, 1974) with the exception of the integration rule for conjunction. Most models of person impression have some kind of adding-type integration, whereas the FLMP has a multiplicative integration. The test among the models, accordingly, becomes quantitative in terms of which integration rule best describes the large body of results.

An important aspect of the present interpretation of person impression task is the role of prototypes in long-term memory. Subjects utilize prototypes to integrate the sources of information and to guide their categorization response or likeableness rating. It is difficult to judge how likeable a person is without evaluating the information with respect to prototypes of likeable and dislikeable people. In the FLMP, prototype matching involves integrating the information by entering the feature values in the relevant prototypes. It should be noted that these prototypes could be generated and modified for the task at hand. They should not be considered to be immutable templates in memory. In the person impression task, it is assumed that the adjectives on a given trial define the relevant descriptors in the likeable and dislikeable prototypes. For example, *meek* and ***well-mannered*** would be evaluated and given truth values defining the likeableness of each adjective. The prototypes in memory can be conceptualized as

Likeable Person: t(Adjective A is Likeable)
        and t(Adjective B is Likeable)
        and ....
Dislikeable Person: 1 - t(Adjective A is Likeable)
        and 1 - t(Adjective B is Likeable)
        and ....

The adjectives in some sense define the prototypes and the theoretical question is how the conjunction "and" is implemented in the integration process.

The outcome of prototype matching is a truth value defining how true it is the person is likeable and how true it is that the person is dislikeable. It should be noted that these truth values are not necessarily the negation of one another. An important operation in the FLMP is that the rating or categorization judgment reflects the truth values of both propositions. The decision is assumed to follow the relative strength assumption given by Luce's (1959) choice rule.

1.1 Previous Results

At first glance, the success of the averaging model in describing previous research dims the prospects for the FLMP. Figure 1 gives the results of a typical experiment involving judgments of the social desirability of hypothetical persons described by two adjectives (Anderson, 1973). Subjects made their judgments on a 20-cm. rating scale between desirable and undesirable. The combination of two factors with 3 and 10 levels, respectively, gives 30 unique descriptions to be judged. As noted in the presentation of the same results in Chapter 7 (Figure 1, Section 1), the results appear to be additive and an averaging model gives a very respectable RMSD of .016. What is striking, however, is that the description given by the FLMP of this same experiment gives an RMSD of .012, a hair's advantage over averaging. The predictions of the FLMP shown in Figure 1 resemble those given by averaging for relatively neutral judgments.

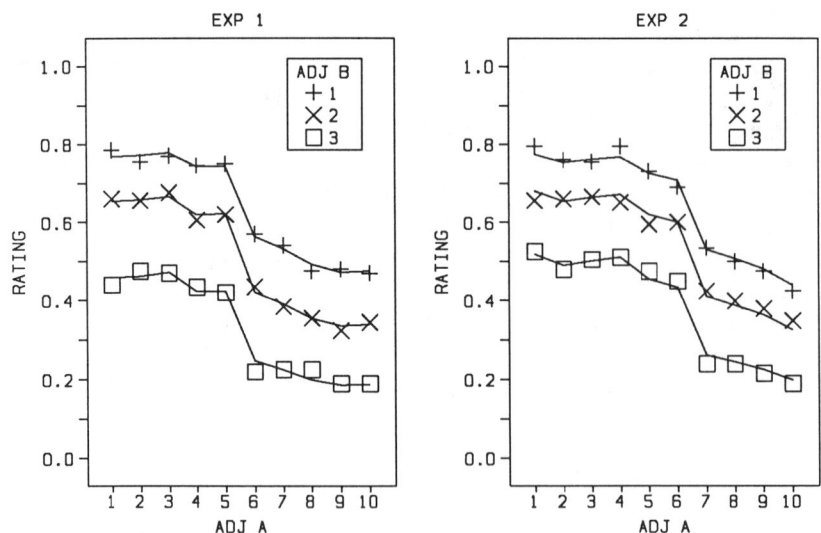

Figure 1. Observed (points) and predicted (lines) judgments of social desirability as a function of two adjectives (observations after Anderson, 1973, and predictions given by the FLMP).

To discriminate between the models, we need combinations of adjectives that produce relatively extreme judgments. Birnbaum (1974) also observed that Anderson's objectives were too neutral to reveal potential interactions, if they existed. Birnbaum chose adjectives covering a wider range of the likeableness scale. The two factors had five adjectives each ranging from *phony* and *mean* to *sincere* and *trustworthy*. Figure 2 gives the results of three experiments. As can be seen in Figure 2, the parallelism prediction given by the averaging rule clearly fails, with RMSDs of .060, .067. and .054. One interpretation of these data is that a negative adjective tends to contribute more than its share to the final judgment. Birnbaum (1974, 1982) argues for increasing weight given to negative adjectives, but still maintaining Anderson's original assumption of an averaging of the individual adjective values.

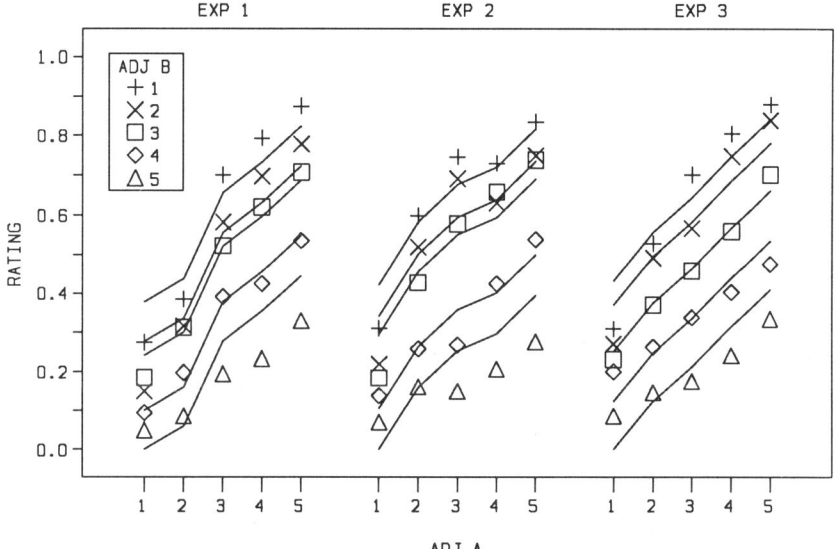

Figure 2. Observed (points) and predicted (lines) likeableness judgments as a function of two adjectives for three different experiments. The predictions are for a simple averaging model (observations after Birnbaum, 1974).

The results of Birnbaum's study are adequately described by the FLMP, as can be seen in Figure 3. The RMSD values across the three experiments were .023, .032, and .036, respectively. The FLMP predicts that the curves should form the shape of an American football, but only half of the football is present in Figure 3. The reason is that extreme negative but not extreme positive ratings are observed. The interpretation resulting from the fit is that negative adjectives are more extreme in truth value than positive adjectives. In this case, a negative

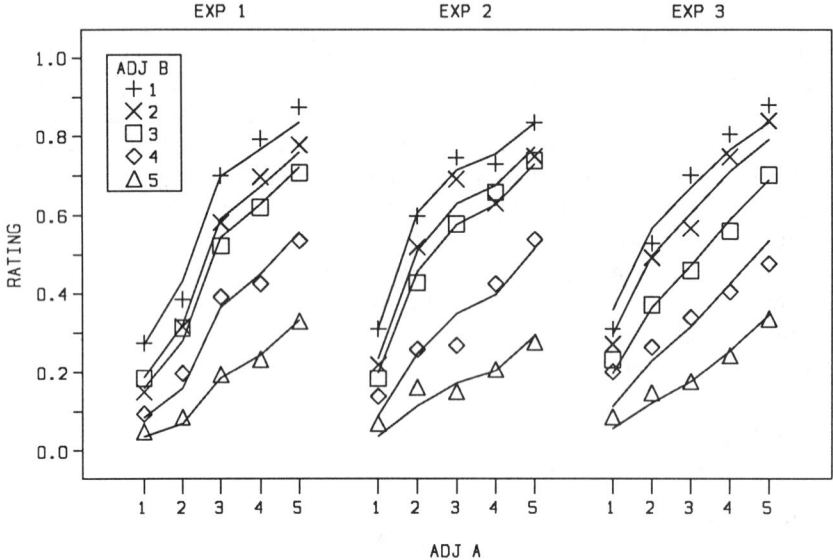

Figure 3. Observed (points) and predicted (lines) likeableness judgments as a function of two adjectives for three different experiments. The predictions are for the FLMP (observations after Birnbaum, 1974).

adjective makes the judgment more negative than a positive adjective makes the judgment positive. This asymmetry might reflect a basic conservatism in that regardless of the number of positive traits a person might have, a single negative trait might decrease the person's likeableness considerably. It follows that positive adjectives tend not to be assigned extreme truth values. Our analysis reveals that previous work on person impression is accounted for nicely within the framework of the FLMP.

1.2 Expanded Factorial Designs.

Including single-factor judgments in the typical two-factor design is a powerful extension of the factorial design typically used to test models of information integration. The correct integration rule should describe judgments in both single-factor and two-factor conditions with the constraint that the truth values of the adjectives be identical in the two conditions. The value of the characteristic behavior *hates* should be identical if this is the only information provided about the man or if it is also stated that the man is *uninteresting*. Although Anderson and his associates (Anderson, 1981) have included presentation of just one of the two factors, we are unaware of any studies that have included both factors presented alone. In a 4 x 4 design, the eight traits would be judged singly as well as the sixteen possible pairings of the two factors. Twenty-four, rather than sixteen, independent data points would be available to test various integration rules and ideally with the same number of free parameters used to describe the standard factorial design.

1.3 Introversion-Extroversion Judgments

To implement a stronger test of the possible integration rules, subjects judged how introverted to extroverted a hypothetical person was, given one or two traits. Four traits were factorially combined with four other traits, giving sixteen possible pairs. In addition, subjects judged a hypothetical person described by each of the eight unique adjectives. Following Anderson (1983), subjects made graphical responses on linear graph paper. The y axis was scaled from introverted to extroverted and numbered from 0 to 1. There were two sheets of paper for the single-adjective condition with four adjectives placed along the x axis on each sheet. A vertical line was drawn above each adjective. A third sheet was used for the sixteen adjective pairs. Four adjectives were placed along the x axis, as on the single-adjective sheets, and the other four adjectives were written on top of the page with a unique symbol next to each of these four adjectives. Subjects were instructed to rate the degree of introversion-extroversion of the hypothetical person on the scale between zero and one. A simple line mark was made on the single adjective sheets, whereas subjects drew the appropriate symbol on the appropriate line in judging pairs of adjectives. Subjects rated the single-adjective descriptions before the double-adjective descriptions. All subjects were tested simultaneously in a classroom.

1.3.1 Method

Subjects. Thirty-two subjects participated during a cognitive psychology class.

Stimuli and Procedure. Subjects judged how introverted to extroverted a hypothetical person was, given one or two adjectives describing the person. Two sets of four adjectives were used. The four A adjectives were: *entertaining, high-strung, meditative,* and *lifeless.* The four B adjectives were: *withdrawn, agreeable, vain,* and *enthusiastic.* Subjects made ratings of each of these eight adjectives and each of the sixteen adjective pairs on a scale from introverted to extroverted. Subjects made their ratings directly on three sheets of graph paper, one for each set of four adjectives and one for the sixteen adjective pairs.

The linear graph paper had 10 squares per inch with 50 squares along the y axis representing values between 0 and 1 going from introverted to extroverted. The scale was labeled every .2 of the unit distance. One set of four adjectives was placed along the x axis. In the case with the adjective pairs, the other set of four adjectives was represented as the curve parameter in a traditional two-dimensional plot. For the data analysis, the ratings were transcribed as values between 0 and 1.

1.3.2 Results

An analysis of variance indicated a highly significant interaction between the A and B variables. The FLMP and the averaging model were fit to the average results. Given only one observation per subject per condition, individual-subject fits are not reasonable. In one analysis, the models were fit to judgments of the 16 unique pairs of adjectives. In the other analysis, the model was fit simultaneously to the 16 unique pairs of adjectives plus the eight adjectives presented alone. In both cases, eight parameters are necessary. In the first case, 16 data points are being predicted, whereas in the second case 24 data points are being predicted. The observed results and the predictions for all 24 data points for the FLMP and the averaging model are shown in Figures 4 and 5, respectively. The FLMP did a somewhat better job in describing the results than did the averaging model in both cases. The RMSD values were .010 and .039 for the FLMP, and .035 and .051 for the averaging model. We conclude that the framework of the FLMP provides an account of the cognitive processes involved in person impression, contrary to what might be expected from modularity.

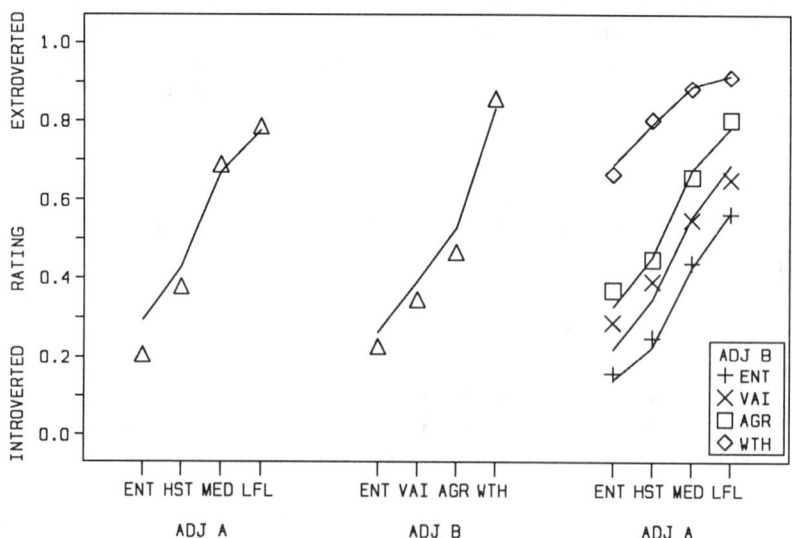

Figure 4. Observed (points) and predicted (lines) judgments for the simple adjectives and pairs of adjectives. Predictions given by the FLMP.

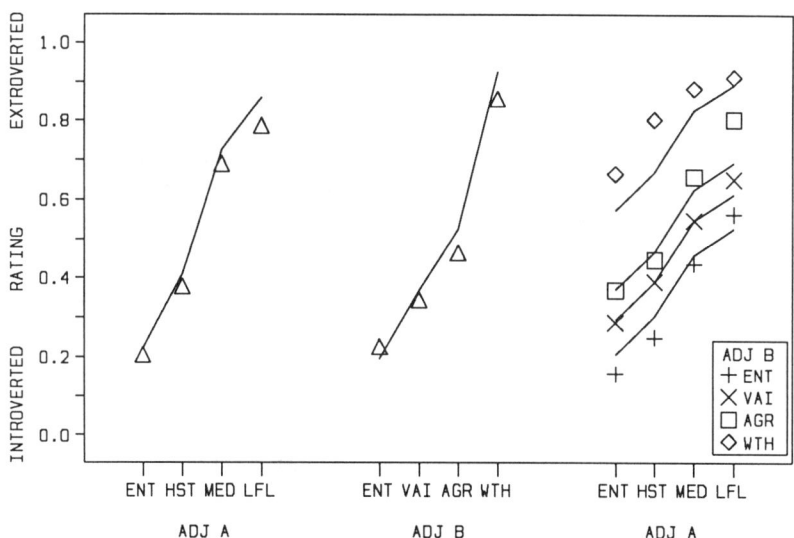

Figure 5. Observed (points) and predicted (lines) judgments for the simple adjectives and pairs of adjectives. Predictions given by the averaging model.

2. Learning Arbitrary Categories

The next line of investigation has one of the oldest traditions in psychological inquiry (Smith & Medin, 1981). Origins can be traced to Hull's (1920) concept-learning studies and the well-known experiments of Bruner, Goodnow, and Austin (1956). The question is how do subjects learn to categorize various objects as instances of different superordinate categories. The work in this area bearing the most similarity to the present framework has been contributed by Medin and his colleagues (Medin & Schaffer, 1978). Consider a prototypical study carried out by Medin, Dewey, and Murphy (1983). Subjects were asked to learn family members from high-school yearbook pictures. The test pictures of women were chosen to give two levels each of hair color, shirt color, smile type, and hair length for a total of $2^4 = 16$ pictures. Table 1 gives the attribute structure used in this experiment and many others carried out by Medin and associates. The specific categories and dimensions differ across experiments, but the task always involves training on the Category A and Category B exemplars and transfer testing on these plus the new instances.

In the Medin et al. (1983) study, the A and B pictures served as training items and the subjects were tested on these and the new pictures. There were four different learning conditions, but we will limit our analysis to just one of these. The analysis of categorization performance during the transfer test provides information about the learning, representation, and utilization of the attributes, dimensions and categories. On each trial, a picture was presented, subjects classified it as a member of the Asch or Boyd family, and then feedback was given about the correctness of the classification. There were 16 blocks of the nine types of pictures and each block had a different realization (photograph) of each type. Subjects were told that they would never see the same photograph twice. The transfer test involved classification of two realizations of each of the 16 types. Thirty-two subjects were tested giving 32 x 2 = 64 observations at each of the 16 item types. The proportion of Asch classifications for each of the 16 types serves as the dependent measure.

Table 1. Attribute structure for the categories used in the Experiments of Medin and his colleagues. The value 1 represents one level of the dimension and the value 0 represents the other.

	Dimension			
Exemplar	D1	D2	D3	D4
Category A				
A1	1	1	1	0
A2	1	0	1	0
A3	1	0	1	1
A4	1	1	0	1
A5	0	1	1	1
Category B				
B1	1	1	0	0
B2	0	1	1	0
B3	0	0	0	1
B4	0	0	0	0
New Stimuli				
N1	1	0	0	1
N2	1	0	0	0
N3	1	1	1	1
N4	0	0	1	0
N5	0	1	0	1
N6	0	0	1	1
N7	0	1	0	0

The direct extension of the present framework is to assume that prototypes for the two families are established. The situation is somewhat different from the speech domain in which there is a distribution of values for a given feature and the distributions for different alternatives overlap to some degree. Ambiguity of features in this categorization task is less important than the presence or absence of features. The two levels of any dimension are clearly discriminable and some members of a given category will have one level and other members will have the other level. In the simplest application of the

FLMP, we assume that each dimension of the prototype for a given category is defined in terms of the most frequent feature value. That is, given a set of instances that define a particular category, the prototype defines for each dimension the level that occurs in the majority of the instances. On the basis of Table 1, the prototype for Asch would contain one feature level (such as dark hair corresponding to Dimension D1) for each of the four attributes, and the prototype for Boyd would contain the negation of the corresponding feature (such as light hair) for each of the four dimensions.

Table 2. Attribute structure for the categories used in the last-name infinite training condition of Medin, Dewey, and Murphy (1983) with proportion of category A judgments during the transfer test and predictions of the FLMP.

	Dimension					
Exemplar	D1	D2	D3	D4	Observed	Predicted
Category A						
A1	1	1	1	0	.81	.78
A2	1	0	1	0	.75	.70
A3	1	0	1	1	.95	.90
A4	1	1	0	1	.77	.72
A5	0	1	1	1	.80	.70
Category B						
B1	1	1	0	0	.42	.39
B2	0	1	1	0	.30	.37
B3	0	0	0	1	.25	.22
B4	0	0	0	0	.11	.07
New Stimuli						
N1	1	0	0	1	.62	.63
N2	1	0	0	0	.31	.30
N3	1	1	1	1	.89	.93
N4	0	0	1	0	.34	.28
N5	0	1	0	1	.31	.30
N6	0	0	1	1	.62	.61
N7	0	1	0	0	.20	.10

The model requires four parameters to predict the 16 data points from the transfer test. Table 2 gives the predicted and observed values. As can be seen in the table, the FLMP gives a reasonably good description of the results with an RMSD = .052, equal to the fit of Medin and Schaffer's (1978) exemplar model. The parameter values for the FLMP reveal that shirt color was less informative relative to the other three attributes. This result is reasonable in light of the fact that shirt color (Dimension D2 in Table 1) did not correlate with the Boyd category. Two of the four Boyds presented in training had one color and two had the other.

2.1 Training Effects

Medin, Altom, and Murphy (1984) evaluated three different training conditions with three different groups of subjects. Subjects in the examples group were given training on only the A and B examples represented in Table 1. In the prototype group, subjects were required to learn prototypical values for each category prior to any training involving the exemplars. The prototypical attributes were presented one at a time and subjects were required to memorize which category was associated with that particular attribute. One problem with the design is that the second dimension for category B did not have a typical value, and the authors do not state how subjects were informed about the prototype value for this dimension. Finally, subjects in the third group, called the concurrent group, received training on the examples and the prototypical attributes simultaneously. Following the initial training, all subjects were asked to categorize the A and B stimuli as well as the new stimuli presented in Table 1.

Table 3. Attribute structure for the categories used in Medin, Altom, & Murphy (1984) and the proportion of category A judgments during the transfer test as a function of the three training conditions and predictions of the FLMP.

	Dimension				Examples		Prototype		Concurrent	
Exemplar	D1	D2	D3	D4	Obs	Pre	Obs	Pre	Obs	Pre
Category A										
A1	1	1	1	0	.73	.73	.88	.82	.95	.91
A2	1	0	1	0	.88	.75	.80	.72	.88	.77
A3	1	0	1	1	.95	.93	.95	.95	.98	.98
A4	1	1	0	1	.77	.70	.81	.81	.94	.88
A5	0	1	1	1	.73	.63	.84	.78	.92	.85
Category B										
B1	1	1	0	0	.25	.35	.31	.34	.28	.35
B2	0	1	1	0	.20	.28	.34	.30	.23	.30
B3	0	0	0	1	.23	.27	.16	.18	.08	.09
B4	0	0	0	0	.06	.08	.02	.03	.05	.01
New Stimuli										
N1	1	0	0	1	.62	.72	.75	.70	.61	.70
N2	1	0	0	0	.50	.37	.34	.22	.28	.15
N3	1	1	1	1	.86	.92	.94	.97	.98	.99
N4	0	0	1	0	.34	.30	.20	.19	.14	.12
N5	0	1	0	1	.42	.25	.42	.28	.36	.23
N6	0	0	1	1	.59	.65	.67	.66	.61	.65
N7	0	1	0	0	.06	.07	.06	.05	.09	.02

The shapes used in the experiment were varied along four binary dimensions of form, color, size, and number. The shape was either an equilateral triangle or a circle, either red or blue, had a diameter height of 1.25 or 2.5 cm, and was either singly or doubly represented on the card. For training and testing of prototypical values, a card would have a single word (for example, red) typed on it, representing one of the two values along one of the four dimensions. Subjects were instructed that each dimension had some information value for determining category membership but no dimension was a perfectly reliable indicator. They were also told to learn the general aspects of each category so that they could then categorize an unfamiliar card. The training procedure involved up to 16 runs through the 9 training cards. Training continued until a participant made no errors on a given run through the set of 9 cards, or until the set had been presented 16 times. The transfer test involved two replications of each of the 16 item types. Given 32 subjects in each of the three groups, 64 observations contribute to each data point.

Table 4. The RMSDs and parameter values for the fit of the FLMP as the function of the three training conditions of Medin, Altom, & Murphy (1984).

Training Condition	RMSD	HC	SC	ST	HL
Examples	.085	.726	.490	.692	.677
Prototype	.058	.765	.573	.747	.739
Concurrent	.072	.828	.636	.810	.782

The FLMP requires four free parameters for each of the three training conditions. The observed and predicted performance during the transfer test is given in Table 3 and the RMSDs and parameter values are given in Table 4. Consistent with the description of the Medin et al. (1983) results, the FLMP is capable of capturing the results of learning arbitrary categories under different training conditions. The model gives the best description of the prototype condition, as it should, given that subjects were taught explicitly the representation assumed by the model.

2.2 Correlated Dimensions

Medin, Altom, Edelson, and Freko (1982) provide an informative assessment of correlated characteristics defining category membership. As the authors observe, models that represent only the separate characteristics and not their correlation cannot predict a contribution of the correlation to categorization. An exemplar model, such as Medin and Schaffer's model, can account for a correlation among characteristics because individual instances are represented and they contain information about correlation. In terms of goodness-of-fit, we have found that the exemplar model and the FLMP provide comparable descriptions of the results of learning arbitrary concepts. If the

FLMP represents only the separate characteristics, it would not be able to account for any influence of the correlation among the characteristics. The question of which characteristics of categories are functional features is primarily an empirical one, however, and there is no reason to preclude the correlation itself from being represented in a prototype model. We will show how this extension of the FLMP provides a reasonable description of learning arbitrary categories with correlated characteristics.

The paradigm used by Medin et al. (1982) was represented in a simulated medical diagnosis task. Hypothetical case studies were presented to teach subjects about one or two fictitious diseases. After the initial training, subjects had to make decisions about both previous case studies and new cases that were not previously presented. In Experiment 4 of Medin et al. (1982), subjects were given four case studies each of *Terrigitis* and *Midosis*. The four symptoms were weight (gain or loss), eyes (puffy or sunken), muscle state (stiffness or spasms), and skin condition (splotches or rash). Table 5 gives the values of the four dimensions for the two diseases. As can be seen, neither the third nor the fourth dimension considered alone predicts category membership. The relationship between the two dimensions is a perfect predictor, however, making their correlation the ecologically valid property. In the learning phase of the experiment, subjects studied the eight learning cases typed individually on index cards. The criterion for learning was successfully sorting the eight cards into the two disease categories. In the transfer test, subjects were presented each of the 16 possible cases in a random order and categorized each case as representing one disease or the other. Thirty-two subjects were tested twice on each of the 16 diseases giving 64 observations per data point.

Table 5 gives the observed and predicted categorizations of the 16 test patterns during the transfer test. The predictions are given for both the FLMP and the exemplar model of Medin and Schaffer (1978). Two versions of the FLMP were applied to the results. In the first, only dimensions 1 and 2 were represented in the prototypes for the two diseases. *Terrigitis* had level 1 for the ideal symptoms and *Midosis* had level 0, because these occurred in three of the four learning cases for each disease (see Table 5). The values of the third and fourth dimensions were not represented because they occurred half the time for both diseases. The fit of the model was very poor, with an RMSD of .216. In the second version, a third feature was added to the prototypes to represent the correlation between dimension 3 and 4. This addition of a single parameter improved the fit considerably, reducing the RMSD to .036 (see Table 5). The parameter values reveal that the correlation was much more informative than the values of the other two dimensions. The parameter values were .580 and .611 for dimensions 1 and 2 respectively, and .725 for the correlation between dimensions 3 and 4. Recall that for two categories the parameter value of a feature represents the degree to which that feature supports one category, and

Table 5. Attribute structure for the cases used in Medin, Altom, Edelson, & Freko (1982; Experiment 4) with observed proportion of *Terrigitis* categorizations and predictions of the FLMP and Exemplar model.

Case	Dimension				Observed	FLMP	Exemplar
	D1	D2	D3	D4			
Terrigitis							
EM	1	1	1	1	.88	.85	.85
RM	1	1	0	0	.89	.85	.86
ST	0	1	1	1	.73	.75	.76
LF	1	0	0	0	.77	.70	.73
Midosis							
AM	0	0	1	0	.12	.15	.15
JJ	0	0	0	1	.17	.15	.14
RL	1	0	1	0	.25	.25	.24
SE	0	1	0	1	.33	.30	.27
New Patterns							
N1	0	0	0	0	.53	.55	.56
N2	0	0	1	1	.53	.55	.54
N3	0	1	0	0	.75	.75	.73
N4	1	0	1	1	.67	.70	.66
N5	1	1	1	0	.45	.45	.46
N6	2	2	0	1	.38	.45	.44
N7	0	1	1	0	.36	.30	.34
N8	1	0	0	1	.28	.25	.27

one minus the feature value represents the degree to which it supports the other category. Thus, the value .5 is neutral and the feature becomes more informative as the value moves away from .5 to either zero or one. It is not surprising that the correlation proved to be more informative because it was perfectly predictive given the learning categories and the separate values of dimensions 1 and 2 were only predictive 75 percent of the time.

The exemplar model's predictions are based on the representations of the eight case studies used in the training session. The probability of categorizing a test case as *Terrigitis* is predicted to be equal to the sum of the similarities of the test case to the four learning cases of *Terrigitis* divided by the sum of the similarities of all eight learning cases. (This is exactly analogous to the pattern-classification operation of the FLMP.) The exemplar model requires four parameters and gave an RMSD value of .031. The four parameters represent the similarity between the two levels of each of the four dimensions. The parameter values were .52, .40, .32, and .06 for the four dimensions.

One question is whether the similarity value for a dimension in the Medin and Schaffer model reflects the distribution of the levels of the dimension, the actual properties of the levels of the dimension, or both. The values are more than similarity estimates because they reflect the distributional properties of the levels of the dimension. Given that the authors counterbalanced the actual dimensions across distribution values given in Table 5, the parameter values should only reflect the latter. In this case, the discrepancy between the values does not make sense because we would expect the values for dimensions 1 and 2 to be equal to one another. Analogously, the values for dimensions 3 and 4 should be equal to one another. It could be that the parameter values are not unique in the fit of the exemplar model. That is, two or more sets of parameters might give the same predictions of the results.

2.3 Summary-Based versus Exemplar-Based Representation

A question that might be considered fundamental to categorization theory is whether a test instance is evaluated against representations of previous instances, summary descriptions of previous instances, or both. The FLMP is firmly grounded in the use of summary descriptions, and this seems particularly suitable for some domains like speech perception. The high frequency of occurrence of instances in speech would seem to make an exemplar-based representation unmanageable. Homa, Sterling, and Trepel (1981) propose that it is only in the initial learning of a concept that the representation might be limited to exemplars. Continued learning would lead to a summary-based representation. The exemplar-based model would appear to become impractical in domains with essentially an unlimited number of exemplars, like speech. As is amply illustrated in category learning experiments, however, exemplar-based representation is reasonable in these domains and it might also be functional in the initial acquisition of speech categories. Although the issue of representation seems fundamental to advances in categorization theory, my feeling is that the question may be undecidable. The FLMP and the exemplar model of Medin and Schaffer (1978) are mathematically very similar and make similar predictions in the category learning experiments (see Table 5).

A summary description cannot represent all categories. As noted by Fried and Holyoak (1984), the category of things stored in my attic is not easy to represent by a summary description (if the goal is to distinguish this category from others, such as things stored in my basement). In this case, a list of each item seems necessary. A summary description might not be represented, if it is not useful, as when the category's instances are highly unrelated. Subjects might also fail to generate summary descriptions even if reasonable descriptions are possible. This might occur when there are only a few instances per category or when the instance learning is stressed and the category structure is disguised.

I feel that the present approach to category learning is similar in spirit to the propositional approach of J. A. Anderson and colleagues (Anderson, 1976, Elio and Anderson, 1981), the Hintzman and Ludlam (1980) and the Fried and Holyoak (1984) models, and the parallel distributed processing (PDP) approach (Knapp & Anderson, 1984; McClelland & Elman, 1986; Rumelhart & McClelland, 1982). These approaches are anti-modularity and address how previous experience influences present performance. Fried and Holyoak (1984) present evidence that subjects can learn not only the ideal values of a category but also the distribution of exemplars of that category. Their model is similar to the FLMP in its Baysean and relative-likelihood assumptions. The authors find support for their model, but do not empirically address the integration of the assumed feature dimensions.

In the "adaptive control of thought" (ACT) model, (Anderson, 1976), a schema is not different in principle from the memory representation of a single experience (Estes, 1986). That is , the development and disruption of a schema would follow the same processing operations as given for exemplars. The same can be said for the prototypes assumed by the FLMP; they are made of the same stuff as representations we feel more comfortable with. In this light, the summary descriptions of the FLMP do not necessarily assume more than what is assumed in exemplar-based models. That is, summary-based theories do not always require greater loans on intelligence than exemplar-based theories. One example is that the FLMP requires only about the same number of free parameters as the exemplar model of Medin and Schaffer, even though the former model is based on a summary description. The FLMP description of the results in Table 5 actually required one fewer parameter than the exemplar model.

As acknowledged by a number of investigators (Busemeyer, Dewey, & Medin, 1984; Elio & Anderson, 1981; Estes, 1986), both summary-based and exemplar-based processes are involved in pattern classification. As noted, they need not be processes of a fundamentally different nature. The PDP model of Knapp and Anderson (1984) stores instances, and given the appropriate input, abstracts a prototype. Following this tack, exemplar-based and summary-based information are easily represented in the FLMP, with no change in the processing assumptions. Consider a prototype for a fraternity member that has summary information and exemplar information. The summary description S and each exemplar E of the fraternity would be represented by a conjunction of features.

$$S = a + b$$

$$E = c + d$$

The complete representation of the prototype would contain both summary and exemplar information, and the question posed is how these different components are matched against a test instance. Logically, someone is a member of the fraternity (relative to being a member of some other fraternity) if they represent a good match to the summary description *or* if they represent a good match to any of the exemplar descriptions. The *or* relation corresponds to the disjunction of the various descriptions and the prototype P for a particular fraternity could be represented as

$$P : S \; or \; E_1 \; or \; E_2$$

Following DeMorgan's Law, the mathematical implementation of disjunction is determined by the definition of conjunction. For simplicity, assume two features *a* and *b* and a prototype consisting of one summary description and one exemplar description. In this case,

$$P : (a + b) \; or \; (c + d)$$

At prototype matching, truth values are inserted in the prototype and combined following the rules for conjunction and disjunction. Assuming a multiplicative integration for conjunction, we have

$$P = ab + cd - (ab)(cd)$$

given the definition of DeMorgan's Law (Chapter 4, Equation 4). As is illustrated in the present example, the FLMP can be extended to represent both summary-based and exemplar-based information. Similarly, multiple summary descriptions can be represented in the same manner as multiple exemplar descriptions. Having multiple summary descriptions is not unreasonable in many situations as, for example, a therapist's concept of suicidal patients. A patient would be considered a good candidate for suicide if his/her symptoms match *any* of the summary descriptions.

Estes (1986) has observed that most theories of categorization and category learning depend on some similarity relationship between the test exemplar and the remembered exemplars (or some kind of summary description derived from them). An important contribution that is seldom addressed, however, is the relative frequencies of the occurrences of the different categories. Categorization is probably dependent on the latter as well as the former, as is easily apparent in the strong effect of base rates or a prior probability in signal detection tasks (Green & Swets, 1966). The FLMP is designed to treat knowledge about relative frequency of category occurrence as an additional (and independent) source of information. This information is integrated with other sources of information following the algorithm that the more ambiguous sources contribute less to the categorization decision. The motivation for this conceptualization can be observed in the analogous treatment of context effects in perception and categorization. A sentence context constraining a word functions as an independent source of information for its recognition (see Chapter 2, Massaro, in press d). Both relative frequency and context can be viewed as informative sources of information influencing perceptual categorization.

Feature and exemplar frequency or probability, important in category learning (Estes, 1986), would also seem to play a less significant role in language. One observational example is the syllable /ðə/. Certainly the most frequent in the language, it remains one of the most difficult to recognize (see Chapter 8 Section). More convincing is the negligible contribution of letter frequency in the visual recognition of printed letters. Appelman and Mayzner (1981) found no overall effect of letter frequency in a careful analysis of 58 previous studies of letter recognition (see also Mason, 1982). Overall frequency would seem to play little role in categorization of common events, even though context-sensitive frequency could still be important. In written language, for example, recognition of a letter critically depends on the surrounding letters. A letter is more easily recognized to the extent that it is predictable by the context letters (Massaro, Jastrzembski, Lucas, 1981; Venezky & Massaro, in press).

3. Sentence Interpretation.

The third domain to serve as a test of the generality of the present framework involves sentence interpretation. Oden (1978) has been one of the pioneers in developing an understanding of sentence interpretation within the framework of multiple continuous sources of information. Subjects were asked to judge the interpretation of sentences generated by the factorial combination of different sources of information. Consider a sentence of the form,

The girl saw the boy with the binoculars.

The two interpretations correspond to whether the girl or the boy are in possession of the binoculars. The verb and the second noun phrase were varied systematically to give a range of interpretations from the girl having the binoculars to the noun in the second noun phrase having the binoculars. The results were well-described by the FLMP, assuming that the verb and second noun phrase function as independent sources of information in sentence interpretation.

When the perceiver is faced with the statement,

the horse the bucket kicked,

it is necessary to assign case roles to the constituents of the sentence, and to determine whether the *horse* or the *bucket* did the kicking. The natural extension is to view sentence interpretation as resulting from the evaluation and integration of multiple sources of information. These sources include syntactic variables such as word order, semantic variables such as animation, and prosodic variables such as stress. Bates and MacWhinney and their colleagues (Bates, McNew, MacWhinney, Devescovi, & Smith, 1982) have carried out both cross-linguistic and developmental studies of sentence interpretation. In the task, subjects are asked to interpret three-word phrases in terms of "which one of the two nouns in the sentence is (the subject of the sentence), that is, (the one who does the action)" (Bates et al., page 266). The task of the subject is to choose between the two noun alternatives based on whatever cues are available. Word order, animacy, and stress were varied in a factorial design. Table 6 gives the description of the independent variables in the studies. There were three possible word orders (NVN, NNV, and VNN), three levels of animacy (both nouns animate, the first noun animate and the second inanimate, and the first noun inanimate and the second animate), and three levels of stress (no stress, stress on first noun, and stress on second noun). The factorial combination of the three independent variables gives a total of 27 unique sentences.

Table 6. Description of independent variables in the sentence interpretation studies. Word order gives the order of the two nouns and verb in the sentence. Animacy, stress, and agreement give the values for the first and second nouns in the sentence. For example, agreement level AD indicates that the verb agreed in number with the first noun and disagreed with the second.

	Levels			
Variable	1	2	3	Abbreviations
Word Order	NVN	NNV	VNN	N = Noun, V = Verb
Animacy	AI	AA	IA	A = Animate, I = Inanimate
Stress	UU	US	SU	U = Unstressed, S = Stressed
Agreement	AD	AA	DA	A = Agree, D = Disagree

3.1 Model Analysis

The application of the FLMP is relatively straightforward. The three independent variables of word order, animacy, and stress can be assumed to influence the choice between the first and the second noun as the subject/agent. These two possible interpretations can be defined as a function of the three cues

First noun as subject or agent: (Appropriate Word Order)
and (Appropriate Animacy) and (Appropriate Stress)
$= w$ and a and s

The second noun can be viewed as the subject or agent to the extent that each of three cues are inappropriate for the first noun being subject or agent. Thus, the second noun as subject or agent can be described as the conjunction of the negations of the three cues for the first noun

Second noun as subject or agent
$= (1-w)$ and $(1-a)$ and $(1-s)$

In terms of the FLMP, nine parameters are necessary to predict the 27 data points corresponding to the 27 unique types of sentences. Three values of W are needed for the three possible word orders. The value of w would be largest for NVN and smaller for NNV and VNN. Using the same logic, three values of a and three values of s are necessary to describe the results.

The parameter values are assumed to be fuzzy truth values between 0 and 1 which indicate the degree to which each of the three sources supports the first noun as subject or agent. According to the FLMP, the conjunction of the three cues is assumed to be multiplicative, followed by the relative goodness determination given by the pattern classification operation. Thus the probability of choosing the first noun as the subject or agent, $P\ (First\ Noun\ )$, is equal to

$$P\ (First\ Noun\ ) = \frac{was}{was + (1-w\ )(1-a\ )(1-s\ )}$$

The alternative choice of interpreting the second noun as subject/agent is predicted to be simply one minus the likelihood of choosing the first noun

$$P\ (First\ Noun\ ) = \frac{(1-w\ )(1-a\ )(1-s\ )}{was + (1-w\ )(1-a\ )(1-s\ )}$$

$$= 1-P\ (First\ Noun\ )$$

Figure 6 gives the observed and predicted results for the English subjects. Word order and animacy had systematic influences on the sentence interpretations, whereas stress had very little systematic effect. As can be seen in the figure, the FLMP provides an accurate description of the results with an RMSD of less than 3 percent. Figure 7 presents the same results for Italian subjects. Although the pattern of results is remarkably different from the pattern of the English subjects, the FLMP also describes the results for the Italian interpretations, with an RMSD of less than 3 percent. Exactly analogous to the life span differences observed in Chapter 8, the linguistic differences are described solely in terms of the information values of the various sources of information; the processes involved in sentence interpretation appear to be identical for the different languages.

The parameter estimates shown in Table 7 for the model descriptions illuminate the cross-linguistic differences that were found. For the English subjects, only the NVN word order supports the first noun as subject agent. Both NNV and VNN are usually interpreted in terms of the second noun as subject/agent. The Italian subjects are less influenced by word order. In addition, NNV is much more supportive of the first noun as the subject/agent than is VNN. The influence of animacy is in the same direction for both linguistic groups, but the effect is much larger for the Italians. Thus, the relative influence of word order and animacy are reversed for the two linguistic groups. Italians show a small effect of stress in that stress on the first noun decreases its

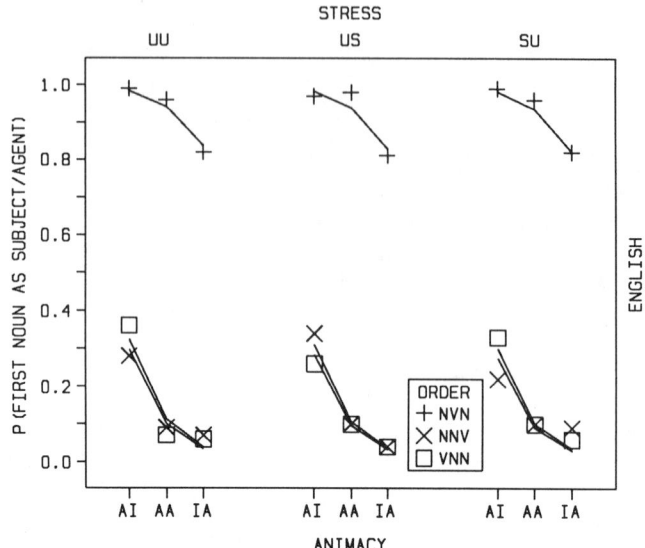

Figure 6. Observed (points) and predicted (lines) probability of identifying the first noun as subject/agent as a function of the animacy of the two nouns, the word order, and the stress level of the two nouns for the English listeners (after Bates et al., 1982).

interpretation as the subject/agent of the sentence.

Table 7. Parameter values for the FLMP for the Bates, et al. (1982) data. The value gives the degree to which the information supports the first noun as subject/agent.

Group	Agreement			Order			Stress		
	AD	AA	DA	NVN	VNN	NNV	UU	US	SU
English	.820	.546	.277	.892	.061	.054	.618	.604	.592
Italian	.932	.530	.086	.802	.377	.605	.611	.594	.439

For English participants, Bates et al. found that both NNV and VNN were usually interpreted in terms of the second noun serving as subject/agent. This result is reasonable if subjects interpret the word order relative to the normally occurring word order. The sequence NNV contains an NV sequence which supports the second noun as subject/agent. Analogously, VNN contains a VN sequence which supports the first noun as object/recipient and thus the second noun as subject/agent. Evaluating the two possible two-word sequences relative to the canonical NVN sentence can explain the observed results.

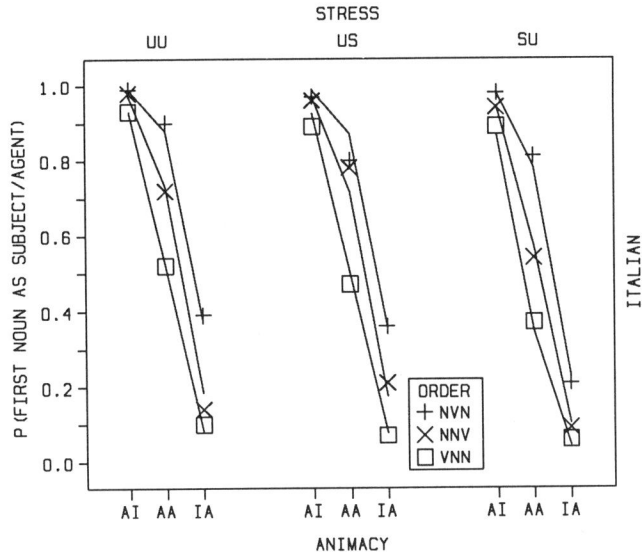

Figure 7. Observed (points) and predicted (lines) probability of identifying the first noun as subject/agent as a function of the animacy of the two nouns, the word order, and the stress level of the two nouns for the Italian listeners (after Bates et al., 1982).

A similar story should describe the Italian subjects, but they interpreted the second noun as subject/agent more often in VNN than in NNV. This result also seems reasonable in light of the time course of processing the test sentence. If the sentence is interpreted as it is produced, then the surface structure constraints would be available earlier in VNN than in NNV. That is, the first noun can be interpreted as object when the second word occurs in VNN, but the second noun cannot be interpreted as subject until the third word occurs in NNV. Once this post-hoc explanation is understood, it is almost surprising that the English subjects did not perform in the same way and differentiate the VNN and NNV orders. Whether these differences between the English and Italian listeners represent something fundamental about language processing remains an issue for future research.

3.2 Four-Factor Design

MacWhinney, Bates, and Kliegl (1984) continued the study of sentence interpretation as a function of multiple sources of information by varying four cues in a factorial design. The design included the three levels of the three factors used in the Bates et al. (1982) experiment and also a fourth variable called noun-verb agreement with three levels. The verb would agree in number with the first noun, with both nouns, or with the second noun of the sentence.

Thus, there were 81 possible sentences and each subject judged each type of sentence only once. There were 24 English, 24 Italian, and 20 German subjects. The dependent measure is the proportion of subjects choosing the first noun as subject/agent for each sentence type.

Table 8. Parameter values for the FLMP for the MacWhinney, Bates, and Kleigl (1984) data. The value gives the degree to which the information supports the first noun as subject/agent.

Group	Agreement			Order			Animacy		
	AD	AA	DA	NVN	VNN	NNV	AI	AA	IA
English	.533	.396	.270	.942	.139	.221	.642	.441	.448
Italian	.977	.543	.012	.757	.352	.440	.851	.570	.166
German	.796	.648	.330	.486	.521	.495	.748	.630	.214

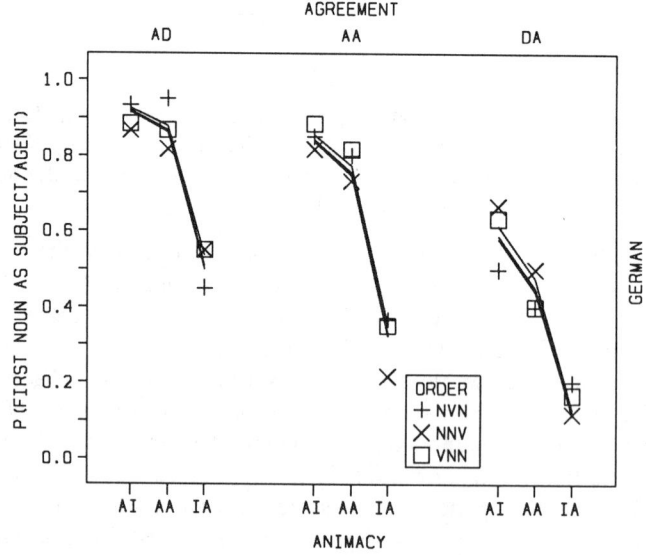

Figure 8. Observed (points) and predicted (lines) probability of identifying the first noun as subject/agent as a function of the animacy of the two nouns, the word order, and the noun-verb agreement for the German listeners (after MacWhinney et al., 1984).

These data were fit by the FLMP in the same manner as in the previous study. Two different models were fit to the results. In the first model, all 81 sentences were described by independent contributions of the four independent variables. In the second model, the 81 sentences were described without assuming any contribution of stress. The average RMSD value of the first fit

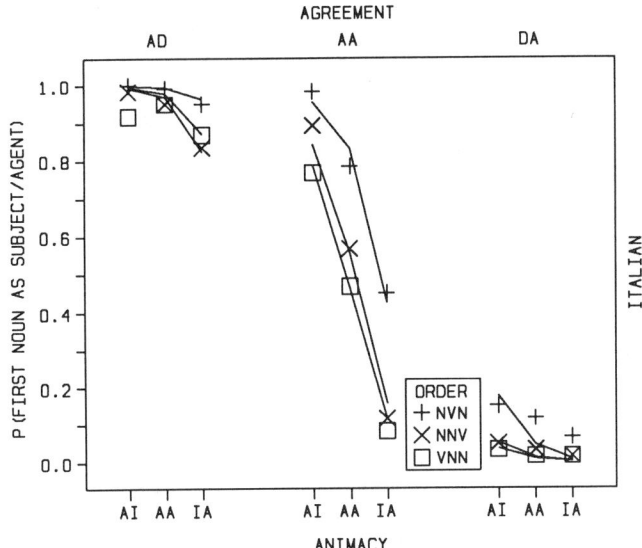

Figure 9. Observed (points) and predicted (lines) probability of identifying the first noun as subject/agent as a function of the animacy of the two nouns, the word order, and the noun-verb agreement for the Italian listeners (after MacWhinney et al., 1984).

was .0659. and the RMSD value of the second fit was .0702. The small difference between these two values provides evidence that stress as manipulated in the study had very little, if any, cue value. Figures 8, 9, and 10 give the observed and predicted results for the 27 sentence types pooled over stress. As can be seen in the figures, the relative effects of the three other variables are critically dependent on language. For the German speakers, there is no effect of word order and large effects of animacy and noun-verb agreement. For the Italian subjects, there are significant effects of all three variables with the largest effect of noun-verb agreement. The effects of word order and animacy are most apparent at the ambiguous level of noun-verb agreement. The English subjects were influenced by word order with significant but relatively small effects of animacy and noun-verb agreement. Table 8 gives the parameter values for the description of the model. These parameter values provide a direct index of the influence of each of the variables and might be considered to be as informative as the judgments themselves but much easier to comprehend.

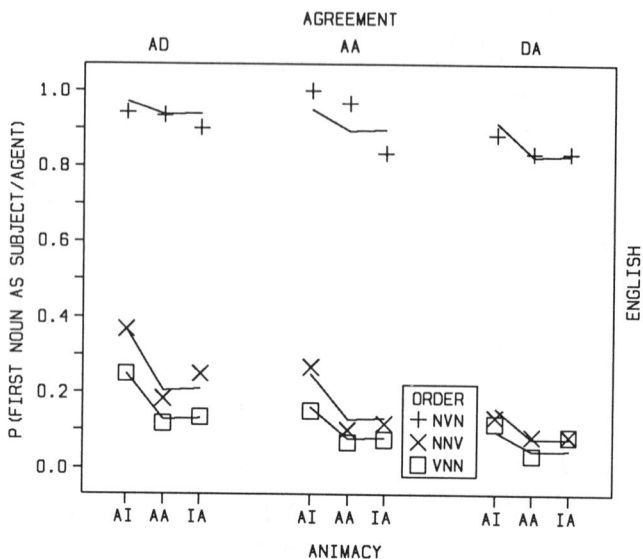

Figure 10. Observed (points) and predicted (lines) probability of identifying the first noun as subject/agent as a function of the animacy of the two nouns, the word order, and the noun-verb agreement for the English listeners (after MacWhinney et al., 1984).

3.3 Developmental Study

Given the success of this paradigm with adult subjects, it was only natural to extend the task to study the development of the processes involved. Bates, MacWhinney, Caselli, Devescovi, Natale, and Venza (1984) tested 40 Italian and 40 English children recruited around the Rome and Denver areas, respectively. In addition, the results of 40 French children provided by MacWhinney (personal communication) will be analyzed. For each language group there were 10 subjects, each at ages 2.5, 3.5, 4.5, and 5.5 years. The same factors were used as in the Bates et al. (1982) study, giving 27 unique types of sentences, and the children were tested with two exemplars of each type. All procedural details were similar to the Bates et al. study except that the children illustrated the meaning of the sentence by manipulating small toy objects.

Figures 11, 12, and 13 give the results for the four age groups for the Italian, English, and French children respectively. Using the model analysis discussed in Section 4.2, stress was found to little cue value at all ages. There was a clear improvement in the use of the other potential sources of information for all languages. The predictions of the model accurately capture the effects of animacy and word order for the Italian subjects. Table 9 gives the parameter values across the four ages and these languages. For the English children, word

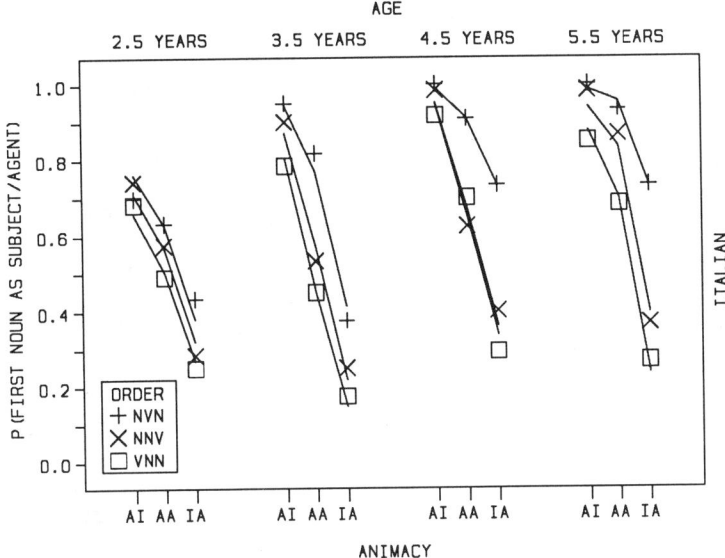

Figure 11. Observed (points) and predicted (lines) probability of identifying the first noun as subject/agent as a function of the animacy of the two nouns, the word order, and the noun-verb agreement for the Italian children (after Bates et al., 1984).

order is more influential, but the effect of animacy is clearly significant for the uncommon word orders. The results of animacy at the uncommon word orders is highly variable but in the appropriate direction. Somewhat similar results are found for the French children although the effect of animacy is much clearer and the model gives a better description of the results. One conclusion is clear; language acquisition is a slow, gradual process rather than one involving sharp transitions or discontinuities.

3.4 Conclusion

Although the Bates, MacWhinney and colleagues provide a general interpretation compatible with the current approach, the present model is the only extant quantitative description of the results. More recently, Rueckl and Oden (1986) varied the featural information in a printed word and the sentence context of the word in a factorial design. According to the FLMP, the bottom-up information and the top-down information should function as independent sources of information about the word identity. This result was obtained and illustrates once again that a positive effect of context does not necessarily imply that low-level processes such as feature analysis are dependent on higher-level processes such as semantic analysis. As Rueckl and Oden (1986) point out, this

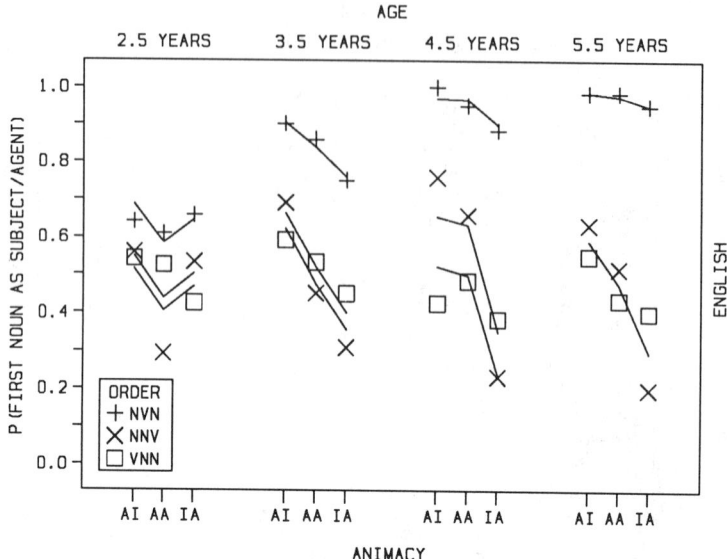

Figure 12. Observed (points) and predicted (lines) probability of identifying the first noun as subject/agent as a function of the animacy of the two nouns, the word order, and the noun-verb agreement for the English children (after Bates et al., 1984).

interpretation represents a synthesis of interactive models and autonomous models of processing. Interactive models assume that the contribution of context results from a direct influence on lower level processes (Marslen-Wilson & Welsh, 1978; McClelland & Elman, 1986; McClelland & Rumelhart, 1981). Autonomous models assume no influence of context on the outcome of a lower level process (Fodor, 1983; Forster, 1979, 1981). In the FLMP, context has a positive effect on the outcome of the process, but without directly modifying the lower level processing feeding into that outcome.

The quantitative analyses of sentence interpretation also provide preliminary answers to important questions that could not be answered otherwise. Following the logic employed throughout our study of bimodal speech perception, the results of sentence interpretation seem to inform a number of alternative explanations. There appear to be multiple sources of information available and these sources appear to be integrated in interpreting a sentence. Furthermore, the sources seem to be continuous rather than categorical and appear to be evaluated independently of one another. Finally, the integration rule has the consequence that the more ambiguous sources of information have less impact on the judgment. One caveat is that our analyses of the Bates and MacWhinney results have been restricted necessarily to group data. Future work

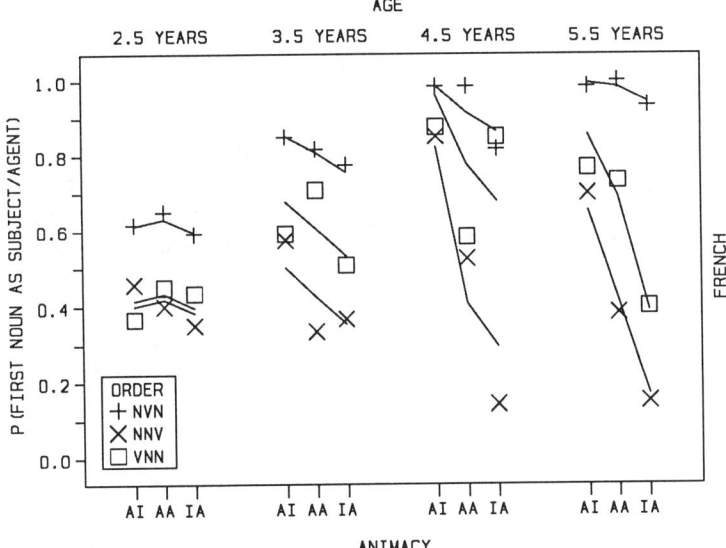

Figure 13. Observed (points) and predicted (lines) probability of identifying the first noun as subject/agent as a function of the animacy of the two nouns, the word order, and the noun-verb agreement for the French children (after Bates et al., 1984).

Table 9. Parameter values for the FLMP for the Bates, et al. (1982) data. The value gives the degree to which the information supports the first noun as subject/agent.

| Group | Age | Order | | | Animacy | | |
		NVN	VNN	NNV	AI	AA	IA
Italian	2.5	.473	.582	.537	.609	.466	.431
	3.5	.607	.738	.485	.772	.412	.368
	4.5	.714	.730	.429	.915	.285	.417
	5.5	.640	.740	.457	.960	.338	.336
English	2.5	.501	.481	.458	.638	.436	.422
	3.5	.611	.676	.532	.743	.498	.322
	4.5	.672	.934	.552	.837	.633	.252
	5.5	.686	.850	.379	.961	.510	.248
French	2.5	.565	.712	.320	.570	.437	.501
	3.5	.623	.894	.259	.667	.331	.444
	4.5	.754	.967	.453	.768	.378	.403
	5.5	.855	.947	.433	.780	.283	.462

should increase the number of observations per subject to permit single-subject analyses and to modify the task to provide more information about the time course of sentence interpretation. Additional judgments such as continuous ratings also will be necessary to resolve completely some of the important issues.

The present framework provides a direct and illuminating description of a challenging new body of data in sentence interpretation. Most of the two or so decades of psycholinguistics has been satisfied with demonstrating the psychological reality of some linguistic concept, rather than confronting the psychological processes involved in language understanding (Tyler, 1981). A reversal of this trend began with a concern for the time course of processing language (Marslen-Wilson, 1973; Massaro, 1972; 1975b). The paradigm used by Bates and MacWhinney is exactly analogous to study of bimodal speech perception and offers a challenge to current theories of language processing.

4. Probability Judgments about Events

The recent literature bears witness to people's judgments about the conjunction of events and how these judgments supposedly violate normative or prescriptive theories of logic, decision, and choice. Tversky and Kahneman (1983) evaluated whether judgments about the conjunction of events agree with the prescription given by probability theory. As an example, subjects were given the now well-known description of a hypothetical person.

Linda is 31 years old, single, outspoken and very bright. She majored in philosophy. As a student, she was deeply concerned with issues of discrimination and social justice, and also participated in anti-nuclear demonstrations.

They judged it more likely that Linda was a feminist bank teller than just a bank teller, supposedly violating the basic qualitative law of conjunction of probability theory. The probability of the conjunction cannot exceed the probably of either of the constituents making it up.

In contrast to some judgmental algorithm based on probability, Tversky and Kahneman's (1983) interpretation is that subjects utilize nonoptimal judgment heuristics. One heuristic is that a person will tend to predict an outcome that is most representative of the evidence. Thus bank teller and feminist is more representative of Linda than is simply bank teller. As pointed out by Anderson (1985), however, the representativeness heuristic falls short of an adequate explanation of decision behavior; it primarily addresses what needs to be explained. One prediction that the representativeness heuristic makes appears to be wrong. Base rate or prior odds are claimed to have no effect, because these do not contribute to representativeness and subjects make their decisions on only the representativeness of the sample. But base rate effects are found in within-subject designs (Leon & Anderson, 1974; Fischhoff, Slovic, & Lichtenstein, 1979) in that subjects' judgments will be influenced by the likelihood of some event as well as the properties of the sample. In the FLMP, base rate would be treated as an additional source of information and both the base rate and the sample are evaluated and integrated for a decision.

The present framework developed in this monograph proposes a general pattern recognition algorithm for a variety of categorization situations. Although the FLMP explanation might be interpreted as similar to the representativeness heuristic, it is fundamentally different. The idea is that the pattern classification algorithm of the FLMP is utilized (erroneously) in the probability judgment task. That is, the situations revealing nonoptimal behavior are almost identical to situations in which this same behavior would be optimal. The argument is that the latter situations supporting "optimal" judgment are more common and the tasks leading to "nonoptimal" judgment are the exception rather than the rule. Analogous to visual perception, we live in a three-dimensional world and the relatively infrequent two-dimensional scene can be misinterpreted if a three-dimensional algorithm is utilized. Given our interpretation, it is necessary to illustrate the similarity between the probability judgment task and the pattern recognition task. In our view, both of these are conjunction tasks in which two or more sources of information have to be evaluated and integrated. The subtle difference between the two tasks has to do with how the outcome of the integration is used. We begin with an analysis of the two different conjunction scenarios to illustrate the similarity between the two tasks.

4.1 Two Conjunction Scenarios

Consider the task of Oden (1977b) involving judgments about the truthfulness of the conjunction of two independent and unrelated propositions such as

A squid is a fish.
A desk is a furniture.

Each of these propositions is more true than false, and the truthfulness of both of them being true should be less than the truthfulness of either one. Either the minimum rule or the multiplicative rule derived from fuzzy set theory can predict this outcome. Oden found a better description of the results for the multiplicative rule, although the important finding is that fuzzy set theory is able to describe the results.

A second conjunction task consists of judgments about the truthfulness of a single proposition based on two independent sources of information such as

An enthusiastic and kind person is likeable.

The judged truthfulness of this proposition should be greater than the judged truthfulness of either of the two different propositions making it up.

> *An enthusiastic person is likeable.*
> *A kind person is likeable.*

The probability of two independent events would not be the appropriate description given that the events can be related to the same proposition or hypothesis. In this case, the scenario is more appropriately described by Bayes Theorem (Section 5.2). Although the second scenario is very similar to the first involving two independent and unrelated propositions, the conjunctional proposition is likely to be judged more truthful than either single statement. The reason is that each adjective (source of information) reduces uncertainty about the likeableness of the hypothetical person. In the first scenario involving the conjunction of unrelated propositions, the assessment in terms of a higher-order prototype is inappropriate given the independent and unrelated propositions. In the second scenario, it is appropriate to assess the conjunction of the two sources of information with respect to prototype representations such as likeable and dislikeable persons. It seems we have a reasonable case to argue for prototype representations being appropriate in the second form of conjunction but not in the first.

4.2 Prototype Representations

An appealing description of the two situations would maintain the same conjunction rule in both cases but would add the contribution of prototype representations in the second situation. In terms of the general pattern recognition model developed in this book, the featural evaluation and integration stage would be identical in the two situations, but the pattern classification stage would be functional in the second case but not the first. Thus, the judgment in the first situation should reflect the conjunction directly, whereas in the second case, the judgment would also contain a relative goodness of match against the appropriate prototypes. In our example, the judged truthfulness of the conjunction would be judged against prototypes of likeable and dislikeable persons. That is, how closely does the enthusiastic and kind person match our prototype of a likeable person and how closely does it match our prototype of a dislikeable person? The truthfulness would be equal to

$$t(x) = \frac{g(a)}{g(a) + g(\neg a)}$$

where $g(a)$ is the goodness of match to the likeable-person prototype and $g(\neg a)$ is the goodness of match to the dislikeable person prototype.

The results of interest, of course, involve those situations in which judgments supposedly violate the normative explanation. In this case, subjects tested within the first scenario judge the conjunction of two events as more likely or more true than either single event. Given a description of Linda, she is judged to be more likely a feminist bank teller than a bank teller. The explanation of these results in the present framework centers on the subject behaving in an instance of the first scenario as if it represents the second kind of scenario. That is, subjects include prototype matching and relative goodness operations even though they are uncalled for by the tenets of normative theory. These operations can lead to a probability judgment of the conjunction that is more true than the probability judgment of either or both of the single propositions. This outcome emerges even though the output of the conjunction operation itself is less true than the truth value of the most true proposition. Thus, in principle, probability theory is not violated by judgments of the conjunction of two events.

Understanding the decision requires understanding the candidate set of alternatives that subjects utilize in the task. The point is that a decision requires assessing the likelihood of any one alternative relative to other alternatives. Assessing whether Linda is a bank teller really asks the degree to which Linda is a bank teller relative to the candidate set of alternatives. In this case, a reasonable alternative candidate might be (not bank teller). Analogously, the contrasting category for the conjunction (bank teller and feminist) might be the conjunction (not bank teller and not feminist). When these respective alternatives are used within Bayes Theorem or the FLMP, we can predict that Linda will be rated as being more likely a feminist and bank teller than just a bank teller. What needs to be considered is that generating alternative categories is a natural part of pattern recognition and this generation is dynamically engaged in pattern recognition tasks and in judgment situations resembling pattern recognition scenarios. We have a direct analogy with how alternatives are generated in speech perception and how the sources of information are evaluated relative to these alternatives. Subjects given bank teller and feminist might evaluate these with respect to the description of Linda and these together match better than just bank teller. Although the verbal description resembles the representativeness heuristic, our explanation is a formal instantiation of a set of processes that are naturally engaged situations resembling pattern recognition.

4.3 Engaging Pattern Recognition Processes

The important question given the present explanation is why do subjects inappropriately behave in scenario one as if it is scenario two. The answer is that scenario two and the processes it entails are most typical of our experience in perception and decision. Pattern recognition involves a situation in which the conjunction of multiple sources of information usually is more informative than any source of information presented alone. Luckily, we are seldom required to consider independent propositions as in Oden's (1977b) task or in the probability judgment task of Tversky and Kahneman (1983). The multiple sources reduce ambiguity of some particular outcome. In contrast, the first scenario represents a situation in which the multiple sources of information are to be assessed with respect to multiple events. As illustrated in bimodal speech perception (Chapter

3, Sections 3 and 5), subjects have difficulty identifying visible and audible syllables as two separate speech events. There is significant cross talk in that each syllable influences the judgment about the other (see also Massaro, 1985a).

The argument is that scenario one is infrequent and unnatural; thus, we are not appropriately equipped to deal with it. Scenario one bears great similarity to scenario two, however, and it is only natural to behave as if it were scenario two. The similarity between the two scenarios is transparent when we consider the following kind of modification of the Tversky and Kahneman experiment. A target person such as Linda is described as usual. Then descriptions of hypothetical people are given and subjects rate the likelihood that each person is the target person. The descriptions vary in terms of the number of attributes. No one would be surprised if some two-attribute descriptions produced more extreme ratings than the corresponding one-attribute ratings. This is exactly the result we found in person impression (see Section 2.3). The question is whether this scenario of pattern recognition differs substantially from the scenario used by Tversky and Kahneman. When they ask which description of Linda is more probable, the question can simply be interpreted as which description best describes Linda, i.e., a pattern recognition situation. Tversky and Kahneman's tasks are engaging pattern recognition processes and these processes are about as rational and optional as they can be. They can be considered to produce nonoptimal behavior only when the experimenter believes that the situation calls for mathematical probability judgment rather than pattern recognition.

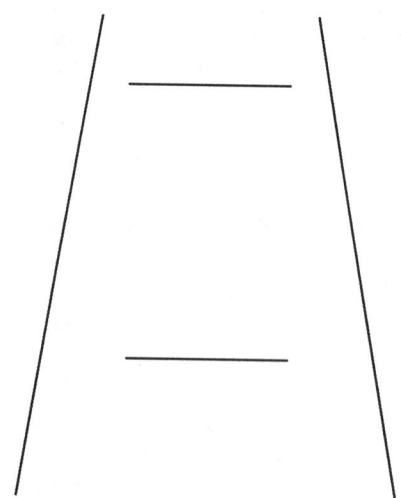

Figure 14. The Ponzo or Railroad Track Illusion

The "inappropriate" behavior in the Tversky and Kahneman experiment has an exact analog in the domain of visual perception. Presented with two-dimensional representations of three-dimensional space, certain illusions occur, such as the Ponzo illusion or railroad track illusion (see Figure 14). One explanation is that the pictorial cues to depth are integrated to give a perceptual interpretation of three-dimensional space (as is appropriate given three-dimensional scenes). Given a two-dimensional scene, however, the processes lead to a perceptual illusion. The illusion is a small price to pay because we encounter two-dimensional scenes so infrequently relative to three-dimensional scenes. Analogously, the pattern recognition scenario is the natural and common one and the processes specified by the present framework are optimal. The inappropriate use of these processes when confronted with the unnatural and infrequent scenario studied by Tversky and Kahneman (1983) should not be taken as evidence for non-optimal behavior (Cohen, 1981). Rather, the behavior should be interpreted as revealing the persistence of optimal algorithms that are overextended (inappropriately) to infrequent judgments.

5. Judgments about Categories

The final line of research has to do with the appropriate description of the assignment of objects to different conceptual categories. As an example, Smith and Osherson (1984) asked subjects to rate the degree to which a pictured object represented a category such as red, apple, or red apple. They found that a pictured object was judged to be a better exemplar of red apple than either of red or of apple. This result violates both the multiplicative or the minimization rule of fuzzy set theory (Goguen, 1969; Zadeh, 1965) for the conjunction of two properties. The truthfulness of the conjunction cannot exceed the minimal truthfulness of its constituents.

It follows that our treatment of the Smith and Osherson (1984) findings should be identical to our analysis of the probability judgments. Subjects that rate the degree to which a pictured object represents a category are utilizing pattern recognition processes and not simply rating the degree to which the pictured object conforms to the designated category. Analogous to the probability judgments, the FLMP can predict that an object can be rated as a better example of red apple than red or apple.

6. Related Developments

The study of visual illusions is as old as psychological inquiry, and most studies have sought the critical cue responsible for the illusion, such as the perceived depth of the central axis in the Müller-Lyer figure or the size of the surrounding circles in the Ebbinghaus illusion. Based on the current theoretical framework, we might expect to find a variety of cues (sources of information) contributing to any given illusion. McClellan, Bernstein, and Garbin (1984) used factorial designs to vary a number of properties of the Muller-Lyer figures (direction of fins, central axis length, fin length, and angle between the fins).

Subjects' magnitude estimations of all combinations of cues revealed that no single "critical" cue accounted for the illusion. Thus we have evidence for the evaluation and integration of multiple sources of information in this perceptual-judgment task, as in the other tasks discussed throughout the monograph. Massaro and Anderson (1971) had already described the Ebbinghaus illusion as a systematic function of the size, distance, and number of surrounding circles relative to the center circle. Erlebacher and Sekuler (1969) also varied a number of properties and concluded that multiple factors contributed to the illusion.

7. Communicating with Multiple Sources

Although watching the face and lip movements of the speaker influences what is perceived, this phenomenon does not appear to be unique. There are several powerful modes of communication that function very much like speech. In addition to the widespread use of sign language, there are other forms of communication that supplement rather than replace speech. Cued speech (Mohay, 1983), for example, supplements lipread information with manual hand movements for communicating to the hearing-impaired. For individuals without sight and sound, the Tadoma method involves the receiver placing his or her hands on the face and neck of the speaker (Norton, Schultz, Reed, Braida, Durlach, Rabinowitz, & Chomsky, 1977). Manual gestures also appear to have properties and functions that are strikingly similar to speech (McNeill, 1985).

7.1 Integrating Sound and Gesture

We have extended our framework to study the integration of a pointing gesture with audible speech (Thompson & Massaro, 1986). Following the strategy of an expanded factorial design, subjects were presented with gesture, speech, and both sources of information. The task was to indicate whether a ball or a doll was intended by the speaker. An auditory continuum of five levels was made between the words ball and doll. The gestural information was also varied by pointing to either the ball or doll objects. The results for both preschoolers and college students were essentially identical to those found in audible and visible speech. There were significant effects of both sources of information and the judgments followed the predictions of the FLMP. The RMSD value for the FLMP fit of individual subjects was .048 compared to an RMSD value of .067 for the fit of the CMP. Interestingly, the preschool children revealed a larger effect of pointing gesture than that previously found for lipreading. Observations such as this one make transparent the power of the present framework for addressing fundamental issues in language acquisition.

7.2 Lipreading with Deficient Sound

A central prediction of the FLMP is that two or more relatively ambiguous sources of information can lead to much better speech perception than can be expected from either source alone or from the simple summation of the two sources. Breeuwer and Plomp (1984) evaluated the contribution of both lipreading and sound pressure information in the understanding of short sentences. Sound pressure information occurring in one or two frequency bands was used to amplitude modulate pure-tone carriers with frequencies equal to the center frequency of the filter bands. As an example, the speech signal was bandpass filtered through a filter centered at 500 Hz. The resulting amplitude of the output of the bandpass filter was used to amplitude modulate a pure tone of 500 Hz.

Although the authors did not compare one-band versus two bands without the presence of lipreading, we can ask how two different sources of auditory information are integrated. With the presence of lipreading, there is a significant improvement given two kinds of auditory energy relative to just one. Correct performance averaged 55, 44, and 81 percent for the 500 Hz, the 3160 Hz, and the additive combination of these two bands, when the bandwidth of the filter was 1/3 of an octave. The analogous percentages were 66, 41, and 87 for the 1-octave bandwidth. These results reveal a superadditive combination of the information from different frequency ranges in the auditory speech signal. Similar results were found when the auditory information was formant-frequency information (Breeuwer & Plomp, 1985). What is important for the present argument is how the visual and auditory sources of information presented together can lead to highly acceptable performance when either presented alone is insufficient. As an example, the percentage of syllables recognized correctly was 33.2 given the auditory source, 22.8 given the visual source and 78.7 given both of these sources of information. This result is strong support for extending the framework of the FLMP to applied domains such as hearing-impairment and communicating over low bandwidth channels.

7.3 Disabled Perceivers

The value of the present perspective is apparent in supplementing sources of information for the disabled individual. One source of information that has been used for profoundly deafened individuals is cochlear prosthesis. This involves electrical stimulation of residual auditory nerve fibers using intracochlear electrodes (Shannon, 1983; Simmons, 1985). Usually, some parameters of the speech signal are derived and used to drive the location, amplitude, and rate of electrode stimulation. Although this information is not sufficient for complete communication, remarkably good performance can be obtained when it is combined with lipreading. In one study, a patient with a multiple-channel cochlear implant was tested with just electrical stimulation, just lipreading, and both of these sources of information (Dowell, Martin, Tong, Clark, Seligman, & Patrick, 1982). Twelve consonants were presented in a VCV context with the vowel /a/. Twenty observations were made on each consonant spoken by a female speaker in one test and a male speaker in the other. The results are of the form of a 12 by 12 confusion matrix under each of the three presentation conditions. The model was applied to the results of female and male speaker separately and gave RMSD values of .023 and 031, respectively. The model is capable of describing the integration of lipread information with electrical stimulation to the cochlear in the same manner as with normal hearing. There is a promising potential for utilizing the present approach as a framework for the assessment and rehabilitation of communication disorders.

7.4 Communicating over Low Bandwidth Channels

Visible speech, like audible speech, has the potential to be communicated over low bandwidth channels. The goal would be to reduce the content of the visible speech to only the critical components. Tartter and Knowlton (1981) placed 27 retroreflective spots on the hands and face of fluent ASL users. Conversation was possible only when the spots were transmitted over TV monitors. Thus, communication in sign language was possible using a highly stylized representation of the hands and body. We would expect that lipreading using a stylized representation of the face is also possible. Not only would the successful use of stylized representation make synthesis possible, it offers the potential for developing lipreading information transmitted over a low bandwidth channel such as a telephone line.

8. Relationship to Connectionist Models

The present framework has anticipated many of the distinguishing properties of a recent but influential movement in psychological inquiry called connectionism. A connectionist model is an information-processing system having and manipulating information. The information is represented in terms of the activations and inhibitions of neural-like units. The units are assumed to exist at different levels; for example, the TRACE model of speech perception (McClelland & Elman, 1986) consists of units at the feature, phoneme, and word levels. The units interact with one another via connections among the units. The connectivity is implemented by positive and negative weights that are either specified in advance or learned through feedback.

A prototypical connectionist model shares several fundamental properties with the current theoretical framework as instantiated in the FLMP. First, both models assume continuous rather than discrete representations; the fuzzy truth values of the FLMP are analogous to the continuous levels of activation and inhibition of connectionist models. Second, both models acknowledge the existence of multiple constraints on human performance. Both models provide an account of the evaluation and integration of multiple sources of information in pattern recognition. Third, there is the parallel assessment of multiple candidates or hypotheses at multiple levels in both models. Fourth, both models provide a common metric for relating qualitatively different sources of information. In the FLMP, each source of information is represented by fuzzy truth values representing the degree to which alternative hypotheses are supported. Activation level plays the analogous role in connectionist models. Fifth, the automatic categorization of a novel instance can be accomplished in both models. Finally, both frameworks conceptualize pattern recognition as finding the best fit between the relevant constraints and the pattern that is perceived. Particularly striking examples of this phenomenon were observed in bimodal speech perception, when for example, subjects perceived /ða/ given an auditory /ba/ paired with a visual /da/ (see Section 2.3 Chapter 3).

The close fit between the present framework and connectionism dictates an exploration of their similarities and differences. Although the two frameworks appear to agree on all metatheoretical criteria, the specific models to date differ in terms of the amount of connectivity in the system. The FLMP assumes no top-down influences of a higher-level unit on activation of a lower-level unit and no inhibition among units at a given level. Connectionist models usually make both of these assumptions. These differences are at the level of specifics and not at the level of metatheory. Thus, it is my belief that the current research provides important constraints on the assumptions that are viable for connectionist models. As presently formulated, many of the connectionist models with two-way connections among different levels of units and connectivity among units at a given level are too powerful. They are capable of predicting not only observed results but also results that do not occur. That is, some connectionist models can simulate both correct and incorrect process models of performance. Although I am sympathetic to the central assumptions of the models within the connectionist framework, my fear is the formal power of the models may distract us from the business at hand—trying to find regularities and laws and eliminating alternative explanations of behavior (Massaro, 1986a; 1986b).

9. Conclusion

If the present generalizations of the current research are reasonable, they strike a blow to the concept of modularity. The reason is that processing in horizontal (cognitive) tasks engages modules that are supposedly encapsulated and specific to a vertical process (input module) such as speech perception. Accordingly, the pessimism that Fodor (1983) has about revealing complex cognitive functioning is deflated. Given the contribution of vertical processes to cognitive skills, insights into the former decrease our uncertainty about the latter. The alternative proposed here is that the same fundamental processes contribute to an impressive variety of perceptual and cognitive actions. Whether the present work has unveiled something about the nature of these processes is now open to examination.

References

Ades, A. E. (1977). Vowels, consonants, speech, and nonspeech. *Psychological Review, 84,* 524-530.

Ainsworth, W. A. (1972). Duration as a cue in the recognition of synthetic vowels. *Journal of the Acoustical Society of America, 51,* 648-651.

Anderson, J. R. (1976). *Language, memory, and thought.* Hillsdale, NJ: Lawrence Erlbaum Associates.

Anderson, J. R. (1985). *Cognitive psychology and its implications,* New York: W. H. Freeman and Company.

Anderson, N. H. (1962). Application of an additive model to impression formation. *Science, 138,* 817-818.

Anderson, N. H. (1965). Averaging versus adding as a stimulus-combination rule in impression formation. *Journal of Experimental Psychology, 70,* 394-400.

Anderson, N. H. (1968). A simple model for information integration. In R. P. Abelson, E. Aronson, W. J. McGuire, T. M. Newcomb, M. J. Rosenberg, & P. H. Tannenbaum (Eds.), *Theories of cognitive consistency: A sourcebook* (pp. 731-743). Chicago: Rand-McNally.

Anderson, N. H. (1973). Functional measurement of social desirability. *Sociometry, 36,* 89-98.

Anderson, N. H. (1974). Information integration theory: A brief survey. In D. H. Krantz, R. C. Atkinson, R. D. Luce, & P. Suppes (Eds.), *Contemporary developments in mathematical psychology, 2* (pp. 236-305). San Francisco: W. H. Freeman.

Anderson, N. H. (1981). *Foundations of information integration theory.* New York: Academic Press.

Anderson, N. H. (1982). *Methods of information integration theory.* New York: Academic Press.

Anderson, N. H. (1983). Intuitive physics: Understanding and learning of physical relations. In T. J. Tighe, & B. E. Shepp (Eds.), *Perception, cognition, and development: Interactional analyses* (pp. 231-265). Hillsdale, NJ: Lawrence Erlbaum Associates.

Anderson, N. H. (1985, August). *A cognitive theory of judgment and decision.* Proceedings of tenth research conference on subjective probability, utility, and decision making, Helsinki, Finland.

Anderson, N. H., & Cuneo, D. O. (1978). The height + width rule in children's judgments of quantity. *Journal of Experimental Psychology: General, 107,* 335-378.

Anderson, N. H., & Shanteau, J. C. (1970). Information integration in risky decision making. *Journal of Experimental Psychology, 84,* 441-451.

Anderson, N. H., & Shanteau, J. C. (1977). Weak inference with linear models. *Psychological Bulletin, 84,* 1155-1170.

Appleman, I. B., & Mayzner, M. S. (1981). The letter-frequency effect and the generality of familiarity effects on perception. *Perception & Psychophysics, 30,* 436-446.

Armstrong, S. L., Gleitman, L. R., & Gleitman, H. (1983). What some concepts might not be. *Cognition, 13,* 263-308.

Aronson, E., & Rosenbloom, S. (1971). Space perception in early infancy: perception within a common auditory visual space. *Science, 172,* 1161-1163.

Asch, S. E. (1946). Forming impressions of personality. *Journal of Abnormal and Social Psychology, 41,* 258-290.

Ashby, F. G., & Townsend, J. T. (1986). Varieties of perceptual independence. *Psychological Review, 93,* 154-179.

Aslin, R. N., Pisoni, D. B., Hennessy, B. L., & Perey, A. J. (1981). Discrimination of voice-onset-time by human infants: New findings concerning phonetic development. *Child Development, 52,* 1135-1145.

Bahrick, L., Walker, A., & Neisser, U. (1978). *Infants' perception of multimodal information in novel events.* Paper presented at the meeting of the Eastern Psychological Association, Washington, DC.

Bates, E., MacWhinney, B., Caselli, C., Devescovi, A., Natale, F., & Venza, V. (1984). A cross-linguistic study of the development of sentence interpretation strategies. *Child Development, 55*, 341-354.

Bates, E., McNew, S., MacWhinney, B., Devescovi, A., & Smith, S. (1982). Functional constraints on sentence processing: A cross-linguistic study. *Cognition, 11*, 245-299.

Bennett, D. C. (1968). Spectral form and duration cues in the recognition of English and German vowels. *Language and Speech, 11*, 65-85.

Berger, K. W. (1972). *Speechreading principles and methods*, Baltimore: National Educational Press.

Bergman, M. (1980). *Aging and the perception of speech.* Baltimore: University Park Press.

Bernstein, I. H., Clark, M. H., & Edelstein, B. A. (1969a). Effects of an auditory signal on visual reaction time. *Journal of Experimental Psychology, 80*, 567-569.

Bernstein, I. H., Clark, M. H., & Edelstein, B. A. (1969b). Intermodal effects in choice reaction time. *Journal of Experimental Psychology, 81*, 405-407.

Bernstein, I. H., & Edelstein, B. A. (1971). Effects of some variations in auditory input upon visual choice reaction time. *Journal of Experimental Psychology, 87*, 241-247.

Bertelson, P., & Radeau, M. (1976). Ventriloquism, sensory interaction, and response bias: Remarks on the paper by Choe, Welch, Gilford, and Juola. *Perception & Psychophysics, 19*, 531-535.

Bertelson, P., & Radeau, M. (1981). Cross-modal bias and perceptual fusion with auditory-visual spatial discordance. *Perception & Psychophysics, 29*, 578-584.

Best, C. T., Morrongiello, B., & Robson, R. (1981). Perceptual equivalence of acoustic cues for speech and nonspeech perception. *Perception & Psychophysics, 29*, 121-211.

Birnbaum, M. H. (1973). The devil rides again: Correlation as an index of fit. *Psychological Bulletin, 79*, 239-242.

Birnbaum, M. H. (1974). The nonadditivity of personality impressions. *Journal of Experimental Psychology, 102*, 543-561.

Birnbaum, M. H. (1982). Controversies in psychological measurement. In B. Wegener (Ed.), *Social attitudes and psychophysical measurement* (pp. 401-485). Hillsdale, NJ: Lawrence Erlbaum Associates.

Breeuwer, M., & Plomp, R. (1984). Speechreading supplemented with frequency-selective sound-pressure information. *Journal of the Acoustical Society of America, 76,* 686-691.

Breeuwer, M., & Plomp, R. (1985). Speechreading supplemented with formant-frequency information for voiced speech. *Journal of the Acoustical Society of America, 77,* 314-317.

Broadbent, D. E. (1958). *Perception and communication.* New York: Pergamon Press.

Broadbent, D. E. (1971). *Decision and stress.* New York: Academic Press.

Broadbent, D. E. (1982). Task combination and selective intake of information. *Acta Psychologica, 50,* 253-290.

Bruner, J. S., Goodnow, J., & Austin, G. A. (1956). *A Study of Thinking.* New York: Wiley.

Brunswik, E. (1934). *Wahrehmung und Gegenstandswelt.* Vienna: Deuticke.

Brunswik, E. (1944). Distal focussing of perception: size-constancy in a representative sample of situations. *Psychological Monographs, 56*(Whole No. 254), 1-49.

Brunswik, E. (1952). *The conceptual framework of psychology.* Chicago: University of Chicago Press.

Brunswik, E. (1955). Representative design and probabilistic theory in a functional psychology. *Psychological Review, 62,* 193-217.

Brunswik, E. (1956). *Perception and the representative design of psychological experiments.* Berkeley, CA: University of California Press.

Brunswik, E., & Kamiya, J. (1953). Ecological cue validity of "proximity" and of other Gestalt factors. *American Journal of Psychology, 66,* 20-32.

Busemeyer, J. R., Dewey, G. I., & Medin, D. L. (1984). Evaluation of exemplar-based generalization and the abstraction of categorical information. *Journal of Experimental Psychology: Learning, Memory and Cognition, 10,* 638-648.

Bush, R. R., Galanter, E., & Luce, R. D. (1963). Characterization and classification of choice experiments. In R. D. Luce, R. R. Bush, & E. Galanter (Eds.), *Handbook of mathematical psychology: Vol. 1.* (pp. 77-102). New York: Wiley.

Butterworth, G. (1981). The origins of auditory-visual perception and visual proprioception in human development. In R. D. Walk, & H. L. Pick (Eds.), *Intersensory perception and sensory integration* (pp. 37-70). New York: Plenum.

Campbell, H. W. (1974). *Phoneme recognition by ear and by eye: A distinctive feature analysis*, Unpublished doctoral dissertation, University of Nijmegen, Holland.

Campbell, R. (in press). Remembering with impurity when pre-categorical acoustic storage is not acoustic, what is it? In D. A. Allport, D. MacKay, W. Prinz, & E. Scheerer (Eds.), *Language perception and production: Common mechanisms in listening, speaking, reading and writing*. London: Academic Press.

Campbell, R., & Dodd, B. (1980). Hearing by eye. *Quarterly Journal of Experimental Psychology, 32*, 85-99.

Campbell, R., & Dodd, B. (1982). Some suffix effects on lipread lists. *Canadian Journal of Psychology, 36*, 509-515.

Carney, A. E., Widin, G. P., & Viemeister, N. F. (1977). Noncategorical perception of stop consonants differing in VOT. *Journal of the Acoustical Society of America, 62*, 961-970.

Chandler, J. P. (1969). Subroutine STEPIT - Finds local minima of a smooth function of several parameters. *Behavioral Science, 14*, 81-82.

Chase, W. G., & Simon, H. A. (1973). The mind's eye in chess. In W. G. Chase (Ed.), *Visual information processing* (pp. 215-281). New York: Academic Press.

Chomsky, N. (1975). *Reflections on language*. New York: Pantheon.

Chomsky, N., & Halle, M. (1968). *The sound pattern of English*. New York: Harper-Row.

Clarke, F. R. (1957). Constant-ratio rule for confusion matrices in speech communication. *Journal of the Acoustical Society of America, 29*, 715-720.

Cleveland, W. S. (1985). *The elements of graphing data* Monterey, CA: Wadsworth Advanced Books and Software.

Cohen, J. L. (1981). Can human irrationality be experimentally demonstrated? *The Behavioral and Brain Sciences, 4*, 317-370.

Cohen, M. M. (1979). *Three cues to voicing of intervocalic velar stops*. Unpublished master's thesis, University of Wisconsin, Madison.

Cohen, M. M. (1984). *Processing of visual and auditory information in speech perception*. Unpublished doctoral dissertation, University of California, Santa Cruz.

Cole, R. A., & Jakimik, J. (1978). Understanding speech: How words are heard. In G. Underwood (Ed.), *Strategies of information-processing* (pp. 67-116). London: Academic Press.

Conant, J. B. (1947). *On understanding science*, New Haven: Yale University Press.

Condry, S. M., Haltom, M., Jr., & Neisser, U. (1977). Infant sensitivity to audio-visual discrepancy. *Bulletin of the Psychonomic Society, 9*, 431-432.

Conrad, R. A. (1979). *The deaf schoolchild*. London: Harper and Row.

Crowder, R. G. (1983). The purity of auditory memory. *Philosophical Transactions of the Royal Society, Section B, 302*, 251-265.

Crowder, R. G., & Morton, J. (1969). Precategorical acoustic storage (PAS) *Perception & Psychophysics, 5*, 365-373.

Cutting, J. E., & Millard, R. T. (1984). Three gradients and the perception of flat and curved surfaces. *Journal of Experimental Psychology: General, 113*, 198-216.

Denes, P. (1955). Effects of duration on the perception of voicing. *Journal of the Acoustical Society of America, 27*, 761-764.

Dodd, B. (1977). The role of vision in the perception of speech. *Perception, 6*, 31-40.

Dodd, B. (1979). Lip reading in infants: Attention to speech presented in-and out-of synchrony. *Cognitive Psychology, 11*, 478-484.

Dowell, R. C., Martin, L. F. A., Tong, Y. C., Clark, G. M., Seligman, P. M., & Patrick, J. F. (1982). A 12-consonant confusion study on a multiple-channel cochlear implant patient. *Journal of Speech and Hearing Research, 25*, 509-516.

Easton, R. D., & Basala, M. (1982). Perceptual dominance during lipreading. *Perception and Psychophysics, 32*, 562-570.

Eimas, P. D. (1963). The relationship between identification and discrimination along speech and non-speech continua. *Language and Speech, 6*, 206-217.

Eimas, P. D. (1974). Auditory and linguistic processing of cues for place of articulation by infants. *Perception & Psychophysics, 16*, 513-521.

Eimas, P. D. (1985, January). The perception of speech in early infancy. *Scientific American, 252*, 1, 46-52.

Eimas, P. D., & Corbit, J. D. (1973). Selective adaptation of linguistic feature detectors. *Cognitive Psychology, 4*, 99-109.

Eimas, P. D., & Miller, J. L. (1980). Discrimination of information for manner of articulation. *Infant Behavior and Development, 3*, 367-375.

Eimas, P. D., Siqueland, E. R., Jusczyk, P., & Vigorito, J. (1971). Speech perception in infants. *Science, 171*, 303-306.

Elio, R., & Anderson, J. R. (1981). The effects of category generalizations and instance similarity on schema abstraction. *Journal of Experimental Psychology: Human Learning and Memory*, 397-418.

Elman, J. L. (1979). Perceptual origins of the phoneme boundary effect and selective adaptation to speech: a signal detection theory analysis. *Journal of the Acoustical Society of America, 65*, 190-207.

Erber, N. P. (1972). Auditory, visual and auditory-visual recognition of consonants by children with normal and impaired hearing. *Journal of Speech and Hearing Research, 15*, 413-422.

Erlebacher, A., & Sekuler, R. (1969). Explanation of the Muller-Lyer illusion: Confusion theory examined. *Journal of Experimental Psychology, 80*, 462-467.

Estes, W. K. (1979). On the descriptive and explanatory functions of theories of memory. In L. Nilsson (Ed.), *Perspectives on memory research* (pp. 35-60). Hillsdale, NJ: Lawrence Erlbaum Associates.

Estes, W. K. (1986). Memory storage and retrieval processes in category learning. *Journal of Experimental Psychology: General, 115*, 155-174.

Falmagne, J. (1985). *Elements of psychophysical theory*. New York: Oxford University Press.

Fechner, G. T. (1966). *Elements of psychophysics: Vol. 1* (H. E. Adler, D. H. Howes, & E. G. Boring, Trans. & Eds.). New York: Holt, Rinehart & Winston. (Original work published 1860).

Fischhoff, B., Slovic, P., & Lichtenstein, S. (1979). Subjective sensitivity analysis. *Organizational Behavior and Human Performance, 23*, 339-359.

Fitch, H. L., Halwes, T., Erickson, D. M., & Liberman, A. M. (1980). Perceptual equivalence of two acoustic cues for stop-consonant manner. *Perception and Psychophysics, 27*, 343-350.

Flavell, J. H. (1985). *Cognitive development*, Englewood Cliffs, NJ: Prentice-Hall, Inc.

Fodor, J. A. (1983). *Modularity of mind*. Cambridge, MA: Bradford books.

Forster, K. I. (1979). Levels of processing and the structure of the language processor. In. W. Cooper, & E. Walker (Eds.), *Sentence processing: Psycholinguistic studies presented to Merrill Garrett* (pp. 27-86). Hillsdale, NJ: Lawrence Erlbaum Associates.

Forster, K. I. (1981). Priming and the effects of sentence and lexical contexts on naming time: Evidence for autonomous lexical processing. *Quarterly Journal of Experimental Psychology, A, 33*, 465-495.

Forster, K. I. (1985). Lexical acquisition and the modular lexicon. *Language and Cognitive Processes, 1*, 87-108.

Frauenfelder, U. H., & Marcus, S. M. (1985). *Phonetic decisions and lexical constraints in the real-time process of speech perception*. (Manuscript No. 488/II). Eindhoven, Netherlands: Institute for Perception Research.

Fried, L. S., & Holyoak, K. J. (1984). Induction of category distributions: A framework for classification learning. *Journal of Experimental Psychology: Learning, Memory, and Cognition, 10*, 234-257.

Fujisaki, H., & Kawashima, T. (1970). Some experiments on speech perception and a model for the perceptual mechanism. *Annual Report of the Engineering Research Institute, 29*, Tokyo: Faculty of Engineering, University of Tokyo, 206-214.

Ganong, W. F. III. (1980) Phonetic categorization in auditory word recognition. *Journal of Experimental Psychology: Human Perception and Performance, 6*, 110-125.

Garner, W. R., Hake, H. W., & Eriksen, C. W. (1956). Operationism and the concept of perception. *Psychological Review, 63*, 149-159.

Gibson, J. J. (1950). *The perception of the visual world.* Cambridge, MA: Riverside Press.

Gibson, J. J. (1966). *The senses considered as perceptual systems.* Boston: Houghton Mifflin.

Gibson, J. J. (1979). *The ecological approach to visual perception.* Boston: Houghton Mifflin Co.

Gielen, S. C., Schmidt, R. A., & Van Den Heuvel, P. J. M. (1983). On the nature of intersensory facilitation of reaction time. *Perception and Psychophysics, 34*, 161-168.

Gleitman, L. R., & Wanner, E. (1982). Language acquisition: the state of the state of the art (pp. 3-48). In E. Wanner, & L. R. Gleitman (Eds.), *Language acquisition: The state of the art.* Cambridge: Cambridge University Press.

Goguen, J. A. (1969). The logic of inexact concepts. *Synthese, 19*, 325-373.

Green, D. M., & Swets, J. A. (1966). *Signal detection theory and psychophysics.* New York: Wiley.

Greene, R. L., & Crowder, R. G. (1984). Modality and suffix effects in the absence of auditory stimulation. *Journal of Verbal Learning and Verbal Behavior, 23*, 371-382.

Greeno, J. G., & Steiner, T. E. (1964). Markovian processes with identifiable states: general considerations and application to all-or-none learning. *Psychometrika, 29*, 309-333.

Haber, R. N. (1983). The impending demise of the icon: A critique of the concept of iconic storage in visual information processing. *The Behavioral and Brain Sciences, 6*, 1-54.

Hary, J. M., & Massaro, D. W. (1982). Categorical results do not imply categorical perception. *Perception & Psychophysics, 32*, 409-418.

Healy, A. F., & Repp, B. H. (1982). Context independence and phonetic mediation in categorical perception. *Journal of Experimental Psychology: Human Perception and Performance, 8*, 68-80.

Heider, F. K., & Heider, G. M. (1940) An experimental investigation of lipreading. *Psychological Monographs, 52*, 124-153.

Helmholtz, H. von (1962). *Treatise on physiological optics. (3rd ed., J. P. C. Southall, Trans. & Ed.). New York: Dover. (Original work published 1856-1866).*

Hershenson, M. (1962). Reaction time as a measure of intersensory facilitation. *Journal of Experimental Psychology, 63*, 289-293.

Hilgard, E. R. (1933). Reinforcement and inhibition of eyelid reflexes. *Journal of General Psychology, 8*, 85-113.

Hilgard, E. R. (1955). Discussion of probabilistic functionalism. *Psychological Review, 62*, 226-228.

Hintzman, D. L., & Ludlam. G. (1980). Differential forgetting of prototypes and old instances: Simulation by an exemplar-based classification model. *Memory & Cognition, 8*, 378-382.

Hofsten, C. von (in press). Catching. In H. Heuer, & A. F. Sanders (Eds.), *Perspectives on perception and action.* Hillsdale, NJ: Lawrence Erlbaum Associates.

Homa, D., Sterling, S., & Trepel, L. (1981). Limitations of exemplar-based generalization and the abstraction of categorical information. *Journal of Experimental Psychology: Human Learning and Memory, 7*, 418-439.

Hull, C. L. (1920). Quantitative aspects of the evolution of concepts. *Psychological Monographs* (Whole No. 123).

Isenberg, D., Walker, E. C. T., & Ryder, J. M. (1980, November). A top-down effect on the identification of function words. Paper presented at the Acoustical Society of America, Los Angeles, CA. *Journal of the Acoustical Society of America, 68,* AA6 (abstract).

James, W. (1890). *The principles of psychology.* New York: Holt. Republished as Dover paperback, 1950.

Jeffers, J., & Barley, M. (1971). *Speechreading (lipreading).* Springfield, IL: Thomas.

Jeffers, J., & Barley, M. (1979). *Look, now hear this.* Springfield, IL: Thomas.

Johnson-Laird, P. N. (1983). *Mental models: Towards a cognitive science of language, inference, and consciousness.* Cambridge, MA: Harvard University Press.

Kahneman, D., & Henik, A. (1981). Perceptual organization and attention. In M. Kubovy, & J. R. Pomerantz (Eds.), *Perceptual organization* (pp. 181-211). Hillsdale, NJ: Lawrence Erlbaum Associates.

Kahneman, D., & Treisman, A. (1984). Changing views of attention and automaticity. In R. Parasuraman, & D. R. Davies (Eds.), *Varieties of attention* (pp. 29-61). New York: Academic Press.

Kemler, D. G., & Smith, L. B. (1978). Assessing similarity and dimensional relations: Effects of integrality and separability on the discovery of complex concepts. *Journal of Experimental Psychology: General, 108,* 133-150.

Kendler, T. S. (1983). Labeling, Overtraining, and levels of function. In T. J. Tighe, & B. E. Shepp (Eds.), *Perception, cognition and development: Interactional analyses* (pp. 129-160). Hillsdale, NJ: Lawrence Erlbaum Associates.

Klatt, D. H. (1980). Software for a cascade/parallel formant synthesizer. *Journal of the Acoustical Society of America, 67,* 971-995.

Knapp, A. G., & Anderson, J. A. (1984). Theory of categorization based on distributed memory storage. *Journal of Experimental Psychology: Learning, Memory, and Cognition, 10,* 616-637.

Krause, S. E. (1982). Vowel duration as a perceptual cue to postvocalic consonant voicing in young children and adults. *Journal of the Acoustical Society of America, 71,* 990-995.

Kuhl, P. K., & Meltzoff, A. N. (1982). The bimodal perception of speech in infancy. *Science, 218,* 1138-1141.

Ladefoged, P., Harshman, R., Goldstein, L., & Rice, L. (1978). Generating vocal tract shapes from formant frequencies. *Journal of the Acoustical Society of America, 64,* 253-257.

Lawson, K. R. (1980). Spatial and temporal congruity and auditory-visual integration in infants. *Developmental Psychology, 16*, 185-192.

Leon, M. (1982). Extent, multiplying, and proportionality rules in children's judgments of area. *Journal of Experimental Child Psychology, 33*, 124-141.

Leon, M., & Anderson, N. H. (1974). A ratio rule from integration theory applied to inference judgments. *Journal of Experimental Psychology, 102*, 27-36.

Lesgold, A. M. (1984a). Acquiring expertise. In J. R. Anderson, & S. M. Kosslyn (Eds.), *Tutorials in learning and memory* (pp. 31-60). New York: W. H. Freeman and Company.

Lesgold, A. M. (1984b). Human skill in a computerized society: Complex skills and their acquisition. *Behavior Research Methods and Instrumentation, 16*, 79-87.

Liberman, A. M. (1982). On finding that speech is special. *American Psychologist, 37*, 148-167.

Liberman, A. M., Cooper, F. S., Shankweiler, D. P., & Studdert-Kennedy, M. (1967). Perception of the speech code. *Psychological Review, 74*, 431-461.

Liberman, A. M., Harris, K. S., Hoffman, H. S., & Griffith, B. C. (1957). The discrimination of speech sounds within and across phoneme boundaries. *Journal of Experimental Psychology, 54*, 358-368. 753-771.

Liberman, A. M., & Mattingly, I. G. (1985). The motor theory of speech perception revised. *Cognition, 21*, 1-36.

Lisker, L. (1978). *Rapid vs rabid: A catalog of of acoustic features that may cue the distinction.* (Status Report on Speech Research, SR-54, 127-132). Haskins Laboratories, Hartford, CT.

Long, J. (1975). Reduced efficiency and capacity limitations in multidimension signal recognition. *Quarterly Journal of Experimental Psychology, 27*, 599-614.

Lopes, L. L. (1976). Model-based decision and inference in stud poker. *Journal of Experimental Psychology: General, 105*, 217-239.

Luce, R. D. (1959). *Individual choice behavior.* New York: Wiley.

Luce, R. D. (1977). The choice axiom after twenty years. *Journal of Mathematical Psychology, 15*, 215-233.

MacDonald, J., & McGurk, H. (1978) Visual influences on speech perception process. *Perception & Psychophysics, 24*, 253-257.

Macmillan, N. A. (in press). Beyond the categorical/continuous distinction: A psychophysical approach to processing modes. In S. Harnad (Ed.), *Categorical perception*. Cambridge: Cambridge University press. New York.

Macmillan, N. A., Kaplan, H. L., & Creelman, C. D. (1977). The psychophysics of categorical perception. *Psychological Review, 84*, 452-471.

MacWhinney, B., Bates, E., & Kliegl, R. (1984). Cue validity and sentence interpretation in English, German, and Italian. *Journal of Verbal Learning and Verbal Behavior, 23*, 127-150.

Marcel, A. J. (1983a). Conscious and unconscious perception: Experiments on visual masking and word recognition. *Cognitive Psychology, 15*, 197-237.

Marcel, A. J. (1983b). Conscious and unconscious perception: An approach to the relations between phenomenal experience and perceptual processes. *Cognitive Psychology, 15*, 238-300.

Marslen-Wilson, W. (1973). Linguistic structure and speech shadowing at very short latencies. *Nature, 244*, 522-523.

Marslen-Wilson, W. (1984). Function and process in spoken word recognition: A tutorial review. In H. Bouma & D. G. Bouwhuis (Eds.), Attention and performance X: Control of language processes. (pp. 125-150). Hillsdale, NJ: Lawrence Erlbaum Associates.

Marslen-Wilson, W., & Welsh, A. (1978). Processing interactions and lexical access during word recognition in continuous speech. *Cognitive Psychology, 10*, 29-63.

Mason, M. (1982). More about the letter-frequency effect. *Perception & Psychophysics, 31*, 589-590.

Massaro, D. W. (1972). Preperceptual images, processing time, and perceptual units in auditory perception. *Psychological Review, 79*, 124-145.

Massaro, D. W. (1975a). *Experimental psychology and information processing.* Chicago: Rand-McNally.

Massaro, D. W. (Ed.). (1975b). *Understanding language: An information processing analysis of speech perception, reading and psycholinguistics.* New York: Academic Press.

Massaro, D. W. (1976). Auditory information processing. In W. K. Estes (Ed.), *Handbook of learning and cognitive processes. Vol. 4: Attention and memory* (pp. 275-320). Hillsdale, NJ: Lawrence Erlbaum Associates.

Massaro, D. W. (1978). A stage model of reading and listening. *Visible Language, 12*, 3-26.

Massaro, D. W. (1979). Reading and listening (Tutorial paper). In P. A. Kolers, M. Wrolstad, & H. Bouma (Eds.), *Processing of visible language: Vol. 1* (pp. 331-354). New York: Plenum.

Massaro, D. W. (1984a). Building and testing models of reading processes. In P. D. Pearson (Ed.), *Handbook of reading research* (pp. 111-146). New York: Longman.

Massaro, D. W. (1984b). Children's perception of auditory and visual speech. *Child Development, 55*, 1777-1788.

Massaro, D. W. (1984c). Time's role for information, processing, and normalization. *Annals of the New York Academy of Sciences, Timing and Time Perception, 423*, 372-384.

Massaro, D. W. (1985a). Attention and perception: An information-integration perspective. *Acta Psychologica, 60*, 211-243.

Massaro, D. W. (1985b). *Brunswik and Gibson: Similarities and contrasts with implications for contemporary psychology*. (Report 67/1985). Research Group on Perception and Action. Zentrum für interdisziplinäre Forshung. Universität Bielefeld, Bielefeld, West Germany.

Massaro, D. W. (1986a, November). *Connectionist models of mind*. Paper given at the twenty-seventh annual meeting of the Psychonomic Society, New Orleans.

Massaro, D. W. (1986b). The computer as a metaphor for psychological inquiry: Considerations and recommendations. *Behavior Research Methods, Instruments, & Computers, 18*, 73-92.

Massaro, D. W. (in press a). A fuzzy logical model of speech perception. In W. A. Lea (Ed.), *Towards robustness in speech recognition*. Apple Valley, Minnesota: Speech Science Publications.

Massaro, D. W. (in press b). Categorical partition: A fuzzy logical model of categorization behavior. In S. Harnad (Ed.), *Categorical perception*. Cambridge: Cambridge University press.

Massaro, D. W. (in press c). Information-processing theory and strong inference: A paradigm for psychological inquiry. In H. Heuer and A. F. Sanders (Eds.), *Perspectives on perception and action*. Hillsdale, NJ: Lawrence Erlbaum Associates.

Massaro, D. W. (in press d). Integrating multiple sources of information in listening and reading. In D. A. Allport, D. G. MacKay, W. Prinz, & E. Scheerer (Eds.), *Language Perception and Production: Shared Mechanisms in Listening, Speaking, Reading and Writing*. London: Academic Press.

Massaro, D. W. (in press e). Speech perception by ear and eye. In B. Dodd and R. Campbell (Eds.), *Hearing by Eye: Experimental studies in the psychology of lipreading.* Hillsdale, NJ: Lawrence Erlbaum Associates.

Massaro, D. W., & Anderson, N. H. (1971). Judgmental model of the Ebbinghaus illusion. *Journal of Experimental Psychology, 89,* 147-151.

Massaro, D. W., & Cohen, M. M. (1976). The contribution of fundamental frequency and voice onset time to the /zi/-/si/ distinction, *Journal of the Acoustical Society of America, 60,* 704-717.

Massaro, D. W., & Cohen, M. M. (1977). The contribution of voice-onset time and fundamental frequency as cues to the /zi/-/si/ distinction. *Perception & Psychophysics, 22,* 373-382.

Massaro, D. W., & Cohen, M. M. (1983a). Categorical or continuous speech perception: A new test. *Speech Communication, 2,* 15-35.

Massaro, D. W., & Cohen, M. M. (1983b). Consonant/vowel ratio: An improbable cue in speech. *Perception & Psychophysics, 33,* 502-505.

Massaro, D. W., & Cohen, M. M. (1983c). Evaluation and integration of visual and auditory information in speech perception. *Journal of Experimental Psychology: Human Perception and Performance, 9,* 753-771.

Massaro, D. W., & Cohen, M. M. (1983d). Phonological context in speech perception. *Perception & Psychophysics, 34,* 338-348.

Massaro, D. W., Cohen, M. M., & Tseng, C-Y. (1985). The evaluation and integration of pitch height and pitch contour in lexical tone perception in Mandarin Chinese. *Journal of Chinese Linguistics, 13,* 267-289.

Massaro, D. W., & Ferguson, E. L. (1986). *Cognitive style and perception: the relationship between category width and speech perception, categorization, and discrimination.* Unpublished manuscript.

Massaro, D. W., & Hary, J. M. (1983). Speech perception and psychophysics: Theory and experiment. *Perception & Psychophysics, 34,* 499-502.

Massaro, D. W., & Hary, J. M. (1984). Categorical results, categorical perception, and hindsight. *Perception & Psychophysics, 35,* 586-588.

Massaro, D. W., Jastrzembski, J. E. & Lucas, P. A. (1981). Frequency, orthographic regularity, and lexical status in letter and word perception. In G. H. Bower (Ed.), *The psychology of learning and motivation* (pp. 163-200). New York: Academic Press.

Massaro, D. W., & Oden, G. C. (1980a). Evaluation and integration of acoustic features in speech perception. *Journal of the Acoustical Society of America, 67,* 996-1013.

Massaro, D. W., & Oden, G. C. (1980b). Speech perception: A framework for research and theory. In N. J. Lass (Ed.), *Speech and language: Advances in basic research and practice: Vol. 3* (pp. 129-165). New York: Academic Press.

Massaro, D. W., Thompson, L. A., Barron, B., & Laren, E. (1986). Developmental changes in visual and auditory contributions to speech perception. *Journal of Experimental Child Psychology, 41*, 93-113.

Massaro, D. W. & Warner, D. S. (1977). Dividing attention between auditory and visual perception. *Perception & Psychophysics, 21*, 569-574.

Mayer, M. J. (1982). A mobile research laboratory. *Behavior Research Methods and Instrumentation, 14*, 505-510.

Mayer, M. J. (unpublished). Visual detection of sinusoidal gratings.

McClellan, P. G., Bernstein, I. H., & Garbin, C. P. (1984). What makes the Mueller a liar: A multiple-cue approach. *Perception & Psychophysics, 36*, 234-244.

McClelland, J. L. (1976). Preliminary letter identification in the perception of words and nonwords. *Journal of Experimental Psychology: Human Perception and Performance, 2*, 80-91.

McClelland, J. L. (1979). On the time relations of mental processes: An examination of systems of processes in cascade. *Psychological Review, 86*, 287-330.

McClelland, J. L., & Elman, J. L. (1986). The TRACE model of speech perception. *Cognitive Psychology, 18*, 1-86.

McClelland, J. L., & Rumelhart, D. E. (1981). An interactive activation model of context effects in letter perception: Part I. An account of basic findings. *Psychological Review, 88*, 375-407.

McGurk, H. (1981). Listening with eye and ear (paper discussion). In T. Myers, J. Laver, & J. Anderson (Eds.), *The cognitive representation of speech.* Amsterdam: North-Holland.

McGurk, H., & Lewis, M. (1974). Space perception in early infancy: perception within a common auditory-visual space. *Science, 186*, 649-650.

McGurk, H., & MacDonald, J. (1976). Hearing lips and seeing voices. *Nature, 264*,

McNabb, S. D. (1974). *Must the output of the phonetic feature detector be binary?* (Progress Report 2, 166-179) Research on Speech Perception, Department of Psychology, Indiana University.

McNeill, D. (1985). So you think gestures are nonverbal? *Psychological Review, 92*, 350-371.

Medin, D. L., Altom, M. W., Edelson, S. M., & Freko, D. (1982). Correlated symptoms and simulated medical classification. *Journal of Experimental Psychology: Learning, Memory and Cognition, 8,* 37-50.

Medin, D. L., Altom, M. W., & Murphy, T. D. (1984). Given versus induced category representations: Use of prototype and exemplar information in classification. *Journal of Experimental Psychology: Learning, Memory and Cognition, 10,* 333-352.

Medin, D. L., Dewey, G. I., & Murphy, T. D. (1983). Relationships between item and category learning: evidence that abstraction is not automatic. *Journal of Experimental Psychology: Learning, Memory and Cognition, 9,* 607-625.

Medin, D. L., & Schaffer, M. M. (1978). Context theory of classification learning. *Psychological Review, 85,* 207-238.

Meltzoff, A. N., & Moore, M. K. (1977). Imitation of facial and manual gestures by human neonates. *Science, 198,* 75-78.

Mervis, C. B., & Rosch, E. (1981). Categorization of natural objects. *Annual Review of Psychology, 32,* 89-115.

Miller, G. A. (1981). *Language and speech.* San Francisco: W. H. Freeman.

Miller, G. A., Heise, G. A., & Lichten, W. (1951). The intelligibility of speech as a function of the context of the test materials. *Journal of Experimental Psychology, 41,* 329-335.

Miller, G. A., & Nicely, P. E. (1955). An analysis of perceptual confusions among some English consonants. *Journal of the Acoustical Society of America, 27,* 338-352.

Miller, J. L. (1977). Nonindependence of feature processing in initial consonants. *Journal of Speech and Hearing Research, 20,* 519-528.

Miller, J. L., & Eimas, P. D. (1983). Studies on the categorization of speech by infants. *Cognition, 13,* 135-165.

Mills, A. E. (1983). Acquisition of speech sounds in the visually-handicapped child. In A. E. Mills (Ed.), *Language acquisition in the blind child* (pp. 46-56). London: Croom Helm Ltd.

Mills, A. E. (in press). The development of phonology in the blind child. In B. Dodd & R. Campbell (Eds.) *Hearing by Eye: Experimental studies in the psychology of lipreading.* Hillsdale, NJ: Lawrence Erlbaum Associates.

Mills, A. E., & Thiem, R. (1980). Auditory-visual fusions and illusions in speech perception. *Linguistische Berichte, 68/80,* 85-108.

Mohay, H. (1983). The effects of cued speech on the language development of three deaf children. *Sign Language Studies, 38,* 25-49.

Montgomery, A. A., & Jackson, P. L. (1983). Physical characteristics of the lips underlying vowel lipreading performance. *Journal of the Acoustical Society of America, 73*, 2134-2144.

Morrell, L. K. (1968). Temporal characteristics of sensory integration in choice reaction time. *Journal of Experimental Psychology, 77*, 14-18.

Navon, D. (1984). Resources--A theoretical soup stone? *Psychological Review, 91*, 216-234.

Neisser, U. (1967). *Cognitive psychology.* New York: Appleton-Century-Crofts.

Neisser, U. (1976). *Cognition and reality.* San Francisco: W. H. Freeman.

Neumann, O. (in press). Beyond capacity: A functional view of attention. In H. Heuer, & A. F. Sanders (Eds.), *Tutorials on perception and action.* Hillsdale, NJ: Lawrence Erlbaum Associates.

Nisbett, R. E., & Wilson, T. D. (1977). Telling more than we can know: Verbal reports on mental processes. *Psychological Review, 84*, 231-259.

Norman, D. A. (1969). *Memory & attention.* New York: Wiley.

Norman, D. A., & Wickelgren, W. (1969). Strength theory of decision rules and latency in retrieval from short term memory. *Journal of Mathematical Psychology, 6*, 192-208.

Norris, D. (1982). Autonomous processes in comprehension: A reply to Marslen-Wilson and Tyler. *Cognition, 11*, 97-101.

Norton, S. J., Schultz, M. C., Reed, C. M., Braida, L. D., Durlach, N. I., Rabinowitz, W. M., & Chomsky, C. (1977). Analytic study of the Tadoma method: Background and preliminary results. *Journal of Speech and Hearing Research, 20*, 574-595.

O'Connor, N., & Hermelin, B. (1981). Coding strategies of normal and handicapped children. In R. D. Walk & H. L. Pick, Jr. (Eds.), *Intersensory perception and sensory integration* (pp. 315-343). New York: Plenum.

Oden, G. C. (1977a). Fuzziness in semantic memory: choosing exemplars of subjective categories. *Memory & Cognition, 5*, 190-204.

Oden, G. C. (1977b). Integration of fuzzy logical information. *Journal of Experimental Psychology: Human Perception and Performance, 3*, 565-575.

Oden, G. C. (1978). Semantic constraints and judged preference for interpretations of ambiguous sentences. *Memory & Cognition, 6*, 26-37.

Oden, G. C. (1981). A fuzzy propositional model of concept structure and use: A case study in object identification. In G. W. Lasker (Ed.), *Applied systems and cybernetics: Vol. VI* (pp. 2890-2897). Elmsford, NY: Pergamon Press.

Oden, G. C. (1984). Everything is a good example of something, and other endorsements of the adequacy of a fuzzy theory of concepts. *Wisconsin Human Information Processing Program (WHIPP 21)*. University of Wisconsin, Madison.

Oden, G. C., & Massaro, D. W. (1978). Integration of featural information in speech perception. *Psychological Review, 85*, 172-191.

O'Leary, A, & Rhodes, G. (1984). Cross-modal effects on visual and auditory object perception. *Perception and Psychophysics, 35*, 565-569.

O'Neill, J. J. (1954). Contributions of the visual components of oral symbols to speech comprehension. *Journal of Speech and Hearing Disorders, 19*, 429-439.

Osherson, D. N., & Smith, E. E. (1981). On the adequacy of prototype theory as a theory of concepts. *Cognition, 9*, 35-58.

Osherson, D. N., & Smith, E. E. (1982). Gradedness and conceptual combination. *Cognition, 12*, 299-318.

Paap, K. R. (1975). Theories of speech perception. In D. W. Massaro (Ed.), *Understanding Language: An information processing analysis of speech perception, reading and psycholinguistics* (pp. 151-204). New York: Academic Press.

Palmer, S. E. (1978). Fundamental aspects of cognitive representation. In E. Rosch, & B. B. Lloyd (Eds.), *Cognition and categorization* (pp. 259-303). Hillsdale, NJ: Lawrence Erlbaum Associates.

Palmer, S. E., & Kimchi. R. (1986). The information processing approach to cognition. In T. J. Knapp, & L. C. Robertson (Eds.), *Approaches to cognition: contrasts and controversies* (pp. 37-77). Hillsdale, NJ: Lawrence Erlbaum Associates.

Peterson, G. E., & Barney, H. L. (1952). Control Methods used in a study of the vowels. *Journal of the Acoustical Society of America, 24*, 175-184.

Peterson, G. E., & Lehiste, I. (1960). Duration of syllable nuclei in English. *Journal of the Acoustical Society of America, 32*, 175-184.

Phatate, D. D., & Umano, H. (1981). Auditory discrimination of voiceless fricatives in children. *Journal of Speech and Hearing Research, 24*, 162-168.

Piaget, J. (1970). Piaget's theory. In P. H. Mussen (Ed.), *Carmichael's manual of child psychology: Vol. 1.* (pp. 703-732). New York: Wiley.

Pisoni, D. B. (1973). Auditory and phonetic memory codes in the discrimination of consonants and vowels. *Perception and Psychophysics, 13*, 253-260.

Pisoni, D. B., & Lazarus, J. H. (1974). Categorical and noncategorical modes of speech perception along the voicing continuum. *Journal of the Acoustical Society of America, 55*, 328-334.

Pisoni, D. B., & Tash, J. (1974). Reaction times to comparisons within and across phonetic categories. *Perception and Psychophysics, 15*, 285-290.

Platt, J. R. (1964). Strong inference. *Science, 146*, 347-353.

Pollack, I., & Pickett, J. M. (1963). The intelligibility of excerpts from conversation. *Language and Speech, 6*, 165-171.

Popper, K. R. (1959). *The logic of scientific discovery.* New York: Basic Books.

Popper, K. R. (1976). *Unended quest.* London: Fontana/Collins.

Port, R. F., & Dalby, J. (1982) Consonant/vowel ratio as a cue for voicing in English. *Perception & Psychophysics, 32*, 141-152.

Posner, M. I. (1978). *Chronometric explorations of mind.* Hillsdale, NJ: Lawrence Erlbaum Associates.

Premack, D. (1986). *Gavagai! Or the future history of the animal language controversy.* Cambridge, MA: MIT Press.

Pylyshyn, Z. N. (1984). *Computation and cognition. Toward a foundation for cognitive science.* Cambridge, MA: MIT Press.

Quine, W. O. van. (1960). *Word and object.* New York: Technology Press of MIT and Wiley & Sons.

Raab, D. H. (1962). Statistical facilitation of simple reaction times. *Transactions of the New York Academy of Sciences, 24*, 574-590.

Radeau, M., & Bertelson, P. (1976). The effect of a textured visual field on modality dominance in a ventriloquism situation. *Perception & Psychophysics , 20*, 227-235.

Radeau, M., & Bertelson, P. (1977). Adaptation to auditory-visual discordance and ventriloquism in semirealistic situations. *Perception & Psychophysics, 22*, 137-146.

Repp, B. H. (1981). Perceptual equivalence of two kinds of ambiguous speech stimuli. *Bulletin of the Psychonomic Society, 18*, 12-14.

Repp, B. H. (1982). Phonetic trading relations and context effects: New evidence of a phonetic mode of perception. *Psychological Bulletin, 92*, 81-110.

Repp, B. H. (1984). Categorical perception: Issues, methods, findings. In N. J. Lass (Ed.), *Speech and language: Advances in basic research and practice: Vol. 10.* (pp. 243-335). New York: Academic Press.

Repp, B. H., Healy, A. F., & Crowder, R. G. (1979). Categories and contexts in the perception of isolated steady-state vowels. *Journal of Experimental Psychology: Human Perception and Performance, 5*, 129-145.

Repp, B. H., Manuel, S. Y., Liberman, A. M., & Studdert-Kennedy, M. (1983, November). Exploring the "McGurk Effect." Paper Presented at the 24th meeting of the Psychonomic Society, San Diego, CA. *Bulletin of the Psychonomic Society*, 358 (abstract).

Roberts, A. H. (1965). *A Statistical analysis of American English*. The Hague: Mouton.

Roberts, M., & Summerfield, Q. (1981). Audiovisual presentation demonstrates that selective adaptation in speech perception is purely auditory. *Perception & Psychophysics, 30*, 309-314.

Rueckl, J. G., Oden G. C. (1986). The integration of contextual and featural information during word identification. *Journal of Memory and Language, 25*, 445-460.

Rumelhart, D. E., & McClelland, J. L. (1982). An interactive activation model of context effects in letter perception: Part 2. The contextual enhancement effect and some tests and extensions of the model. *Psychological Review, 89*, 60-94.

Rumelhart, D. E., & Norman, D. A. (1983). Representation in memory. *Center for Human Information Processing, 116*, 1-117.

Salthouse, T. A. (1985). *A theory of cognitive aging*. Amsterdam: North Holland.

Samar, V. J., & Sims, D. G. (1983). Visual evoked-response correlates of speechreading performance in normal-hearing adults: a replication and factor analytic extension. *Journal of Speech and Hearing Research, 26*, 2-9.

Samuel, A. G. (1977). The effect of discrimination training on speech perception: non-categorical perception. *Perception & Psychophysics, 22*, 321-330.

Sanders, A. F. (1980). Stage analysis of reaction processes, In G. E. Stelmach & J. Requin (Eds.), *Tutorials in motor behavior* (pp. 331-354). The Netherlands: North Holland Publishing Co.

Sawusch, J. R. (1977). Peripheral and central processes in selective adaptation of place of articulation in stop consonants. *Journal of the Acoustical Society of America, 62*, 738-750.

Selfridge, O. G. (1959). Pandemonium: A paradigm for learning. In *Mechanization of thought processes* (pp. 511-526). London: Her Majesty's Stationery Office.

Shannon, R. V. (1983). Multichannel electrical stimulation of the auditory nerve in man. I. Basic psychophysics. *Hearing Research, 11*, 157-189.

Shebilske, W. L. (in press). An ecological efference theory of natural event perception. In H. Heuer & A. F. Sanders (Eds.), *Perspectives on perception and action*. Hillsdale, NJ: Lawrence Erlbaum Associates.

Shepherd, D. C. (1982). Visual-neural correlate of speechreading ability in normal-hearing adults. *Journal of Speech and Hearing Research, 25*, 521-527.

Shepherd, D. C., DeLavergne, R. W., Frueh, F. X., & Clobridge, C. (1977). Visual-neural correlate of speechreading ability in normal-hearing adults. *Journal of Speech and Hearing Research, 25*, 521-527.

Shepp, B. E. (1978). From perceived similarity to dimensional structure. In E. Rosch & B. Lloyd (Eds.), *Cognition and categorization* (pp. 135-167). Hillsdale, NJ: Lawrence Erlbaum Associates.

Shepp, B. E. (1983). The analyzability of multidimensional objects: Some constraints on perceived structure, the development of perceived structure, and attention. In T. J. Tighe & B. E. Shepp (Eds.), *Perception, cognition, and development: Interaction analyses* (pp. 39-75). Hillsdale, NJ: Lawrence Erlbaum Associates.

Shepp, B. E., Burns, B., & McDonough, D. (1980). The relation of stimulus structure to perceptual and cognitive development: further tests of a separability hypothesis. In F. Wilkening, J. Becker, & T. Trabasso (Eds.), *Information integration by children* (pp. 113-145). Hillsdale, NJ: Lawrence Erlbaum Associates.

Simmons, F. B. (1985). History of cochlear implants in the United States: A personal perspective. In R. A. Schindler, & M. M. Merzenich (Eds.), *Cochlear implants* (pp. 1-11). New York: Raven Press.

Smith, E. E., & Medin, D. L. (1981). *Categories and concepts*. Cambridge, MA: Harvard University Press.

Smith, E. E., & Osherson, D. N. (1984). Conceptual combination with prototype concepts. *Cognitive Science, 8*, 337-361.

Smith, L. B., & Kemler, D. G. (1977). Developmental trends in free classification: evidence for a new conceptualization of perceptual development. *Journal of Experimental Child Psychology, 24*, 279-298.

Smith, L. B., & Kemler, D. G. (1978). Levels of experienced dimensionality in children and adults. *Cognitive Psychology, 10*, 502-532.

Smith, P. T. (1968). Cost, discriminability and response bias. *The British Journal of Mathematical and Statistical Psychology, 21*, 35-60.

Snyder, R. T., & Pope, P. (1970). New norms for an item analysis of the Wepman test at the first grade, six-year-level. *Perceptual and Motor Skills, 31*, 1007-1010.

Spelke, E. S. (1976). Infants' intermodal perception of events. *Cognitive Psychology, 8*, 553-560.

Spelke, E. S. (1979a). Exploring audible and visible events in infancy. In A. D. Pick (Ed.), *Perception and its development: A tribute to Eleanor J. Gibson* (pp. 221-235). Hillsdale, NJ: Lawrence Erlbaum Associates.

Spelke, E. S. (1979b). Perceiving bimodally specified events in infancy. *Developmental Psychology, 15*, 626-636.

Spelke, E. S., & Owsley, C. (1979). Intermodal exploration and knowledge in infancy. *Infant Behavior and Development, 2*, 13-27.

Spoehr, K. T., & Corin, W. J. (1978). The stimulus suffix effect as a memory coding phenomenon. *Memory & Cognition, 6*, 583-589.

Sternberg, S. (1969). The discovery of processing stages: Extensions of Donders' method. *Acta Psychologica, 30*, 276-315.

Sternberg, S. (1975). Memory scanning: New findings and current controversies. *Quarterly Journal of Experimental Psychology, 27*, 1-32.

Stroop, J. R. (1935). Studies of interference in serial verbal reactions. *Journal of Experimental Psychology, 18*, 643-662.

Studdert-Kennedy, M., Liberman, A. M., Harris, K. S., & Cooper, F. S. (1970). Motor theory of speech perception: A reply to Lane's critical review. *Psychological Review, 77*, 234-249.

Studdert-Kennedy, M., Liberman, A. M., & Stevens, K. N. (1963). Reaction times to synthetic stops and vowels at phoneme centers and at phoneme boundaries. *Journal of the Acoustical Society of America, 35*, 1900.

Sumby, W. H., & Pollack, I. (1954). Visual contribution to speech intelligibility in noise. *Journal of the Acoustical Society of America, 26*, 212-215.

Summerfield, A. Q. (1979). Use of visual information in phonetic perception. *Phonetica, 36*, 314-331.

Summerfield, A. Q. (1983). Audio-visual speech perception, lipreading and artificial stimulation. In M. E. Lutman, & M. P. Haggard (Eds.), *Hearing science and hearing disorders*. London: Academic.

Summerfield, A. Q. (in press). *Preliminaries to a comprehensive account of audio-visual speech perception.* In B. Dodd & R. Campbell (Eds.) *Hearing by Eye: Experimental studies in the psychology of lipreading.* Hillsdale, NJ: Lawrence Erlbaum Associates.

Tartter, V. C., & Knowlton, K. C. (1981). Perception of sign language from an array of 27 moving spots. *Nature, 289,* 676-678.

Theios, J. (1975). The components of response latency in human information processing. In S. Dornic, & P. M. A. Rabbitt (Eds.), *Attention and performance: Vol. V* (pp. 418-440). New York: Academic Press.

Theios, J., & Walter, D. G. (1974). Stimulus and response frequency and sequential effects in memory scanning reaction times. *Journal of Experimental Psychology, 102,* 1092-1099.

Thomas, E. A. C., & Myers, J. L. (1972). Implications of latency data for threshold and nonthreshold models of signal detection. *Journal of Mathematical Psychology, 9,* 253-285.

Thompson, L. A., & Massaro, D. W. (1986). Evaluation and integration of speech and pointing gestures during referential understanding. *Journal of Experimental Child Psychology, 42,* 144-168.

Thurstone, L. L. (1927). A law of comparative judgment. *Psychological Review, 34,* 273-286.

Tillmann, H. G. (1985). Personal communication, Munich, West Germany, July.

Todd, J. W. (1912). Reaction to multiple stimuli. *Archives of Psychology, 3,* 1-65.

Townsend, J. T. (1984). Uncovering mental processes with factorial experiments. *Journal of Mathematical Psychology, 28,* 363-400.

Townsend, J. T., & Landon, D. E. (1982). An experiment and theoretical investigation of the constant-ratio rule and other models of visual letter confusion. *Journal of Mathematical Psychology, 25,* 119-162.

Townsend, J. T., & Landon, D. E. (1983). Mathematical models of recognition and confusion in psychology. *Mathematical Social Sciences, 4,* 25-71.

Treisman, A. (1969). Strategies and models of selective attention. *Psychological Review, 76,* 282-299.

Treisman, A., & Gelade, G. (1980). Feature-integration theory of attention. *Cognitive Psychology, 12,* 97-136.

Treisman, A., Kahneman, D., & Burkell, J. (1983). Perceptual objects and the cost of filtering. *Perception & Psychophysics, 33,* 527-530.

Trevarthen, C. (1977). Descriptive analyses of infant communication behaviour. In H. R. Schaffer (Ed.), *Mother-infant interaction* (pp. 227-270). London: Academic Press.

Turvey, M. T. (1977). Contrasting orientations to the theory of visual information processing. *Psychological Review, 84,* 67-88.

Turvey, M. T., & Shaw, R. (1979). The primacy of perceiving: An ecological formulation of perception as a point of departure for understanding memory. In L. G. Nilsson (Ed.), *Perspectives on memory research: Essays in honor of Uppsala University's 500th Anniversary* (pp. 167-222). Hillsdale, NJ: Lawrence Erlbaum Associates.

Tversky, A., & Kahneman, D. (1983). Extension versus intuitive reasoning: The conjunction fallacy in probability judgment. *Psychological Review, 90,* 293-315.

Tyler, L. K. (1981). Serial and interactive-parallel theories of sentence processing. *Theoretical Linguistics, 8,* 29-65.

Tyler, L. K., & Wessels, J. (1983). Quantifying contextual contributions to word-recognition processes. *Perception & Psychophysics, 34,* 409-420.

Ulrich, R., & Giray, M. (1986). Separate-activation models with variable base times: Testability and checking of cross-channel dependency. *Perception & Psychophysics, 39,* 248-254.

Utley, J. A. (1946). A test of lipreading ability. *Journal of Speech and Hearing Disorders, 11,* 109-116.

Van der Heijden, A. H. C., Hagenaar, R., & Bloem, W. (1984). Two stages in postcategorical filtering and selection. *Memory & Cognition, 12,* 458-469.

Venezky, R. L., & Massaro, D. W. (in press). Orthographic structure and spelling-to-sound mappings in reading english words. In A. Allport, D. MacKay, W. Prinz, & E. Scheerer (Eds.), *Language perception and production: shared mechanisms in listening, speaking, reading and writing.* London: Academic Press.

Vinter, A., De Nobili, G. L., Pellegrinetti, G., & Cioni, G. (1982). Auditory-visual coordination in neonates and infants. *Infant Behavior and Development, 5,* 250.

Vinter, A., De Nobili, G. L., Pellegrinetti, G., & Cioni, G. (1984). Auditory-visual coordination: Does it imply an external world for the newborn? *Cahiers de Psychologie Cognitive, 4,* 309-322.

Walden, B. E., Montgomery, A. A., Holum-Hardegen, L. L., & Prosek, R. A. (1984). *Categorical versus continuous perception of synthetic visual consonant-vowel articulations.* Unpublished manuscript, Walter Reed Army Medical Center, Washington DC.

Walden, B. E., Prosek, R., Montgomery, A., Scherr, C. K., & Jones, C. J. (1977). Effects of training on the visual recognition of consonants. *Journal of Speech and Hearing Research, 20,* 130-145.

Ward, T. B. (1980). Separable and integral responding by children and adults to the dimensions of length and density. *Child Development, 51,* 676-684.

Ward, T. B. (1983). Response tempo and separable-integral responding: Evidence for an integral-to-separable processing sequence in visual perception. *Journal of Experimental Psychology: Human Perception and Performance, 9,* 103-112.

Ward, T. B., Foley, C. M., & Cole, J. (1986). Classifying multidimensional stimuli: Stimulus, task, and observer factors. *Journal of Experimental Psychology: Human Perception and Performance, 12,* 211-225.

Warren, D. H., McCarthy, T. J., & Welch, R. B. (1983). Discrepancy and non-discrepancy methods of assessing visual-auditory interaction. *Perception & Psychophysics, 33,* 413-419.

Watson, C. S., Rilling, M. E., & Bourbon, W. T. (1964). Receiver-operating characteristics determined by a mechanical analog to the rating scale. *Journal of the Acoustical Society of America, 36,* 283-288.

Welch, R. B., & Warren, D. H. (1980). Immediate perceptual response to inter-sensory discrepancy. *Psychological Bulletin, 88,* 638-667.

Werner, H. (1957). *Comparative psychology of mental development.* New York: International Universities Press.

Zadeh, L. A. (1965). Fuzzy sets. *Information and Control, 8,* 338-353.

Zadeh, L. A. (1982). A note on prototype theory and fuzzy sets. *Cognition, 12,* 291-297.

Zadeh, L. A. (1984). Making computers think like people. *IEEE, 21,* 26-32.

Zlatin, M. A., & Koeningsknecht, R. A. (1975). Development of the voicing contrast: Perception of stop consonants. *Journal of Speech and Hearing Research, 18,* 541-553.

Author Index

Subject Index